A SOUTHERN R

BRIG. GEN. BEN. MCCULLOCH

A SOUTHERN RECORD

The History
of the
Third Regiment
Louisiana Infantry

By W. H. TUNNARD

CONTAINING A COMPLETE RECORD OF THE CAMPAIGNS IN ARKANSAS AND
MISSOURI; THE BATTLES OF OAK HILLS, ELK HORN, IUKA, CORINTH; THE SECOND
SIEGE OF VICKSBURG, ANECDOTES, CAMPS, SCENERY, AND DESCRIPTION OF THE
COUNTRY THROUGH WHICH THE REGIMENT MARCHED, ETC., ETC.

"Let us then be up and doing,
With a heart for every fate;
Still achieving, still pursuing,
Learn to labor and to wait."

LONGFELLOW

BATON ROUGE, LA.:
PRINTED FOR THE AUTHOR
1866

INTRODUCTION BY WILLIAM L. SHEA

THE UNIVERSITY OF ARKANSAS PRESS
Fayetteville 1997

Library of Congress Cataloging-in-Publication Data

Tunnard, W. H. (William H.), b. 1837.
      A southern record : the history of the Third Regiment, Louisiana Infantry /
by W. H. Tunnard.
            p.   cm.
      Originally published: Baton Rouge : W. H. Tunnard, 1866.
      Includes bibliographical references and index.
      ISBN 1-55728-493-8 (pbk. : alk. paper)
            1. Confederate States of America. Army. Louisiana Infantry Regiment, 3rd.
      2. United States—History—Civil War, 1861–1896—Regimental histories.
      3. Louisiana—History—Civil War, 1861–1865—Regimental histories.   I. Title.
      E565.5 3rd.T8   1997
      973.7'463—dc21   97-26285
                                                                       CIP

Reprinted from the original edition published in 1866 by W. H. Tunnard. An introduction and index has been added to this edition. Some regularizations in spelling and punctuation in the text have been made by the University of Arkansas Press.

DEDICATION

To the cherished memory of the revered dead, and the
undaunted gallantry of the heroic living,
officers and men, of the
THIRD REGIMENT LOUISIANA INFANTRY

I respectfully dedicate this volume.

"And while adversity's chill blast
Sweeps like a besom o'er our land,
And round her bleeding form are cast
The hated tyrant's chains at last,
We still possess the glorious Past—
The victories of our patriot band,
The memories of the fields of glory,
Which aye shall live in song and story,
To cheer the brave and shame the coward—
By that blue heaven bending o'er us,
By that green earth spread out before us,
By that dear fame of those who bore us,
We are not whipped, but overpowered."

PAUL CRIMSON

PREFACE

THAT "truth is stranger than fiction" is an axiom as correct as it is trite. Thus I claim for these pages of history a strict adherence to truthfulness in recording actual occurrences, facts garnered from the great and bloody drama of the late war, around which lingers the halo of imperishable glory, possessing all the fascination and interest of romance. This record has been dotted down on the long and weary march, in the quiet camp, within breastworks and besieged strongholds, before and after the fierce conflict of deadly strife—a correct record of events as they actually occurred, they are presented to the public. I have indulged in few fancies of the imagination, nor do I claim for this work any peculiar literary excellence. Simple in construction of sentences, unpretending in style of composition, it is given to the public for perusal as one of the many bloody chapters in the history of the late Revolution, when Southerners endeavored, by force of arms, to establish their independence and preserve untarnished the principles of constitutional liberty bequeathed to them by their ancestors, and baptized and consecrated with their best blood, from the despotic domination of Radicalism. The attempt has most signally failed; and while the Southern people accept the issue of the struggle as the unalterable decree of a mysterious Providence, such records of the past, as contained in this volume, will be regarded as priceless mementoes of heroic deeds, an imperishable epitome of gallant achievements, fierce conflicts, determined valor and patient and long-enduring suffering of those brave men who sacrificed their lives, devoted their energies and efforts toward the establishment of long-cherished principles and institutions.

Mere history can furnish only a tithe of the vivid reality of warlike scenes. Perusing its pages, the reader gleans only the record of gallant achievements, lives in the midst of scenes befitting a romance, and not stern realities. Thus there is a strange fascination in such compilations.

War has existed almost since the creation of the universe, and its records, from ancient days down to modern times, when Napoleon electrified the world with his brilliant victories, possess peculiar attractions, deep interest. Yet the reader gathers not from the pages of history, with its glowing descriptions and all the attendant pomp and glory of the struggle, its attendant horrors, the deadly conflict, the untold agony, the accumulated trials, the unspeakable suffering, unbearable anguish which accompany the dark side of the brilliant, fascinating picture.

'Tis well that it should be so. There are few, however, especially in this suffering, ruined Southern land, who do not understand, ay, know from experience dearly purchased, what war means in the fullest signification of the term.

This book is a chapter from its bloodiest record. It has been compiled amid business pursuits, and the bustle and turmoil of a great commercial city, in the still hours of the night and the gray dawn of morn; from published letters written during the war, private notes, and such official documents as have been preserved from the ruin of defeat. The author has labored under peculiar disadvantages, being deprived of official records and documents, and has been compelled to rely on his present experience and information, and such notes and papers as could be obtained from the surviving members of the Regiment.

If he has failed in presenting as complete and interesting a work as the subject demands, it is a fault not of the head or heart, but simply as stated, because his sources for obtaining necessary information have been not only limited, but very meagre.

Few organizations during the late war gained a more enviable reputation than the Third Regiment Louisiana Infantry.

An isolated Regiment, among other troops, its gallant men bore their banner triumphantly through the sulphureous canopy and thunder-voices of deadly conflicts, making, by their heroic deeds and undaunted bravery, an imperishable record on the scroll of time; a name that "shall live in song and story," and of which Louisiana may well be proud. Its honored dead slumber 'neath the soil of many States; its gallant survivors, with a spirit worthy their self-sacrificing devotion, have accepted the *finale* of the fierce contest, and are now found both in positions of honor and trust as well as the humbler stations of life, striving to regain and repair their shattered fortunes. I know of no more satisfactory labor, no pleasanter mental task, than this self-imposed work of commemorating the sacrifices of the former, and the unconquerable valor of the latter, rendered still more distinguished by the spirit with which they have received and accepted their defeat. Our revered dead shall live ever fresh and green in our memories, while the living are united in those indissoluble bonds which bind brave spirits to each other, cemented by common dangers and sufferings, and a stern defence of cherished principles.

Imperfect as this record may be, it is given to the public not for criticism, but as a compilation of facts, exhibiting some of the innumerable thrilling scenes through which Southerners bore their banner, now furled forever— scenes in which they participated as votive actors.

I regret exceedingly that this record is so meagre, my sources of information so limited, but believe and know that I have written nothing save actual occurrences, which, I trust, may meet the approval and commendation of my friends and former comrades.

W. H. TUNNARD

BATON ROUGE, LA., *August,* 1866

PERSONAL

I DEEM it but an act of justice to myself to state, that I have been compelled to mention my own name, in connection with the several occurrences in this History, not that I desire to arrogate to myself any undue share of the fame gained by the Regiment, nor do I wish to be considered egotistical. To others is given the privilege of praising or condemning my actions. I was an active participator in the battles of Oak Hills and Elk Horn; but, at the reorganization of the Regiment, May 8, 1862, was detailed in the Commissary Department, and followed the fortunes of the Regiment as a non-combatant. I do not desire my motives to be misunderstood, nor my record to become the subject of uncalled-for criticism. Hence this explanation.

THE AUTHOR

CONTENTS

CHAPTER XIX

CHAPTER XX

CHAPTER XXI

CHAPTER XXII

CHAPTER XXIII

CHAPTER XXIV

CHAPTER XXV

CHAPTER XXVI

CHAPTER XXVII

CHAPTER XXVIII

CHAPTER XXIX

CHAPTER XXXVII

Camp near Pineville, Louisiana—The Louisiana Brigade—Its *Morale*—Quietude—Exchange—Organization of the Third Louisiana Infantry—Activity—Military Executions—The Ladies of New Orleans and the Confederate Prisoners—General Polignac's Troops—A Visit from Captains Gallagher and Charles A. Bruslé,

CHAPTER XXXVIII

Ho! For Shreveport—The "Lelia"—Arrival at Grand Ecore—A Warm Welcome—Generosity of Prudhomme Hyams—Arrival at "Lac des Meures" Plantation—Colonel S. M. Hyam's Generosity and Hospitality—Captain Isaacson a Prisoner—The Barbecue—"Farewell"—Up the River,

CHAPTER XXXIX

Camp "Boggs"—Shreveport—Provost Guard—Details—Conscripts—Frost—Concert—Governor H. W. Allen's Generosity to the Regiment—Reconstruction—Dissatisfaction—Desertions—Sufferings at Soldiers' Homes,

CHAPTER XL

The Holidays—Christmas Dinner in Camp—Festivities in Shreveport—Clothing at Last—Forney's Review—The Third Regiment Louisiana Infantry Honored—The Sham Battle—Reception of the Third Regiment—General Forney Introduces them to his Division—Speeches—Good Cheer—The Flag of the Regiment—Robberies in Shreveport—Arrival of Yankee Commissioners—Aspect of Camp—The Regiment Protects Shreveport from Destruction, May 17th, 1865—The Missourians—Indignation—Disbanding—Farewell of the Veterans—Scenes of Destruction—The Last of the Regiment—Darkness and Gloom,

CHAPTER XLI

Scenes from Camp Life at Camp Boggs—Music—Preaching—The Storm—"Here's Your Honey"—Our Quarters—Our Southern Women—Unmarked Graves—The *Personnel* of the Regiment—How They Accept the Situation,

INTRODUCTION

BY WILLIAM L. SHEA

MEMOIRS written by Confederate soldiers who campaigned in the West are relatively rare; rarer still are accounts of service in the vast expanses of the Trans-Mississippi. With this in mind, the literary legacy of the 3rd Louisiana Infantry is something of a marvel. The 3rd Louisiana was a highly-regarded regiment that took part in every major campaign and engagement in Arkansas, Missouri, and Mississippi during the first two years of the war. While that record is impressive enough, what is even more remarkable is that two notable first-person accounts of the trials and tribulations of the 3rd Louisiana made their way into print.

The first of these books was William H. Tunnard's *A Southern Record: The History of the Third Regiment Louisiana Infantry*. It was published in Baton Rouge in 1866 when the experiences described by the author were still vivid in his memory. The second was William Watson's *Life in the Confederate Army*, which did not appear for another twenty-one years. It is a more polished literary effort, but it also demonstrates how the passage of time affects the human memory. The two books are different in other ways as well. Tunnard was a native of Louisiana and a staunch secessionist who served from the outbreak of hostilities to the bitter end four long years later. He took part in the capture of the Baton Rouge Arsenal in 1861 and was present for the final surrender at Shreveport in 1865. His account is the story of the regiment. It is based on primary documents—many of which are printed in full in the text—and has the ring of authenticity throughout. Watson, by contrast, was a British subject who had no particular attachment to the Southern Confederacy and who decided that one year as a Rebel was enough for him. His story is essentially that of a personal odyssey. It was published in London and intended for a British audience. Both accounts are valuable, but most veterans of the 3rd Louisiana, were they available to be polled on the subject, undoubtedly would agree that Tunnard's is the more reliable of the two because of its immediacy and scope.[1]

William H. Tunnard—Will or Willie to his family and friends—was born in New Jersey in 1837. He was the youngest son of a successful carriage maker named William F. Tunnard, a capable artisan blessed with a keen business sense. When Will was still a toddler, the elder Tunnard moved his family to Baton Rouge, Louisiana's small but growing capital city on the Mississippi River. The carriage business prospered, and the Tunnard family soon achieved a considerable measure of wealth and social standing. Young Will attended private schools in Baton Rouge before being sent off to Kenyon College in Ohio to obtain the kind of education that was not then available in Louisiana. After graduation in 1856 at the age of nineteen, he returned home to work in the family business. Like many antebellum Americans, particularly in the South, the Tunnards were interested in military affairs. Father and sons were among the original members of the Pelican Rifles, an East Baton Rouge Parish militia company formed in November 1859, shortly after John Brown's raid on Harper's Ferry, Virginia, had electrified the nation and unleashed a frenzy of paramilitary activity in the South. Despite their northern birth and education (at least in Will's case), the Tunnards were staunchly southern in their views on states' rights and secession.[2]

When Louisiana seceded in January 1861, the Pelican Rifles, along with similar militia companies from across south Louisiana, marched to the U.S. Arsenal in Baton Rouge and demanded its surrender. Shortly thereafter, the members of the company volunteered for active duty and proceeded downriver to Camp Walker in Metairie, a suburb of New Orleans, where they and thousands like them were introduced to the mysteries of formal military life, or at least as formal as it ever got in the Confederate army. It was at Camp Walker that the 3rd Louisiana Infantry was organized as a one-year regiment under the command of Col. Louis Hébert, a bilingual Acadian graduate of West Point who proved to be an exemplary officer. Under his demanding tutelage, the 3rd Louisiana earned a reputation as a crack outfit. As the regiment took shape, Will Tunnard found himself well connected. His father was elected major of the regiment and his older brother a second lieutenant in Company K. Why the youngest Tunnard remained in the ranks despite family connections and a college education is not known.

Contrary to popular belief, not all Louisiana regiments were composed of French-speaking Creoles and Acadians who lived in galleried townhouses or paddled pirogues through the swamps. It is quite true that most people in antebellum south Louisiana were of French, Spanish, or West African ancestry, but even as early as 1850 the population in that part of the state was remarkably diverse by southern standards. Several of Louisiana's best-known Confederate units, especially those from the booming metropolis of New Orleans, were largely composed of men from more recently-arrived immigrant groups, especially Irish. What is even more often overlooked is that while south Louisiana was an ethnic gumbo, the rest of the state was very different. Antebellum north Louisiana was settled primarily by persons of English and Scottish background, the same sort of people who populated most of the interior South from Virginia to Texas.

The 3rd Louisiana was a bit of a geographic and cultural anomaly in that it was primarily a north Louisiana regiment that included two companies from the southern part of the state. One of these was Company A from Iberville Parish, located between Baton Rouge and New Orleans, whose members were predominantly of French descent. The other was Tunnard's Company K, formerly the Pelican Rifles of East Baton Rouge Parish. Like all of the bustling ports along the Mississippi River, Baton Rouge was a cosmopolitan place, and the muster roll of Company K included names of English, Scottish, German, French, Irish, Italian, and Spanish origin. Tunnard, a transplant from New Jersey whose comrades in Company K included a Scottish immigrant named William Watson, does not mention any significant difficulties among soldiers of such different cultural backgrounds, but we can certainly imagine that there were times when "Cajuns" and "Crackers" and members of other ethnic groups were amused, baffled, intrigued, or annoyed by the antics and comments of their compatriots.

Another point worth remembering is that the composition of early Civil War regiments, formed during the initial flush of idealism and enthusiasm in 1861, was far different from that of the conscript regiments raised later in the war. The membership of each company in the 3rd Louisiana was a representative cross section of its home parish. This certainly was true of Company K—the Pelican Rifles presented a fairly accurate demographic profile of the white male population of Baton Rouge and its vicinity. Officers were older, better educated, and more prosperous members of their communities, often businessmen or attorneys. Enlisted men were a mix of artisans, tradesmen, clerks, farmers, laborers, and students, who often were sons of the more prosperous families. All would have been respectable; few would have been impoverished. In the language of the era, the volunteers of '61 were the flower of the Confederacy. It was not yet a rich man's war and a poor man's fight.

Tunnard begins with a brief description of the events that led to secession and the formation of the regiment, but the most valuable portion of his account is the story of the 3rd Louisiana's participation in most of the events that determined the course of the war in the upper Trans-Mississippi and the lower Mississippi Valley. The men expected and hoped to be sent to Virginia along with the other regiments training at Camp Walker, but when the 3rd Louisiana left New Orleans it proceeded to Fort Smith, Arkansas, where a small army was being assembled to defend the northwestern corner of the Confederacy. After an unhurried journey up the Mississippi and Arkansas Rivers, the Louisianians reached Fort Smith on the border of the Indian Territory (present-day Oklahoma). There they came under the command—and the charismatic spell—of the celebrated Texas Ranger, Benjamin McCulloch, who deeply impressed Tunnard and apparently every other man in the regiment with his common-sense approach to warfare, his devotion to his troops, and his commitment to the Confederate cause. It is telling that the frontispiece to the original edition of *A Southern Record* is an engraving of McCulloch rather than a portrait of any of the regiment's popular commanders.

In mid-summer of 1861 McCulloch's army struggled over the Boston Mountains and marched northward across the Ozark Plateau to Missouri. The purpose of this movement was to support Sterling Price's Missouri State Guard, a pro-secessionist army opposing Union activities in Missouri. En route, Tunnard encountered "backwoods Arkansians" for the first time and made humorous observations about their lack of intelligence and sophistication, which seems to have been common practice among Ozark travelers even at that early date. On August 10 the combined armies of McCulloch and Price were camped along Wilson's Creek a few miles southwest of Springfield when they were attacked by a small Union army commanded by Nathaniel Lyon. The battle raged all day and the 3rd Louisiana figured prominently in the fighting, helping to parry one Union thrust from the north, then turning about and driving off another assault from the south.

Wilson's Creek (or Oak Hills) was a Confederate victory, but logistical difficulties and a falling out with Price compelled McCulloch to withdraw into northwest Arkansas. The 3rd Louisiana spent the fall and winter of 1861–1862 in chilly but comfortable surroundings atop the Ozark Plateau. McCulloch moved heaven and earth to ensure that his men were properly sheltered and supplied even at the very edge of the Confederacy, and they loved him for it. Most of the regiment rode out the winter in sturdy frame huts constructed in Cross Hollows. Two companies—one of which was Company K—were lodged nearby in the hilltop community of Fayetteville. In October the regiment became the only unit in McCulloch's frontier army to receive uniforms, courtesy of the state of Louisiana. Most of the men were issued coats and pants of more-or-less regulation bluish-gray denim, but for some reason Tunnard and his fellows in Company K received coats and pants of dark brown denim. This Ozark winter interlude was also memorable in that it was the first time many of the Louisianians had ever experienced frozen precipitation. A heavy snowfall just before Christmas triggered "the great snowball fight" in which officers and men alike took part. Fortunately, a shipment of wool overcoats from Louisiana reached the regiment before the worst of the winter weather. The winter was a special occasion for the Tunnard family. When Colonel Hébert was placed in charge of McCulloch's infantry brigade, Major Tunnard assumed command of the regiment.

To this point, service in the 3rd Louisiana had been relatively mild, and even enjoyable in some respects. All that came to an end in late February when the war unexpectedly intruded. A Union army led by Samuel R. Curtis drove Price out of Missouri and into Arkansas. Caught completely off guard by the bold enemy winter offensive, Price and McCulloch were compelled to retreat southward into the Boston Mountains. The impressive cantonment at Cross Hollows and a good part of Fayetteville were burned by the retreating Confederates, along with a vast amount of accumulated stores. It was a dismal experience and was a foretaste of things to come. The Civil War in the Trans-Mississippi was becoming a serious affair.

Two weeks later the Confederates received a new commander, Earl Van Dorn. Bold and reckless to a fault, Van Dorn named his new command the Army of the West and immediately led it northward to drive the enemy back into Missouri. After an exhausting three-day advance through a blizzard, the Confederates struck the Union army at Pea Ridge on March 7–8, 1862. The 3rd Louisiana was in the thick of the fighting near the village of Leetown and suffered substantial casualties. McCulloch was killed, Colonel Hébert and Major Tunnard were captured, and the worn-out Confederates eventually gave way. Pea Ridge (or Elk Horn) was a Union victory that more than off-set the Confederate triumph at Wilson's Creek seven months earlier. Worse was to come. The disorganized Confederate retreat was a disaster, and the regiment returned to camp near Fort Smith "in straggling squads, tired, hatless, barefooted, hungry, dirty, and ragged."

After Pea Ridge the Army of the West was transferred by steamboat and railroad across the Mississippi River to Corinth, Mississippi. For weeks the soldiers of the 3rd Louisiana participated in the defense of that valuable railroad junction. Skirmishing and digging of field fortifications occupied much of their time; skimping along on insufficient rations and enduring unpalatable water occupied most of their thoughts. In May came the stunning news that a Union fleet had captured New Orleans and Baton Rouge. This must have been particularly demoralizing for the men of Company K, but Tunnard says little of it.

The 3rd Louisiana was a one-year regiment, and under the rules of the recent Conscript Act it was reorganized in May 1862. New officers were chosen at all levels. Major Tunnard, exchanged after Pea Ridge, resigned due to ill health and returned to Baton Rouge. Will Tunnard remained with the regiment but received assignment to the commissary department as a sergeant, from which vantage point he gained a different perspective on how a military organization functioned.

The Confederates abandoned Corinth in the summer of 1862 and fell back to Tupelo. While there every unit in the Army of the West received a "Van Dorn pattern" battleflag. This was a solid red ensign decorated with yellow stars and a crescent moon. It was somewhat reminiscent of banners carried by Muslim armies and was unquestionably the most distinctive of all Confederate battleflags. When most of the Confederate army departed for an invasion of Kentucky, Van Dorn and his Army of the West were left behind to recover northern Mississippi. The result was a confused but intense clash in a forest near Iuka, Mississippi, on September 19, 1862. The 3rd Louisiana bore the brunt of the battle and lost its new flag and well over a third of its men. Van Dorn attacked the Federals again, this time at Corinth on October 3–4. The Confederates made a series of head-on assaults against strong fortifications and suffered a crushing defeat. The much-reduced 3rd Louisiana played only a modest role in the battle but still lost a third of its surviving strength. Van Dorn was relieved of command after the catastrophe at Corinth, and the weakened Confederates retired once more, first to Holly Springs, then to Grenada. It was the lowest point in the war for the Louisianians. "The Third Regiment was in a terrible condition," recalled Tunnard without exaggeration. At Iuka and Corinth over half of the officers and men of the 3rd Louisiana had been killed, wounded, or captured. Food, equipment, and clothing were in short supply and morale was at rock bottom.

At the end of 1862 the 3rd Louisiana finally left the dismal forest-covered hills of north Mississippi, the scene of so much failure and misery, and headed for Vicksburg, the vital Confederate strongpoint on the Mississippi River. The overall Confederate commander, John C. Pemberton, assigned the regiment to the defense of Snyder's Bluffs along the Yazoo River, about fifteen miles north of Vicksburg, and there they remained for the next five months. The soldiers engaged in occasional skirmishing, but for the most part the winter of 1862–1863 atop Snyder's Bluffs was an uneventful period in the regiment's history. The men dug shallow caves into the loess hills and even constructed porches over their entrances. Supplies flowed steadily from nearby Vicksburg and, perhaps equally as important for the urbanites of the Pelican Rifles, newspapers arrived daily. Also during this period the surviving members of the 3rd Louisiana were issued crude Confederate-made Mississippi Rifles (which proved worthless and had to be replaced with Enfields from the United Kingdom) and equally crude uniforms of coarse and undyed wool (which the men despised).

The Louisianians lived in their caves, enjoyed the relatively mild weather, and wondered what the enemy was doing. Morale gradually improved as wounded and exchanged comrades returned and a small number of replacements dribbled in. It was during this period that Tunnard made his only reference to dining on crawfish (or crayfish, as he spelled and probably pronounced the term). While preparing a spicy pot of crawfish stew, he observed that soldiers from north Louisiana companies and neighboring regiments were amazed at the culinary inclinations of the "Cre-owl" Louisianians. "They could not appreciate such a peculiar taste," sniffed Tunnard. This brings up another interesting point. For the first two years of its existence the 3rd Louisiana was an "orphan" regiment. Confederate regulations required that regiments from a particular state be brigaded together, but the 3rd Louisiana was the only Louisiana unit ever to serve in the upper Trans-Mississippi and the only Louisiana unit in Van Dorn's Army of the West during its service in north Mississippi. Consequently, the men found themselves associating with regiments from Arkansas, Missouri, and Texas. This may have helped to broaden experiences and promote tolerance on the part of all concerned, though the crawfish episode seems to indicate otherwise.

On May 17 the 3rd Louisiana and other units guarding Snyder's Bluffs were shocked out of their complacency by the startling news that Ulysses S. Grant's Union army had crossed the Mississippi River and was approaching Vicksburg from the east; they were in danger of being cut off. A large amount of weapons, ammunition, and provisions were destroyed or left behind as the Confederates abandoned Snyder's Bluffs and hastened into the ring of fortifications surrounding Vicksburg. Now, finally, the regiment was brigaded with other Louisiana units under their original commander, Louis Hébert, and given the dubious honor of manning the defenses in the center of the Confederate line, directly athwart the Union advance.

What follows is Tunnard's detailed day-by-day account of the siege of Vicksburg, which lasted from May 19 to July 4, 1863. He was appalled by this very different form of warfare. A stand-up fight Tunnard viewed as a true if

terrible test of manly virtues, but siege warfare with its mix of danger, deprivation, and boredom struck him as inhuman. "A more deadly, vindictive, and
determined species of warfare was never waged." Conditions deteriorated
throughout the six-week siege as stocks of food dwindled, Union forces crept
closer, and the overpowering heat and humidity took its toll. The lifeblood of
the regiment drained away as every day brought additional casualties from
sniper and artillery fire.

As luck would have it, the pitifully understrength 3rd Louisiana was
involved in the most dramatic incident of the siege. The regiment occupied a
redan—a V-shaped fort—where the Jackson Road passed through the
Confederate fortifications. Union soldiers dug an approach trench to the point
or angle of the redan, then began tunneling directly underneath the fort. The
Confederates dug a countermine but failed to intercept the Union tunnel,
which soon was filled with barrels of gunpowder. On June 25 a massive explosion demolished the front of the redan. A Union infantry assault followed but
was repulsed after desperate fighting. The one great Union opportunity to
breach the Confederate fortifications failed, largely because of the tenacity of
the men of the 3rd Louisiana. (The massive remains of the 3rd Louisiana
Redan, as the damaged fort has been known for over a century, can be visited
today in Vicksburg National Military Park, where a thicket of markers and
monuments provides the details of this extraordinary episode.)

The end came on July 4, 1863, when Pemberton surrendered Vicksburg
and its garrison of nearly 30,000 men to Grant. Tunnard was paroled rather
than imprisoned, but for him and most of the men in the 3rd Louisiana, the
war was effectively over. The defeated army dissolved as weary and demoralized Confederates simply marched out of town and headed home. "Thus
melted away the gallant army of Vicksburg," lamented Tunnard. Unable to
prevent its soldiers from leaving, the Confederate government did the only
thing possible and granted everyone a furlough, in the desperate hope that
most men would return to the ranks after they had recovered from their trav-
ails. And most did. Because of Union control of the Mississippi River, some
members of the 3rd Louisiana reassembled at a parole camp near Demopolis,
Alabama; a larger number reported to a similar camp near Alexandria,
Louisiana. Tunnard was part of the former group, but in October he and eight
others made their way across the Mississippi River to Alexandria, and shortly
thereafter to Grand Ecore near Natchitoches.

For all practical purposes the history of the 3rd Louisiana ends at this point;
never again would the two surviving fragments of the regiment serve together.

The troops in Alabama finally were exchanged (released from their parole) in December 1863 and were consolidated with other bands of stray Louisianians into the 22nd Louisiana. They went on to defend Mobile and to fight in the battle of Spanish Fort near the close of the war, suffering additional casualties in the process.

The members of the 3rd Louisiana at Grand Ecore were not exchanged until July 1864, a full year after the fall of Vicksburg. They were inactive for that entire period and often were furloughed home to relieve the strain on the Confederate supply system, which was on its last legs. A return to active service meant little change, however, for there was nothing to do in the Trans-Mississippi, where the war had largely petered out. The regiment proceeded up the Red River to Shreveport where officers and men waited for the conflict to be decided elsewhere. The Louisianians were bored and restless during the winter of 1864–1865 but tried hard to keep their spirits up. They held reviews, enjoyed such parties as could be managed in straightened circumstances, and even put on a mock battle for the local citizens, which must have been an odd experience for veterans of so many bloody clashes.

Finally, inevitably, the curtain came down. The Confederate army in the Trans-Mississippi did not so much surrender as disintegrate. When news of military disasters in Virginia and the Carolinas reached Shreveport, discipline broke down in many units and desertion became rampant. Confederate authorities assigned the most reliable regiments—including the 3rd Louisiana —to patrol the streets of Shreveport to prevent looting and vandalism. The collapse of the Confederacy was chaotic and utterly disheartening, especially to men like Tunnard who had stuck it out from the beginning. "The condition of affairs was terrible, awful, heart-rending," he wrote. The end came on May 20, 1865, when the survivors of one of the Confederacy's first and finest regiments were discharged and told to make their way home as best they could.

Like other Confederate soldiers who served in the West, the men of the 3rd Louisiana were all too familiar with withdrawals, defeats, retreats, and surrenders (not once but twice). Only at Wilson's Creek in 1861 did Tunnard and his compatriots experience the grim joy of victory. Pea Ridge, Iuka, Corinth, Vicksburg, and for a fragment of the regiment Spanish Fort, comprised a depressing litany of dashed hopes, missed opportunities, and wasted valor. Of the 1,136 men who served in the 3rd Louisiana, 123 were killed in battle and 80 died of other causes. Hundreds more were crippled by wounds or debilitated by disease. Tragically, few of the men who assembled at Camp Walker in 1861 were destined to live out their threescore years and ten.[3]

Tunnard prepared his history of the 3rd Louisiana during a year filled with distractions and hardships as he and millions of other southerners tried to resume their lives amidst the wreckage of the Confederacy. He completed the manuscript within fifteen months of the surrender at Shreveport, working at night or whenever he could spend some time away from his business pursuits. Tunnard was an educated man, but he was not a particularly gifted stylist. His narrative contains too many verbose passages extolling the virtues of southern womanhood and the gallantry of southern soldiers. But his richly detailed descriptions of experiences in camp, on the march, and in battle are clear and often compelling. Tunnard clearly tried to be as accurate as possible, no small task considering his strong personal feelings and the disordered period in which he wrote. From time to time his bitterness is obvious, but on the whole he is reasonably fair minded, even when discussing Yankees. He notes, for example, the generous behavior of Union soldiers toward hungry Confederates after the surrender of Vicksburg.

The basis of *A Southern Record* was a detailed journal that Tunnard maintained during his four years of military service. He copied from this source quite closely at times, especially when recounting daily events during the siege of Vicksburg, and on occasion he even slipped into the present tense he used during the war. He also relied heavily on official Confederate military records and on letters, diaries, and memories provided by nearly two dozen former comrades. Tunnard printed many of the official documents in full and included lengthy excerpts from several of the private documents. He was unable to find a copy of the regimental muster roll and was compelled to include what he termed a "necessarily incomplete" list of his former comrades, living and dead. In almost every other way, however, he succeeded in his quest to set the record straight and to ensure that the accomplishments achieved and sacrifices made by the men of the 3rd Louisiana would not be forgotten.

For Will Tunnard, as with so many other veterans, the years of arduous military service comprised the most important and most memorable period of his life. Indeed, it is probably no exaggeration to say that the Civil War never really ended for Tunnard. The publication of *A Southern Record* marked the beginning of a lifetime of commemorative activities. He joined various Confederate veterans' organizations and regularly attended reunions across the South. In the 1890s he was elected major general of the Louisiana Division of the United Confederate Veterans, at long last obtaining the "officer's commission" that had eluded him (or that he had avoided) during the war.

A Southern Record is among the best of all Confederate memoirs and regimental histories. Merton Coulter, the dean of southern Civil War historians, praised the book as an "exceptionally valuable commentary" on military affairs in the West, and the distinguished historian Allan Nevins considered it to be an "excellent composite of personal accounts of battles and army life." Tunnard undoubtedly would be pleased to know that his work has been so well received. He would perhaps be even more pleased to learn that with the publication of this paperback edition by the University of Arkansas Press, *A Southern Record* is now available to a wider audience than ever before.[4]

NOTES

1. William Watson, *Life in the Confederate Army* (London: n.p., 1887).

2. "Maj. Gen. Will H. Tunnard," *Confederate Veteran* 7 (1899): 22.

3. Arthur W. Bergeron, Jr., *Guide to Louisiana Confederate Military Units, 1861–1865* (Baton Rouge: Louisiana State University Press, 1989), 76–79.

4. E. Merton Coulter, ed., *Travels in the Confederate States, A Bibliography* (Norman: University of Oklahoma Press, 1948), 249; Allan Nevins, et al, eds., *Civil War Books: A Critical Bibliography* 2 vols. (Baton Rouge: Louisiana State University Press, 1967), 1:171.

A SOUTHERN RECORD

CHAPTER I

TRUTHFULNESS is the gem which gives to History its greatest charm; the golden light which adorns it with mellow rays for all coming time. Hence in making History by our own deeds, or writing them for present and future ages, we should adhere strictly to the promulgation of facts alone. It is a lamentable circumstance that deep-seated, ineradicable prejudices have been ingrafted into every published record which has been given to the public concerning the late struggle. Men must be governed by fixed principles, must adhere to cherished thoughts and feelings, and hence act, speak and write in conformity with these controlling influences. Thus the Northern mind thinks of the war as a gigantic rebellion to destroy the American Government, while the South conceived it to be a struggle for the preservation of constitutional freedom and their peculiar institutions. No one at the present time can properly determine the truth. Justice, with her nicely-balanced scales, must wait for historians of the next century to properly weigh facts, in order to discriminate between the North and South, and give to the world a correct record of events connected with this gigantic internecine strife. Fanaticism, that foul demon of discord and strife, first reared its hydra-head among the mountains and hills of New England. From an insignificant birth, it grew in strength and power until its influence extended over the whole North. The first aim and object of this foul spirit was the eradication of slavery on this continent, an interference with the peculiar institutions of one section by the powerful arm of the opposing section. In opposition to fanaticism grew up an equally malignant spirit in the South. As years passed by, feelings of hatred and enmity first engendered, grew in intensity and bitterness until all compromise was rejected and the sword was unsheathed to settle the differences which existed. Of the opening acts of the war it is needless to write. They are known by every man, woman and child in the land, and are engraven in characters of living light upon millions of throbbing hearts. After the election of Abraham Lincoln by a sectional minority, the Southern States, commencing with South Carolina, one by one severed the chains which had bound them in loving ties to the General Government. Banished was the starry flag which had floated so proudly over a great and powerful nation, forgotten were the wise teachings of a

Washington, when fanatical hate, marshaling its hosts, was confronted by a spirit of stern and uncompromising resistance. Human thought fails to express, in its conception of material objects, and their concomitant surroundings, the magnitude of this struggle. Neither can human mind place the blame where it justly belongs, without introducing amid its conceptions prejudices which, expressed, would destroy its reliability. Hence we infinitely prefer that others discuss this question *pro* and *con,* rather than make it a subject of conjecture and speculation in the pages of this volume.

In December, 1860, the General Assembly of Louisiana met in extraordinary session in obedience to the call of the Governor, Thomas O. Moore. After a short session acts were passed for the organization of the militia, in view of the threatening aspect of affairs between the General Government and the Southern States, and also for a convention of representatives from the people, to assemble January 23, 1861, to determine the future course and policy of Louisiana. At this time there was a state of feverish excitement all over the land. South Carolina had already taken the initiative, and severed her connection with the Federal Union, and State conventions had been called in Florida, Alabama, Mississippi, Texas, and Georgia. Previous to the assembling of the Louisiana Convention, on January 12, 1861, the United States Arsenal and Barracks at Baton Rouge were taken formal possession of by the State authorities, being surrendered to Gov. Moore by the officer then in command, Maj. Haskin, of the U.S. Army. This important event was achieved without bloodshed, although accomplished amid intense excitement. This victory, so important, was gained through the instrumentality of a battalion from New Orleans under command of J. B. Walton, composed of the Crescent City Rifles, Chasseurs-a-Pied, Louisiana Guards, Washington Artillery, Orleans Cadets, Sarsfield Rifles, and Louisiana Grays, with a Grosse Tête Company, Delta Rifles, Pelican Rifles, National Guards, and Creole Guards of Baton Rouge. By this prompt action of seizure, an immense quantity of arms, artillery, and munitions of war of every description, fell into the possession of the State. On the 23d of January, 1861, the Convention assembled, and after four days' deliberation passed the ordinance of secession, with nearly a unanimous vote. As elsewhere, the action of this body was received with the wildest enthusiasm, and the State flag everywhere floated in the breeze. The whole State and land were turned from peaceful pursuits into preparations for the expected fierce, bloody, and deadly struggle.

The arms captured at the arsenal were rapidly distributed to the volunteer organizations, and forwarded to the forts and troops elsewhere. At Pensacola, Fla., and Charleston, S.C., the opposing forces confronted each other, both parties preparing for the coming strife, February 9th, 1861. At Montgomery,

Ala., was formed the Provisional Government of the Confederate States, by South Carolina, Florida, Mississippi, Alabama, Georgia and Louisiana, a constellation around which clustered in radiant beauty nearly all the remainder of the Southern States. Jefferson Davis, of Mississippi, was chosen President, and Alexander H. Stephens, of Georgia, Vice-President. After the organization of the Confederate Government, scenes (familiar now as household words) full of excitement followed each other in rapid succession. All attempts to settle the sectional difficulties and differences on some peaceable basis were rejected by the Federal Government, until they at last culminated, on April 12th, 1861, into an open rupture. The U.S. Government then attempted to convey reinforcements and supplies into Fort Sumter, off Charleston, S.C. The attempt was frustrated by the batteries under General Beauregard opening fire on the approaching vessel, and preventing her entrance. A fierce conflict took place between Fort Sumter and the Confederate States batteries. Thus the gun that bellowed out its hoarse thunder across the waters of Charleston harbor, proclaimed the momentous fact that war had actually begun. Peaceful arbitration was a failure, now that the sword must determine the issue.

In obedience to instructions from Governor Moore, the Pelican Rifles★ of Baton Rouge (organized November 25th, 1859, and of which the author was a member) entered upon garrison duty in the barracks, having already offered their services to the State. At this time nearly every steamer going down the Mississippi River was loaded with volunteer companies hastening to New Orleans preparatory to being organized into regiments for muster into the Confederate service. Impatiently already organized companies waited for the call which would permit them to hasten to the seat of war. It came at last, in the following proclamation of the Governor:

"HEADQUARTERS LOUISIANA MILITIA,⎱
Adjutant-General's Office, N. O., April 21, 1861 ⎰

"The President of the Confederate States having made a requisition upon the Governor of Louisiana for five thousand infantry to serve for twelve months, unless sooner discharged, (this force being in addition to the three thousand already called for,) I, Thomas O. Moore, Governor of the State of

---

★This company was organized during the excitement occasioned by the raid of John Brown into Virginia, and in anticipation of a general insurrection throughout the Southern States. Their banner was manufactured out of rich blue silk and the most costly trimmings. On one side was painted the seal of the State, and on the reverse side the motto "Southern Rights Inviolate," surrounded with a golden wreath, thus proclaiming it the first Southern rights flag unfurled in Louisiana.

Louisiana, do hereby proclaim that volunteers will be received in accordance
with the requisition of the President of the Confederate States, each company
to be composed of not less than sixty-four privates, four sergeants, four cor-
porals, one captain, one first lieutenant and one second lieutenant. Volunteers
will be received by companies, battalions or regiments. Those offering will
address Adjutant-General M. Grivot, at New Orleans, stating the force of their
command, will remain in the parish in which they form, perfect themselves
in drill, etc., and hold themselves in readiness at a moment's notice, subject to
the orders of the Governor. The Governor appeals to the patriotic citizens of
this State to respond to this proclamation for the protection of the rights of
the State. By order of

"THOMAS O. MOORE,
"*Governor and Commander-in-Chief.*

"M. Grivot, *Adjutant and Inspector-General, La.*"

The above order was promptly and eagerly responded to, and the question
was not who shall go, but rather who will remain at home. Creole and
American, Celt and Gaul, old and young, rich and poor, all were ready for the
fray. Southern blood had already been shed, and Southern hearts grew strong
in defence of their homes and firesides, which sheltered the dear ones. Among
the first companies who responded to the proclamation of the Governor was
the Pelican Rifles of Baton Rouge. Its departure was marked by one of those
indescribable scenes which were just at this period so numerous in the land, and
which each survivor of our early volunteers remembers as if emblazoned in the
heavens in characters of living light. What one among the thousands who then
went forth to peril life and limbs in defence of cherished principles, does not
remember the last farewell of loved ones, the clasp of soft arms around manly
forms, the unspeakable eloquence of tearful eyes, the hopeless despair of whose
glance followed him through long and weary campaigns, and came back to
memory amid the din, uproar, and carnage of battle? Yet there was no flinching in those loving hearts, no appeals to remain, and Omnipotence alone could
note the wild agony of the loved ones, as, with warm kisses and cheerful words,
they bade sons, husbands, brothers and fathers go forth to the defence of their
own sunny land. Such scenes may well become a part of history, for they exhibit
the deep patriotism which actuates the human heart in the hour of peril to the
land we love.

On the broad stream of the turbid Mississippi—away from homes, from
friends—parted, "it may be for years, it may be forever;" mingling with like
brave spirits actuated by the same feelings of patriotic devotion to country and

principle. In New Orleans at last;—the great throbbing commercial emporium of the State and the South, swelling the list of companies already present. All is bustle and activity. Ladies in countless numbers throng the galleries, and strong-hearted men crowd the banquets to greet with smile and cheer each organization as it marches with steady tread over the paved streets.

The spot selected as a place of encampment for the rapidly arriving volunteers is known as the Metairie Course, then called Camp Walker. Some of the companies which were to form part of the Third Regiment Louisiana Infantry had already arrived, and others on the way when we reached the camp. What a scene for one unaccustomed to witness a regular encampment! In the early part of May upward of 3,000 troops were present, and still rapidly arriving. It was a somewhat different affair from holiday soldiering at home. The enforcement of strict and rigid military discipline, the daily compulsory drill, guard mounting and duty, caused many a high-toned and independent spirit to rebel against restrictions upon personal liberty. Yet the duties imposed were bravely, and at last cheerfully, discharged. It was a spectacle both strange and new to see young men, reared amid the luxuries and comforts at home, whose fair faces and white hands had never been soiled by contact with work, doing soldier duty, bending over the camp-fire, preparing meals or boiling coffee, tears streaming from their eyes, caused by villainous smoke from these same camp-fires, carrying wood and water, and when the day's duties were completed, lying down upon a board or the bare ground with knapsack or billet of wood for a pillow, and a single blanket for covering. Without doubt visions of soft beds and downy pillows haunted the young soldier's first dreams in camp. The companies present were immediately organized into regiments, preparatory to being mustered into the Confederate States service and proceeding to the seat of war.

CHAPTER II

In May, 1861, the Third Regiment, Louisiana Infantry, was organized by the selection of the following officers: Colonel, Louis Hebert; Lieutenant-Colonel, S. M. Hyams, Sr., of Natchitoches; Major, W. F. Tunnard, of Baton Rouge.

FIELD AND STAFF.—Quartermaster, Theodore Johnson, Iberville; Commissary, T. L. Maxwell; Surgeon, ——— Breedlove; Chaplain, Rev. P. F. Dicharry; Adjutant-Lieutenant, J. Harvey Brigham.

The regiment was composed of the following companies:

Company "A," Iberville Greys: Captain, Charles A. Bruslé; First Lieutenant, T. C. Brown; Second Lieutenant, T. G. Stringer; Second Lieutenant, Jr., T. R. Verbois; Non-Commissioned Officers and Privates, 87 strong.

Company "B," Morehouse Guards: Captain, R. M. Hinson; First Lieutenant, W. S. Hall; Second Lieutenant, D. C. Morgan; Second Lieutenant, Jr., J. H. Brigham; Non-Commissioned Officers and Privates, 124 strong.

Company "C," Winn Rifles: Captain, David Pierson; First Lieutenant, Asa Emanuel; Second Lieutenant, William Strother; Second Lieutenant, Jr., W. C. Lurry; Non-Commissioned Officers and Privates, 89 strong.

Company "D," Pelican Rangers, No. 2: Captain, J. D. Blair; First Lieutenant, S. D. Russell; Second Lieutenant, W. E. Russell; Second Lieutenant, Jr., S. M. Hyams, Jr.; Non-Commissioned Officers and Privates, 77 strong.

Company "E," Morehouse Fencibles: Captain, J. F. Harris; First Lieutenant, P. C. Brigham; Second Lieutenant, P. Brooks; Second Lieutenant, Jr., W. D. Brigham; Non-Commissioned Officers and Privates, 78 strong.

Company "F," Shreveport Rangers: Captain, J. B. Gilmore; First Lieutenant, W. A. Lacey; Second Lieutenant, O. J. Wells; Second Lieutenant, Jr., A. Jewell; Non-Commissioned Officers and Privates, 115 strong.

Company "G," Pelican Rangers, No. 1: Captain, W. W. Brezeale; First Lieutenant, W. O. Brezeale; Second Lieutenant, G. W. Halloway; Second Lieutenant, Jr., L. Caspari; Non-Commissioned Officers and Privates, 157 strong.

Company "H," Monticello Rifles: Captain, J. S. Richards; First Lieutenant, W. D. Hardiman; Second Lieutenant, W. H. Corbin; Second Lieutenant, Jr., Cy. A. Hedrick; Non-Commissioned Officers and Privates, 107 strong.

Company "I," Caldwell Guards: Captain, W. S. Gunnell; First Lieutenant, J. C. Evans; Second Lieutenant, L. B. Fluitt; Second Lieutenant, Jr., T. J. Humble; Non-Commissioned Officers and Privates, 116 strong.

Company "K," Pelican Rifles: Captain, John P. Viglini; First Lieutenant, John B. Irvin; Second Lieutenant, F. D. Tunnard; Second Lieutenant, Jr., F. R. Brunot; Non-Commissioned Officers and Privates, 87 strong.

Total strength of the Regiment: Field Officers, 8; Line Officers, 40; Non-Commissioned Officers, 92; Privates, 945. Grand total, 1085.

The various companies were mustered into the State service in April and May, and the Regiment was formally received into the Confederate service on the 17th day of May, 1861.

This body of stalwart men were from the country parishes, represented as follows: Company "A," Plaquemine; Companies "B" and "E," Morehouse; Company "C," Winn; Companies "D" and "G," Natchitoches; Company "F," Caddo; Company "H," Carroll; Company "I," Caldwell; and Company "K," East Baton Rouge.

This Regiment, numbering 1085 men, were the bone and sinew, some of the choicest spirits from the parishes which they represented, mostly young men, with the glow of health upon their features and the fire of a patriotic devotion and enthusiasm sparkling in their clear eyes; men who went forth actuated by a firm conviction of right, earnest adherents to principle; whose brave spirits met the issue squarely, and would not quail or flinch when the day of danger and trial arrived. Strange as it may seem, this organization of robust young men were commanded by field officers whose heads were streaked with gray—men of age and experience.

General Louis Hebert was born in the parish of Iberville, La., March 13, 1820. He graduated at Jefferson College, St. James' Parish, La., December 10, 1840; entered West Point as a cadet in June, 1841, and graduated third in his class, in all his studies, on June 19, 1845. He was appointed Brevet Second Lieutenant in the Corps of Engineers, U.S.A., and served as such until February, 1846, when, on account of sickness in his family, he resigned from the army to superintend his father's affairs.

In 1853 General Hebert was elected State Senator, from the senatorial district then composed of the parishes of West Baton Rouge and Iberville, for a term of four years, but only served in the session of 1854 and 1855. During the session of 1855 he was appointed and confirmed State Engineer which office he accepted, and resigned his Senatorship. He continued State Engineer (being repeatedly re-appointed) until the office was abolished in 1859. In 1860 he was elected a member of the Board of Public Works of the State; but the Board was abolished by the Legislature in 1861. From 1856 to 1861, General Hebert held the commission of Colonel of Militia of East Baton Rouge. Such is the brief outline of the history of the first colonel of the Third Louisiana Infantry. After the fall of Vicksburg, General Hebert was stationed at Wilmington, N.C., where he constructed fortifications which exhibited his splendid talents for engineering, an occupation in which he was skilled, and for which he was pre-eminently fitted by education.

As an officer, he was a strict disciplinarian, punctilious in enforcing a rigid adherence to all orders; as a man, he was genial and kind in manner and conversation. The old members of the Third Regiment may remember now how exacting the Colonel was in demanding a ready and close adherance to his orders, and how they writhed under the rule of his iron hand. Yet, after all, the Colonel became a great favorite with the Regiment, which manifested its feelings on every favorable opportunity. As the leader of a regiment or the commander of a brigade, General Hebert was cool, and exhibited his military training and education.

Lieutenant-Colonel S. M. Hyams, of Natchitoches, was born in Charleston, S.C., September 16, 1813, and was a student at Charleston College under President Adams. He came to New Orleans in 1830, and was a student at Centenary College, Jackson, up to 1834. Went to Natchitoches in 1834 and returned to New Orleans the succeeding year. He held the office successively as U.S. Deputy Surveyor and Clerk of the District Court, Natchitoches. In 1846, on the call of Governor Johnson for six months' men to serve in Mexico, he raised a company, and was Captain in the Fifth Regiment, Louisiana Volunteers, but was mustered out the same year with his regiment and returned home. He was then elected Sheriff, which office he filled for six years, and was afterward U.S. Marshal, Western District of Louisiana, and Register of the Land Office.

He brought to New Orleans a company of fine men, showing conclusively the confidence reposed in his ability as a tactician and soldier. His military experience needed no better recommendation than the fact that he was chosen as captain of Company "G."

As a man, Colonel Hyams is hospitable to a fault. Both lawyer and planter, his name is known far and near for his generosity and affability. Often have we known the Colonel to forget his position and rank in his feelings as a man. His men were always pleasantly welcomed to his quarters. Though almost a confirmed cripple from the rheumatism, the Colonel exhibited his devotion to his country by thus braving the hardships of a soldier's life while subject to an almost incurable disease. We never think of Lieutenant-Colonel Hyams but what the heart grows warm with eloquent feelings.

Major W. F. Tunnard, a native of New York, born in N. Y. City on June 17, 1809, came to the South many years ago, and was identified with it in heart, feeling and principle. A mechanic by trade, he built up a fortune and reputation by close application to business, gaining an enviable reputation for fairness and truthfulness in all his business relations. Of untiring energy, activity and perseverance, firm and resolute in his views and plans, unbending in his prejudices and determination, of iron nerve and great activity, he linked his fortunes to the young Confederacy, and went forth to battle in defence of his home and the land of his choice. He gathered about him the flower of Baton Rouge, the choice spirits of the city, mostly young men just entering the threshold of manhood. Devotedly attached to military pursuits, with years of experience as a tactician, he was eminently fitted to command. His voice was trumpet-toned, clear and distinct. As a soldier and commander, Major Tunnard was beloved by the whole of the Regiment, among the survivors of which are now some of his warmest friends. He was a strict disciplinarian, but when released from his position as commander, mingled freely with the men, often joining in their sports and games. Like Colonel Hyams, he left family and business behind him, and, with his sons, joined the early volunteers. Colonel Hyams had three sons in the Regiment and Major Tunnard two.

Under men of years and experience such as these, was the Third Regiment organized for active service.

On the 7th of May there was a grand review of all the troops in Camp Walker by Governor Moore and staff. The affair was grand and imposing at this early date, and attracted an immense concourse of people, the majority of whom were our fair Southern ladies, always present with their bright smiles and cheering words to encourage the young volunteers. Among the participants in this were the following companies, afterward belonging to the Third Regiment: A, C, D, F, G, I and K. The men at this period were becoming initiated into the mysteries of camp life, and accustomed to its daily routine, which were by no means light. At early dawn the reveille roused them from slumber. Roll being called, the companies were dismissed to put their quarters in order. Breakfast at 6 o'clock A.M. In the mean time ten men from each company were detailed to serve in the main guard, to enforce discipline and guard the camp. A police guard was also appointed, who cleaned up all dirt and filth about the tents, brought water for the company, wood for the cooks, and, in fact, kept everything in order and cleanliness. During the afternoon, squad drills. Who does not remember those squad drills, and the double-quick around the race-track? The boys became equal to racers. Living on a race-course made the disease for running contagious. At sundown, company muster for roll-call and supper. Tattoo at 9 o'clock P.M., when the men retired to their respective tents; fifteen minutes later, three taps of the drum compelled every light to be extinguished, and the camp was in darkness and quietude. These duties were conducted with regularity and precision, and performed with a promptitude and cheerfulness surprising in men who had never known restraint, and were fresh from the luxuries and pleasures of home. Everything necessary for the comfort and convenience of the troops was furnished, and laugh, jest and song attested the general satisfaction and good feeling of the men.

On the 17th of May, 1861, the Third Regiment was mustered into the Confederate service by Lieutenant Pfiffer, and shortly afterward receiving marching orders, prepared to leave for a field of active service. All was bustle and confusion, and the men were in high spirits, full of enthusiasm and joviality at the prospect of the change. To them anything seemed preferable to a longer stay in the low, marshy grounds of Camp Walker, with its myriads of mosquitoes and other inconveniences. At 4 P.M., May 20th, the regiment formed and took up the line of march for the river. There is something solemn yet soul-stirring in the solid tramp of a large body of armed men, as they depart for some scene of deadly strife, with ensigns fluttering in the breeze, and the strains of martial music or the roll of the stirring drum. From Camp Walker the march of the regiment was one grand ovation, the balconies of the houses, banquets and streets being crowded with countless thousands of men, women and children, bidding the brave boys farewell. Many knew that it was a last farewell to the enthusiastic and noble soldiers of this command, and they duly appreciated the heartfelt expressions of sympathy showered upon them, and the emotion manifested upon many fair and lovely faces. As the regiment passed down Canal Street, a gentleman remarked: "There goes a body of men who will make their mark on the battle-field." Let history prove the correctness of this spontaneous sentiment. On the arrival of the regiment at the river, they were marched on board the steamers Arkansas, Arkansaw, Indian No. 2, and Countess, their destination being announced as Fort Smith, to aid in checking a threatened invasion of our Western border. This announcement was a sad blow to the expectations of a large mass of the regiment, as they anticipated being ordered to Virginia. "Man proposes, but God disposes." At 9 P.M. the regiment cheered its last adieu to New Orleans. The next evening the boats arrived at Baton Rouge. It having been telegraphed from New Orleans that the regiment would reach Baton Rouge early on the 21st, the population turned out *en masse* to give them a reception and take a last farewell of Company K, Pelican Rifles. The Arkansas having on board the Monticello and Pelican Rifles and Iberville Greys alone, touched at the landing, and a half hour was given the members of Company K to bid a final adieu to friends and relatives. The landing was packed to its utmost capacity with citizens of both sexes; the scene that ensued beggars all description. Language grows weak and impotent in the attempt to portray these early parting scenes of the war. The warm embrace, the streaming eyes, agonizing expressions of sorrow, loving words of cheer and advice, the whispered prayers for the loved ones' safety, the tokens of love and remembrance are memories as ineffaceable as the foot-prints of time. Regardless in the abandonment of the excitement and deep feel-ings of the moment, the members of the different companies were seized by the ladies, kissed and embraced indiscriminately. Those soft, encircling arms, and the warm pressure of loving lips, lingers with the soldier to his dying hour, and often comes back with irrepressible influence to the hearts of those who survive the dread carnage of battling hosts. Many a sly joke and rich story did the members of Companies A and H have to relate concerning their recep-tion at Baton Rouge. Fair countrywomen! 'twas but the expression of your woman's sympathy, deep affection and abiding hope, in the cause which your loved ones had espoused. Tuesday, May 21st, will long be remembered by those who participated in those parting scenes. Many of those warmly throb-bing hearts now mouldering lie 'neath the green sod of distant States in the soldier's humble grave, but the survivors cherish the memory of those by-gone scenes with deep reverence and holy affection. At the expiration of the given time the men promptly returned to the boat and cheered their adieu. As the steamers passed up the river, an innumerable number and variety of fire-works were discharged, presenting a beautiful and exciting spectacle, the farewell offering of a large number of patriotic ladies who had collected for this pur-pose. Scenes similar to this occurred at Plaquemine, Lake Providence, where-ever the regiment had friends and relatives, while the river banks at every plantation, hamlet, city and village poured forth their inhabitants to wave an adieu to the men. Such enthusiasm, unanimity of sentiment and feeling, was never before known and exhibited. On the 23d the boats landed opposite Vicksburg to await the arrival of Colonel Hebert, who had been detained in New Orleans. The next day left this city and proceeded up the river. Again a halt was made at Napoleon, in expectation of the arrival of the Colonel. Up to this period little had occurred to mar the hilarious spirits and reckless jovi-ality of the men. Several men had died on the trip, the joint effects of a change of diet and manner of living. Here occurred the first funeral of the regiment, being the burial of one of the members of Company F, private Thomas D. Smith. As the sad and silent procession followed a comrade in arms to his final resting-place, gloomy thoughts arose in many a manly bosom. How mournful thus to die among rough but sympathizing comrades, with no soft hand to wipe the death-damp from the clammy brow, no loved voice to whisper words of hope and consolation to the departing spirit! Yet such was "the beginning of the end" to many a sorrowful scene through which the soldier is destined to pass. Now scenes of suffering and death have not blunted the feelings or familiarized the mind with human agony, and the heart must needs go out in tender sympathy toward the far-distant relatives of the buried volunteer.

"WAS IT THE SERGEANT OR CAPTAIN?"

When the regiment left New Orleans, on board the steamer Countess were Companies F, G and D, commanded by Lieutenant Colonel S. M. Hyams, Lieutenant A. W. Jewell, appointed Adjutant, and Sergeant Kinney, Sergeant-Major of the detachment. "This was our first starting out in search of war," says the narrator, "and to illustrate how much we knew of military matters, I will relate the following circumstance. The boat on which we were, the Countess, as stated, had on board three companies. We had our regular guard, officer of the day, officer of the guard, and guard mounting every morning. One evening, not long after leaving New Orleans, Captain Gilmore (afterward Colonel) made the following remarks to his Orderly Sergeant:

"Sergeant, you have put all the company on guard now, and I think it is about time you were going on guard yourself."

"Very well, Sir," replied the Orderly, who went and seized a gun, relieved the man on duty, and stood guard there all night, no one coming to relieve him. In the morning the Lieutenant of the Guard asked the Sergeant if he was Orderly of Company F? The Sergeant replied, "Yes, Sir."

"How comes it, then," inquired the Lieut., "that you are on guard?"

"Why," replied the Sergeant, "the Captain ordered me to stand guard."

"But the Captain has no right to order you on guard," and with this remark the Lieutenant turned on his heel and left, laughing heartily. The Orderly goes up stairs, went into the cabin, rushes up to his Captain, who was reading a paper, and very quietly remarked: "Captain, you have no right to put me on guard."

"I have, Sir," said the Captain, jumping up from his chair, "and I wish you to distinctly understand that I am Captain of this company, and when I order a man to go on guard or do anything else, he shall do it."

"I'll go and see Colonel Hyams, then," replied the Sergeant.

"Very well, Sir," spoke the Captain, and sat down.

The Sergeant went to Colonel H., who was reading in the ladies' cabin, and asked him if the Captain could put him (the Sergeant) on guard.

"No, Sir," replied the Colonel, "you are the man to make the guard detail in your company."

This information tickled the Sergeant, who straightway went to his Captain and said:

"Captain, I am the man who puts every man on guard in the company, and I'll put you on next."

The Captain dropped his paper, jumped up and went to the Colonel. What the conversation was between them I have not the means of knowing, as the Captain would never speak on that subject. Anyway, the Captain and the Sergeant never ordered each other on guard afterward.

CHAPTER III

LITTLE ROCK

ON the 27th of May the regiment reached Little Rock, Ark. The journey toward Fort Smith was brought to a sudden termination by a request from the authorities that the regiment should quarter here, as rumors were prevalent that Jim Lane, of Kansas notoriety, was about to assail this post. The next day the command was disembarked, under the leadership of Col. Hyams, and marched to the former U.S. Arsenal grounds, already occupied by a large body of State troops, composed of cavalry and artillery, and a large force of militia, armed with the formidable long-barreled rifle, which rendered the backwoodsmen of Kentucky so famed in the first revolutionary struggle. The same spirit which throbbed and pulsated in every Southern heart animated the volunteers of Arkansas, who hastened to the common defence, armed and equipped with every conceivable weapon. The camp here was very comfortable. The grounds beautifully laid out, and shaded by large and handsome oaks. The Arsenal buildings at Little Rock are fine and of durable construction. Here a number of the regiment were detailed to construct cartridges for the command, which was soon amply supplied and prepared to meet the foe. While camped here they participated in one of those thrilling and affecting scenes which were then so frequent, but yet always full of deep interest, being the occasion of a flag presentation to a company of Churchill's cavalry regiment, by one of Little Rock's fairest daughters, Miss Faulkner. The address of the lady orator was one of peculiar force and unsurpassed eloquence. Her clear, ringing voice was heard by all, and her manner and words sent a thrill of enthusiasm to every manly bosom, attested by frequent, loud and prolonged bursts of applause. As the regiment marched from the grounds each company, in passing the splendid banner, greeted it with hearty cheers, which were lustily returned by the cavalry troop, in loud huzzas for the Louisiana regiment.

The ladies of Little Rock daily visited the encampment, and seemed to be particularly fond of certain members of the Regiment. Unsurpassed for beauty of person, refinement, and elegance of manners, it was not surprising that they became the objects of devoted admiration. Could the green turf or the rustling trees o'erhead have spoken, many would be the tales they would unfold of the soft pressure of loving hands, and whispered words of affectionate devotion. Alas! for the forgotten charms of those fair ones, so recently left in sorrow and tears!

CHAPTER IV

CAMP POTEAU

ON the 5th of June the Regiment embarked for Fort Smith. The river having risen suddenly, rendered unnecessary a march to Fort Smith, much to the relief of the men. They reached Fort Smith on the 7th, and became a portion of the Western army under the command of Gen. Ben McCulloch, the famed Texas Ranger. The camp selected was an open field, one and a half miles south of Fort Smith, near a stream called Poteau, on the neutral ground that separates Arkansas from Indian Territory. The Poteau is a deep, sluggish stream, with rocky banks, and empties into the Arkansas River above Fort Smith. This stream afforded a fine bathing-place for the men, and its precipitous rocky banks, crowned with huge trees, furnished abundant shade for those disposed to lounge beneath their protecting shelter. The men suffered severely from the heat, day succeeding day, clear and sultry, with scarcely a breath of air to stir the leaves of the trees or cool the suffocating atmosphere. Early in June, General McCulloch returned to Fort Smith from the Indian Nation, where he had been, endeavoring to form an alliance with the different tribes and obtain their assistance in achieving Southern independence. His mission had proved unsuccessful, and another conference had been appointed to take place on the 20th of June. The success of his mission was anxiously watched, as the tribes on the Western frontier would prove powerful and desirable auxiliaries at this period. General McCulloch at this time did not visit the Regiment, although the men were eager to see their future leader, already so famed as a Ranger on the Texan frontier. Rumors were prevalent that Lane, of Kansas notoriety, was about advancing on Fort Smith. His approach was anticipated, and his coming would have received a *warm* welcome. The force encamped near Fort Smith at this period consisted of two infantry and one cavalry regiment, and a company of artillery.

Col. Hebert reached the Regiment in company with Surgeon Breedlove on the 16th. He inaugurated immediately a strict observance of military rules and regulations. The regiment imagined Col. Hyams had been rigid enough as a commander, but he was surpassed by Col. Hebert. Drills and parades, a close adherence to issued orders were required and enforced, until the regiment became equal to regulars in the discharge of their various duties. Of course numbers complained at the rigid discipline to which they were subjected, having scarcely gained the important knowledge as yet that the first duty of a soldier was obedience to orders, and next, that troops were the most efficient when most thoroughly trained. On the 19th of June the first Regimental Court-Martial was convened, consisting of Col. Louis Hebert, President; Maj. Tunnard, Lieuts. Evans, Lacy, Russell, and Hyams; Capt. C. A. Bruslé, Judge Advocate; Lieut. F. Brunot, Recorder. The measles became epidemic in camp, and several of the regiment died and found soldiers' graves. All through the hot and sultry days of June did the regiment remain at Camp Poteau, watching anxiously the incipient stages of the war breaking out in various portions of the land, destined at last to sweep with simoom blast over the whole country. During this time Missouri awakened from her lethargy like a giant aroused from deep slumber, and her hardy sons began to prepare for the coming struggle. Bound in the strong chains of military power with foes within and without her borders, yet did she not quail, cower or shrink from the issue. With the uprising of the Missourians, the troops of the Confederate States began hastening to the rescue. The Third Regiment received marching orders on the 28th of June, and began active preparations for their first march. Generals Lyon and Lane were both reported approaching Fort Wayne, our probable destination. Gen. McCulloch's little army was rapidly increasing in strength. His activity, energy and determination infused life into all the command. The men grew hilarious over the anticipation of an active campaign, and rejoiced at the prospect of a change from an idle camp life to scenes more worthy the spirit which had led them thus far from home. On the first of July the First Division, comprising companies A, B, G, D, and F, left Camp Poteau under command of Col. S. M. Hyams, *en route* for some point northward, and camped opposite Van Buren.

2nd. Crossed the river and marched four miles. 3rd. Marched eighteen miles and camped at Natural Dam. 4th. Marched twenty miles, crossed Baston Mountain, and camped at Evansville. To-day Col. Hyams made a neat, appropriate and patriotic speech, of which no record was preserved. 5th. Marched twenty-two and one-half miles, and camped at Cincinnati. 6th. Marched twenty miles to "Double Springs." 7th. Marched fourteen miles to Maysville. Dr. Kendall was sent to Gen. McCulloch with a special dispatch, announcing the arrival of the detachment, and the desire to push forward and join him, if needed. He returned the next day, having ridden 114 miles in 23 hours.

THE MARCH TO CAMP JACKSON

The Second Division, comprising Companies C, E, H, I and K, under command of Major W. F. Tunnard, left Camp Poteau on the morning of the 4th. This was to be no holiday parade amid peaceful pursuits as in days gone by. At 2 o'clock A.M. the reveille aroused the men from their slumbers. Knapsacks for the first time were strapped on shoulders all unused to the burden. The shelters which had so long protected the men from the scorching summer's heat were given to the flames, and amid the wildest enthusiasm the men commenced the march. What a day of severe experience it was, all who participated therein will remember. Shoulders grew sore under the burden of supporting knapsacks; limbs wearied from the painful march, and feet grew swollen and blistered as the troops marched along the dusty road. Knapsacks were recklessly thrown by the roadside or relieved of a large portion of their contents, under the intolerable agony of that first march of only nine miles. Each morning the detachment was aroused at 1 A.M., and taking a hasty meal, consisting of crackers and a cup of coffee, resumed the march. The country was rocky, and the road hard and precipitous. The men, however, soon became accustomed to marching, and bore its hardships with fortitude and courage, keeping up their spirits with songs and jokes as they tramped steadily forward. The myriad of stars looked down on a strange scene indeed as this band of reckless soldiers proceeded on their journey. On the 6th crossed Baston Mountain. The ascent was gradual, yet in places precipitous, the road being a mass of solid rock, full of boulders and loose stones, extending upward for a distance of over a mile. The Major dismounted and led the men on foot, and while they threw themselves in perfect exhaustion on the ground to recover breath after the severe climb, exhibited his activity by a run and jump over some of the prostrate forms. The descent was very precipitous, and the boys made it at a double-quick, being unable to halt after getting under full speed. Few are there who do not remember that rocky ascent, and if you wished to make one of the Louisianians swear for weeks afterward, say "Baston Mountain." It was quite sufficient to make expletives innumerable. The detachment usually arrived in camp between 10 A.M. and 12, thus making their marches mostly before the heat of the day. When the day's journey was ended, the men generally threw themselves upon the ground and slept long and soundly ere thinking of preparing anything to eat. Just beyond Baston Mountain is the village of Cincinnati, near which the detachment encamped. They were enthusiastically greeted by the inhabitants, and here, as elsewhere along the route, the people exhibited their generosity by furnishing the men with milk and eatables, such as they possessed. These acts of kindness were appreciated and properly acknowledged. While in camp, near Cincinnati, a great, awkward specimen of the young Arkansas backwoodsman came into camp. He strolled among the men with mouth and eyes wide open, with a mingled expression of amazement, astonishment and curiosity on his features, much to the amusement of the men. His wonder increased the longer he looked about him, until, approaching a piece of artillery, his thoughts found expression. Addressing a Captain standing near by, he remarked:

"I say, meister, what is this yere thing?"

"A cannon," remarked the Captain, as the muscles of his mouth began to twitch and his eyes to sparkle.

"A cannon, hey! What in thunder is that fur, I should like to know?"

The Captain explained.

His eyes grew yet more distended.

"Well," drawing a long breath, "that's the darndest gun ever I seed."

Coming close to the Captain with an inquiring glance and whispered words, he asked:

"I say, meister, how much might that ere cannon cost?"

"Oh, about two dimes like these," said the officer, pulling them from his pocket.

"Is them ere dimes?—well I declare;" and, turning away, he walked off muttering indistinctly the words "cannons" and "dimes." Of course the conversation was frequently interrupted by explosions of laughter from the circle who had gathered around this green specimen of *genus homo*.

One redeeming feature of this rocky, mountainous country was the number of cold springs. Ah! it was a delicious luxury after the day's weary march to bathe the swollen, feverish and blistered feet in these streams of clear, sparkling water; a luxury scarcely to be exchanged for a place in Mahomet's paradise.

While on the march information reached us that a fight had taken place at Neosho, Mo. General McCulloch had surprised the enemy there, and Captain McIntosh, Adjutant-General of the Brigade, reported the capture of eighty Federals, one hundred rifles, and seven wagons loaded with provisions. Two of these wagons were loaded with delicacies and provisions sent by the ladies as a Fourth of July dinner for the Republicans. Unfortunately both the intended recipients and their luxuries fell into the hands of the Southerners, and the Union dinner well suited rebel appetites.

The country, as you approach Maysville, becomes more level, until finally it merges into a fine open rolling prairie land, interspersed with belts of timber. The detachment reached Camp Jackson at 10 A.M. on the morning of the 9th, in fine spirits and health, having performed their first march from Fort Smith, a distance of over 100 miles, over a rough road and in the midst of the hottest season of the year, in five days and two hours. The first detachment were in camp awaiting our arrival. Quite a number of troops, comprising artillery, infantry and cavalry, had already assembled here from Missouri and Arkansas. McCulloch arrived at the same time from his trip to Neosho, bringing with him abundant evidence of his success. It was here the Third Regiment had their first good look at their leader. He was enthusiastically welcomed, and complimented the regiment highly upon their fine military appearance and bearing. A good story was told of General McCulloch's strategy in learning the enemy's force and plans. Disguised as a drover he went boldly into the Federal camp to sell his cattle, of which he had a number. He succeeded admirably without his rank or intentions being discovered, and having gained all necessary information, made the attack which proved so successful. Of undaunted courage, iron nerve and will, never for a moment losing his self-control under the most trying circumstances, he delighted in such perilous adventures. The Federals at this time were in force near Springfield, and the General went energetically to work organizing his little army preparatory to an early move on the foe.

CHAPTER V

CAMP JACKSON

CAMP JACKSON, so named in honor of the Governor of Missouri, was located about three miles east of Maysville, in a belt of woods skirting the eastern limits of a broad expanse of prairie stretching its bosom far away south, north and west. The prairie in front of the encampment furnished a fine and ample parade-ground, and the grass was not left to grow undisturbed by the evolutions of armed men.

On the 12th the troops were once more under marching orders, and at 8 A.M. next morning left Camp Jackson for Bentonville, distant 28 miles. There were about three thousand men on the road, which was terribly dusty, and the weather, as usual, clear and sultry. Ammunition was distributed to the troops, and everything pointed to an early engagement. Marched fifteen and a half miles. On the 14th passed through Bentonville, a small but pleasant village, situated in Benton County, on the outskirts of an extended prairie. This was the Sabbath, yet to the soldier all days seemed alike. How different this dusty, long march, from the quiet Sabbaths at home, where matin-bells summon a Christian people to the houses of worship! War is a hard task-master, and heeds not the calls of conscience. As usual, springs of cool, clear water were abundant along the route. Marched 12 miles. On the 15th we encamped amid the hills of Arkansas at a spot known as Camp McCulloch, being a small field on the level surface of one of the numerous rocky promontories of the country. The rain poured down in torrents, and we began to experience some of the inconveniences of a soldier's varied existence. The men made beds of the rails from a worm-fence close at hand, to keep their bodies from the damp ground, covering their rough edges with straw and shucks, which they deemed an especial luxury, and upon which they laid down to pleasant dreams. Receiving marching orders early the next day, the troops moved forward a short distance and encamped on Sugar Creek, a small mountain stream winding its tortuous way amid the surrounding hills. This was known as Camp Stephens, in honor of our Vice-President, being seven miles east of Bentonville. Here Gratiot's

Arkansas regiment joined us. The weather was unusually fine, our encampment pleasant, yet many of the extra duty men will remember the severe labor of clearing a parade-ground where they obtained their first experience in digging up stumps and grubbing out roots. While remaining here a tremendous storm occurred at night, flooding the camp with water, which flowed in a miniature river through its centre, sweeping away pans, basins, tables, etc. Amid the lightning's vivid flash and the deep roll of the thunder could be heard the shouts of the men, exclamations and expletives, as they were literally drowned out of their beds. "Knee-deep," one would shout. "Quarter less twain," came from another direction. "Quack! quack! quack!" answered a third, thus displaying an indifference to their inconveniences, and a commendable endeavor to make sport out of each other's mishaps. The morning after the storm exhibited scenes which, under other circumstances, would have been considered lamentable, but which the boys called ludicrous. On impromptu elevations the men were lying in the mud and water, oblivious to all their mishaps, curled up like snakes, and one of them actually making a bed of the drumhead. On Sunday, 22d, one of Churchill's scouting parties had a brisk skirmish with a like party of the enemy, whom they succeeded in driving back, although largely superior in numbers. A few of the Southerners were wounded, none killed, while the foe suffered severely. A prisoner was brought into camp, and the men rushed to obtain a view of him, as if he was some great curiosity and not a mortal similar to themselves.

Camp Stephens was daily visited by numbers of ladies from the surrounding country, who always had pleasant smiles and cheerful words for the soldiers. A brass band attached to one of the Arkansas regiments discoursed most excellent music, and was a great feature of our camp life and a source of great gratification to our men. Soldiers, as a class, are passionately fond of music. Well do we remember with what deep emotions we have listened to the harmonious strains as they floated out on the air some still moonlight night, returning in murmuring echoes from the surrounding hills. Truthfully has the great English bard written:

> "He who hath not music in himself, and whose soul is not moved by a
> sweet concourse of sounds, is fit for treason, stratagem and spoils."

An unfortunate accident occurred on the 23d, resulting in the instantaneous death of James Howard, a member of Company "F," by the discharge of a gun through the carelessness of ———— Nagle, of Company "G." Nagle became frightened, and immediately deserted. This event was the cause of great excitement, resulting in a quarrel between the Colonel and several officers, who, being reported to General McCulloch, were placed under arrest. Differences were, however, finally adjusted, and the regiment and other troops under marching orders once more on the 26th. From this time we were in the midst of continued scenes of excitement. On the 28th crossed the line and entered Missouri. While on the march, received intelligence of the secession of Missouri. Reached Keatsville in the middle of the day, the roads being very dusty and the heat almost intolerable. It being reported that there was fighting ahead, the regiment closed up and pushed rapidly forward with loud cheers. The exhausted stragglers in the rear came up at a full run, forgetting their fatigue in the excitement of an anticipated fight. Churchill's regiment had already pushed forward, and already had a brisk encounter with the foe. On the 29th reached Cassville, where the regiment was greeted with the wildest enthusiasm by the Missourians. Amid vociferous cheers, the thunder of artillery and waving of banners, the regiment marched past the camp of the State troops, eliciting numerous remarks of praise and admiration by their steady and regular tread and their deportment as a disciplined body of troops. An isolated regiment amid Arkansas and Missouri troops, each member felt as if in his individual person was concentrated the honor and fair name of Louisiana—a feeling which undoubtedly contributed largely to their subsequent deeds of valor and unconquerable determination never to yield to the foe. From the first organization of the army the Louisianians became the favorites of the other troops, between whom and themselves grew up a strong feeling of friendship, which neither time nor any other circumstance could destroy.

On the 29th a lady came into camp from beyond Springfield with important dispatches sewed up in her clothing. Her husband had been engaged to take these dispatches, but became very ill. She volunteered to supply his place; and leaving home and the sick husband's bedside, successfully accomplished her mission, having passed through the whole Federal army. Such heroism was the theme of every tongue, and showed what Southern women would do for their country. It is to be regretted that her name was not dotted down to adorn the pages of this history. Yet is she not forgotten.

CHAPTER VI

THE ADVANCE

AT Cassville the army was thoroughly organized for an advance on Springfield, and separated into three divisions as follows: First Division, under command of Colonel L. Hebert, 4,000 strong, to march on the 30th; the other Divisions, of about equal strength, the two following days. On the 1st of August our army encamped on Crane Creek, distant twenty-seven miles from Springfield, Mo., where we soon received intelligence that the enemy were rapidly advancing on our position with a strong force, supposing that McCulloch's army was weak in numbers and could be easily defeated. In fact, it was stated that General Lyons boasted that he would *drive us back into Mexico and drown us in the Gulf.* He little dreamed what brave and indomitable spirits he must conquer.

August 2d the camp was thrown into a state of feverish excitement by orders to arm, as the enemy was advancing. It seems, however, that our advanced guard, composed chiefly of Missourians (mounted), had suddenly come upon the enemy, nine miles distant, who had fired upon them, when they precipitately fled without returning the fire or attempting to show fight. Some few Arkansas troops, however, who were with them, engaged the enemy, and a brisk skirmish fight ensued, our loss being only one man killed. Captain Stanley, a brave and dashing officer of the United States Regular Army, was killed in the fight by a negro attached to the Missouri troops. On the 3d Churchill's Regiment of mounted infantry—a gallant, daring and dashing body of men—were sent forward with instructions to decoy the enemy into our camp, where a well-planned ambuscade had been prepared for their reception. General Lyons, it seems, had discovered the strength of our forces and the plan to welcome his arrival from a deserter out of our camp. His men pursued only within three miles of our position.

In order that the situation of the army may be fully comprehended, we give the following explanation: The road ran from the valley of Crane Creek through a ravine flanked by steep hills, where it would be impossible for one army to attack another without suffering terribly from an ambuscade or masked batteries. The hill-sides, extending close down to the road, were covered with a dense, almost impenetrable growth of black jacks and hazel-bushes. The Louisianians were placed in position on the extreme right of the whole army, and where a fight seemed inevitable, went to work with their knives and sabre-bayonets, lopping off the branches of the trees and bushes which obstructed a good view of the road, in order to render their aim and fire more effective. The retreat of Churchill's Regiment was a helter-skelter flight, in accordance with previous instructions; and as they rushed by our position amid clouds of dust, the rapid flight of horsemen, artillery, and wagons sounded like the roar of many waters. The men waited and watched for the foe, compressed lips and blanched faces betokening the inward excitement, while not a man moved from his allotted place. The night of the 3d, Companies A and K, under command of Captain Viglini, were placed in position as sharpshooters on the rocky hill-side, commanding a full view of the road, with instructions to support the advance picket and keep back the enemy in case of an attack. Directly in front of their position the road ascended a steep hill, in a direct line, at whose base, right and left, two more roads branched off along the adjacent valleys. The main road, directly in front of our line, composed of white pulverized stone, stood out a bold, clearly-defined line in the darkness, along which no living object could travel without being instantly discovered. No moon, with its silvery rays, lighted up the hill-tops, only myriad stars shone from the clear heavens above, while the cold dews chilled the forms of the watchful soldiers. The hill on which we were stationed was composed of small, angular, flinty rocks, on which the men reposed after various and sundry contortions of body to find a "soft part" and remove their *cutting* acquaintance. Every other man along the line of skirmishers slept at stated intervals, while the remainder kept a close watch on the roads. The foe came not; and late in the afternoon of the succeeding day the detachment of sharpshooters were relieved from duty and permitted to return to camp, Companies E and I taking their places. During this time the Third Regiment was still kept in position, the remainder of the army being on their camping-grounds. The boys did not fully appreciate the honor bestowed or confidence placed in them as efficient and brave soldiers.

The next day was the Sabbath, bright, beautiful and golden. All remained quiet until early noon, when a balloon was discovered hovering over our camp, which sailed eastward in the direction of the enemy. All was bustle and activity, as the troops rapidly assembled in their respective quarters. A report soon prevailed that the enemy had penetrated the left of our position, and the balloon was a preconcerted signal for an advance on our front and flank. It proved a false rumor, and the army reposed in security and quietude.

During this time the generals had assembled for consultation as to the future movements of the army, as it was found impossible to remain longer in its present position, the water being actually offensive from filth, and provisions for the army very scarce. We must either retreat or advance. Desperate as was the alternative, it was determined to advance. The order was issued to prepare to march Sunday night, the 4th inst., at 11 o'clock P.M. All realized the desperation of such a move, yet not a man quailed or was found missing from his place in the regiment. Last messages were delivered to those detailed to remain with the wagons, packages for the loved ones at home made up, and the men laid down to what many deemed their final living sleep, ere the march commenced. When the hour for departure arrived, the regiment was ready and equipped, the gallant boys on the right of the whole army, led by Company K. Not a man free from detailed duty was absent from his place. At 11½ o'clock the whole army was in motion. In sections, six abreast, and close order, the men took up the line of march in anticipation of meeting almost certain death, but with undaunted, unquailing spirits. In breathless silence, with the bright and glittering stars looking down upon them through dark and deep defiles and beneath frowning hill-sides, marched the dense array of men, moving steadily forward; not a whisper was heard, no sound of clanking sabre, or rattle of canteen and cup.

Tramp! tramp! tramp! firm and undaunted, the army proceeded on its perilous journey like a band of dark spirits, over the hard and rocky road, accompanied by the dull rumbling of the artillery carriages over hills, along a road skirted by dense underbrush and tall trees, and through those narrow defiles the army proceeded. That was a night that tried men's souls. Although moving forward in momentary expectation of being attacked, nothing special occurred. As the first roseate hues of morn tinged the eastern horizon, our advance came upon the picket of the enemy, who were so completely taken by surprise that they precipitately fled, leaving behind them coats, provisions and utensils. Greer's Texas regiment of cavalry joined us at this time. They were a splendid body of daring, dashing Texan Rangers, magnificently armed and mounted. The army moved steadily forward, with cavalry on both flanks, scouting the surrounding hills and woods. About 10 o'clock in the morning, while halting near a well for the purpose of resting and procuring water, the men were watching the general as he sat perched on the top of a corn-crib. The head of the column had been halted just within the limits of a woodland, ere the road emerged into an open, rolling prairie-land as far as the eye could reach. Soon the General was observed to look long and anxiously through his field-glass. A wave of his hand summoned an aid-de-camp to his side, who soon brought orders for the regiment to take position on the right, in a dense growth of hazel skirting the road. Every man was ordered to conceal himself, a section of artillery run to the front, rapidly unlimbered, loaded and pointed so as to sweep the road. What could it mean? Shortly, far away over the prairie, a cloud of dust was seen to mount upward. Nearer and nearer it approached, until a body of the enemy's cavalry was discovered in hot pursuit of one of General McCulloch's scouts. They rode boldly to within point blank of the concealed line of battle ere they discovered their mistake, when, wheeling suddenly, they fled rapidly, not a shot being fired at them. Through the excessive heat and over dusty roads the march was continued, the enemy retreating as we advanced. The men suffered terribly from thirst, there being little or no water on the route. Their sufferings became so intolerable that finally the General marched them one and a half miles away from the road to procure water, in order to allay their burning thirst. The army then pushed rapidly forward in pursuit of the retreating foe, who were reported but a short distance in advance at a spring. It was soon discovered, however, that they were still retreating. As soon as this was known, the Missouri *horsemen* came rushing up from the rear, riding heedlessly through the ranks of hot, tired, thirsty and dusty men, almost suffocating them. The regiment, in order to protect themselves, halted, fixed bayonets, and determinedly compelled them to quit the road. Arriving at Big Spring, the men and animals made an indiscriminate rush for the water, which was fortunately abundant and fine. The enemy had been gone but about three hours, having left many things behind them in their precipitate retreat. That night our army laid down in an open field without shelter. The regiment had thus lain out all night previous to the march, traveled all the succeeding night in great suspense and anxiety, pursued a retreating enemy all day over dusty roads and in extremely sultry weather, and the night of August 5th slept in the open air without blankets or food, the next morning proceeded about two miles and encamped near Wilson's Creek, nine miles from Springfield. The position was as follows: we were on a hill-side, at whose western base flowed a stream, the hill sloping away north and east, along which ran the main road to Springfield. Opposite our encampment, west and northwest rose in a gradual slope a succession of hills extending as far as the eye could reach. The hillside northwest was about three-quarters of a mile distant, the intervening space being covered by corn-fields in the valley formed by Wilson's Creek. On the north was a slight rise beyond the ravine, covered as usual with a dense undergrowth of black jack and hazel, skirting a large and open corn and hay-field.

CHAPTER VII

OAK HILLS

ON Friday, the 9th inst., the order was to prepare to march at 8 P.M. on the position of the enemy, in order to surprise them. The post of honor and danger as usual being assigned to the Third Regiment, the van guard of the center division on the main road leading to Springfield. Providence prevented the consummation of these proposed plans. Early in the morning the sky became overcast with dark, dense and lowering clouds, accompanied by thunder and lightning, and in the afternoon of the same day a light rain began to fall. Many of the Arkansas and Missouri troops were armed with the old fashioned flint-lock guns, carrying their ammunition in a buckskin pouch, as is customary with the backwoods hunters. It would not do to expose the ammunition to the elements, and thus render unserviceable the assistance of a large force of our army. At 9 o'clock the order for an advance was countermanded, but the troops required to hold themselves in readiness to march at a moment's notice. The picket guards had been recalled so as to be ready to march with their respective commands, and in expectation of momentarily receiving marching orders, the different regimental commanders objected to sending them out again. It was a serious blunder, yet who was responsible for the mistake or oversight we cannot truthfully determine. Thus all unguarded the army sank to repose, the men to dream of home and coming exciting scenes, after bitterly expressing their disappointment at the delay. All eager for battle, they little dreamed of the fearful scenes of slaughter and bloodshed. The morning of August 10th had scarcely tinged the Eastern horizon with the grayish dawn, and ere many of the men were out of their tents, when the battle opened. Looking to the hill northwest of our camp, could be seen the wagons, ambulances, and many horsemen of the advance encampment fleeing from the coming battle storm. The couriers and aids-de-camp, with furious speed, were delivering orders. The Third Regiment promptly formed on the hill, many of them minus coats in their eager haste. Scarcely had they formed line ere McCulloch dashed up, furious with excitement and rage, and shouted,

"Colonel, why in hell don't you lead your men out?" The question was not repeated. Company K had been transferred from the left to the right, which, with Company A, was under the leadership of Captain J. P. Viglini. Captain Woodruff of Little Rock was in position with his guns commanding the valley and adjacent hill sides. As the regiment began to move into position, a puff of smoke arose from a clump of trees northwest of our position, followed by another accompanied by the ugly scream of shot and their sudden, dull thug into the ground. The men shouted at each iron messenger as it approached, many indulging in jokes and witticisms, such as exclaiming, "this ball music is fine for dancing." "Here comes another iron pill." "Dodge, boys, but don't tumble." But the majority were calm, pale with excitement, compressed lips, and blazing eyes betokening the spirit of their determination. We quickly entered the ravine north of our encampment, marching in close columns of companies, and approached the corn field already described. During this time the battle had opened on all sides, and Woodruff and Totten were fighting a lively artillery duel. As the regiment advanced through the dense undergrowth towards the open field, a terrible and scathing fire was opened on them by nearly double their numbers of U.S. Regulars, the flower of General Lyons' army. The regiment rapidly wheeled into line of battle, each company taking its position with prompt celerity. Numbers of the men had already fallen.

The enemy were securely posted behind the fence, while our position among the bushes rendered it almost an utter impossibility to obtain a good view of them, even by our coolest and clearest sighted marksmen. Seeking every possible protection and shelter, the fight was maintained with a stubborn and determined valor. Not a stone's throw from each other these lines of men, composed of old regulars and a virgin volunteer regiment of Louisianians, were combating each other with dogged obstinacy. The fight lasted upwards of an hour, and those who listened to the musketry declared it to have been terrific in its volume of sound. Men were dropping all along the line; it was becoming uncomfortably hot, when Captain McIntosh dashed along the line, shouting "Get up, Louisianians, and charge them! Do you all wish to be killed?" With a tremendous cheer, so fearful, coming from men under fierce excitement, they rushed on the foe with fixed bayonets, led by the field and line officers and Capt. McIntosh. The regulars fled from the deadly charge, with but few exceptions, and as the regiment reached the fence, they poured a heavy, rapid fire into their ranks, killing and wounding large numbers, punishing them thoroughly for the damage already inflicted upon us. Over the fence, across the field, after the foe, did the boys charge with loud cheers, until they once more approached the enemy's battery within point-blank range. Beneath its protecting fire the beaten foe had taken shelter. The battery immediately concentrated its fire upon the regiment as it began to form a new line of battle. Canister shot and shell were rained upon them until it became too uncomfortable to be withstood. The order was given to retire behind the protection of a hill immediately in the rear of the field. It was obeyed with zealous alacrity, and the men decamped instanter, watching the flash of the enemy's guns as they retreated, and falling prostrate on the ground permitted the iron hail to pass over them, and then rise only to run and repeat the same manœuvre. It was taking very practical lessons in the manual *a la Zouave*. Not half a dozen men were injured in this retreat. None killed. The officers immediately began to form the regiment, which had become much scattered in their precipitate retreat, when Gen. McCulloch rode up to the right of the line and, after making some inquiries and remarks, said, "Come, my brave lads, I have a battery for you to charge, and the day is ours!" The regiment at this time were only partially organized, mostly from the right companies, with some scattering men from the others. The men, however, followed the leadership of their brave General with steady, regular tread along the valley, crossing around the base of the hill, over the creek, where the road took an abrupt turn westward, and ascended a precipitous rocky hill, to the left of which was posted Siegel's battery. At the creek numbers momentarily halted to gulp down a few mouthfulls of water to quench their burning thirst. It mattered little to them that it was filthy and loathsome, that it was red with blood, and blackened men lined its banks and bathed their burning limbs and torturing ghastly wounds in its waters. After crossing the creek, the General halted at intervals, while in point blank range of the battery, and taking a survey through his field-glass, would coolly turn in his saddle, wave his hand, and simply utter the monosyllables, "Come on!" His actions and features were a study for the closest scrutinizer of physiognomy. Not a quiver on his face, not the movement of a muscle to betray anxiety or emotion. Only his grey eyes flashed forth from beneath his shaggy eyebrows a glittering, scrutinizing and penetrating glance. As the men reached the protection of the hill on which the battery was stationed, and ere an order had been given, a man stepped from behind the shelter of a huge oak on its summit. The general abruptly halted and inquired in a calm, clear voice: "Whose forces are those?" The reply came back, in distinct tones: "Siegel's." "Whose did you say?" "Union. Siegel." At the same time raising his rifle with deliberate aim to fire. Ere his purpose was accomplished, the sharp crack of a Mississippi rifle proclaimed the flight of a death messenger on its fearful errand. That shot was fired by Corporal Henry

Gentles, of Company K. The aim was quick and accurate, and as the man dropped heavily to the ground without a groan, the General turned to the corporal remarking simply, "That was a good shot." The remark was characteristic of his coolness under the most perilous and trying circumstances. The General turned to Captain Viglini, standing close to him, and said: "Captain, take your men up and give them hell." The men scaled the rocky hill-side and came abruptly upon the enemy's guns. With loud huzzas they rushed upon the battery, sweeping it at the point of the bayonet, ere the amazed foe could recover from their astonishment. They fled into a corn-field and along the road in the rear of their lost battery, with the victors in close pursuit. In the field upwards of 200 were killed and wounded, so close and deadly was the fire poured into their retreating columns. This gallant charge resulted in the capture of three 12-pounder howitzers, and two 6-pounder field guns. Here fell Capt. Hinson, of Company B, and his brother-in-law, Mr. Whitstone, killed by an unfortunate shot from one of our own batteries under charge of Capt. Reed, which, unknown to the regiment, had been pouring a heavy and destructive fire upon these guns. The loss of these gallant men was deeply deplored, under such circumstances. The guns were rolled down the hill-side, and the regiment, including the remainder who had arrived under Major Tunnard, formed once more and marched about a mile northward to attempt the capture of Totten's battery, which had given them such a hot reception early in the day. After flanking their position, owing to an unfortunate delay, they managed to escape. Around these guns the fight had been deadly and furious. The hill-sides were literally covered with the dead and wounded of friend and foe. Here Gen. Lyon met his fate, a just reward for his murder of innocent women and children in the streets of St. Louis. The enemy, completely discomforted, began a precipitous flight at about 2 o'clock P.M. The battle was over; the foe repulsed at every point; Gen. Lyon killed; the colors in our possession, and Siegel's battery captured. The different regiments were marched to their respective camps. The loss of the Third Regiment was 9 killed, 47 wounded, and 3 missing; that of the army 265 killed and about 700 wounded. The men eagerly scouted the battle-field and brought in the killed and wounded. Our dead, dressed in their best clothes, and with a blanket for a winding sheet, were sadly committed to soldiers' graves by their friends. The Texans under Col. Greer won an enviable reputation by their dashing and reckless bravery. They pursued the foe into Springfield, killing and capturing numbers on the road, and taking Siegel's remaining gun and stand of colors, and planting the first secession flag in Springfield.

The loss of the enemy in this fight was estimated at about 800 killed, 1,200 wounded, and 350 prisoners, while a large number of the most approved small arms fell into the possession of our victorious army. So hasty was the flight, that the foe threw away small arms, blankets, coats, and knapsacks, which were strewn along the road for miles. Their dead were deserted, and their wounded filling every available dwelling and building in Springfield, left to the care of the Confederates. An officer, with a flag of truce, came for Lyon's body, which was taken to Springfield, but even it was deserted in their hurried retreat, and was buried by Mrs. Phillips, the wife of the U.S. Congressman from that district. This second general battle of the war, fought under such disadvantageous circumstances by the Southerners against fully equal numbers, better armed and disciplined, was a complete, thorough victory. Yet the Northern press and Northern historical records of the war have falsified its correct details in almost every particular.

The following are the official reports of the field-officers of the regiment:

"HEADQUARTERS THIRD REGIMENT LOUISIANA INFANTRY, }
Camp at Wilson's Creek, Mo., August 12, 1861. }

"To Brigadier Ben. McCulloch, commanding Confederate States Army:

"SIR,—I have the honor to report the part that my regiment took in the battle of Oak Hills on Saturday the 10th. Aroused by yourself early in the morning, I formed my regiment, and following the direction of Captain James McIntosh, Brigadier-Adjutant-General, followed the Springfield road for a short distance to a narrow by-road, flanked on both sides by the thickest kind of underbrush, and on one side by a rail fence. This road led to a corn-field. At the moment of deploying into line of battle, and when only two companies had reached their position, the enemy opened their fire on our front within five paces. Deploying the other companies, an advance was ordered, led gallantly and bravely by Captain McIntosh, to whom I owe all thanks for assistance.

"The enemy posted behind a fence in the corn-field. The companies moved up bravely, broke the enemy, pursued them gallantly into the corn-field and routed them completely. On emerging from the corn-field, the regiment found themselves on a naked oat-field, where a battery on the left opened upon us a severe fire. The order was given to fall back to a wooded ground higher up to the right. The order was obeyed, but by some misunderstanding the right of the regiment and some of the left were separated from the left and found themselves under the command of Lieutenant-Colonel Hyams, who there received your order to march to attack Siegel's battery, and command on the left of the field of battle. His report is herewith transmitted, giving an account of the operations of his battalion up to the time of my joining him. I remained myself near the above-named corn-field, rallying and reforming the left into a detachment of some one hundred men. I advanced towards Totten's (enemy's) battery. I advanced to a position some five hundred yards from the battery, where I remained before the line of the enemy some twenty-five or thirty minutes, when, falling back, I again rallied some stray portions of the regiment, and marched, by orders, to join the right wing on the left of the field. This I did; and having reformed the regiment, I received orders to move, so as to place myself in the rear of the enemy's battery (Totten's) then closely engaged in front. Although moving as expeditiously as possible, I did not reach the proper position until Totten's battery had been drawn back in retreat. Some of the enemy still remained on the hill and in a ravine. I, however, hesitated to attack, having discovered a force immediately in my rear, whom I did not ascertain to be friends for some twenty minutes. I then ordered the advance, attacked the enemy and put them to flight. In this the regiment was very gallantly assisted by a detachment of Missourians and others, whom I then supposed to be under the immediate command of Captain Johnson. This fight ended the engagement of my regiment for the day. The Regiment was formed on the hill previously occupied by the enemy, and, by orders, was marched back to their camp. The first of the engagement of the regiment commenced at $6^{1}/_{2}$ o'clock A.M. and ended at $1^{1}/_{2}$ o'clock P.M., when the enemy made their final retreat. I transmit a list of the killed, wounded and missing, recapitulating as follows: Killed, 1 commissioned officer, 1 non-commissioned officer and 7 privates; total killed, 9. Wounded, 3 commissioned officers, 6 non-commissioned officers and 39 privates; total, 48. Missing, 3 privates.

"Proud of the manner in which my regiment behaved in their first fight against the enemy of our Confederate States (a fight in which officers and men displayed endurance, bravery and determination), it is difficult for me to particularize the service of officers and men. I will, however, bring to the notice of the Commanding General some cases. The whole of my staff acted with great coolness and bravery; the Lieutenant-Colonel leading a battalion, in my absence, against Siegel's battery, and the Major assisting constantly in the rear wing. Captain Theodore Johnston, Quartermaster, was of invaluable service in transmitting orders, rallying the men and encouraging them to stand by their colors, often exposing himself to the fire of the enemy. Adjutant S. M. Hyams, Jr., left his horse and fought bravely on foot. Captain Thomas L. Maxwell, Commissary, followed the regiment in battle, and assisted much in rallying the men. The lamented Captain, R. M. Hinson, fell while gallantly leading his company against Siegel's battery. A nobler gentleman and a braver soldier could not have been found. Sergeant-Major J. O. Renwick was shot down in my presence in the first fight whilst bravely fronting and fighting the enemy. He was the first killed of the regiment. Dr. George W. Kendall, a volunteer surgeon on the field, was active and untiring in his exertions to relieve the wounded. In the reports of Company Commanders, many acts of bravery and gallantry by non-commissioned officers and privates are mentioned.

"With the consent of the General, I shall seek hereafter occasions to show that their conduct has been noticed. I cannot conclude without saying that the conduct of Captain James McIntosh, in throwing himself with my regiment in our first fight, and in the attack on Siegel's battery, greatly contributed to the success of our arms, and deserves unlimited praise.

"I must not forget also to return to the Commanding General himself the thanks of the Regiment and my own for his presence at the head of the right wing at the charge on Siegel's battery.

"With high respect, I remain, your obedient servant.

"LOUIS HEBERT, *Colonel Commanding.*"

"Report of Lieutenant-Colonel Hyams to Colonel Hebert, of Third Louisiana Regiment:

"SIR,—In the morning of the 10th of August, 1861, after forming with the regiment and marching to the thicket and corn-field, and your command on the order of a charge in the thicket, I dismounted and was on foot with the command in the charge. The Sergeant-Major Renwick was killed, as was Private Placide Bossier, of Pelican Rangers, No. 1. After crossing the fencing and running the enemy through the corn-field, where the enemy's artillery were showering grape and shell, with Minie muskets, I was met by General McCulloch, who ordered the regiment to face to the right and march by flank movement towards the creek, and sent an aid to communicate the order to you further on the right of the regiment.

"In this first encounter in the bushes, where all behaved well, it was impossible to designate any particular individual. Here I first noticed the fearlessness and undaunted bravery and activity of Captain Theodore Johnson, Quartermaster, in communicating orders from headquarters.

"Learning from him that you was separated from the command, he attached himself to that portion of the regiment under me, composed of the Pelican Rifles, Captain Viglini; Iberville Grays, Lieutenant Verbois; Morehouse Guards, Captain Hinson; Pelican Rangers, No. 2, Captain Blair; Winn Rifles, Captain Pierson; Morehouse Fencibles, Captain Harris; Shreveport Rangers, Captain Gilmore; Pelican Rangers, No. 1, Captain Brazeale; and a few of the Monticello Rifles under Sergeant Walcott, and seventy of the Missouri troops (who had attached themselves to my command) under Captain Johnson. We were conducted by the gallant Captain McIntosh across the ford to Siegel's battery where, having deployed in line, the charge was ordered. On my giving the order and arriving on the brow of the hill, Lieutenant Lacy, of the Shreveport Rangers, sprang on a log, waved his sword and called, "Come on, Caddo." The whole command pushed forward, carried the guard, rushed to the fence and drove the enemy off. Here the gallant Captain Hinson, in cheering his men, was killed by a shot from our own battery taking us in flank. Private Whitstone, of the Morehouse Guards (brother-in-law of Captain Hinson), was killed at his side by the same shot. I cannot speak in too high commendation of both officers and men for their coolness and bravery. They had charged and taken five guns out of six of the battery, and passed beyond them without knowing we had them, except those companies immediately in front of the guns.

"The standard-bearer of the regiment, Felix Chaler, of Pelican Rangers, No. 1, behaved with great coolness and courage, advancing and bearing them to the front in every charge. Corporal Hicock, of the Shreveport Rangers, Private J. P. Hyams, of Pelican Rangers, No. 1, and Corporal Gentles, of Pelican Rifles, rushed forward and captured one cannon that was just in rear of the first guns captured (about one hundred yards), where they killed the only man who remained with his gun, the rest of the cannoniers having abandoned the gun at their approach.

"Orderly Sergeant Alphonse Prudhomme is reported to have cheered and acted with coolness. The Color Company stuck to the colors, as did the Shreveport Rangers, and all rallied to the flag. I cannot speak too highly of the courage and activity of all our gallant officers and men in this charge. It is impossible to say which company was in advance, where all obeyed orders and went so gallantly into action. But for the unfortunate casualty created by our own battery firing into our flank and raking us, killing several and wounding many, we would have had but few regrets.

"Poor Hicock, having advanced in front of the regiment in driving the enemy from the corn-field round the large white house, was shot in the breast. Here I beg to call attention to the gallantry of Captain McIntosh, who conducted us to the front of the attack. Quartermaster Theodore Johnson, of our regiment, was of great assistance, and behaved with distinguished bravery. We rolled their captured guns down the hill, and one cannon was conducted with its horses to our artillery. We then marched back to the valley below the hill, and were in line when you joined us with the rest of the regiment. Drum-Major Patterson, of the Pelican Rifles, left his drum, shot the first man of the enemy, after calling themselves friends, thereby stopping our fire and their treacherously firing upon us.

"I am, respectfully, your obedient servant,

"S. M. HYAMS, *Lieut.-Col. Third Regt. La. Vols.*"

Colonel Hyams' report contains some inaccuracies, as will be easily discovered from the author's version of the battle. The first detachment was led
by General McCulloch in person, and not by Captain McIntosh, who was,
however, present at the charge.

REPORT OF MAJOR W. F. TUNNARD

"Colonel L. Hebert, commanding Third Regiment La. Volunteers:

"Sir,—In accordance with your request I have the honor to make the
following report of events that occurred under my immediate notice in the
battle of Oak Hills:

"When the regiment was ordered to form at 6 A.M., I assisted in getting
the companies in line, and marched out of camp with the left wing, the
enemy's batteries having opened on our forces before we left camp. We
marched out to the right, and by order of Adjutant-General McIntosh, I
assisted in deploying the regiment in a thick oak under-brush to the left of
the road, and before we were in the field ten minutes we were fired on by
the enemy, 1,800 strong, who were ambushed in a corn-field behind a fence.
After exchanging several shots with them, and a number of our men being
killed and wounded, an order to charge was given by Colonel McIntosh,
which was immediately responded to by our men with a cheer and shout.
On rushing to the fence, the enemy immediately turned and fled in disorder, our regiment pursuing and shooting them as they ran. In this pursuit I
was with the left wing, cheering them on until we reached an open field,
where we found the enemy protected by Totten's battery, which at once
opened on us as we attempted to form. I immediately ordered the regiment
to scatter and move to the right, where, under cover of a hill, with the assistance of Captain Maxwell, the line was formed. While I was engaged in getting our scattered forces together in line General McCulloch rode up and
led off the right to attack Siegel's battery, and I found the left companies,
with a large number of the right wing, had become separated from the right
in passing through the bushes. We marched on to join the right of the
Regiment. In crossing the ford in the valley, we received a discharge of grape
and canister from Siegel's battery, which wounded several of the men and
shot my horse. I then led the detachment on foot, the battery having been
taken and the enemy again repulsed by the right wing and in full retreat
before we joined the regiment. The regiment being formed, marched out
under your command to attack Totten's battery. On arriving at the point of
attack, we found the battery removed and the enemy in full retreat, except
a reserve, which fired several shots at us, which were promptly returned. This

ended the battle for the day. An accidental discharge of a musket by one of our men wounded three of our number, one very severely.

"In each engagement our men behaved gallantly, and under the severe fire of the batteries, that poured a continual shower of grape, shot and shell, they never faltered.

"I have the honor to be, yours respectfully, etc.,

"W. F. TUNNARD, *Major, Third Regiment La. Vols.*"

The following official dispatch speaks for itself:

"HEADQUARTERS MISSOURI STATE GUARDS, ⎫
Springfield, August 15, 1861. ⎭

"COLONEL,—General Price instructs me to say that the discipline and bravery which your regiment displayed in the late battle were so marked, and your services and theirs so efficient in winning that important victory, that he would fail in his duty were he not to express to you and to them his own high appreciation of the distinguished services of the Louisiana Regiment on that occasion, and the gratitude with which the officers and men of this army and the people of Missouri will always remember you, your officers and men.

"I have the honor to be, with the greatest respect,

"Your obedient servant,

"THOMAS L. SMEAD, *Acting Adjutant-General.*

"To Colonel L. Hebert, Louisiana Regiment."
[A true copy of the original.]

LOUIS HEBERT, *Colonel Third Regiment, La. Vols.*

War viewed from the standpoint of the peaceful home circle, with its surroundings of happy and loved faces, and the comforts and conveniences of life, exhibits none of that hideous deformity which environs its dread reality. The battle of Oak Hills enlightened many ignorant minds as to the seriousness and fearful certainty of the contest. It did not, however, unnerve a single arm to strike a fresh blow, or dampen the ardor of a single heart. It proved thoroughly the dashing bravery of the Southern soldier, contending under every disadvantage against almost inevitable defeat, and taught the enemy also a severe lesson of what the future contained. So sudden and unexpected the attack, so close, terrible and obstinate the contest, that numbers thought the day irretrievably lost and gave up in hopeless despair. Not so with the Louisianians, who *never for an instant felt that they were whipped.* Through the thickest and hottest of the fight, where shot and shell fell fastest, and the rifles poured their storm of leaden hail, the regiment forced its way, charging the foe with loud cheers, and always driving them from their positions. For more than six hours the desperate conflict continued, beneath the cloudless sky and in the sultry atmosphere of an August day.

When the enemy were finally repulsed and driven in dismay from the field, an opportunity was afforded to view the result and obtain some definite information of the slaughter.

Soon after the battle ended the enemy, under a flag of truce, commenced attending to their dead, dying and wounded. All the remainder of the 10th, after the conclusion of the battle, and during the whole night, seven of their six-mule teams were busily engaged carrying off their dead and wounded. Early Sunday morning, Sergt. W. H. Tunnard, of Co. K, was detailed as sergeant of a large force to finish the burial of the enemy's dead. Armed with shovel, pick-axe and spade, the detail proceeded to the principal point of the battle-field to complete this mournful task, which the enemy, unable to accomplish, had abandoned in despair. The ground was still thickly strewn with the ghastly and mangled forms. Fifty-three bodies were placed in a single grave, all gathered within the compass of one hundred yards. These were hastily covered with brush and stones, when the detail precipitately departed. The effluvia from the swollen, festering, blackened forms, already covered with worms was too horrible for human endurance. Hundreds unburied were left food for the worms, fowls and beast of the earth. No conception of the imagination, no power of human language could do justice to such a horrible scene.

OFFICIAL REPORTS OF KILLED
AND WOUNDED AT OAK HILLS

The force under Gen. Price engaged numbered 5,300; killed 156; wounded 517. Among the casualties were the names of a number of gallant officers, as the following list shows:

Killed.—Colonels R. H. Weitman and Ben. Brown; Lieutenant-Colonels Austin and G. W. Allen; Major Charles Rogers; Captains Blackwell, Enghart, Farris, Halleck, and Coleman; Lieutenants Hughes, and Haskins; Adjutant C. H. Bennet.

Wounded.—Brig. Gens. Slack and Clark; Colonels Benbridge, Foster, Kelly and Crawford; Captains Nichols, Dougherty, and Armstrong.

Col. McIntosh, Adjutant Gen. McCulloch's Brigade, reported losses as follows:

Third Louisiana Regiment: 9 killed, 48 wounded, 3 missing; Lt.-Col. McRae's Battalion: 2 killed, 6 wounded; Col. McIntosh's Regiment: 11 killed, 55 wounded; Capt. Woodruff's Battery: 2 killed, 2 wounded, 1 missing; Capt. Reid's Battery: 1 wounded; Col. Churchill's Regiment: 42 killed, 153 wounded; Greer's Regiment, Texas Cavalry, loss not known.

Churchill's Regiment were the greatest sufferers, the first attack being made on this regiment, the enemy capturing their camp and wagons, and baggage, which they destroyed. The standard-bearer of one company was changed four times, three being shot while carrying the colors.

Amid the early scenes and incidents of the war it was not an unusual occurrence to find men of high position in society, leaving home, profession, and the pursuits of daily life, to unite their fortunes with the humblest and most unobtrusive citizens of the land.

The history of the Third Regiment and the account of its first initiation into the scenes of the bloody drama of the war, would be incomplete without the mention of two persons, who participated in the hard fought field of Oak Hills. We refer to Dr. W. G. Kendall, and the Hon. Wm. Robson. These gentlemen were from Shreveport, joined the regiment at Van Buren as amateur soldiers, continued with the regiment until after the battle of Oak Hills, on which occasion they rendered most efficient service.

Dr. Kendall, a gentleman of refined manners, cultivated intellect, and high position in his profession, made innumerable friends in the regiment by his kind and affable manner, and genial good nature. At Oak Hills he was in the hottest of the fight, exhibiting a cool courage worthy of one who had voluntarily attached himself to the fortunes of one of Louisiana's most gallant organizations. Col. Hyams wrote under date of August 13, 1861: "Dr. Kendall was in the fight, assisted the wounded, and occasionally took a pass at the enemy. He rendered great service as aid to the surgeons after the battle."

The Hon. Wm. Robson, at the commencement of hostilities, was a member of the Legislature, but this did not deter him from uniting his fortunes to those of the Third Infantry, and often could he be found with a musket, doing duty as a private, in the ranks. He is a man of undoubted bravery, calm, cool, self-possessed under the most trying circumstances. "W. Robson," Col. Hyams said, "acted as aid to Col. Hebert, and was in the thickest of the fight, rallying stragglers, and conveying orders. He showed great coolness and bravery."

Dr. Kendall tells the following anecdote of Robson. "The Union men fought as guerrillas, to some extent picking off stragglers on the field. One of these parties got near Robson and took a clear 'clatter' at him at about 120 yards, one of the shots killing a negro boy's horse alongside of R. He thought that was no place for him, bent down to the saddle bow and gallopped over a hill at 'double-quick.' They took the negro boy to Springfield, thinking he belonged to R., and said they had killed his master, and now he belonged to them. A man by the name of Phelps, a son of the U.S. Congressman, was the leader, and claimed the honor of killing Robson. The boy escaped, and was rejoiced to find R. alive. He had on his person his master's watch and $300 in gold, which he brought back with him."

"Robson rallied the stragglers, and at one time brought up forty-five men to where the regiment was engaged. Some were rather inclined to remain behind, but finally, seeing that R. was not afraid to ride through the fire, concluded to follow him. He and his sorrel pony were conspicuous characters. He was known in the regiment as Capt. Robson."

ADDITIONAL INTERESTING PARTICULARS

On Tuesday after the battle the Federal prisoners were in the public square at Springfield under guard, and outside was a crowd of Missourians, Arkansians, and camp followers generally. Directly a party commenced singing "Dixie," a new version for the occasion. One of the prisoners after they got through said, "Ah, well! I only wish you had stayed in Dixie." At one time, just after the capture of Siegel's battery, the rumor prevailed that Col. Hebert was down. Dr. Hebert anxiously inquired for him, and at that moment, far above the crashing of the small-arms, could be heard the stern, clear tones of the gallant colonel urging on the Louisiana regiment: "Steady, my men—steady!" Just then Gen. Price was rallying the stragglers of the Missouri line, urging them on to a final attack, "for in twenty minutes the Louisiana regiment will charge again, and if we rally to the front this battery will be taken."

Gen. Price behaved with great gallantry, exposing his own person freely and not hesitating to send his men into danger. He was slightly wounded. Col. Weightman, of Atchison, Mo., was in command of a Missouri brigade (infantry), with a battery which was so badly provided with ammunition that they took iron bars one and one-half inch square and cut them up into chunks, using them as grape. These pieces made most horrible wounds, but were soon exhausted. His brigade fought like heroes both here and at Carthage, but the colonel fell early in the action, mortally wounded, and died before the battle was over. He was formerly in the U.S. Army, and was a very highly accomplished and able officer; his death was an almost irreparable loss to Missouri, and cast a gloom over the whole army.

Col. Hebert was actively employed throughout the day, and added another chaplet to his already high reputation as an officer. At no time were the enemy able to force any of the regiments back, and the men would get in so close to their lines that the shot-guns loaded with buckshot told with fearful effect, and the much valued Minié guns of the foe overshot the Southerners.

Capt. Theodore Johnson (Quartermaster of the regiment) acted as aid to Col. Hebert, and was actively engaged in carrying orders, and showed great coolness and courage.

Lieut. J. O. Wells, of Co. F, had been on the sick-list, reduced by flux from 159 pounds to 124, but staggered to his place and stood at his post, bravely doing his duty throughout the whole fight.

Of the activity, courage, and valuable assistance rendered by Dr. G. W. Kendall and Wm. Robson too much cannot be said. The former, a citizen of Shreveport, a gentleman of polished manners, refined education, and standing high in his profession, with Wm. Robson, Esq., then a member of the Louisiana Legislature, joined the regiment at Van Buren as independent volunteers. Dr. Kendall was in the fight, cool and courageous, often joining in the fray; assisted the wounded, and rendered valuable and great assistance as aid to the surgeons after the battle. He had a horse killed under him during the fight.

Gen. Lyon was killed about half-past one o'clock, while bravely leading his men. His uniform coat was cut up into small pieces and carried away as relics. His horse, a magnificent gray stallion, imported from England by Mr. January, of St. Louis, was also killed, and the boys cut all the hair from his mane and tail, and distributed it.

Maj. Tunnard, of the Louisiana regiment, had his horse shot under him.

Col. McIntosh was seriously bruised by a grape-shot in the side. Churchill's First Arkansas Regiment fought desperately, as did McIntosh's and Gratiot's Third Arkansas, and were under a tremendous fire for a long time from a superior force, but kept up such a furious fire with shot-guns, flint-lock muskets, etc., that the enemy could not be brought to charge them. McRae's Battalion won its share of laurels. When he heard of Weightman's death, with a wild shout for vengeance, he led his man into the fray where most needed. When marching from Crane Creek, Lieut.-Col. Hyams was on the sick-list, suffering intensely from rheumatism and a kick from a sore-backed Indian pony; but, at the rumored approach of the enemy, mounted his horse, reported himself at headquarters ready for duty, and was with the regiment on the march, in their ambuscades, and through the battle, coolly and calmly directing the men.

HOW THEY FLED

After the arrival of the troops at Wilson's Creek, eight of Woodruff's artillerymen, guided by a tall Missourian, left camp to obtain some forage for their horses. The Missourian stopped at a creek, the artillerymen went on. The Missourian started after them, but had not proceeded far when he met four men on horseback, with white bands around their hats. He inquired of them, "Have you seen any artillerymen ahead?" They replied, "Oh! yes, some of the U.S. artillerymen are in a field a little way ahead." The Missourian replied, "You are mistaken, those men belong to Uncle Jeff."

They waited to hear no more; wheeled their horses "right about," and fled to the woods.

INCIDENTS PREVIOUS TO
AND CONNECTED WITH THE
BATTLE OF OAK HILLS

When the army reached Crane Creek, August 1, a rumor came that the enemy was approaching. Captain McIntosh, with that reckless daring and dashing bravery so characteristic of the man, dashed up the road with a detachment to see what was the matter. About 4 o'clock a few horsemen came down the road past the camp, and following on, in hot haste, came the main body of the advance-guard, mixed up with the wagons, and all coming as hard as whip and spur could urge the horses. They went sweeping by, giving the alarming intelligence that the enemy had advanced in great force and cut them off and killed McIntosh. Still no message came to McCulloch. The Sergeant-Major of the regiment, without orders, had the "long roll" beaten, and the men "fell in" in double-quick time. General McCulloch dashed up the road fairly foaming with rage, exhausting his whole vocabulary of vituperation (no meagre one) in denunciations of Rains' Missouri Cavalry, who had thus most disgracefully stampeded without any apparent cause. Every man was eagerly questioned about Colonel McIntosh, and finally one old fellow had seen a man, answering his description, as he came by. "Well! what was he doing?" "Cussin' the Missourians," was the prompt reply. A roar of laughter, followed by a cheer, arose, for the identification was certain and satisfactory, and all knew that McIntosh was safe.

THE LOUISIANIANS' SPIRIT

A rumor prevailed that General Lyon had issued from Springfield and was about to surround us. One of the boys suggested that "it didn't make much difference to the Louisiana boys which side he attacked them on, as they were so far from home that all points of the compass seemed alike to them, and if Lyon wanted to attack us in the rear, and he were McCulloch, he would give him a pass through his camp *and then lick him like hell."*

THE MIDNIGHT MARCH

As the men, in breathless expectation, cautiously moved forward, not the sound of a voice, the rattle of a canteen or sabre to be heard, the midnight silence alone was disturbed by the heavy monotonous *tramp, tramp* of the men, and the dull rumbling of the artillery carriages. As the army defiled through gorge after gorge, the anxiety became painfully intense. At one time, while the column had halted, the colonel's orderly (Prud. Hyams) struck a match for the purpose of lighting a segar, and as the light flashed out in the darkness, a murmur ran through the line: "There it comes at last;" "Now we have got it;" and many expected to hear the roar of a gun. The stern command of an officer to "put out that match," was the only result, and the orderly missed his smoke that time.

TREACHERY OF THE ENEMY

So close and desperate was the first engagement of the regiment in their fight with the enemy that every command and word spoken could be distinctly heard even amid the uproar of the fight. When the head of the regiment approached close to the fence of the corn-field, Drum-Major Patterson was in the immediate front of the column. A United States regular got up on the fence, in plain view, and seeing our advance, cried out, "We are friends." His answer was the report of Patterson's rifle, who simply remarked, as he fired, "No you don't, I have seen you before." R. Patterson originally belonged to this regiment, which he early left, to unite his fortunes with those of the South. It was the first shot and death of the battle.

A sergeant of one of the companies was standing in a small byroad intersecting the fence, a short distance to the left, when two of the enemy climbed upon it in full view. Raising his rifle to fire, one of them waved his hand and quietly said, "Don't shoot, we are friends." At that moment Lieutenant Irvin, of Company K, stepped into the road. Some one ordered the sergeant out of the road, in the words: "Get out of that you damned fool, you'll be killed." As he did so, one of the enemy fired at Lieutenant Irvin, seriously wounding him in the throat, remarking, as he saw the Lieutenant double up in pain, "I got that son of a ———"

The heroism of many of the wounded was astonishing, who cheered the men on as they laid on the ground, shouting for Jeff Davis, regardless of their agony.

WAITMAN'S TWO-GUN BATTERY

This battery was as famed as it was singular and grotesque in its appointments. One gun was a small iron piece, mounted on wagon-wheels and a roughly-constructed carriage; the other was a huge long twelve-pound howitzer, known as "Sacramento," a Mexican gun, composed of brass and silver, the ringing boom of whose voice was peculiar, and heard above all other sounds. This battery had taken a position within point-blank range of Siegel's guns, with the disadvantage of being in the valley. As the Louisiana Regiment passed this battery to charge the enemy's guns, only a single man stood near it, his head bandaged with a red handkerchief, his face and person blackened with powder and smeared with blood. One gun was upset, the ammunition-wagon scattered in pieces around, the horses lying around dead, horribly mangled, the ground trodden down in many places, and, in others, torn up by the plunging shot, actually crimson with gore. As the regiment passed the spot, the man exclaimed, "Give it to them boys. They have ruined our battery, killed our men and our ammunition is all gone." He looked the impersonification of one of war's grim demons. That scene will not soon be forgotten by those who witnessed it.

A DEATH NOT REPORTED
IN OFFICIAL REPORTS

When the army first left Camp Jackson on the march, a large dark-and-tan-colored dog attached himself to the regiment, and soon became a universal pet. When on the march he invariably trotted along the road a few paces in advance of the van, and hence earned the sobriquet of "Sergeant." He seldom left his position in front of the moving column, when the regiment was ordered out of camp. On the morning of the battle of Oak Hills, "Sergeant" was on hand to participate in the events of the day. Amid the storm of leaden bullets and the fierce rattle of musketry in the first close, deadly and obstinate engagement with the enemy, "Sergeant" charged through the bushes, leaping over logs and obstacles, barking furiously all the time. He seemed to enjoy the fight exceedingly. As he passed down the line his sharp voice attracted the attention of some of the men, one of whom shouted to him, "Get out of that Sergeant, you d——d fool, you'll be killed." The words were scarcely uttered ere a fatal ball struck him, and, with a long piteous whine, he rolled on the ground never to rise. The intelligent animal fell among the prostrate forms of many who had fed and caressed him, the victim of his own fearless temerity.

GENERAL PRICE'S REPORT

HEADQUARTERS MISSOURI STATE GUARD, ⎱
Springfield, August 12, 1861. ⎰

"To his Excellency CLAIBORNE F. JACKSON, *Governor of the State of Missouri:*

I have the honor to submit to your Excellency the following report of the operations of the army under my command, at and immediately preceding the battle of Springfield.

I began to move my command from its encampment on Cowskin Prairie, in McDonald County, on the 25th of July, towards Cassville, in Barry County, at which place it had been agreed between Generals McCulloch, Pearce and myself, that our respective forces, together with those of Brigadier-General McBride should be concentrated preparatory to a forward movement. We reached Cassville on Sunday, the 28th of July, and on the next day effected a junction with the armies of Generals McCulloch and Pearce.

The combined armies were then put under marching orders, and the First Division, General McCulloch commanding, left Cassville on the 1st of July, upon the road to this city. The Second Division, under General Pearce of Arkansas, left on the 1st day of August; and the Third Division, Brigadier-General Steen of this State commanding, left on the 2d day of August. I went forward with the Second Division, which embraced the greater portion of my infantry, and encamped with it some twelve miles northwest of Cassville. The next morning a messenger from General McCulloch informed me that he had reason to believe that the enemy were in force on the road to Springfield, and that he should remain at his then encampment on Crane

Creek until the Second and Third Divisions of the army had come up. The Second Division consequently moved forward to Crane Creek, and I ordered the Third Division to a position within three miles of the same place.

The advance guard of the army, consisting of six companies of mounted Missourians, under command of Brigadier-General Rains as at that time, (Friday, August 2d,) encamped on the Springfield road about five miles beyond Crane Creek. About 9 o'clock A.M., of that day, General Rains' pickets reported to him that they had been driven in by the enemy's advance-guard, and that officer immediately led forward his whole force, amounting to nearly 400 men, until he found the enemy in position, some three miles on the road. He sent back at once to General McCulloch for reinforcements, and Colonel McIntosh, C. S. A., was sent forward with 150 men; but a reconnoissance of the ground having satisfied the latter that the enemy did not have more than 150 men on the ground, he withdrew his men and returned to Crane Creek. General Rains soon discovered, however, that he was in presence of the main body of the enemy, numbering, according to his estimate, more than 5,000 men, with eight pieces of artillery, and supported by a considerable body of cavalry. A severe skirmish ensued, which lasted several hours, until the enemy opened their batteries and compelled our troops to retire. In this engagement the greater portion of General Rains' command, and especially that part which acted as infantry, behaved with great gallantry, as the result demonstrates; for our loss was only one killed (Lieutenant Northcut) and five wounded, while five of the enemy's dead were buried on the field, and a large number are known to have been wounded.

Our whole forces were concentrated the next day near Crane Creek, and during the same night the Texan Regiment, under Colonel Greer, came up within a few miles of the same place.

Reasons which will be hereafter assigned, induced me, on Sunday, the 4th inst., to put the Missouri forces, under the direction, for the time being, of General McCulloch, who accordingly assumed the command-in-chief of the combined armies. A little after midnight we took up the line of march, leaving our baggage trains, and expecting to find the enemy near the scene of the late skirmish, but we found, as we advanced, that they were retreating rapidly towards Springfield. We followed them hastily about seventeen miles, to a place known as Moody's Spring, where we were compelled to halt our forces, who were already exhausted by the intense heat of the weather, and the dustiness of the roads.

Early the next morning we moved forward to Wilson's Creek, ten miles southwest of Springfield, where we encamped. Our forces were here put in readiness to meet the enemy, who were posted at Springfield to the number of about 10,000. It was finally decided to march against them; and on Friday afternoon orders were issued to march in four separate columns, at 9 o'clock that night, so as to surround the city and begin a simultaneous attack at daybreak. The darkness of the night and a threatened storm caused General McCulloch, just as the army was about to march, to countermand this order, and to direct that the troops should hold themselves in readiness to move whenever ordered. Our men were consequently kept under arms till towards daybreak, expecting momentarily an order to march. The morning of Saturday, August 10, found them still encamped at Wilson's Creek, fatigued by a night's watching and loss of rest.

About 6 o'clock I received a messenger from General Rains that the enemy were advancing in great force from the direction of Springfield, and were already within 200 or 300 yards of the position, where he was encamped with the Second Brigade of his Division, consisting of about 1,200 mounted men under Colonel Cawthorn. A second messenger came immediately afterwards from General Rains to announce that the main body of the enemy was upon him, but that he would endeavor to hold them in check until he could receive reinforcements. General McCulloch was with me when these messengers came, and left at once for his own headquarters to make the necessary disposition of our forces.

I rode forward instantly towards General Rains' position, at the same time ordering Generals Slack, McBride, Clark and Parsons to move their infantry and artillery rapidly forward. I had ridden but a few hundred yards when I came suddenly upon the main body of the enemy, commanded by General Lyon in person. The infantry and artillery which I had ordered to follow me came up immediately to the number of 2,036 men, and engaged the enemy. A severe and bloody conflict ensued, my officers and men behaving with the greatest bravery, and, with the assistance of a portion of the Confederate forces, successfully holding the enemy in check. Meanwhile, and almost simultaneously with the opening of the enemy's batteries in this quarter, a heavy cannonading was opened upon the rear of our position, where a large body of the enemy under Colonel Siegel had taken position in close proximity to Colonel Churchill's Regiment, Colonel Greer's Texan Rangers and 679 mounted Missourians, under command of Colonel Brown and Lieutenant-Colonel Major.

The action now became general, and was conducted with the greatest gallantly and vigor on both sides for more than five hours, when the enemy retreated in great confusion, leaving their Commander-in-Chief, General Lyon, dead upon the battle field, over 500 killed, and a great number wounded.

The forces under my command have possession of three twelve-pounder howitzers, two brass six-pounders, and a great quantity of small arms and ammunition, taken from the enemy; also, the standard of Siegel's Regiment, captured by Captain Staples. They have also a large number of prisoners.

The brilliant victory thus achieved upon this hard fought field was won only by the most determined bravery and distinguished gallantry of the combined armies, which fought nobly side by side in defence of their common rights and liberties, with as much courage and constancy as were ever exhibited upon any battle field.

Where all behaved so well, it is invidious to make any distinction, but I cannot refrain from expressing my sense of the splendid services rendered, under my own eyes, by the Arkansas Infantry, under General Pearce, the Louisiana Regiment of Colonel Hebert, and Colonel Churchill's Regiment of Mounted Riflemen. These gallant officers and their brave soldiers won upon that day the lasting gratitude of every true Missourian.

This great victory was dearly bought by the blood of many a skillful officer and brave man. Others will report the losses sustained by the Confederate forces; I shall willingly confine myself to the losses within my own army.

Among those who fell mortally wounded upon the battle field, none deserves a dearer place in the memory of Missourians than Richard Hanson Weightman, Colonel commanding the First Brigade of the Second Division of the army. Taking up arms at the very beginning of this unhappy contest, he had already done distinguished services at the battle of Rock Creek, where he commanded the State forces after the death of the lamented Holloway; and at Carthage, where he won unfading laurels by the display of extraordinary coolness, courage and skill. He fell at the head of his brigade, wounded in three places, and died just as the victorious shouts of our army began to rise upon the air.

Here, too, died, in the discharge of his duty, Colonel Benjamin Brown of Ray County, President of the Senate, a good man and true.

Brigadier-General Slack's Division suffered severely. He himself fell, dangerously wounded, at the head of his column. Of his regiment of infantry, under Colonel John T. Hughes, consisting of about 650 men, thirty-six were killed, seventy-six wounded, many of them mortally, and thirty are missing. Among the killed were C. H. Bennet, Adjutant of the regiment, Captain Blackwell and Lieutenant Hughes. Colonel Rives' squadron of cavalry, (dismounted) numbering some 234 men, lost four killed and eight wounded. Among the former were Lieutenant-Colonel Austin and Captain Engart.

Brigadier-General Clark was also wounded. His infantry (290 men) lost, in killed seventeen, and wounded 71. Colonel Burbridge was severely wounded. Captains Farris and Halleck and Lieutenant Haskins were killed. General Clark's cavalry, together with the Windsor Guards, were under the command of Lieutenant-Colonel Major, who did good service. They lost six killed and five wounded.

Brigadier-General McBride's Division (605 men) lost twenty-two killed, sixty-seven severely wounded, and fifty-seven slightly wounded. Colonel

Foster and Captains Nichols, Dougherty, Armstrong and Mings were wounded while gallantly leading their respective commands.

General Parsons' Brigade, 256 infantry and artillery, under command respectively of Colonel Kelly and Captain Guibor, and 406 cavalry, Colonel Brown, lost, the artillery, three killed and seven wounded; the infantry, nine killed and thirty-eight wounded; the cavalry, three killed and two wounded. Colonel Kelly was wounded in the hand. Captain Coleman was mortally wounded, and has since died.

General Rains' Division was composed of two brigades—the first, under Colonel Weightman, embracing infantry and artillery, 1,306 strong, lost, not only their commander, but thirty-four others killed and 111 wounded. The Second Brigade, mounted men, Colonel Cawthorn commanding, about 1,200 men, lost twenty-one killed and seventy-five wounded. Colonel Cawthorn was himself wounded. Major Charles Rogers, of St. Louis, Adjutant of the brigade, was mortally wounded, and died the day after the battle. He was a gallant officer, at all times vigilant and attentive to his duties, and fearless upon the field of battle.

Your Excellency will perceive that our State forces consisted of only 5,221 officers and men; that of these no less than 156 died upon the field, while 517 were wounded. These facts attest more powerfully than any words can, the severity of the conflict, and the dauntless courage of our brave soldiers.

It is also my painful duty to announce the death of one of my aids, Lieutenant-Colonel George W. Allen, of Saline County. He was shot down while communicating an order, and we left him buried on the field. I have appointed to the position thus sadly vacated, Captain James T. Cearnal, in recognition of his gallant conduct and valuable services throughout the battle, as a Volunteer Aid. Another of my staff, Colonel Horace H. Brand, was made prisoner by the enemy, but has since been released.

My thanks are due to three of your staff, Colonel William M. Cooke, Colonel Richard Gaines, and Colonel Thomas L. Snead, for services which they rendered me as Volunteer Aids, and also to my Aid-de-Camp, Colonel A. W. Jones.

In conclusion, I beg leave to say to your Excellency, that the army under my command, both officers and men, did their duty nobly as became men fighting in defence of their homes and their honor, and that they deserve well of the State.

I have the honor to be, with the greatest respect,

Your Excellency's obedient servant,

STERLING PRICE.
Major-General, Commanding Missouri State Guard.

BEN M'CULLOCH'S REPORT

"HEADQUARTERS MCCULLOCH'S BRIGADE, ⎫
"*Camp Weightman, near Springfield, Mo., Aug.* 12, 1861. ⎰

"*Brig.-Gen. J. Cooper, Adjt.-Gen., C. S. A.*

GENERAL—I have the honor to make the following official report of the battle of Oak Hills on the 10th inst. Having taken position about ten miles from Springfield, I endeavored to gain the necessary information of the strength and position of the enemy stationed in and about the town. The information was very conflicting and unsatisfactory. I, however, made up my mind to attack the enemy in their position, and issued orders on the 9th inst. to my force to start at 9 o'clock at night, to attack at four different points at daylight. A few days before, Gen. Price, in command of the Missouri forces, turned over his command to me, and I assumed command of the entire force, comprising my own brigade, the brigade of Arkansas State forces under Gen. Pearce, and Gen. Price's command of Missourians. My effective force was 5,300 infantry, fifteen pieces of artillery, and 6,000 horsemen armed with flint-lock muskets, rifles, and shot-guns. There were other horsemen with the army who were entirely unarmed, and instead of being a help, were continually in the way. When the time arrived for the night march, it began to rain slightly, and fearing, from the want of cartridge-boxes, that my ammunition would be ruined, I ordered the movement to be stopped, hoping to move the next morning. My men had but twenty-five rounds of cartridges apiece, and there was no more to be had. While still hesitating in the morning, the enemy was reported advancing, and I made arrangements to meet him. The attack was made simultaneously at half-past 5 A.M. on our right and left flanks, and the enemy had gained the positions they desired.

Gen. Lyon attacked us on our left, and Gen. Siegel on our right and rear. From these points batteries opened on us. My command was soon ready. The Missourians, under Gens. Slack, Clark, McBride, Parsons, and Rains, were nearest to the position taken by Gen. Lyon with his main force; they were instantly turned to the left, and opened the battle with an incessant fire of small-arms. Woodruff opposed his battery to the battery of the enemy under Capt. Totten, and a constant cannonading was kept up between these batteries during the engagement. Hebert's regiment of Louisiana Volunteers and McIntosh's regiment of Arkansas Mounted Riflemen were ordered to the front, and after passing the battery (Totten's), turned to the left and soon engaged the enemy with the regiments deployed. Col. McIntosh dismounted his regiment, and the two marched up abreast to a fence around a large corn-field, where they met the left of the enemy already posted. A terrible conflict of small-arms took place here. The opposing force was a body of regular United States Infantry, commanded by Capts. Plummer and Gilbert.

Notwithstanding the galling fire poured on these two regiments, they leaped over the fence, and gallantly led by their colonels, drove the enemy before them back upon the main body. During this time the Missourians under Gen. Price were nobly attempting to sustain themselves in the centre, and were hotly engaged on the sides of the heights upon which the enemy were posted. Far on the right Siegel had opened his battery upon Churchill's and Greer's regiments, and had gradually made his way to the Springfield road, upon each side of which the army was encamped, and in a prominent position he established his battery. I at once took two companies of the Louisiana regiment who were nearest me and marched them rapidly from the front and right to the rear, with order to Col. McIntosh to bring up the rest. When we arrived near the enemy's battery, we found that Reid's battery had opened upon it, and it was already in confusion. Advantage was taken of it, and soon the Louisianians were gallantly charging among the guns and swept the cannoneers away. Five guns were here taken, and Siegel's command, completely routed, were in rapid retreat with a single gun, followed by some companies of the Texan regiment and a portion of Col. Major's Missouri cavalry. In the pursuit many of the enemy were killed and taken prisoners, and their last gun captured.

Having cleared our right and rear, it was necessary to turn all our attention to the centre, under Gen. Lyon, who was pressing upon the Missourians, having driven them back. To this point McIntosh's regiment, under Lieut.-Col. Embry, and Churchill's regiment on foot, and Gratiot's regiment, and McRae's battalion, were sent to their aid.

The terrible fire of musketry was now kept up along the whole side and top of the hill upon which the enemy was posted. Masses of infantry fell back and again rushed forward. The summit of the hill was covered with the dead and wounded—both sides were fighting with desperation for the day. Carroll's and Greer's regiments, led gallantly by Capt. Bradfute, charged the battery, but the whole strength of the enemy was immediately in the rear, and a deadly fire was opened upon them. At this critical period, when the fortune of the day seemed to be at the turning-point, two regiments of General Pearce's brigade were ordered to march from their position (as reserves) to support the centre. The order was obeyed with alacrity, and Gen. Pearce gallantly rushed with his brigade to the rescue. Reid's battery was also ordered to move forward, and the Louisiana regiment was again called into action on the left of it. The battle then became general, and probably no two opposing forces ever fought with greater desperation; inch by inch the enemy gave way and were driven from their position. Totten's battery fell back; Missourians, Arkansians, Louisianians, and Texans pushed forward. The incessant roll of musketry was deafening, and the balls fell as thick as hail-stones; but still our gallant Southerners pushed onward and with one wild yell broke upon the enemy, pushing them back and strewing the ground with their dead. Nothing could withstand the impetuosity of our final charge; the enemy fled, and could not be rallied again, and they were last seen at 12 M., retreating among the hills in the distance. Thus ended the battle. It lasted six hours and a half.

The force of the enemy, between nine and ten thousand, was composed of well-disciplined troops, well armed, and a large part of them belonging to the old army of the United States.

With every advantage on their side, they have met with a signal repulse. The loss of the enemy is at least 800 killed, 1,000 wounded and 300 prisoners. We captured six pieces of artillery, and several hundred stand of small-arms, and several of their standards.

Maj.-Gen. Lyon, chief in command, was killed. Many of the officers high in rank were wounded. Our loss was also severe, and we mourn the death of many a gallant officer and soldier. Our killed amount to 265; 800 wounded, and 30 missing. Col. Weightman fell at the head of his brigade of Missourians, while gallantly charging upon the enemy. His place cannot be easily filled. Generals Slack and Clark, of Missouri, were severely wounded, Gen. Price slightly. Capt. Hinson, of the Louisiana regiment, Capt. McAlexander, of Churchill's regiment, Capts. Bell and Brown, of Pearce's brigade, Lieuts. Walton and Weaver—all fell while nobly and gallantly doing their duty. Col. McIntosh was slightly wounded by a grape-shot, while charging with the Louisiana regiment; Lieut.-Col. Neal, Maj. H. Ward, Capts. King, Pearsons, Gibbs, Ramsaur, Porter, Lieuts. Dawson, Chambers, Johnson, King, Adams, Hardista, McIvor, and Saddler were wounded while at the head of their companies.

Where all were doing their duty so gallantly it is almost unfair to discriminate. I must, however, bring to your notice the gallant conduct of the Missouri Generals McBride, Parsons, Clark, Black and their officers. To Gen. Price I am under many obligations for assistance on the battle-field. He was at the head of his force leading them on, and sustaining them by his gallant bearing. Gen. Pearce, with his Arkansas brigade (Gratiot's, Walker's, and Dockery's regiments of infantry), came gallantly to the rescue when sent for; leading his men into the thickest of the fight, he contributed much to the success of the day. The commanders of regiments of my own brigade, Cols. Churchill, Greer, Embry, McIntosh, Hebert, and McRae, led their different regiments into action with great coolness and bravery, and were always in front of their men, cheering them on. Woodruff and Reid managed their batteries with great ability, and did much execution. For those officers and men who were particularly conspicuous, I will refer the Department to the reports of the different commanders.

To my personal staff I am much indebted for the coolness and rapidity with which they carried orders about the field, and would call particular attention to my volunteer aids, Capt. Bledsoe, Messrs. F. C. Armstrong, Ben Johnson (whose horse was killed under him), Hamilton Pike, and Major King. To Maj. Montgomery, Quartermaster, I am also indebted for much service as an aid during the battle; he was of much use to me. To Col. McIntosh, at one time at the head of his regiment, and at other times in his capacity as Adjutant-General, I cannot give too much praise. Wherever the balls flew he was gallantly leading different regiments into action, and his presence gave confidence everywhere.

I have the honor to be, sir,

Your obedient servant,

BEN McCULLOCH,
Brig.-Gen. Commanding.

CHAPTER VIII

THE day after the battle the troops marched three miles nearer Springfield, in order to escape from the terrible effluvia occasioned by the festering bodies lying unburied on the battle-field, camping near Wilson's Springs, whose clear, cool water escaped in abundant profusion from a large chasm in the rocks. This encampment was near an open, rolling prairie, and six miles from Springfield. The Missourians proceeded to Springfield, taking possession of the place. The night of the 11th a severe thunder-storm arose, and the next day it cleared off cool. Here General McCulloch issued the following congratulatory order:

"HEADQUARTERS, CAMP NEAR SPRINGFIELD, MO. ⎱
General Orders, No. 27, August 12, 1861. ⎰

"The General commanding takes great pleasure in announcing to the army under his command the signal victory it has just gained.

"Soldiers of Louisiana, of Arkansas, of Missouri and of Texas, nobly have you sustained yourselves. Shoulder to shoulder you have met the enemy. Your first battle has been glorious, and your General is proud of you. The opposing force, composed mostly of the old regular army of the North, have thrown themselves upon you, but, by great gallantry and determined courage, you have entirely routed it with great slaughter. Several pieces of artillery and many prisoners are now in your hands. The commander-in-chief of the enemy is slain and many of the general officers wounded. The flag of the Confederacy now floats over Springfield, the stronghold of the enemy. The friends of our cause who have been imprisoned there are released. While announcing to the army the great victory, the General hopes that the laurels you have gained will not be tarnished by a single outrage. The private property of citizens of either party must be respected. Soldiers who fought as you did day before yesterday cannot rob or plunder.

"By order.　　　　　　GENERAL MCCULLOCH.
"JAMES MCINTOSH, *Captain and Adjutant-General.*"

In their departure from McCulloch, the Missourians carried with them the battery taken by the Louisiana troops, by what authority was not discovered. They claimed the honor of capturing the guns, causing much exasperation among the men of the regiment. This soon became a subject of serious dissension between the State Guards and the Confederate troops, being the foundation of the differences, heart-burnings and jealousies which existed afterwards and followed McCulloch to his death. The guns, however, were finally returned stripped of almost everything movable about them. Orders were issued to move on the morning of the 16th at 6 A.M. The troops moved in obedience to orders, marching about seven miles, and encamped in a pleasant spot near some fine springs. The weather kept clear and pleasant. The Arkansas State troops here left the brigade, having enlisted for only three months, and being unwilling to enter the Confederate service. Thus the fruit of our golden victory was being thrown away at the very moment when, if properly seized, it would have resulted gloriously for the Southern cause. The enemy were in full retreat toward St. Louis, and if a unanimity of action had actuated all who participated in the late battle, and the enemy been rapidly followed into Missouri, her downtrodden people would have risen *en masse* and thrown aside the chains which bound them hand and foot. General McCulloch in vain appealed to their patriotism and bravery. Home! was the only response. Thus the ruinous policy of organizing State troops crippled the Confederate cause and environed our gallant commander with difficulties, completely annulling the advantage which he had gained, making him a victor over a foe, a leader without an army. McCulloch returned from his fruitless mission to the Arkansas troops furious with anger at his failure. While in this camp much dissatisfaction existed in the regiment. They were living in the open air without blankets, tents, or scarcely provisions enough to keep them alive, subject to all the inclemencies of the weather. Frequent thunder storms arose to add to and increase their accumulated miseries. The sick-list began to grow alarmingly large. Wagons were sent out to gather green corn to distribute as food to the men, oftentimes three ears being the day's rations. When these wagons arrived in camp, the boys invariably indulged freely in the propensity for fun, so proverbial among soldiers in their hour of sorest need and most trying situation. A general outburst would commence; "Here's your corn;" "Come up and draw your oats;" "I say, Colonel, any fodder to-day with this corn," were a few of the numerous expressions. While encamped here we visited the deserted camp-grounds of the Federal troops. It was situated in a broad, rolling prairie, near a strip of woods, through which ran a small stream. Their bake-ovens (quite models in their way), built of stone and mud and brush-shelters, were scattered in all directions. In a prominent position a large smooth stone was planted firmly in the ground. On its face were traced, in quite artistic style, a pick-axe, spade and axe crossed, interspersed with the words, "Pioneer Company A, Missouri Volunteers, July 19, 1861." Near by, on a large tree, was the inscription: "Headquarters First Iowa Regiment, Company A, Captain Cummins, Lyon commanding." This was the regiment so terribly used up in the fight. This regiment was mustered out shortly after the battle, and the remnant, doubtless, carried home with them ample testimony to the desperate valor and daring of the "Secesh," as the Dutch called the Southerners.

On the 24th August, Captain Gilmore, Sergeant Kenney and Private Cole, of Company F, visited the battle-ground. The dead of the enemy were strewn all over the field unburied. They found 150 of them. Dead horses, old clothes, broken wagons, canteens, haversacks, were strewn over the field. They noticed particularly the hill that Woodruff's battery had been playing on (Bloody Hill). Oak trees a foot in diameter were cut into by the canon-balls. More dead men were scattered here than at any other point of the field. Here fell General Lyon. Here the last of the battle was fought. Some of the wounded had crawled into the shade of the trees and died there, while others died in the ranks where they fell. The whole scene was a mournful picture of war's desolation.

In obedience to orders, the camp in Missouri was broken up, August 25, and McCulloch's little army turned their faces southward. All day long the men marched in a cold, drenching rain, reaching camp only to lie upon the wet ground, racked with pains, and many with burning fever. The country was beautiful, being an open, rolling prairie land, extending, as far as the eye could reach, in gentle undulations. The men had little heart, however, for the beauties of nature. Some conception may be formed of the increasing powers of endurance exhibited by the men when it is stated that, notwithstanding the inclemency of the weather and heavy roads, they marched fourteen miles in four hours, halting but once. All along the line of march the people turned out to see the Louisianians, their name already having spread far and wide for their undautned courage and intrepid valor. Many a smile on fair faces, and loving glances from bright eyes greeted them; aye, and cheering words also, conclusively showing how beauty appreciates valor, and that the fair thought the brave eminently deserving of their smiles. At Mount Vernon, Mo., one of our camping-places, the regiment was enthusiastically greeted and honored, especially by the ladies. Ah! the numerous kindnesses shown by the heroic women of the land have encouraged them beyond the power of expression. The regiment remained several days at Mount Vernon, which was principally noted for its handsome ladies, making it quite an attraction for the boys. A hospital was here established, in which the numerous sick men were placed. Little attention was bestowed upon them save by personal friends, and no proper food provided for them. Placed in rows upon hard beds on the floor of a church, these brave men slowly wasted away from that fell disease of the soldier, typhoid fever, finding peace at last in death, to be buried by sympathizing comrades, in a distant State, away, far away, from the dear ones whose loving care might have snatched them from the grave. Oh, the crying evils of these wayside hospitals! The wanton neglect and indifference shown, the wrongs practiced upon sick soldiers all over the land, will some day meet with a fearful reckoning.

One fair afternoon some ladies made a call upon a prominent officer of the regiment, entering his tent in all the amplitude of crinoline. One thought to seat herself and have a cosy chat, but hoops (oh! hoops) upset the chair, and the fair visitant suddenly found herself *(mirabile dictu)* on the ground. The officer who had been playing the host most polite from a front face, was incapacited from rendering any assistance, a portion of his apparel giving unmistakeable evidence that he belonged to the "Ragged Brigade." Here was a predicament. A gallant Captain, however, relieved both the distressed lady and the embarrassed host by offering immediate assistance.

On the 30th of August the march was once more resumed, much to the delight and satisfaction of the men. Soldiers are proverbial for their restlessness, and, strange as it may seem, infinitely prefer the tedious and toilsome march to the quietude of camp life for any length of time. The road lay through a country of alternate woodland and prairie. Some of the landscape views were exquisite in their groupings of wood and prairie land, with their contrasts of dark lines and smooth, emerald surfaces. Marched twenty-two miles, and encamped at a small place known as Sarcoxie. The march was over a dusty road, and through a country almost devoid of water. The men were glad when the halt was ordered. The camp was soon thronged with ladies from the surrounding country, eager to get a look at the Louisianians. Questions innumerable were propounded, many of which cased *audible* smiles on the part of the men. The cannon and shells attracted particular attention, many never having seen such curiosities before, or heard the roar of such huge guns. All asked to have one fired off—a request much easier made than granted. Much to the chagrin of the men, the request was refused. Miss Kate Wilson, a truly handsome lassie, attracted marked attention. How many, we wonder, now remember her fair face and handsome form, tastefully arrayed in a dark riding habit, as, seated on her beautiful pony, she distributed her sweet smiles and kind words to the crowd of admirers who surrounded her. We wonder, too, whether she ever dreamed that her kind and genial manner to the soiled, travel-stained, yet noble-hearted soldiers, would place her name in history.

Sunday morning, September 1, 1861, was a bright, beautiful one, a lovely harbinger of one of those dreamy days when the soul drinks in with intoxicating pleasure every scene of beauty. At daylight, the men were in line ready to proceed, Colonel Hebert in command of the brigade, General McCulloch having left him in charge of the army and proceeded to Bentonville. We crossed in our march a broad, open prairie, extending as far as vision could reach, an emerald sea of tall, waving grass, thickly interspersed with nature's wildflowers in rich profusion of variegated colors. Guns and hats were ornamented with these floral beauties, which gave to the troops quite a holiday attire, notwithstanding their soiled and tattered uniforms and rough, bronzed features. Camped, after a march of fourteen miles, on Black or Shoal Creek, two miles from Granby. This was a deep stream of cold water, in whose limpid depths the men eagerly bathed their sore and wearied limbs. The Lieutenant-Colonel, S. M. Hyams, here played a rich joke on Major Tunnard, by spreading the report that he was General McCulloch. While the Major was washing and dressing himself, a dense throng of men gathered about his tent, much to his discomfiture and astonishment, all eager to catch a glimpse of the supposed famed Texan Ranger. It was some time before they were undeceived. Colonel Hyams loved a good joke, indicative of the genial spirit of the man, and enjoyed the fun hugely.

Resuming the march, the command passed through Granby. This place is situated seven miles from Neosho, the seat of Newton County, with a population of 2,500, nine-tenths of whom live in log cabins and shanties, being employed mostly in mining. It is on a range of bare, desolate, bleak-looking hills. The miners are what are termed "floaters," and comprised of every variety and class of people—Irish, German, English, Scotch and "Yankees." There were two smelting establishments in this town, which did an extensive business. We were informed that in 1860 there was procured from these mines something like 7,000,000 pounds of ore, out of which had been manufactured 50,000 pigs of lead. The mines are the richest in the known world, the *Galena* producing *nine-tenths* of pure metal. Of course the possession of these mines was of the utmost importance to the Confederates, furnishing as they did all the "blue pills" used by the army. The inhabitants enthusiastically greeted the troops as they passed through the town, Confederate flags being unfurled everywhere. The troops encamped at Neosho, the place of McCulloch's first exploit with the enemy. It is a place of considerable size, situated in a valley surrounded by hills. The march from this town was in the midst of constant rain, and the men of the regiment were in a terrible condition. Large numbers were shoeless, and the uniforms hung in shreds and tatters about their forms after their arduous campaign. On the 5th the regiment once more reached Camp Jackson. As the regiment crossed the Missouri line, and when in sight of Camp Jackson, they cheered long and vociferously. It seemed like reaching home once more, after having traveled over 500 miles, fought a desperate battle, and endured untold hardships and sufferings.

CHAPTER IX

DOUBTLESS many will inquire why General McCulloch left Missouri. The reasons are obvious and forcible. First, the disbanding of the Arkansas troops; second, the departure of the Missouri forces under Generals Rains and Price. Thus, with reduced forces, insufficient supplies and clothing, it was deemed advisable, nay, was absolutely necessary, to move to some point where the army could be reorganized, strengthened and rendered efficient for the fall campaign. The new troops must be disciplined and drilled, and properly prepared for a soldier's life.

Camp Jackson was the best location for these purposes. Another cause for the movement was the treatment received at the hands of the Missourians, and the disposition of many of their generals to arrogate to themselves the honor of the victory gained at Oak Hills. Even the genial, warm-hearted Sterling Price, the leader of the Missourians, allowed his judgment to be warped by the general prejudice. In his official report he said: "I have gained a great victory with the assistance of a few Confederate troops." We do not believe that General Price intended any disparagement to the Louisiana or other troops, for the Third Regiment, as has already been shown, received an appropriate acknowledgment from him for their distinguished services. Yet such statements as above, in official reports, raised a storm of indignation among both officers and men against the Missourians for a usurpation of all the glory of August 10th. The Third Louisiana Regiment performed deeds that day which gave them a name for daring and bravery imperishable as history itself, endearing them to the people of Missouri and Arkansas in ties cemented in blood. The gallant Missourians who entered the Confederate service feel and know this, for they stood side by side and shoulder to shoulder like brothers, in many battles and campaigns afterwards. But on this topic more anon. Early in September came information of the declaration of the Indians in favor of the South. This nerved anew the unflagging spirits and unfaltering energies of our troops. Four months in the Confederate service! Four months had we been away from home, making long and wearisome marches over rough and rocky roads, through valleys, over hill-tops, in rain and sunshine, dust and mud, heat and cold. Leaving tents behind to facilitate our movements, we had encamped without shelter, making the damp, chilly ground our couch, and the azure sky our only covering. Add to this the tortures of hunger, want of sufficient apparel, and up to this period not a cent of pay, all endured with comparatively little murmuring or complaining, and it shows a spirit which nothing could break or conquer.

> "We're the sons of sires that baffled
>   Crowned and martyred tyranny;
> They defied the field and scaffold
>   For their birthrights—so have we."

"MON BLONKET"

Who does not remember Johnny Crasson, of Co. K? He was a Frenchman of undoubted descent, imperfectly versed in the English language, yet very ambitious to learn its intricate meaning. Diminutive in person, when first in the army unusually credulous, good-natured, and yet loving fun, Johnny was the subject of many practical jokes. Eventually he became thoroughly initiated into the mysteries of soldier life. His first lessons in English were obtained from one more versed in profane than polite idioms of the language. Thus Johnny could be heard at all hours practicing his lessons. We remember his coming into camp after a fatiguing day's march, and relieving his overburdened soul, under trials inflicted by some Confederate mules, in this wise: "Sacre tonnere! by gar! mes amis, one tarn miyule, he com'ee to ze wagoon and eat'ee mon blonket off my knopsock! Ze tam tevil! Sacre by gar! he no satisfy to eat ze wagoon into what you call ze scalloop, but he eat'ee ze only blonket of one poor soldat, tam my soul!" Johnny never heard the last of his "blonket" and his "knopsock."

CHAPTER X

DURING our return march and after the arrival at Camp Jackson, the men indulged their appetites freely in the fruit everywhere so abundant, the apples being large and mellow, the peaches luscious and juicy. Yet many a poor fellow paid dearly by extra camp and guard duty for eating "forbidden fruit." On the 6th of September commenced drilling and all the regular minutiæ of camp life. McCulloch informed the men that as soon as he was prepared he would march on the enemy wherever he could find them. At this time provisions were poor and scanty, tents very scarce, and the men in large numbers actually naked and barefooted. They expressed the very sensible opinion that they must have more shelter, clothing, food and pay if their "idolized Ben" expected them to render efficient service—be ready for action. Major Tunnard was taken sick on the 6th, and becoming rapidly worse, was finally carried to the residence of Mrs. Cunningham, a half-breed Cherokee in the Indian Territory. At one time his life was despaired of, and but for necessary medicines furnished from Gen. McCulloch's headquarters, the prompt medical assistance of Dr. Cross, Brigade Surgeon, and the unwearying kindness and tender care of Mrs. Cunningham, would undoubtedly have died September 13th. His son takes an especial pleasure in thus noticing the services of these kind friends in the hour of sore need. Under Mrs. Cunningham's careful nursing he soon fully recovered, to resume his duties as a soldier. On the 9th a large supply of provisions and funds arrived to gladden the hearts of the men. It was a day of general rejoicing in camp. The next day McCulloch, having received the proper authority from the Secretary of War, published the following proclamation:

HEADQUARTERS CAMP JACKSON, ARK., ⎫
September 10th, 1861. ⎭

Citizens of Arkansas, Texas, and Louisiana:

Every exertion is now being made on the part of our enemies of the North to retrieve their late disastrous defeats on the plains of Manassas, and the late battle-field of Oak Hills. It now becomes necessary, in order to maintain the glorious achievements of our arms, that a large force should be thrown into the field on this frontier; and having received instructions from the War Department at Richmond to increase the force under my command, I will receive and muster into the service of the Confederate States five regiments of infantry from each of the above-named States, by companies, battalions and regiments, for three years or during the war. Those from Arkansas will rendezvous at Fort Smith and Camp Jackson. I have in my possession arms sufficient to equip two regiments of Arkansas troops; the remaining three are required to equip themselves with the best they can procure. The forces from Texas will rendezvous at Sherman. Those from Louisiana will rendezvous at Little Rock. Both of the above are expected to equip themselves with the best arms they can procure. An officer will be detailed to muster into service the forces from each State at their respective places of rendezvous. The commanding officers of companies, battalions and regiments, as soon as they have been mustered into service, will procure the necessary transportation for their several commands, and march them at once to Camp Jackson, unless otherwise ordered. Each man will be provided with two suits of winter clothing and two blankets, also tents, if they can be procured. It is desirable that the forces of the several States should be in the field at as early a date as possible.

I call upon you, therefore, to rally to the defence of your sister State, Missouri. Her cause is your cause, and the cause of justice and independence. Then rally, my countrymen, and assist your friends in Missouri to drive back the Republican myrmidons that still pollute her soil and threaten to invade your own country, confiscate your property, liberate your slaves, and put to the sword every true Southern man who dares to take up arms in defence of his rights.

The principles inaugurated in this war by the proclamation of Maj.-Gen. Fremont should warn the South of the ultimate intentions of the North, and show them the necessity of rallying to the standard of their country (for the time specified above), prepared to fight in defence of their homes, their altars, and their firesides, until our independence shall be recognized and its blessings secured to our posterity.

BEN McCULLOCH,
Brigadier-General Commanding.

At the time of this proclamation several companies of Texans arrived in camp. One, Goode's Artillery, was a splendidly equipped company, well drilled and disciplined, and a fine-looking body of men. They became devotedly attached to the Louisiana regiment.

Mixed amid the sweets of life are the bitter dregs. Almost daily news reached camp of the death of members of the regiment at the hospitals in Mt. Vernon and other places, from disease and wounds. After the departure of the regiment the ladies of Mt. Vernon were unceasing in their attention and untiring in their kindness to those left in their midst. Yet notwithstanding all that these kind and gentle hearts could do to stay the ebbing tide of life, the soldier sank to his final rest, and sleeps quietly in the burial-ground of Mt. Vernon, where the battle's fierce din can never reach him, until the last reveille shall have summoned the countless dead from their narrow tombs.

The men of the regiment were united in the strong bonds of more than brotherly affection, and when death's keen arrow found its victim among their number, there was heartfelt sorrow. Ah! those early graves of our first dead! What memories come back at the thought of them!

> As softly as starlight melts into day,
> On pinions of angels their souls passed away.
> Strong men are bowed—in anguish they weep,
> O'er the dead still so dear—in death's quiet sleep.
> But ah! far away o'er mountain and glen,
> Lie the homes, that they ne'er shall enter again,
> Where loving ones wait to welcome in joy
> Back to their sunlight their own soldier boy.
> But above them now sweeps the blue azure dome,
> Ne'er shall parents or friends welcome them home;
> Dear comrades, farewell, your battles are o'er,
> Together in conflict we'll rally no more.
> Farewell! life is o'er, earth fades from your sight,
> Around you has closed death's long dreamless night.

Day after day passed away at Camp Jackson during the month of September with little that proved of much interest. There were morning company drills and evening parades, the latter being largely attended by ladies from the surrounding country, to witness the evolutions of the regiment. The fine manly appearance of the men, their soldierly bearing, discipline, splendid evolutions, and marching elicited the admiration of the spectators and the wonder of the new troops. The weather, most of the time, was beautiful, the atmosphere genial and pleasant. The sun looked lovingly down on the broad expanse of prairie lying stretched out before the camp, while the gently stirring air through the trees which sheltered the camp, inclined the men to gather in groups and quietly talk of home or discuss the latest sensational item of the war.

On the 20th, Major Tunnard received a commission to proceed to Little Rock to muster in troops, obtain recruits for the regiment, and use his influence to strengthen McCulloch's forces. He departed on the 21st, accompanied by the best wishes of the regiment, who were much attached to him.

On the evening of the 25th, while the different regiments were drilling on the open prairie, Captain Goode's Battery was also out practicing. By some unaccountable means one of the caissons blew up, fortunately injuring no one. The horses attached ran away with the remains, while the Arkansas troops stampeded in utter confusion amid the shouts and cheers of the Louisianians, who stood their ground without a man leaving the ranks. They had already seen "the elephant" in all his huge proportions, and could not run from an exploding caisson. The incident furnished food for many a hearty laugh at the expense of the Arkansians. The men were now suffering intensely from the want of proper clothing, as the weather began to change, the nights growing cold and frosty. However, they were consoled somewhat amid their sufferings with the intelligence that the State had forwarded a fine supply of everything necessary for their comfort. Hon. A. Talbot, of Iberville, was appointed by Gov. Moore to have these supplies safely and speedily transported to the regiment.

On the last day of the month occurred the first scene of punishment witnessed in the brigade, one of the Arkansians having been condemned to be drummed out of camp with his head shaved for stealing. In the afternoon the whole brigade assembled to witness the execution. They were formed in two lines, facing each other, with space sufficient to permit the criminal to march between the ranks. At the appointed hour he was brought forth, marched down the extended lines to the tune of the "Rogue's March," followed by a file of men with fixed bayonets, his head shaved bare, and a large placard attached to his back marked "THIEF." This punishment was a novelty, and was witnessed by the brigade with serious faces and in silence. It became a frequent occurrence, however, in the soldier's experience. The prisoner was conducted a mile from camp, released and ordered to leave, under penalty, if caught, of being shot. The spectacle, most assuredly, was not a very agreeable one.

During this period General Price had been achieving some important successes in Missouri, having captured Lexington, with the Federal forces there, arms, ammunition, etc. His forces had rapidly augmented in numbers. The people of Missouri, under the spur of Fremont's proclamation, to kill every Secessionist caught in arms against the United States, were everywhere organizing for a desperate armed resistance to the invading foe. Everything pointed to the early resumption of active operations.

Captain Theodore Johnson had been appointed Brigade Quartermaster, and Lieutenant W. D. Hardiman, of Company H, filled his post in the regiment. On the 1st of October, Captain T. L. Maxwell, Regimental Commissary, left the regiment on furlough, and Felix R. Brunot, of Company K, was appointed in his place during his absence. Many of the men, disabled from wounds and constitutional infirmities, were discharged. One-half the regiment were on the sick-list, and the rest, if anything, worse off. Such was the state of affairs in the beginning of October.

On the night of the 4th, the camp was visited by one of those terrific storms so prevalent during this season of the year, and which the open nature of the country rendered all the more furious in its force and grandeur. Late in the afternoon huge masses of clouds, inky in their darkness, gathered in the north-west. In fantastic forms, they were piled up like a succession of jagged mountain-peaks, their rough edges tinged with a pale-yellowish light. Anon a vivid flash of lightning would dart its forked tongue athwart the blackness, followed by the rumbling thunder's roll. The storm drove down with furious speed upon our encampment. The men hurried hither and thither, driving down tent-pegs and tightening the cords. From experience, dearly bought, they knew what to expect. It burst at last upon the camp with ten-fold fury. The lightning's blinding flash was followed by the thunder's peal, crash upon crash, in rapid succession. The trees groaned and shivered with the wind-king's mighty power. Then came down the rain, first in large pattering drops, succeeded finally by a deluge of water as if all the flood-gates of heaven had been loosed. Cries, shouts and laughter were heard on all sides, according to the nature of the men's mishaps; tents tumbled upon their occupants, from beneath which the men would emerge like drowned rats, much to the amusement of their more fortunate comrades. Such scenes as these were no rare occurrence, and formed a part of the soldier's experience at Camp Jackson.

CHAPTER XI

AMUSEMENTS

THE boys whiled away the idle hours of camp life with games and amusements of every description. Racing, athletic sports, wrestling, trials of skill and strength, pitching quoits, gymnastic performances, and last, but not least, football. Kind reader, did you ever witness the game? If not, we will enlighten your understanding. It is a favorite amusement with college-boys, where, if played with roughness, yet is the game conducted according to systematic rule. A football is usually about the size of a man's head, or a thirty-six pound cannon-ball. It is manufactured out of four oval pieces of leather, so shaped as to be as round as possible. An opening is left in this cover, with a tongue to cover the opening, on both sides of which are holes, at regular intervals, so that it could be tightly laced up. Through this opening was inserted a fresh beef bladder, which was then blown up to the utmost capacity of the cover. The mouth of the bladder was then securely tied, the end thrust inside the cover, which was tightly laced up, and the ball is ready for the game—a light, bounding thing, to be rudely kicked, cuffed and scrambled over. The ground being chosen, free from all obstructions, two stakes are driven down securely, about fifteen or twenty yards apart, at a distance of fifty or seventy-five yards, or further if deemed necessary. Sides are then chosen, equal in numbers, whose object is to drive the ball through each other's base, or "home," with the foot alone. Behold, then these weather-beaten men, strong, active, athletic, inured to hardship, thus arrayed. There is to be no schoolboys' work here, but a trial of muscular strength, united with skill and fleetness of foot. The scene is so grotesque and peculiar that it would astonish and amuse our friends at home. The players are dressed in every variety of fanciful costumes. Shirts of gaudy hues, colored handkerchiefs tightly tied around their bodies, pants stuffed into socks, turbans, fanciful, indeed, formed of woolen tippets, red, blue, green and yellow, all showing that the "boys" appreciate the "phunny" scenes of more peaceful times. At a distance the men look like a collection of revelers on Mardi-gras day.

A single player, with ball in hand, steps midway between the two opposing forces, and, with a tremendous kick, "camps" it. Both parties make a rush
at the rolling, bounding plaything, in their desperate efforts to force it through
each other's base. They scramble, fight, wrestle over it, all in good-humor.
Shins suffer tremendously in the struggle, often receiving the blow intended
for the ball. At times two opposing players make a rush at it, and with fearful
force strike it at the same time, and, performing a flying leap through the air,
measure their full length in opposite directions of the greensward.

Captains and lieutenants and privates, officers and men, joined in the sport,
affording the privates a rare chance to repay some personal pique or fancied
wrong. Woe betide the unpopular officer who joined in this game, for he was
certain to come from it sore and bruised. Such is an imperfect outline of this
"rough-and-tumble" sport, which was the favorite amusement at Camp Jackson.

We turn from these sports to a scene more interesting as well as exciting.
On the 5th of October several boxes arrived in camp for Company K, containing donations of clothing, etc., from their friends and relatives at home.
Notwithstanding the day was dark, gloomy and stormy, the air chill and damp,
all tuned out and gathered in anxious expectation and excitement around the
boxes. Bundle after bundle found its way to the proper owner, amid cheers,
cries and shouts. Surely could the ladies of the "Baton Rouge Campaign Sewing
Society" have witnessed the scenes around those boxes, heard the expressions
of gratitude, and viewed the demonstrations of joy on all sides, they would
have felt that their labors were properly appreciated. Members from the other
companies, and from McNair's and McRae's Arkansas Regiments, gathered
around to witness the delivery of the clothing, until there was a dense mass of
jostling, crowding, noisy men, of which the boxes formed the nucleus and centre of attraction. Each uniform contained either letters, pictures of dear ones at
home, souvenirs from sweethearts, gloves or tippets, pockets and arms being
stuffed with these mementoes. Accompanying this supply of clothing was a
mysterious-looking box, the gift of a friend and citizen to the company. On
being opened it was found to contain liquors of all kinds, "rara avis" in camp;
yea! much "forbidden fruit," such as brandy, whisky, cordials, etc., with ink,
lemons, looking-glasses, combs, brushes, tobacco, pipes, pickles; in fact, a perfect assortment of "knick-knacks" and groceries. The donor was enthusiastically toasted for his munificence, and the name of "Tony" Montau became a
synonym for joviality and fun. It was but a short time before the whole regiment received their supply of clothing, the munificent gift of Louisiana to her

Truly Yours &c
Willie. H. Tunnard.

brave sons. This clothing was manufactured at the State Penitentiary, and was of substantial material, known as jeans, being of a grayish-blue color, with the exception of Company K, which was of a dark brown. The outfit of the regiment exceeded their most sanguine expectations, and infused a new feeling and spirit among the men, and they felt that now were they fully prepared for active operations, regardless of winter's approaching rigorous weather.

We consider the annexed tribute to the ladies of the Campaign Sewing Society no innovation to the pages of this volume, an expression of sentiments equally applicable to other companies of the regiment, and which but few soldiers of the South did not experience at some period of their lives in the army, for the patriotic devotion, unceasing labors, patient toil, and heroic fortitude and self-sacrificing spirit of our fair Southern women, in aiding and strengthening the cause which their sons, fathers, husbands, brothers and lovers had espoused.

HEADQUARTERS CO. K, THIRD REGT. LA. VOLS., }
Camp Jackson, Ark. Oct. 8th, 1861. }

To the President and Members of the Ladies' Campaign Sewing Society:

KIND FRIENDS,—When the heart is fullest, the lips fail in giving expression to the strength and depth of the inward emotions. Yet such is the case as I now attempt to pen these lines. False indeed would I be to *my own* feelings, did I not express to you in *some* manner *my* heartfelt thanks for the untiring zeal and energy which you have displayed in the equipment of the Pelican Rifles for their winter campaign.

Mere words, mere language, will not convey a tithe of the emotions stirred within me, or the gratitude felt for your munificence. Surely our arms will be nerved anew to strike fresh blows, and our hearts strengthened by this exhibition of your interest in us and the cause of Southern Independence.

Though there may not be among you any Molly Pitchers to avenge, at the cannon's mouth, amid the din and strife of the battle-field, a loved one's death, or thus exhibit your interest in our country's cause, yours is none the less a work of patriotism—more a work of love. Loved ones have departed from your midst, and many are the vacant places at the quiet fireside and in the home circles of those who have gone forth to aid in driving the invader and despoiler from Southern soil. They are enduring the privations and sufferings of a soldier's life, living in tents and the open air, braving the dangers of the battle-field, the rigors of a severe climate. Yet, while husbands, fathers, sons, and friends are thus evincing their devotion to the common cause, your interesting perseverance and energy, your noble, self-sacrificing spirit and unceasing labors of love aid as materially the success and onward march of our independence, our freedom of thought, speech and action.

Dark clouds of battle in gloom o'er us lower;

Armed legions have gathered to join in the fight;

A despot has called his hordes to o'erpower

A people all free, now battling for right.

From workshop and counter, from lowly cottage and lordly mansion, freemen have hastened and now stand shoulder to shoulder, regardless of former place or position, to make a despot's minions feel the strength of *freemen's* arms, of freemen's daring and bravery.

You, mothers and daughters at home, are aiding the cause of "Rebellion," and so long as your patriotism lasts, evinced in such works of love and remembrance as we have lately been the recipients of, so long is there reason to hope for the eventual triumph of Southern freemen. Woman's love, woman's patriotism and devotion will achieve more than armed legions, and do now accomplish more than aught else in aiding to turn back the tide of Northern hate and fanaticism.

Kind friends, what more can I say? How evince to you the thanks, the gratitude of a soldier's heart? Let deeds of future daring and bravery convince you that soldiers are not unmindful of the interest exhibited towards and felt in them by loved and fair ones at home. With a prayer for blessings on your labors and the final success of our cause,

I subscribe myself your friend,

W. H. TUNNARD, *Acting Orderly Sergeant.*
In behalf of Company K.

CHAPTER XII

THE FALL CAMPAIGN

OCTOBER 7th, 1861, was a beautiful, clear day, such as we often experience in the Fall. Orders were issued to prepare to break up camp and move on the following morning at 10 o'clock A.M. All was bustle and confusion, the men hurrying, scampering to and fro, packing knapsacks, etc. The order, however, was rescinded, as it was found impossible to complete the necessary preparations to march. Rumors began to prevail that General Price was retreating, closely followed by Fremont with an army of 30,000 men. On the 11th, under orders, we left Camp Jackson, and ere night had once more crossed the line into Missouri, our destination being reported as Carthage, camping in an open field, surrounded by dense woods. On the 12th an election was held for officers to fill vacancies in the various companies, Company A choosing E. Gourrier as Second Junior Lieutenant; Company K, H. H. Gentles.

On this day also the regiment received their first pay from the Confederates States for May and June in scrip, a species of money not very available to the soldier. The country abounded in wild fruit and nuts, such as pawpaws, grapes, hawes, hazel-nuts, and apples also in profusion, of which the men gathered eagerly and devoured. 13th. Camped at Scott's Mills, on Elk River. The next day, while on the march, the regiment met the family and effects of Governor Jackson, of Missouri, *en route* for Arkansas. The meeting between the Governor and the regiment, there, in the lonely woods of Missouri, was a scene such as few can ever forget. The day was bright and beautiful; the sunbeams glancing smilingly down through the o'ershadowing branches of the forest trees. As the Governor approached, the regiment formed in line along the roadside and welcomed him with three hearty cheers, at the same time presenting arms, as he moved along the line, with head uncovered. Reaching the extreme left of the line, Governor Jackson faced the men, and, in tones trembling from the depth of his agitation and emotion, thus addressed them: "I am glad to meet you. I welcome you to Missouri. You will find many warm-hearted brothers here who will warmly, nobly greet you. I feel that

Missouri is free, and hope to announce on my return that she is *legally* a member of the Southern Confederacy, even as she now is *virtually*. There are troops enough, I hope, to drive every foe from her soil. We have plenty to feed them, and if we are blessed with pleasant weather, one of our old-fashioned autumns, not an enemy will remain in the State. I hope and expect that you will winter in the heart of Missouri, if not in St. Louis. I have heard of you before at the battle of Oak Hills, and for your deeds there I thank you. Once again I welcome you to Missouri." This simple-worded address of the Governor, delivered with impressive force and eloquence of manner, elicited another burst of applause from the warm-hearted Louisianians. Lieutenant-Colonel Hyams replied in the following expressive language: "In behalf of the Louisiana Regiment I would simply answer—*let their past deeds speak for their future*."

Such is the outline of the most pleasant incident of our campaign. The march was resumed. Camped at night on the right of an open field, in woods, near the roadside, the spot being known as Camp Pike. Goode's Texas Battery joined us to-day. In this camp occurred a fearful tragedy, always a matter of deep regret and sorrow, but especially among those who should be united in the strong bonds of unity of feeling, interest, and purpose. Two members of the Morehouse Fencibles, Co. E, were engaged in a game of cards, when a dispute arose, ending in blows. The result was that Mayo shot Hays in the abdomen, inflicting a mortal wound; Hays drew a Bowie-knife, after being shot, stabbing and instantly killing Mayo. Hays died the next day in Neosho. Thus two valuable lives were sacrificed needlessly, and the regiment lost two efficient members. On the 17th the march was resumed, the regiment passing through Neosho, and camped eighteen miles from Carthage, on Shoal Creek. Rumors of the enemy's approach began to be very prevalent, it being supposed that they would attempt to gain possession of Neosho before the 23d, the day appointed for the convening of the Legislature of Missouri for the purpose of passing the secession ordinance. The regiment still continued to advance, arriving on the 18th at Centre Creek. The 20th they began their retreat, Price's army, computed at 18,000 men, arriving at Neosho and filling the whole valley in which it was situated with the uproar, confusion and bustle incident to the camping of a large force, especially one in rapid retreat from a pursuing foe. This morning the air was chill and cold, the ground covered with a heavy hoar-frost. Yet the day turned out clear, serene and beautiful. It always seemed as if these quiet Sabbath-days must mark some important event and stirring scenes! McCulloch's Division was in the neighborhood, wild rumors prevalent, added to which was the arrival of General McCulloch and staff, Gov. Jackson, Generals Rains, Harris, and Price, making a scene of excitement seldom witnessed, beyond portrayal by human language. The next morning the Louisiana regiment, after marching nearly all night, passed through Neosho, *en route* for Arkansas, followed by the mounted forces. As regiment after regiment poured through the same place, the excitement became intense, and affairs began to assume a serious aspect. The Missourians complained loudly against Arkansas for not re-enforcing McCulloch. It did, indeed, seem strange, that the people of Arkansas should have remained idle spectators of these events, when their own State was threatened with invasion, and no barrier to oppose it save General McCulloch's brave little army, and the gallant Missourians, struggling so nobly and desperately to free their State from the presence of the foe. This sudden retreat, however, seemed to awaken the dormant energies of the Arkansians, and they began to organize and hasten to the rescue. Stone's Texas Regiment passed the regiment while on the retreat, uttering loud, shrill Indian war-whoops as they dashed by at the top of their horses' speed. They were a splendidly mounted body of men. The retrograde movement of McCulloch's forces continued through Pineville, until the regiment once more struck camp at Cavendish Springs, called "Camp McCulloch," two miles above Camp Stevens, in Arkansas, but a short distance from the Missouri line. Thus the men, after an absence of fifteen days, once more found rest, much to their relief. The weather was becoming very cold, still nothing was said or thought about winter-quarters. In the mean time, General Price was once more on the advance. He seemed indefatigable in his efforts, undaunted in his determination to keep within the borders of Missouri.

General McCulloch's mounted forces had gone to the front to feel the enemy's position, and, if possible, ascertain his strength.

Numerous laughable incidents occurred on the retreat, but we give place only to the following good joke, told on Colonel Hebert. It seems that at one of the camps, between Carthage and Neosho, several of the regiment found a pen full of very fine fat hogs, or, as the boys termed them, "bear," for whose flesh they had a "lamentable" love. It was the work of but a few moments to kill several of the largest and finest. A dispute arose as to whether they should scald them or skin them, the usual *modus operandi* in such cases. The Colonel, unnoticed, had approached the group, and after listening to the dispute, quietly remarked: "Skin them, my men, skin them; no time for scalding now." The boys were completely astonished, both at the interruption and such a relaxation from the enforcement of strict military discipline by the Colonel. However, they followed his advice, and told the joke much to the amusement of the whole regiment.

RETROGRADING

Just after leaving the vicinity of Carthage, and while crossing an open prairie, a bright light became visible, and several of the men in their feverish excitement declared that they saw horsemen galloping by. Adjutant Hyams and several others were sent to reconnoitre but discovered nothing. The men then began to question Colonel Hebert eagerly as to where they were going, inquiring anxiously if they were retreating. "Retreating?" said the Colonel: "Oh no, my men—only retrograding." The regiment learned thoroughly the meaning of the word ere they finally rested from the wearisome march.

In the account of the battle of Oak Hills it is mentioned that Companies A and K, Third Louisiana, were united under the command of Captain J. P. Viglini (Co. K). The following orders explain the absence of Captain Bruslé on that memorable occasion:

HEADQUARTERS MCCULLOCH'S BRIGADE, }
Camp Stephens, Ark., July 21, 1861. }

CAPT.—You will proceed without delay to the Creek Agency in the Indian Territory, and there muster in a regiment of Creek Indians. It appears from treaty stipulations made by Captain Pike, Commissioner, that this regiment is to be composed of eight companies of Creeks and two of Seminoles.

It will be proper for you, as soon as you reach the Indian Territory, to make Captain Pike, the Commissioner, aware of your mission, who will, no doubt, give you valuable information in regard to this regiment. As soon as the regiment is organized and mustered into service, an election will be held for a colonel and other field officers, whom you will also muster into service.

Major Clark, Quartermaster at Fort Smith, will be directed to send to you an agent of the Quartermaster and Commissary Departments, to furnish the necessary supplies. Beef and flour can be furnished in the country, or certainly from Texas. It will therefore only be necessary to furnish the regiment with coffee, sugar, and salt from Fort Smith, and directions will be given to that effect. A quantity of powder and lead will also be sent from Fort Smith to the regiment.

I have the honor to be, Captain,

Your obedient servant,

JAMES MCINTOSH, *Capt. C. S. A. and Adjt.-Gen.*

HEADQUARTERS McCULLOCH'S BRIGADE, }
Special Orders, }   *Camp Stephens, Ark., July 22,* 1861. }
No. 16. }

I. Captain C. A. Bruslé, of the Louisiana Regiment of Volunteers, will proceed without delay to the Creek Agency, and muster in a regiment of Creek and Seminole Indians, which is being organized there.

II. Major Clark, Brigade Quartermaster at Fort Smith, will send with Captain Bruslé an agent of the Quartermaster and Subsistence Departments, to furnish the necessary supplies to the different companies of the regiment as they are mustered into service.

By order General McCulloch.

JAMES McINTOSH,
Capt. C. S. A. and Adjt.-Gen. of Brigade.

Perhaps no more interesting subject could be presented than a few items concerning the Indians, their country, method of living, and connection with the late struggle. The part which they took in the war seems to have been totally ignored. Availing ourself of the privilege given by the notes of Captain Bruslé, we give a chapter on this subject.

In obedience to the above order, Captain Bruslé immediately proceeded to Fort Smith to carry out the object of his instructions. He left Fort Smith July 30th, at 12 M., and reached Scullyville at 6 P.M., fourteen miles from Fort Smith. The country up to within five miles of the place resembles the wild lands of Lower Louisiana in appearance. The soil is very fertile, and produces large crops of corn, oats and wheat. There were few farms along the road, yet these compare favorably in every respect with the best farms in Northwestern Arkansas.

Although the land between Fort Smith and Scullyville cannot be excelled in fertility, yet, at this period, there were but three farms to be seen. The country beyond Scullyville is a rolling prairie, mostly sterile. The houses on the farms are built of logs, and are not very comfortable in appearance.

On the 31st, Captain B. gives the following bill of fare for dinner: Corn-bread, milk and hominy, with rancid bacon; "not very palatable," says the Captain, "but I take a little to prevent from starving. Now add to this most detestable water, and a man's misery is complete." The scarcity and impurity of water on this route is a noticeable fact. Traveled eighteen miles without water; found some impossible to drink, as it smells too strong of carrion. Traveled eight miles more and succeeded in getting some of an Indian farmer, which I managed to drink, although smelling badly and having an oily surface.

After traveling two miles more, Captain B. stopped at Mr. Jones' farm. He drew some water from the well, and found it filled with those "bugs" which infest all well-traveled roads. This caused a sudden weakness about the Captain's stomach, which shocked his whole system. The very worthy Captain attempts to become stoical and determined as an Indian, yet he breaks out: "I begin to think that McCulloch ought to have sent some one else on this mission."

Mr. and Mrs. Jones (of *the* Jones family) are Choctaws; live like the other farmers; had a family—three boys and as many girls. No fruit of any kind is to be found. A neglected peach-tree in some corner of a yard is occasionally seen, but few water-melons even; yet the soil is good, and capable of producing such fruit in abundance.

On the 1st August Captain B. was stopping at Mr. J. Brebb's, a half-breed Choctaw. "His wife is a very large squaw, weighing over two hundred pounds. Still she appears active. Their house, although of logs, was about as comfortable as any seen in the Western country. It is as neatly and as comfortably furnished as log-houses can well be. They own a family of negroes, who work a goodly-sized farm for them."

"The prairies cannot be surpassed in beauty. For a distance of ten or fifteen miles all around, you behold a rolling prairie, covered with excellent, luxuriant grass, whose emerald surface rolls away in long waves 'neath the autumnal breeze. Even the hills are covered with this growth of nature's covering. The whole country has the appearance of being hemmed in by a tall, blue, vapory wall, which are the mountains, raising their tall summits, at a great distance, north, south, east and west. The sight is grand, imposing and picturesque, filling the soul of the beholder with unexpressible emotions."

August 22d. Saw the famous Tom Star, a Cherokee Indian, who was rendered notorious by the perils which he encountered a few years since while upon terms of deadly hatred against the whole Cherokee Nation. He was not alone, however, in his opposition, for he had fourteen brothers who all espoused his cause. For a period of upwards of four years the Cherokee Nation was the theatre of the most revolting scenes. Murder followed murder in rapid succession. The Cherokees finally succeeded in killing all the Stars but Tom and one of his brothers (both living now), who still annoyed them to such an extent that they sued for peace. Old Tom, who had often fled for his life and made many hairbreadth and miraculous escapes, was now handsomely paid to cease hostilities. The old man is very intelligent, and is very familiar with all portions of the Indian Territory, as well as parts of Texas, Missouri and Arkansas. These States he paid a hurried visit to while fleeing from the pursuit of the Cherokees. He is said, at present, to be one of the most peaceful men in the Nation. I acquired much valuable information from him during his short stay at Mr. Rubbs'. He promised to join us at Springfield, where he can see a "big fight." Here I met another character in the person of a straggling Indian. His name is Moses Riddle; is very poor; lives wherever he has an opportunity, and is very stupid, the effects of whisky, doubtless, as he has the appearance of a confirmed drunkard. He seems to be very anxious to join the army, and promises to unite with the Creeks, if he can only find his pony, who, like the chief characteristic of his owner, is much given to straying or straggling. This man Riddle said he had two brothers in the army; one of them, he seemed to think, was a very gallant fellow. He went on to say, "One of my brothers is a murderer," in that exalted tone in which a white man would have acquainted you with the fact that his brother was colonel of a regiment or general of an army. It appears that his brother had a dispute with a Cherokee about a horse, which was the cause of his shooting the Cherokee. His second feat was performed on the person of the Sheriff of the county, who attempted, in obedience to the law of the Nation, to seize some whisky he carried with him.

This picture is too revolting for more particulars. "Last night," continues Captain B., "I had the *pleasure* of sleeping in the same room with this apologist of the crime of murder."

Mr. Rubbs is a half-breed, stands about six feet two or three inches in his socks. His frame is well formed both for strength and activity; seems to be very resolute, and, at the same time, kind-hearted. His children are unusually badly spoiled. Indian babies are generally the most noisy in the world except negroes.

Arrived at North Fork at 2 P.M., August 3. This place contains about eight stores and several indifferent residences, together with a boarding-house, kept by a half-breed Creek named Smith, who is absent with Captain Pike, making treaties with the wild Western Indian tribes. Mrs. Smith is nearly white, dresses quite neatly, and is "much of a lady." Here I was visited by a number of celebrities, among whom were Captain W. F. McIntosh, Captain Napoleon, Moore and Walker. These gentlemen show the very smallest evidence of Indian blood, are very affable, courteous and polite in manners. One would imagine he was among the most refined of the American race, did he not know them to be half-breeds. They are similar in dress to the Americans, and intensely Southern in feeling and sentiments. They despise a Yankee as they would a rattlesnake, with all that deadly hatred so characteristic of the race, surpassing a Spaniard in intensity, with that tenacity of feeling which nothing can eradicate. They were delighted at the idea of being mustered into the service, and were proud to see Captain B., to whom they paid every attention.

The country in this region is well settled, the crops abundant, and the people are exultant over the defeat of the Federals at Manassas. They say they will never rest satisfied until they invade Kansas and pay the villains there back in their own coin. The inhabitants are well-behaved, orderly and moral in their habits. I have, as yet, seen no full-blooded Indians. To-morrow will leave for the Creek Agency to meet the soldiers. Have been awaiting the arrival of the Colonel of the regiment.

The heat here is suffocating; the thermometer stands 110°, and the prairie breezes are as refreshing as steam from an escape-pipe.

I left Mr. Smith's at 5 o'clock A.M., August 4, and arrived at R. Ross' place at 11½ A.M., after taking advantage of many of the shade-trees about the creeks I crossed. The distance traveled is twenty-three miles. This may look like slow traveling, but it is accomplishing a great deal when there is taken into consideration the effect of the sun in these large prairies, the heat being terrible. The nights are somewhat pleasant, but the days perfectly awful with their suffocating atmosphere.

If you wish to imagine yourself in this country, just get into a hot oven, and if there be any difference, it will be in favor of the oven. Had I not brought an umbrella and a pair of goggles, I feel confident I never would have reached my destination. Saw a few full-bloods along the road. They are exceedingly lazy and slovenly, a thousand times more so than the negroes. The women perform all the labor, and are more active and energetic than the men. The majority of them speak no English, and exhibit no disposition to be on friendly terms with the whites. They are the most independent people in the world.

August 5. Arrived at the Creek Agency, where I met a handsome reception from the Indians. There was a rush during the entire day for the hotel where I stopped. Had an interview with D. N. McIntosh, son of General McIntosh, of Red-Stick war fame. This gentleman, with Mr. Stedham, were appointed Commissioners to treat with the Confederate States. They are both refined and educated gentlemen, half-breeds.

It is surprising to find the number of old Indians who are anxious to enlist for the war. Their enthusiasm is worthy the emulation of our own people.

In the large crowd who soon congregated around me, I was peculiarly impressed with one very old full-blood, who had seen at least seventy summers. I indulged my curiosity by asking him, through the interpreter, if he too was willing to fight for his country. The reply was as laconic as it was characteristic of the race. He replied: "*I am a man.*"

The full-bloods dread nothing so much as to meet death in their homes. They say it is a disgrace for a man to die at home like a woman. Hence they are rejoiced at the opportunity to distinguish themselves on the battle-field, or of meeting an honorable death.

Among the companies eventually mustered into service were William F. McIntosh's, hideously painted with all the insignia about them, to proclaim that the hatchet had been dug up; D. N. McIntosh's, James McHenry's, Samuel Miller's, Thlar Keta's, William McIntosh's, Herrod's, Sam Chicotah's, Uchee and Cusetah.

Having accomplished his mission, Captain Bruslé returned to Camp Jackson late in August, when he was furnished with a leave of absence for sixty days, at the expiration of which period he reported to the regiment at Camp McCulloch.

CHAPTER XIII

CAMP M'CULLOCH

CAMP MCCULLOCH was situated on a rough rocky hill, almost surrounded by valleys. On the east was a deserted field, well adapted to the exercise of drilling. Of course camps were *always* selected in view of such *very agreeable* contingencies. The first order issued for the enforcement of the rules and regulations of camp was on the 28th October, which the men considered as equivalent to being informed that, for some time, at least, there would be no more marching. Thus once more commenced the regular routine of camp-life. 'Twas the season of the "sere and yellow leaf." The forest, for some time, had been clothed in crimson and gold; all those varied and gorgeous hues of nature's painting, which have made the Autumns of the North so famed in the poet's song. During the march from Missouri, through the deep valleys shut up by high hills, some of the most beautiful landscape views that the eye of man ever gazed upon, greeted the vision. The golden sunlight glancing along the hill-sides, lighting up the tree-tops ornamented with a multiplicity of various-colored leaves, while the valley beneath slumbered in shadows, formed pictures of such rare and exquisite coloring that few of the way-worn and weary soldiers failed to appreciate by expressions of enthusiastic admiration. The weather during this period was delightful. The days bright and beautiful, the atmosphere mild and pleasant, but at night cold and frosty.

Thanks, however, to the labor and love of fair ones "far awa'," we were abundantly supplied with warm and comfortable clothing, and prepared to bid defiance to the approach of white-bearded winter. On the 31st there was a grand review of the regiment, muster, and general policing the parade-ground. The regiment also saw the munificent gift of Tennessee to General Price pass the encampment. This present from the "Volunteer State" consisted of fourteen wagons loaded with camp equipage and munitions of war, and twelve pieces of artillery, six and twelve-pounder guns. Everything about them perfectly new and in the most complete order. The horses were superb-looking animals. These guns were the finest that had yet come to the Western army; each one has point and breech sights. We thought, as we gazed at them, that

Tennessee would soon hear something *pointed* from these messengers of war, whose arrival was most opportune, and would be greeted with wild demonstrations of joy by the gallant, noble, and patriotic men under General Price.

November 1st dawned clear and pleasant. Being All-Saints' day, the usual drills, etc., were omitted, and many of the men went to the houses of the surrounding farmers to visit fair acquaintances. It was wonderful with what rapidity the men ingratiated themselves into the favor of these same sturdy farmers and the good graces of their fair daughters. Yet so it was, and they were frequent visitors to the camp, enjoying the scenes of a soldier's life, as well as their lively sallies of wit and small talk. Many amusing incidents arose from this intercourse, one of which we here chronicle as too good to be lost. We have already stated that the men visited the farmers' dwellings, whose chief charms concentrated in some fair, bright-eyed lassie, thus exhibiting that fondness for feminine society and companionship which characterized them when at home. A worthy corporal of one of the companies, with his "chums," comprising an entire mess, had been frequent visitors at a lowly cot near the encampment, where two really handsome young ladies resided. Rising one day from an agreeable tête-à-tête over the dinner-table, two or three of the men considered it nothing more than an act of politeness to invite the farmer and his family to take dinner with them the following day. "I shall certainly do so with pleasure," was the reply. Nothing more was thought of the invitation until the next morning near the dinner hour, when who should make their appearance in camp but the farmer, wife, daughters, and small members of the family (as he had promised), to dine with the "boys." There was nothing prepared, and, worse of all, no provisions on hand with which to prepare a suitable dinner. The joke was soon known all over camp. The men strolled negligently about the unfortunate victims in groups to enjoy and add to their discomfiture, and sly jokes, witticisms, and suppressed laughter greeted them on all sides as they escorted their visitors through the encampment. They determined not to be made the subject of fun for the whole regiment. So, "nil desperandum," with commendable zeal a portion of the mess made preparations for dinner, while the remainder "played the agreeable." By dint of borrowing and begging a really nice meal was served up. The mess, for once in the history of the company to which they belonged, were excused from drill that day, and a *fashionable* meal eaten in the encampment.

One of the most agreeable features of Camp McCulloch was the immense flocks of wild pigeons that roosted near this spot. The boys killed large numbers of them, and feasted "right royally" on their flesh, to them a great delicacy after living for months on fresh beef and salt pork. They were broiled, stewed, roasted, baked in pies, in fact, prepared in every conceivable variety of style which the ingenuity of the men could devise, and let the reader be informed that a soldier's ingenuity in the culinary line was by no means to be made sport of.

The Major rejoined the regiment here on the 2nd, and was most cordially, enthusiastically, and warmly greeted by the men. He brought with him funds in specie to pay off Company K for services rendered in the State previous to entering the Confederate service. Of course to this company his arrival was a source of great rejoicing, aside from their love for him as their first commander. At this period General Price's army was at Cassville, while McCulloch's Division were scattered between Camp McCulloch and Springfield, awaiting the movements of the enemy. Here the General issued another stirring appeal, calling the Arkansians "to arms," in view of the threatened invasion. On the 6th, Generals McCulloch and Price and Governor Jackson held a consultation at Keatsville to determine the future movements to be made. All was excitement and anxious expectation in view of the approaching hostilities. Colonel McIntosh's command, from this date, were actively engaged in devastating the country between our position and the enemy. Everything that would or could aid them was destroyed—corn, fodder, oats, hay and wheat-stacks—while the roads were thoroughly and completely blockaded by felling timber across them. It showed how imminent the danger was considered. A good joke was told on a sergeant who was very active in this work of destruction. Entering one day a large cornfield near a dwelling, he exhibited his usual zeal in applying the torch to the grain. As he was setting fire to a corn-chock the owner exclaimed, "Look out, there's a gun in there!" The words were scarcely spoken, when the gun exploded in the stack just behind him, the ball whizzing by in dangerous proximity to his head. Dropping his torch, he turned to Col. McIntosh near by, exclaiming, "Look here, Colonel, I don't mind being killed by a Dutchman, but I'll be hanged if I want to be shot at by an infernal corn-shock." The enemy were constantly annoyed and harassed by the cavalry, their trains captured, their pickets driven in, and their army kept in constant commotion, in anticipation of an attack from the Confederates.

On the 6th the regiment cast 518 votes for the President and Vice-President of the Confederate States; proper returns were made out and forwarded to Louisiana. Orders were also read out for all lights to be extinguished at 8 o'clock, and the men prepared to fall in, no noise in camp, the "long roll" to be beaten in case of firing. The excitement caused by these orders was too intense to allow any rest that night. Stone's, Greer's, and the two Indian regiments left for Kansas. The Indians were half naked—in all the hideousness of their war paint, and armed with long rifles, tomahawks, and scalping-knives, apparently as savage and untamed as when, in years long passed, they alone inhabited the American continent.

The enemy precipitately left Springfield about the middle of November. This sudden and unexpected move disappointed the expectations of the troops, as it was hoped to have led them among the hills of Arkansas, and, turning upon them, utterly to have routed them.

The regiment was in splendid health and spirits, more so than at any time during its formation. The men passed their idle hours in foot-racing, wrestling, jumping, singing, and dancing. They entered with keen relish into all kinds of mischief. One would scarcely have supposed that they had just been facing a powerful foe, anticipating a fearful and deadly combat. To all intents and purposes our fall campaign was finished, although little was said about winter-quarters. The night of November 16th there was a light fall of sleet; General McCulloch left to-day for Springfield with 4,000 cavalry; the 17th was a dark, cloudy, gloomy day, but not cold. We anticipated now the opening of winter weather; cold, rain, sleet, and snow. How rejoiced would the men then have been could they have been transferred to some field of active service, instead of remaining inactive and confined to winter-quarters during the coming months! Inured to hardship, brave and daring, the men of the Third Regiment would have infinitely preferred an active campaign to a winter of idleness. But as the fates willed so must its destiny be accomplished. They had "learned to labor," but not to wait while there was work to do, or a blow to be struck for the independence of their country. On the 18th, Major W. F. Tunnard, at the head of 150 men, departed at 12 o'clock at night, with three days' rations, to clear out the blockaded roads leading to Springfield. Making a march of ten miles, they halted, and commenced the task assigned them. The men worked with the same alacrity and perseverance which always characterized them. Whether work, play or fight, they entered into it with a zeal and energy truly commendable. Having accomplished the duty assigned them, they returned to camp on the afternoon of the 20th. The weather at this time was very wintry; tremendous storms arose, followed by bitter cold weather. Everything became frozen solid and hard. The men suffered from the weather, tents being very insufficient protection against the penetrating air, and now began to look forward to more comfortable quarters. Advices from General McCulloch reached the command, giving information that Siegel was at Rolla with a portion of the Federal forces, and Hunter at Sidalia with the remainder.

General Price was marching, with his army largely reinforced, upon the latter, while General McCulloch, using Springfield as a base of operations, was making a demonstration on Rolla, to prevent Siegel from reinforcing Hunter. Such was the condition of affairs at this date. On the 24th, Major Theodore Johnson and Captain Bruslé reached the regiment. The weather continued too cold to permit the men to engage in their customary drills, and they passed the time principally by indulging in their favorite amusement, foot-ball. The weather was fine for the violent exercise of this rough game. November 25th was a marked day in the army. On this day the Infantry Division was reviewed by Colonel L. Hebert. Although there were present no "knights of the quill" to write about the manly appearance and military bearing of the men; no fair ones to wave cambric handkerchiefs and lend the charm of their beauty and presence to the scene, yet was the display none the less creditable to all concerned. The soiled and worn uniforms of the men, with their determined features, unshaven beard and unshorn locks, spoke of war in all its grim reality, and proclaimed the review no light pageantry or holiday festival. On this same day a musical club was organized in the regiment, for the purpose of enlivening the coming winter evenings with "strains of harmonious melody." The instruments were two flutes, a piccolo, violin and guitar. The artillery and cavalry passed camp, *en route* for their winter-quarters. On the 27th, General McCulloch arrived in our camp, *en route* to Richmond, Va. The *personnel* of this remarkable character was striking. His face was nearly concealed with brown beard and moustache. Keen gray eyes looked with piercing glance from beneath the overshadowing eyebrows; a brown felt hat placed firmly on his head; black and white checked overcoat, pants of blue army cloth, the inside half of the legs being lined with buckskin, and hands incased in soiled buckskin gauntlets, with not a mark or ornament visible to betoken his rank or attract attention. An observer would little have supposed him to be the famed and dreaded Ben McCulloch.

Though late in the season, the fall races took place on this day, an event of much excitement and fun among the men. The race-track was a lane about a quarter of a mile long, near the camp, level and smooth. Bets were freely offered and taken, the first entry being Dr. Hebert and Captain Richards, two noted racers, in a single dash of a quarter. Behold, then, the scene. The chosen judges at the stand; the fences lined with excited, eager men; the riders stripped, and handkerchiefs tied about their heads. The start was made, and Richards, amid shouts and cheers, won the race by four feet exact measurement. The next race was between Adjutant Hyams' filly and Richards, a dead heat. The race being repeated, Hyams' filly won by six inches. The fourth and last race was between two ponies, Brigham and Hedrick, the latter being successful. Such was one of the scenes of November 27th. We chronicle another. A mysterious-looking wagon drove up to the encampment, which seemed to immediately attract great attention, the men thronging around it in numbers. The Argus-eyed officers were on the alert, and soon made a descent upon the contents of the wagon, when, "oh, lud!" it was discovered to contain *a keg of whisky.* How *could* the boys discover such *stuff,* we wonder? Passing strange, indeed. The contents were immediately seized and confiscated by Lieutenant-Colonel S. M. Hyams, as contraband of war. The Lieutenant-Colonel did not, then and there, spill the whisky. Not he. He had too keen an appreciation of what was good for a soldier on a cold day, if not taken in too large doses. The men were forthwith summoned to his quarters, and every one given a drink of the forbidden nectar. He was vociferously cheered for his kind remembrance of the soldiers' wants.

On the evening of the 28th a daring robbery was committed in camp. While Quartermaster Hardiman was eating his supper, some person or persons unknown succeeded in abstracting from his quarters his trunk containing all the funds belonging to the regiment, and papers. It contained about $5,000. The theft was quickly discovered, and details immediately made to scour the surrounding country, and an eager, energetic search instituted for the capture of the thief and recovery of the money. The trunk was soon discovered by a squad from Company K, in the woods, back of the Quartermaster's tent, broken open; but so hot and close had been the pursuit, that the robber only succeeded in partially rifling the trunk of its contenets. He obtained about $2,100, which was in an envelope, leaving behind a package of Confederate bills, and some silver, amounting to nearly $3,000 more. The perpetrator of the deed was never discovered. It was evidently committed by some person who knew the Quartermaster's habits and the place where he kept his funds for paying the teamsters, as this fund alone was taken.

Orders were issued at this time for the men to go to winter-quarters. The morning of November 29th was cold, the sky overcast, as the regiment bade adieu to Camp McCulloch. They marched off in fine spirits, and soon accomplished the journey of sixteen miles, stepping it off at a lively pace. On arriving at Cross Hollows the quarters were found unprepared for their reception, and so they were once more encamped in the open air, exposed to the inclemency of the weather. Cross Hollows was a deep valley, running east and west, shut in by high acclivities. The country here is a succession of high, rocky hills, and deep, dark and narrow defiles. Surrounded on all sides by these frowning hills, the camp was protected from the cold, piercing wintry winds, yet it also seemed like imprisoning the men to winter them here, far distant from any society or regular communication with friends at home. The country abounded in wild game of all kinds, such as bear, deer, quails, pigeons, ducks, turkey, while White River, distant about two miles, furnished a fine place for fishing and skating. Thus, to those so inclined, amusements could be found to while away the wintry days. The people in the neighborhood were rough specimens of the backwoods Arkansians, and spoke a language peculiarly their own—a language that would puzzle one deeply versed in all the idioms of the King's English; as for instance: *"We'ens* is going to-morrow; is *you'ens* all going?" Quartermaster H. asked an old farmer if he had any forage. "No," he replied, "I hev spore all I kin spare."

CHAPTER XIV

CAMP BENJAMIN

THE quarters of the Louisiana Regiment were situated in one of the valleys of Cross Hollows, protected from the chilly, wintry winds by high, rocky hills, covered with a heavy growth of timber. They were substantial wooden buildings, constructed of tongued and grooved planks placed upright, with roofing of the same material. The flooring was the very best, and would have been a credit to the handsomest of private residences. Each building was 36 by 20 feet, divided into two rooms by a partition meeting in the centre at the chimney, constructed of brick, with a fire-place in each room, with a smooth brick hearth. The privates' quarters were in two parallel rows facing each other, while the officers' ran perpendicular to them, forming a square at one end. The men were not too much crowded, and slept in berths placed one above the other, similar to those in a state-room of a river steamer. The utmost contentment and good feeling prevailed among the men, and all seemed determined to enjoy the days of the winter months. With abundant material for the purpose, they soon manufactured chairs, tables, shelves, and mantle-pieces over the fire-places. Most agreeably were they disappointed at their situation and surroundings. They soon gathered about them all those little comforts and conveniences which so materially contributed to the happiness of a soldier's precarious existence. The buildings were soon named according to the inclination of the occupants, and a stroll through the quarters exhibted to the view grotesque lettering, telling of all kinds of "Dens," "Retreats," and "Quarters," while you could easily discover "Bull Run," "Leesburg," "Belmont," and other streets. "Manassas Gap" opening into "Capital Square," the officers' quarters. Companies A and K were ordered to Fayetteville as provost-guard for that place during the winter months, and left Camp Benjamin December 4th.

Behold now these war-worn, yet jovial soldiers, preparing to pass the winter months! On the 11th of December the scene in Camp Benjamin was one of peculiar activity and bustle, for the announcement had been made that the

buildings were ready for occupation. They were apportioned to the companies, and the men eagerly and zealously proceeded to fit them up for permanent residences. The day was a fine one, the atmosphere cool and bracing.
Halloo, song, and laughter echoed along the valley, and over the hill-tops,
while from a grist-mill near by came the monotonous splash of its huge water-
wheel, mingled with the clank of machinery and the peculiar whirr and
rumble of its mill-stones. The frowning hill-sides there never looked down
upon such a scene of bustle, activity, and hilarity.

Thus the regiment became established in their winter-quarters, surrounded
with nearly every comfort a soldier's heart could desire. There was a sad defi-
ciency, however, in the Medical Department, and numbers of the men on the
sick-list with diseases so dangerous to those unaccustomed to such a rigorous
climate. These sons of a sunnier clime felt most acutely the piercing wintry air,
and from exposure and negligence in providing against the constant atmospheric
changes, made themselves victims to the approach of insidious diseases.

Captain T. L. Maxwell, A. C. S., arrived in camp on the 12th. He was
most cordially greeted by the men. There was not a single member of the regiment who did not love Captain Maxwell. His constant geniality of disposition, general kindness and affability, won every heart. He had a smile for all,
was fond of a good joke, loved the bright and sunny side of existence. In time
of need and danger he was always found at his post, a true soldier, a brave man.
No wonder he found firm friends in the regiment, and was highly respected
deep in the hearts of the noble men whose wants he supplied. To-day Captain
M. is the same affable, polite, courteous, smiling, warm-hearted man, and loves
nothing better than to meet some of his old comrades and chat over the days
of "auld lang syne." On this same day overcoats, sent to the regiment by
Governor Thomas O. Moore, arrived, and were distributed. Louisiana seemed
never to weary in supplying the necessities of her gallant sons.

At this period the regiment was commanded by Major W. F. Tunnard,
Colonel Hebert being in command of the brigade, with headquarters at
Fayetteville, and Lieutenant-Colonel Hyams absent on furlough. The Major
instituted a system of the strictest discipline. Of unbending determination and
strong will, as already stated, he never flinched from the prompt execution of
every order which he promulgated. *He meant what he said.*

On the 14th Private L. Devlin, of Company E, was drummed out of the
regiment for stealing. He had disobeyed orders. It was the first punishment in
the regiment. The next day a man from Fayetteville was detected in selling liquor
to the men, and swindling them out of their money by some gambling device.

He was turned over to the tender mercies of the boys. Ready for every species of mischief, they did full justice to the subject thus furnished. They so worked on the man's fears that he imagined he was about to be hung, drawn and quartered. Most piteously did he beg to be released. His tormentors were obdurate, and every appeal was answered with threats and scowls.

A sharp rail was procured, upon which he was mounted, with feet tied together. As they dangled beneath, two stalwart men raised it on their shoulders, while one man, on each side of the victim, with fixed bayonet pointed at him, prevented the possibility of the victim losing his balance, and away they all went. The bearers were rough trotters; very, indeed; and amid shouts, laughter and jeers, mingled with the groans of the victim, he was rode through the whole encampment. Such "a ridin' on a rail" no mortal ever got. It is needless to state "that man never visited the Louisianians again."

On the 21st a court-martial was organized for the trial of petty offences. President—Captain O. E. Hull; Members—Lieutenant S. D. Russell and Lieutenant Brigham; Judge-Advocate—Captain J. S. Richards.

The next day there was a heavy fall of snow. A scene of uproarious mirth ensued. There was a general "ducking" of all, irrespective of rank, and fierce battles with snow-balls. It was hazardous for any one to venture in sight, as he would be most unmercifully pelted with snow.

On the 24th Lieutenant J. H. Brigham was appointed A. A. Q. M., in place of Captain Hardiman, absent on furlough. At this period Lieutenant W. M. Washburn, Company B, was the Acting Adjutant, S. M. Hyams, Jr., having received the appointment of Adjutant-General of the brigade.

Christmas Eve, the holiday festivities, and foaming bowls of egg-nog, with raw liquor, seemed as plentiful as the spring water near by. Uproarious hilarity prevailed, the absent were toasted in many a cup, and songs sung with eventually discordant chorus. The next day was Christmas. Soldiers loved to dispense hospitality, consequently there were numerous gatherings of convivial spirits, and egg-nog was drank with all the éclat and formality of a drawing-room assembly, or hilariously tossed off with a jovial toast and upraised cups.

The 1st of January witnessed a new spectacle in camp-life. A tall pole was formally raised in front of Major Tunnard's quarters, and the regimental flag flung to the breeze. The Major made a terse, neat, appropriate and stirring speech to the men on this interesting occasion, which was enthusiastically and vociferously cheered.

At this time the boys were having gay times, going to parties given every night in the neighbors' houses. Doubtless to this day the buxom Arkansas lasses in that vicinity remember the Louisianians, with their manly bearing, good looks, polished ease and elegance of manner and graceful movements. The majority of these men were gentlemen, once moving in refined society at home, and nothing more delighted them than to exhibit their accomplishments before the astonished gaze of these same plain, honest, country people.

On the 11th of January the regiment was paid off.

On the 24th the mumps broke out in camp. The Major had instituted a regimental hospital, which he daily visited, and used every exertion to have the sick properly cared for. This wise measure was highly appreciated by the men, and such kindness for their welfare and comfort implanted in their strong hearts imperishable feelings of gratitude and respect. Dr. Lowther here officiated as physician. He was an efficient physician, and, as a man, was unsurpassed for his kindliness and affability.

On the 25th orders were received from headquarters for the regimental commanders to have their respective commands thoroughly prepared and organized for marching immediately. The last day of January found the ground covered with a heavy fall of snow, and the anticipation of an early campaign subsided.

February 7. Orders read at dress parade for company drills, four hours each day. There was a very alarming increase of the sick. Drill! What! and give up all other schemes? Verily, no! The life of ease and pleasure which had made the hours pass so smilingly away, had, undoubtedly, incapacitated the men from doing soldier's duty. Was it really so? Let us see how the sequel proves.

February 11. General McCulloch forbids the granting of furloughs or leaves of absence under any circumstances.

On the 12th an order was received to have all the mules shod and the wagons repaired with the quickest possible dispatch, and for the troops to hold themselves in readiness to move immediately.

14th, about 12 o'clock at night, the camp was alarmed by the cry of fire. A fearful scene of excitement ensued, and the men indiscriminately rushed *en déshabille* into the open air, regardless of the biting wintry weather. The sentry-box in the rear of the hospital had, by some means, caught fire, and was burned up. No other damage done. We leave imagination to picture that night-scene, as mere word-painting could not do the subject full justice.

The 16th of February was a memorable day at Camp Benjamin. That day, at 1 o'clock, an order was received to cook six days' rations, and to be ready to move in one hour.

A large number of ladies assembled to witness the departure, and as the regiment moved away, "Good-bye," "God bless you," was on the lips of all.

Marched up the telegraph road and reached Price's Camp, at Trat's store, at 9 o'clock P.M. The enemy's camp-fires were visible four miles distant.

Few of the men took either blankets or clothing with them, little dreaming of the events which were about to occur. As they lay around their camp-fires, they thought of the happy days at Camp Benjamin; how halcyon hours, all brimming with pleasure, had winged their swift flight; of festivities within and without their camp; of hunts, rambles into the country; of the abundance and plenty which surrounded them there. Ah! those scenes of the past, surrounded with the frame-work of winter sports, had fled forever, and now a reality, to contain horrors never before experienced or dreamed of, hovered over them with its restless, sable pinions. Camp Benjamin, a long, a last farewell bade we to thee!

CHAPTER XV

WINTER AT FAYETTEVILLE

AWAY once more on the tramp, with a single companion as company. That night we laid under a hay-stack and slept till morning. The next day the detachment reached Fayetteville early in the morning, and were given the college building for quarters. This was a fine edifice—the main building extending east and west, with two wings on the north and south sides. The grounds around it were beautifully laid out, and interspersed with fine oak-trees.

Here, then, we must rest for a time. The boys seemed to find Fayetteville a pleasant little town, and becoming acquainted with the lassies of the place, entered with keen relish and peculiar zest into all the amusements of the season. Balls and parties were no rarity, while the young men exhibited, by their attention to the ladies, the fact that a soldier's rough experiences had in nowise blunted their refinement of feelings or polish of gentlemanly deportment, or that the charms of women were not as powerful to attract as in "days of yore." The days succeeded each other in rapid succession, with little to vary their monotony save such excitement as the boys manufactured themselves. There was the usual guard-mounting for the day's duties, roll-calls and evening parades. At night the men usually gathered in their quarters to laugh, talk and joke over occurring events, often ending with an uproarious "stag-dance." The members of Company A had among them a fine glee-club, and often would they serenade the young ladies of the place, or, gathering in front of the quarters during the pleasant evenings, fill the quiet air with their harmonious voices, the pleasant songs floating away in the quietude in soft echoing refrains. It was not an unusual occurrence to have their vocal music returned by the appreciative young ladies of Fayetteville, who would come to the fence surrounding the quarters and charm the soldiers' senses with exquisite songs, warbled in the clear bell-like tones of woman's rich voice. The fair singers were never rudely interrupted or disturbed in their efforts to show their appreciation of the compliments paid them; but when the song was finished the men could not refrain always from expressing their admiration and gratification by a burst of applause.

During this month another battery of six guns, and seventy-two wagons loaded with supplies, passed through the place, *en route* for Price's army. Two of these guns were long, rifled cannon, very old, and said to have played a prominent part in the battle of Yorktown—a very doubtful supposition. Siegel, in his return towards Springfield, attempted to capture these supplies, but General Price learning his intentions, by forced marches, reached Springfield twenty-four hours in advance of him, and thus frustrated his designs. General Price having received a commission as a general in the Confederate service, soon organized out of the State Guard a large force—men who, like all the first volunteers, went into the army actuated by principle, in the firm belief that the cause they espoused was right and just. This was the nucleus of that splendid body of men who became so famed; who seemed to be strangers to fear, and with reckless daring and undaunted bravery fought all through the war, never quailing in the hour of most imminent peril. Between these troops and Louisianian Regiment grew up an attachment cemented in bonds of blood, and which no dissensions, trials or danger could ever sunder. The Louisianians will ever keep green in their memory their association with the first Missouri Volunteers, and admire their heroic deeds as brave men should.

On the 21st December we were visited by a cold, freezing rainstorm, which at night changed into snow, and the next morning we arose to find the ground hidden 'neath winter's white mantle, while the light feathery flakes were rapidly descending from the dark clouds o'erhead. The sun rose the next day on a wintry scene of dazzling beauty, such as the eye seldom gazes on. The air was sharp and biting, the ground beautiful in its smooth whiteness, while the limbs, twigs and boughs of the trees glittered and glistened as the sun shone upon their crystal covering of ice as if incased in diamonds. It was one of winter's most magnificent pictures, calling forth unbounded expressions of admiration from those who had never witnessed such a spectacle. It was, indeed, something new to those who had been accustomed only to the softly-smiling skies and balmy atmosphere of a land filled with orange groves and budding blossoms. Thus gathering around him gorgeous wintry scenes of nature's unrivaled paintings, the old year was rapidly passing away. Christmas was generally observed and celebrated by the detachment. Early in the morning the bell over our quarters commenced a rapid tintinnabulation not customary to it, accompanied by the dread cry of "Fire!" "Fire!" There was rolling, tumbling and jumping out of one, two and three-story berths; a general scramble for clothing, intermingled with all kinds of cires and exclamations. "Where are my shoes?" "Who has my pants?" "Where in the devil is my coat?" etc., etc. We went out of the only door, from which a flight of steep steps led to the ground, at the imminent risk of broken necks and limbs, some clothed, others in *déshabille,* hatless and shoeless—a motley crowd, indeed—only to find a pleasant moonlit morn and nothing astir. We had been incontinently "sold" by some soldier who remembered it was Christmas morning and loved a practical joke. Many enjoyed the fun, while others commenced the day by using the king's English in a manner not taught in the Bible.

The men were consoled, however, by an early invitation to Captain Viglini's quarters, where they drowned the remembrance of their early disturbance in a "smile" of delicious, fragrant, *all hot, piping hot* egg-nog, "nidding and nodding" at each other over the favorite beverage of the holidays.

Of the many toasts drank, we give the following: "Our first Christmas in the Southern Confederacy. When bright-winged peace shall have dispelled the dark gloom of war, may we each sit down 'neath the shadow of his own vine and fig-tree to relate the incidents of the Western Campaign, remembering this as one of the most pleasant." An admirer of *himself* abroad and the ladies at home, gave "Company K—first in peace at home, first in war abroad, and first in the hearts of the ladies." The conceited ragamuffin!

Permission having been obtained, during the morning one of Siegel's captured six-pounder pieces was dragged from the arsenal and made to thunder forth its deep-toned voice in honor of the occasion. When last we heard its tone it spoke only to proclaim the coming storm of death and ruin which it was sending amid battling hosts. Now it caused the hills and villages to re-echo in honor of the glad tidings borne from heaven to earth by angels proclaiming "Peace on earth, good-will to men." Then its thunder proclaimed war; now it spoke of peace. How strange the contrast! The soldiers on duty were not forgotten, for some kind lady friends sent them a repast of all manner of dainties and substantials, and once again they feasted most sumptuously and royally. The festivities of the day ended in a large ball at the court-house, where assembled the beauty of Fayetteville—the gay laddie and fair lassie—who "tripped it on the light fantastic toe" until the "wee sma'" hours of the succeeding morn. The boys enjoyed their Christmas, although not greeted by the smiling faces and cheerful voices of "loved ones at home."

The weather was usually very cold, but the year went out in mildness and serenity. The gray-haired '61 was laid in the grave of the Past, and from its ashes, Phoenix like, sprang into existence the newborn '62. The past year had been freighted with momentous events—the ruin of the greatest of republican governments being the chiefest. The mind in vain attempted to grasp futurity as we stood upon the threshold of the new year; in vain endeavored to penetrate its hidden folds and gather there the record of our future destiny. No light came from its obscurity, and weak man must go blindly forward, and with his puny arm and impotent strength carve out the inevitable decrees of fate. The new year opened bright and promising for the success and hopes of the Young Republic, born under such a fierce baptism of blood. Yet the war was only in its incipiency, only the beginning of the tremendous proportions which it afterwards assumed. Missouri was in a deplorable condition, filled with scenes of violence and dark crime, and her people at this period were pouring through Arkansas in a continuous stream, moving with their household goods, negroes and stock to Texas, where they expected to find homes, security and peace.

Col. McIntosh commenced the new year by gaining a decisive victory over some disaffected Indians, under the leadership of a chief known as Opothleyhola. This decisive victory was gained by the combined cavalry forces of McCulloch's Brigade, comprising Texans, Arkansians, and Indians. A general court-martial was also in session nearly all the winter, disposing of the numerous cases brought for trial for various offences against military regulations and discipline. This court-martial was convened in accordance with the following order:

HEADQUARTERS SECOND BRIGADE, }
Special Order, }   *December 13th*, 1861. }
No. 7. }

A general court-martial is hereby appointed to meet at Fayetteville, Ark., on the 26th day of December, 1861, or as soon thereafter as practicable, for the trial of such persons as may be brought before it.

DETAIL OF THE COURT

Colonel McRae, of McRae's Regiment; Major Matheson, of Colonel Rector's Regiment; Captain J. S. Richards, of Third Regiment Louisiana Infantry; Captain W. T. Hall, do.; Captain J. B. Gilmore, do.; Captain McCulloch, of Colonel McNair's Regiment; Captain Provence, of Provence's Battery; Captain Hawkins, of Whitfield's Battalion; Captain W. R. Bradfute, Chief of Artillery; Captain Griffith, of Colonel Rector's Regiment; Captain Swaggerty, of Colonel Hill's Regiment; Lieutenant Davis, of Goode's Battery.

Captain Charles A. Bruslé, of the Third Regiment Louisiana Infantry, is hereby appointed Judge-Advocate of the Court. No other officers than those named can be assembled, without manifest injury to the service.

By order   COLONEL LOUIS HEBERT,
                                            Commanding Second Brigade.

                                            S. M. HYAMS, JUNR.,
                                            Adjutant Second Brigade.

The author was the provost marshal of this court, and made many long rides to Bentonville, Camp Benjamin, and Fort Reagan, in carrying out the bequests of the court.

The 8th of January was celebrated by the detachment firing a national salute. The day is enshrined in every Louisianian's heart, and we could not pass it by in silence.

The Major having received money on the 9th to pay the troops for four months, and being appointed paymaster, visited our quarters both to see the men and instruct the officers to prepare pay-rolls. The intelligence was most joyfully received, for the men were all sadly in need of funds. At this time there existed a great deal of ill-feeling regarding the future leadership of the army. General Price's claims were advocated by a portable paper which went with the Missouri forces and was edited by J. W. Tucker, a bitter, uncompromising opponent of General McCulloch. This called into existence a paper named the "War Bulletin," edited by J. H. Brown, Esq., a talented gentleman, well known in Texas, and an enthusiastic, devoted friend of General McCulloch. It was a matter to be regretted that these differences arose, or that the Southern press should impugn the motives of General McCulloch, attacking his character as a man and a General. We do not intend or desire in this History to enter upon the merits or demerits of this controversy. Yet we cannot refrain from stating in behalf of McCulloch (who now fills a soldier's honored grave), that he was generally beloved, nay, idolized, by the Louisianians and Texans, and the volunteers under him "had undiminshed confidence in his heroism, skill and ability, having been with him and witnessed his indefatigable perseverance and labors in the face of a thousand difficulties." Let this controversy end as it would, the men then felt that it was a matter of small moment who commanded, so that the brave and chivalrous sons of the South, be they Texans, Lousianians, Arkansans or Missourians, were united heart and soul, determined to drive the Northern invaders out of Missouri. General Price was doing a noble work in Missouri, enlisting her sons in the Confederate service, thus forming a permanently organized army, which, becoming drilled and disciplined, would be better prepared to meet the foe. McCulloch's Division in the latter part of January was composed of fourteen regiments, three battalions, one independent company, and four light artillery companies, all in excellent health and splendid spirits. Such was the condition of affairs when rumors began to circulate pointing to an early, active Spring campaign, and the men became feverish with excitement. General Price was reported to have received the appointment of Brigadier-General. General McCulloch was to return to the command of his old brigade, and all differences merged in the leadership of Major-General Earl Van Dorn. On the 23d of January General Price sent a messenger to Fayetteville, that the enemy were advancing upon him in large force; that he was unable to hold his position. The Federals had been concentrating their forces for some time previous to this date, but it was scarcely anticipated that they would open the campaign so early, ere the winter had begun to break up. His dispatch, therefore, was astounding, yet not altogether unexpected. The intelligence was immediately telegraphed to General McIntosh, and orders issued by Colonel Hebert to the troops to prepare to move at an early date. The news was received by the men with much enthusiasm at this prospect of once again meeting the foe, though it required them to leave their comfortable winter-quarters, and make a long, tedious march in the inclement weather. While in expectation of receiving marching orders, Providence most opportunely interposed its mysterious hand to stay the fierce tide of war. It was a fortunate circumstance both for the comfort as well as safety and health of the troops. For several days previous to the 28th it had been dark, damp, and cloudy weather; on this day it commenced raining briskly, and continued all day until night, when it suddenly turned cold; the rain froze on the ground as it fell, then turned into sleet, and eventually into a heavy blinding snow-storm. The next morning the white flakes still descended, until the ground was covered to the depth of fifteen inches. It was winter indeed now, and all hopes of an expedition into Missouri ended, as the roads were rendered impassable for many days to come. Perhaps a more grand, gloomy as well as beautiful picture of winter scenery was never witnessed than after this storm. The sky had been obscured by heavy gray clouds in bold outline, against which were defined the delicate tracery of limbs and twigs of the trees, covered with an incrustation of ice, and filled with long, pendant icicles, while the black trunks stood out in fine contrast with the white mantle of snow covering the earth beneath. The sun shone out brightly, making the scene a picturesque one truly. The trees glittered with their crystallization, reflecting the rays with innumerable sparkles and prismatic coloring, while the undulating hills presented the appearance of burnished silver. Of course the Louisianians had an immense amount of sport out of this snow-storm, to many of them an entirely new spectacle. They snow-balled each other with desperate energy, and finally gathering into a strong band, commenced an indiscriminate "ducking" of every one with whom they came in contact. This process consisted in seizing the victims and rolling them in the snow, completely covering them with the light substance. Perhaps such a scene of winter sport was never witnessed in Fayetteville, as then occurred. Colonels, majors, captains, lieutenants, merchants, lawyers, doctors, and citizens, all alike shared the same fate. It was something rare and amusing to see a squad of privates in full chase after a colonel with shouts and laughter, or dragging a major from some hiding-place, only to give them a good rolling in the snow. It was a useless undertaking to attempt to escape. The men respected neither persons nor places in their uproarious sport. Gray hairs alone saved the victim. They even made a descent upon Colonel (now acting General) Hebert's headquarters. They found the house closed, but they were not to be cheated out of a single victim. The Colonel's dignity and position could not protect him now. He held a parley with the leaders, and finally compromised the matter by inviting the whole party into his fine quarters and giving them some "refreshments," very acceptable, indeed, to the boys, after their violent exercise, and wet as they were from the snow. Every one joined in the sport with perfect good-humor. General McCulloch's whole staff shared the fate of every one else. Doubtless many years will roll away ere the good people of Fayetteville will forget this winter-day frolic of the Louisianians.

There was no certainty now of an early campaign. The enemy had returned to Rolla, having suffered intensely from the cold weather. The roads were impassable, and would be so for many days to come. Below they were almost completely blockaded with trees, broken down by the weight of ice which had accumulated on them. A strong appeal was made to the Third Regiment to re-enlist at the expiration of their approaching term of service; but the men expressed the determination of returning home rather than serve in a campaign in this section. There was a general desire and disposition to serve the country, but they wished a different field of operations. The regiment already had a reputation that extended from the Missouri River to the most distant boundaries of the Confederacy, and the brave spirits who composed the organization felt no desire to remain idly at home while their country needed their strong arms and stout and willing hearts. Their campaigns had already been severe, and they felt as if they needed rest and companionship of friends and relatives from whom they had so long been separated. The course of events, however, determined their destiny, without any action of themselves, as the sequel will show.

CHAPTER XVI

THE SPRING CAMPAIGN, 1862

EARLY in February rumors were in circulation that General Price was in full retreat from Springfield, closely pursued by a large and powerful foe under command of General Hunter.

On Saturday, the 15th of February, these rumors were confirmed, as courier after courier arrived asking for assistance.

General Price was really in the State of Arkansas, daily fighting the enemy's advance-guard like a tiger at bay. On Saturday afternoon the detachment left Fayetteville to join Price's army, marching all night, and joining the regiment early the next morning. They crossed Cross Hollows at a double-quick, lustily cheering as they hastened towards the foe. Everything was in confusion at winter-quarters, the troops having left behind everything—clothing, etc.—in their sudden departure and eager haste. Along the road leading to Fayetteville was a scene that beggared description. Long trains of wagons, loaded with army stores, provisions, arms, tents, utensils, etc.; carriages and buggies filled with women and children, whose blanched faces betokened their fears; horsemen, footmen, little children and delicate young women hastening away from the simoom blast of war's desolation. The scene was heightened as we encountered Price's army. McCulloch's infantry on hand at this trying juncture consisted of the Louisiana Regiment, McRae's and McNair's Arkansas regiments, who joined the retreating army only to be turned back by the retrograding column. All day Monday we fell back slowly, but in good order. In the afternoon the advance-guard of the enemy made a rush on our rear, and for nearly an hour a desperate fight ensued, in which artillery was freely used on both sides. A line of battle was formed, in anticipation of a general engagement. The Confederates succeeded in repulsing the enemy, our loss being three killed and seventeen wounded; enemy's about forty. The dash of the Federal cavalry was so impetuous that they became intermingled with our troops, and there was a free use of sabres and small-arms. They could not stand, however, the deadly fire of the Missourian shot-guns. Monday our forces reached their winter-quarters, to spend the night, while Price's army occupied Cross Hollows, distant two and a half miles. Young's Texas regiment arrived, and camped with the regiment. The next day we marched to Cross Hollows and camped in an open field in the valley, shut in by the high hills. This day Rector's and Mitchell's Arkansas Regiments joined the army. The latter regiment had marched forty-five miles in twenty-four hours without halting. General McCulloch also arrived, and was met with such a storm of enthusiasm as seldom greets any man. Such a deafening cheer as the Louisianians gave him attested *their satisfaction*. They were wild with joy, throwing up their hats and elevating them on the points of their bayonets in their enthusiasm. General McCulloch bared his head, and while his eagle eye lighted up with a unwonted fire, remarked, "Men, I am glad to see you;" a greeting which was responded to with a heartfelt burst of applause. The men, on account of the suddenness of the demand for their services and hasty departure from their quarters, were without tents, blankets and provisions. That night they laid down on the frozen ground, around huge fires, to snatch, if possible, a short sleep while expecting the enemy. To add to the hardships which they had encountered, it commenced a cold, freezing rain, which continued nearly all night. Some few, fortunate in the possession of blankets, slept through it all, their covering becoming a mass of ice, from which they had to be released by the assistance of their friends; but the majority of the troops gathered, in shivering groups, around their camp-fires. A line of battle, under General McCulloch's energetic supervision, was formed, and soon every hill-side glistened with bayonets, and batteries frowned upon every avenue of approach. While thus awaiting the enemy's approach, they suddenly appeared in Bentonville, on our extreme left flank, taking possession of the quarters of Rector's regiment. Two of their scouts were also captured on White River, on our extreme right, indicating a design to flank our position. Of course they destroyed the greater portion of the clothing, etc., of Rector's men, besides killing some of the citizens and committing other outrages. On Tuesday morning, very early, our army began to retreat, in the midst of a bitter cold storm of sleet and snow. The road was a mass of solid ice, slippery and as hard as rock. Yet the Louisianian Regiment began the march with buoyant spirits, joking, laughing and singing as they tramped over the slippery road. All day long the weary march continued, while the beards of the men became white with their frozen breath, even the water in the canteens turning into ice. Weary, foot-sore, hungry and cold, they arrived at Fayetteville on the night of the 19th, only to find nearly every house deserted by the women and children, while every man had shouldered his rifle for the deadly strife. The Northern heavens, lighted up with a reddening glow, telling the men that their winter-quarters had been given to the flames, to prevent their occupation by the enemy, proclaiming also the destruction of their clothing, utensils and equipage. The scene was by no means a consoling one, under such reflections. Thus, as these fine and comfortable quarters melted away into ashes, it entailed on the regiment the loss of nearly everything they had, besides a large quantity of quartermaster and commissary stores and forage. The regiment remained at Fayetteville on the 20th, the detachment composed of Companies A and K occupying their old quarters, while Price's trains, artillery, infantry and cavalry poured through the place in a continuous stream.

The scene in Fayetteville beggared all description. Stores broken open and rifled of their contents, private residences left unoccupied, invaded and pillaged, while commissary stores were scattered in wanton profusion in every direction. Upwards of 500,000 pounds of pork—bacon, shoulders and hams—were distributed among the retreating and half-starved troops. Every man and horse had a share of the burden, while it was scattered in every direction over the streets and on the side-walks. The men even made fires of it to warm their chilled and freezing bodies. But why dwell on this gloomy picture of war? The destruction entailed on individual and Government property was occasioned by a want of transportation.

General Price had conducted a masterly retreat, protecting, as he did, a train of 3,500 wagons, and moving over 50 pieces of artillery without loss. Through icy streams, over rough roads, in the midst of winter, and pursued closely by a powerful and victorious foe, had he fallen back, step by step, over the plains of Missouri, among the hills of Arkansas, with complete success. When the Louisiana Regiment reached the retreating column they were greeted on all sides with enthusiastic acclamations by the Missourians. "Here's the Louisiana Regiment;" "It's all right now;" "Give 'em h—ll, boys," etc., were some of the expressions used, while the fatigued troops seemed to gather new strength and energy from their arrival. It spoke volumes for the confidence reposed in the regiment, the reputation they had gained for untiring energy, unfaltering nerves and distinguished bravery.

The enemy had one of the largest, best disciplined, and equipped armies yet sent into the field, and the object of our retreat was to draw them as far from their base of supplies as possible among the hills of Arkansas, and give them battle in a position of our own choosing. The immense number of horses in the army, and the scarcity of forage, rendered it necessary that the Southern army should fall back so as to obtain access to supplies more conveniently, and to gain a position where the enemy could not penetrate to the rear. Baston

Mountain was looked upon as the stand-point, the proper position, where the undisciplined troops of the command would be more than a match for the superiority of the foe. The weather grew milder, and the frozen roads became a mass of sloppy mire over ankle deep, ere the army resumed the march. On the 20th we were once again in motion. The sky was overcast with lowering, grayish clouds, indicating rain, while the roads were almost impassable on account of the mire and mud. Soon after departing from Fayetteville, a glance backward revealed one of those spectacles attendant on war, which arouse indescribable emotions of sorrow and indignation. Lurid flames, with their forked tongues, began to appear in several places, until a sea of fire, leaping heavenward, accompanied with a dark volume of smoke, rolled over the town, proclaiming the destruction and ruin left behind us. As the cloud rolled away northward, it must have spoken volumes to the foe of the sullen determination which animated the Southerners. The men tightened their grasp on their rifles, while the muttered curse, contracted brows, and blazing eyes plainly betokened the spirit aroused in them by this scene of ruin and destruction. The Commissary and Quartermaster buildings, containing stores, arsenal, mills, together with several residences, including a large quantity of provisions, ammunition, and some arms, were destroyed. Nothing was left behind that could in any manner contribute to the comfort or support of the enemy. However much this wholesale destruction was to be deprecated, as a military necessity no one could question its wisdom and justice who at all comprehended the situation of affairs. It was no time, in the face of a powerful and pursuing foe, to query into the motives and policy of a course of procedure, prompted by dire necessity, the salvation of the army, and the ultimate good of the country. All day long the retreat was continued, and a camp selected at night, only that the men might lie down on the saturated ground, in a cold and drenching rain, as usual short of provisions, and with little or no shelter. The Third Regiment, as usual, was the rear-guard of the whole army.

Perhaps nothing could more forcibly demonstrate the spirit that animated the Louisianians than an incident that occurred on their arrival at Fayetteville. One of the regiment, who showed the white feather at Oak Hills, and had been taken so violently ill every time there was a prospect of a fight, was found in hospital here. "The boys" called on him, sympathized with him, regretted exceedingly that he was so unfortunate, but they had determined that no member of the Third Louisiana should be taken alive by the Yankees, and producing a rope with a running noose, threw it over his head, around his neck, and apparently were about to apply the "Hemp Practice." His recovery was instantaneous, and his protestations that the cure was a permanent one were very emphatic.

Saturday, February 22d, 1862, was a day which those who composed the Army of the West will not readily forget. Amid a terrific storm of rain and hail the men once more journeyed on, sinking ankle deep in mud. Yet cold and drenched as they were, the Louisianians marched cheerfully forward, shouting forth with stentorian voices the chorus of the "Bonny Blue Flag," and other patriotic songs. It seemed as if they were determined their spirits should not succumb to their accumulated sufferings, hardships, and trials. It appears almost incredible that men could exhibit such reckless indifference, such strength of will and determination, after such a week of bitter experiences as these men were taught. The war, however, developed and decided some strange theories as to the amount of physical powers which the human frame contained— powers of enduring fatigue, hunger, thirst, heat and cold, which would scarcely have been believed before, if asserted. The troops arrived at their destination on Baston Mountain late at night, the 22d inst., with provisions so scarce that bread was hoarded as a miser hoards his gold, and dealt out in very limited quantities. Provisions, however, soon arrived, the weather changed to bright, clear, and pleasant days, tents sufficient to shelter, and blankets to make the men comfortable, soon being supplied. Few of those at home who celebrated the 22d of February amid scenes of festivity and rejoicing, from mere description and word-painting, can ever realize how the Western Army of the South spent this natal day of our loved Washington, the first inauguration-day of the young Confederacy.

CHAPTER XVII

BASTON MOUNTAIN

GENERAL MCCULLOCH'S Division camped on the main or telegraph road leading to Van Buren, while General Price's army occupied a position on Cane Hill road, some three miles further west, defending the road over Baston Mountain. The strength of the position, together with much-needed rest and a good supply of provisions, soon placed the army in splendid fighting trim, and the enemy's approach was quietly awaited.

Our cavalry were out between our position and the enemy watching their movements. On the 23d a picket guard was scattered about Fayetteville, when they were surrounded by a large cavalry force of the Federals, who surprised them. Several were killed, wounded and taken prisoners, in their attempt to escape. A scout killed a Federal at Mud Town, a place between Baston Mountain and Fayettevile. He was out foraging on his own responsibility; he was ordered to surrender, which he refused to do, when the Texan killed him, as he drew his revolver to fire.

The days passed away without materially changing the relative positions of the two armies. A large force of cavalry were sent out to penetrate to the enemy's rear, cut off their supplies, and destroy their trains. The expedition proved eminently successful. The Federals reported that their trains had been destroyed and mules killed by *Missouri Jayhawkers*. The army knew who "struck Billy Patterson," as the Texans returned on the 24th, bringing with them ten prisoners. They destroyed a sutler's train, attacked 300 of the enemy, killing 27 without having a man injured, penetrating as far as Keatsville, Mo. One of the prisoners brought in, an officer, stated that he had seen considerable scouting in the bushes, but the Texans beat the Devil for reckless riding in the woods. His uniform was in rags, almost torn from his person, by contact with the bushes. The raiders never struck a road in their expedition, but kept to the woods, nearly altogether. The Federals soon retreated from Fayetteville, and took up a position at Cross Hollows, announcing their determination not to attack the Confederate forces among the hills of Arkansas. Colonel Churchill's regiment dismounted on the 25th, consenting to this step only on condition that they should have a position next to the Louisiana boys. The regiment was now supported by McRae's and Churchill's regiments, all animated by a spirit of emulation as to which would most distinguish themselves in the coming battle for deeds of daring and bravery. February closed with clear and pleasant weather. There was a general muster, review, and inspection on the last day. The troops were in execellent health and spirits. The discipline was very rigid at this time, and orders very strict. The closest guard was kept around the camps, and on the roads, so that it was an utter impossibility for either soldier or citizen to travel without a correct permit. In a practical degree, martial law prevailed. On the evening of March 2d, Major-General Earl Van Dorn arrived, and was welcomed by salutes from nearly all the Missouri artillery. He at once assumed command, and immediately issued orders to prepare to march on the enemy. Impetuous, at times rash and reckless, brave and daring to a fault, with his usual spirit, he was about to hurl his army on the foe. The men felt that there was to be no more retreating, no more waiting. The two forces having at length been united, he hesitated not a day as to his course. All extra clothing, baggage, tents, etc., were ordered to be left behind. Provisions (such as were on hand) were prepared, and all was once again bustle and excitement. The army took up the line of march on the 4th, left in front, as follows: Price's army, with strong flankers, on the left. Next came McCulloch's Division, as follows: Rector's, Hill's, Mitchell's, McNair's, McIntosh's (dismounted), Whitfield's Battalion (dismounted Texans), McRae's Arkansas Regiment, Province's Battery, Churchill's Regiment (dismounted), Hart's Battery, and Third Louisiana Regiment, with Goode's Battery in front. Then the trains of the various regiments. On the night of the 4th, the College buildings in Fayetteville, occupied by Companies A and K as winter-quarters, were fired by some incendiary, supposed to be a signal to the enemy of our occupation of the place.

The army arrived at Elm Springs, fifteen miles north of Fayetteville, on the evening of the 5th, to find the enemy gone. Here two spies sent out by Siegel were captured. A more ragged, forlorn, dirty, miserable-looking couple could not possibly have been found. They were *splendidly* rigged for the *occasion,* and did credit to the inventive genius of the *Deutshe* General Siegel. The cavalry also captured seven forage wagons, and thirty-eight Federals, out hunting forage. The next morning ten more were added to the number. They evidently had not been informed of our advance, and were surprised most completely. During this time the weather was very cold, and we were visited with several

snow-storms, and making forced marches every day. It seemed as if General
Van Dorn imagined the men were made of cast-steel, with the strength and
powers of endurance of a horse, whose mettle he was testing to its utmost capacity and tension. Scarcely time was given the men to prepare food and snatch a
little rest. On the 6th we started very early, and arrived at Bentonville soon after
noon. The army looked splendidly as the long line marched across the open
prairie with their flags fluttering in the breeze. We reached Bentonville just in
time to see Siegel's Division, who had been west of this place, disappear with
his column *en route* for the main body of the enemy. An hour sooner and he
would have been cut off. On what slight events do the fate of armies depend!
General McIntosh made a dashing charge upon the rear of the retreating column, plunging into the midst of a large force of infantry and in face of a battery, with Greer's Texas Regiment, ere he was aware of the peril of his position.
There was a fierce rattle of musketry, mingled with the roar of artillery, for a
few moments, proclaiming how sharp was the skirmish. Although obliged to
retire, he killed a number of the foe, captured forty prisoners, and one piece of
artillery, knocked into *pi* by a well-directed shot from one of Price's rifled
pieces. Our loss two killed and eight wounded. That night we laid down once
more in Camp Stephens, only to resume the march after two hours' rest. We
were being rushed upon the foe like a thunderbolt. But they were prepared for
our coming. Ere morning our army was slumbering within three miles of the
enemy, while General Price had penetrated to their front, cutting off their
retreat towards Missouri. He had succeeded in cutting out a blockaded cross-
road, leading to the main road in front of the enemy, without being discovered or molested. When we halted on the night of the 6th fires were built with
rails from an adjoining fence. General McCulloch came among the men of the
Louisiana Regiment, and sitting down on a rail near one of the fires, commenced chatting with the officers and men, who gathered thickly around him.
He was dressed in a complete suit of beautiful dark and heavy velvet. One of
the men approached the fire, and, not observing who the General was, tapped
him on the shoulder with a bundle of sticks which he had in his hand, remarking, "I wish you would put these in that fire and give me a light." The General,
without moving his position, quietly took the splinters and thrust them into
the fire. As soon as they were lighted he took them out, and turning to the private, quietly said: "Here my good fellow, is your fire." The man was dum-
founded, confused, when he saw who it was that he had treated so familiarly,
and, muttering an apology, hastened from the spot. His astonishment and confusion created much laughter among the men who witnessed the incident. After

chatting quietly and calmly for some moments as to the issue of the approaching battle, he energetically exclaimed: "I tell you, men, the army that is defeated
in this fight will get a h—l of a whipping!" Was it prophecy? Did the unseen
Angel of Death, which threw the shadow of its dark wings over his brave spirit,
whisper to his soul his approaching doom? We know not, yet that night the
men all remarked how different he seemed from his usual manner. He was
unusually reticent, and spoke in a quiet, subdued voice, so unlike his customary energetic, determined actions and speech.

CHAPTER XVIII

THE BATTLE OF ELK HORN

WEARIED, hungry, and broken as the men were from their rapid march, the loss of rest and want of food, early on the morning of March 7, 1862, they were marched on the position known as Pea Ridge, near Elk Horn Tavern and ravine, about thirty miles north of Fayetteville. The road towards Missouri led through a deep and narrow defile, darkened with the shadows of the over-hanging hills. The division started to join Price, but were soon turned back as the enemy were making a demonstration in our rear. The morning was bright and beautiful, the air fresh, pleasant and bracing. Soon the deep boom of a single gun echoed over the hills and along the valleys, followed by another and another, until the sound became a continuous roar. General Price had opened the fight. While marching towards the enemy's position, Hart's Battery in front, supported by the Louisianians, along the east end of an open corn-field extending far down the valley, the enemy opened a battery of rifled guns on the moving column from a cluster of trees near the centre of the field. Our cavalry, under the leadership of the intrepid and dashing McIntosh, were in this field, close to the right of the infantry. The ground sloped very gently towards the position taken by the Federal battery. As soon as the guns opened, the cavalry commenced manœuvring until they formed a half circle, extending the whole width of the field. The shells began to pass in dangerous prox-imity with their shrill scream, when suddenly a hundred bugles pealed forth the charge, their clarion notes rising clear and distinct above the din of battle. With shrill whoops, and yelling like demons, upwards of 5,000 painted Indians and Texan Rangers, under the lead of the gallant McIntosh, swept down like a whirlwind on the doomed battery. So impetuous, so sudden was the charge, that no time was given the foe to meet the rushing host of horsemen. In less than five minutes the battery was captured, the infantry force supporting it shot down, ridden over and scattered like chaff before a whirlwind. It was a gallant charge—a brave feat seldom occurring, and, once witnessed, never to be forgotten. Napoleon's Life Guards never swept upon a foe with more impetuosity and gallantry than did our cavalry in this charge. The uproar died away in spattering shots, and then ceased altogether.

These guns were given in charge of the Indians, to whom such huge guns seemed not only a mystery, but endowed with supernatural powers. Their use was a new feature in warfare, to which they were totally unaccustomed. They immediately took to the bushes; then, suddenly darting out, shot down the horses, at the same time uttering a guttural "Boom!" They next piled rails on the carriages and put fire to them. When it was reduced to ashes, and the guns lay useless on the ground, they expressed their satisfaction by saying, "No more boom"—"Good!" They shot at every one having on a blue coat, whether friend or foe, using their scalping-knives in the same manner—some of the Confederate dead having been found subjected to this barbarous custom of these untutored savages. The half-breeds were better trained, and practiced no such barbarities. After the capture of this battery, the infantry was marched to the top of a high cone-shaped hill, overlooking the valley extending westward. They were soon discovered and opened on by another battery. Here they laid down, the shot passing harmlessly over them with their shrill, ugly scream. The surrounding country was covered with dense underbrush and heavy timber, interspersed with open corn-fields, surrounded by high, rocky hills. In company with Mitchell's, McRae's and McNair's Arkansas regiment, the Louisianians were led to meet the foe. As the line of battle cautiously felt its way through the dense undergrowth, the whole line was opened on with a fire so close and deadly that they wavered and staggered before the storm in some places, being thrown into great confusion. Quickly rallying, under the lead of Colonel Hebert, commanding the brigade, and Major Tunnard at the head of the regiment, with loud cheers we rushed on the foe, driving them back in confusion. Five times they rallied, and five times were they charged and routed. It seemed as if nothing could withstand the reckless, furious courage which animated the men. The foe retreated within cover of a masked battery which was planted in a thicket skirting a corn-field. So close and hot was our pursuit that no opportunity was given to use the guns. As the men caught sight of these guns, they rushed upon them with deafening cheers across the open corn-field, driving back the foe with irresistible fury. Around these guns the contest raged fearfully; the musketry was close, heavy and deadly. But the men held their position, and once more defeated the foe, fighting a largely superior force. The line was in great confusion at this time. Captain Gunnels, of Company I, assisted by other officers, made an attempt to form a new line, in which he partially succeeded, as the men were so wild with excitement as to be almost uncontrollable. This new line was immediately in front of the captured guns in the open field, just outside the skirting woods. Another battery suddenly opened on our right, far down the field, while a regiment of cavalry made a dashing charge through a gap in the fence upon our left and rear. With our forces in confusion, tired and worn down with their long marches, hard fighting and eager pursuit of the enemy, without our leaders (Major Tunnard, Colonel Hebert and many officers having disappeared), the men turned upon the cavalry like tigers at bay. So close and deadly was the concentrated fire of the line upon the head of the charging squadron, that scarcely a man who entered the field in the charge escaped. Men and horses rolled in death upon that blood-stained field. The remainder of the cavalry wheeled away in rapid flight. Thus surrounded, not reinforced or aided by cavalry or infantry, the order was given to fall back, which was accomplished in good order under a heavy fire from the enemy's artillery. The battery captured and then abandoned belonged to Siegel's division of the army. With sorrow and dismay was it then learned that Generals McCulloch and McIntosh had both fallen early in the day—the former killed while reconnoitering the enemy's position; the latter while leading a charge at the head of his old regiment. Hence the inactivity of our cavalry and reserved infantry forces, who impatiently awaited, where they were stationed, orders from the generals to enter the arena of strife. The Lousiana Regiment fought with brave, reckless desperation, and suffered very severely.

The growth of underbrush on the battle-field was so dense that the field officers were compelled to dismount. Thus the Major, with a sword in one hand and a flag in the other, rallied and cheered on the men until he sank upon the ground completely exhausted. He attempted to find his horse, but failed to do so, on account of his helpless condition. We extract from his private diary the following particulars of his capture: "I remained lying on the ground more than an hour, not knowing where our forces were, or whether we were victorious or defeated, when I was startled by the approach of a regiment. On discovering me, one company fired a volley at me, the balls striking all around me, but fortunately none hitting my person. I at once waved my handkerchief in token of my helpless condition. Lieutenant Gale, of the Forty-forth Illinois Regiment, rode up to me and demanded my arms, which I handed him. On discovering my complete physical exhaustion, he sent for a horse, which I mounted, and was escorted to their camp."

During the fight, McRae's and Mitchell's Regiments being thrown into confusion, fell in the rear of the Third Regiment. Major Tunnard, assisted by

Lieutenant Humble, of Company I, and Lieutenant Johnson, besides other officers, made the most strenuous exertions to form them into line, but without
effect. They dropped behind, firing upon the Louisianians from the rear, doing
a great deal of mischief. This was caused by undisciplined "Minute-men," who
had joined the different regiments for the battle. Private Caton, of Company
E, and one of Company C, were thus shot from the rear. Colonel Hebert fought
bravely throughout the battle, leading the men gallantly in every charge. While
attempting to lead a portion of the troops, including some sixty of the regiment, from the field of battle, they were thus surrounded and taken prisoners.
Besides Colonel Hebert, the enemy captured Captain Viglini, Company K,
Lieutenant Washburn, Company B, and Lieutenant Emanuel, Company C.
The death of Generals McIntosh and McCulloch undoubtedly lost the
battle. The enemy were completely beaten at every point, and had our reserve
forces been ordered up at the proper moment, the victory would have been
most signal.

When the Louisianians learned the certainty of their idolized chieftain's
death, many of these lion-hearted men threw themselves in wild grief upon
the ground, weeping scalding tears in their bitter sorrow. It is a fearful spectacle to see a strong-hearted man thus give way to his feelings. It demonstrated
the devotion felt for General McCulloch, and showed how deeply he was
enshrined in these brave souls. The sun went down amid the roar of artillery
and the rattle of musketry. We slept on the field of battle, burrowing amid
heaps of dry forest-leaves, to, in some measure, protect our weary frames from
the chilling mountain air. A deep gloom settled over the spirits of the men,
and they were nearly disheartened.

At 1 o'clock A.M. we were aroused from our weary, restless slumbers, and
ordered to join Price's command. This brave general had also driven the enemy
from every position, capturing seven pieces of artillery, a large number of prisoners, the enemy's camps, etc. Early on the morning of the 8th the battle
recommenced with redoubled fury. The cannonading was terrific—the thunder of the guns reverberating among the hills in a continuous roar. As
McCulloch's Division approached the line of battle, the men stripped for the
fight, throwing aside their few remaining blankets and overcoats, and evincing their eagerness by hastening forward at a double-quick. A line of battle
was formed immediately in the rear of the engaged forces, near an open field,
and the men were once more within range of the enemy's shot and shell,
which passed harmlessly over them. While the struggle went on, several of our
batteries were ordered to a point of one of the hills. It was in point-blank range

of a concentrated fire of the enemy's batteries, and our guns were successively silenced, with fearful loss. Here Captain Clark, the gallant commander of one of Price's most effective and distinguished batteries, lost his life. A gun of one battery was brought out by a single cannoneer, all his comrades having fallen, the last one being killed as he was hooking the sponge to the carriage.

The subjoined official report of Captain Gilmore, commanding Company F, and a letter written by Sergeant W. Kinney, Company F, furnish some interesting particulars of the battle, and portray not only the desperate valor of the members of Company F, but also of the remainder of the regiment who fought with them:

SERGEANT KINNEY'S
ACCOUNT OF THE BATTLE

VAN BUREN, *March 16th, 1862.*

A few words of the great battle may be interesting. We left Baston Mountain on Tuesday, March 4th, and camped near Fayetteville; General Price's command in advance. Wednesday morning we passed through Fayetteville, our train being left behind; we camped for the night at Elm Springs, twelve miles from Fayetteville. It snowed heavily all day, making the roads almost impassable. We learned next morning that the enemy was at Bentonville, about 13,000 strong, and we took up the line of march for that place. The weather was piercing cold. Our advance-guard engaged the enemy, who were in full retreat, one mile north of Bentonville, and fought them all the way to Camp Stephens, a distance of seven miles. I have not learned the loss of the enemy; ours was three wounded.

We saw two of the enemy dead and one wounded on the roadside. The woods all along the road were strewn with dead horses. We arrived at Camp Stephens about dark, almost frozen and starved, having only one biscuit for breakfast that morning, and no prospect of supper. We built fires, and sat around them waiting for the wagons to arrive. Just as they came up we were ordered to march. We left camp at ten o'clock that night without supper, or blankets to keep off the damp night air. We marched about seven miles, when we were ordered to rest, which we needed very much, having marched twenty-six miles that day and night. We made fires of fence-rails, and laid around them until morning.

It was impossible to sleep, for the night was bitter cold; no one will ever know how much we suffered from cold and hunger; no tongue or pen can paint it. Friday morning, March 7th, came at last, and with it the order, "Fall in!"

The Rangers "fell in" to a man, but such a worn-out set of men I never saw. They had not one single mouthful of food to eat. We marched about five miles and countermarched three miles; General Price had opened the battle on the Telegraph road, near Elk Horn Tavern, at 10 A.M. The enemy had possession of the hills between the Telegraph and the road we were on. All the infantry and cavalry of McCulloch's Division were drawn up in line; Third Louisiana was sent forward to open the engagement on our side. While we were marching through a lane, with some Texas and Indian cavalry on our right, we were suddenly fired on by a masked battery about 300 yards distant; not expecting an attack so soon, we were thrown into considerable confusion, from which, however, we soon recovered, to witness one of the most brilliant charges of the campaign by Young's and other Texas cavalry. As soon as the battery opened on us the cavalry bugles sounded the charge. Like a flash of lightning the columns of cavalry dashed out, completely surrounding the battery, and capturing it in less time than it takes to write it.

The enemy's infantry and cavalry who were supporting the battery fired one round and ran.

We now marched in a south-easterly direction. Major W. F. Tunnard, commanding; Captain Hart's Battery in advance.

We had marched about one mile, when we were fired on by a mountain howitzer, stationed on a high hill on our right. The enemy made some very close shots; fortunately not one of our boys was injured by them.

Colonel Hebert came riding down, and was requested by the men not to leave them. This was the highest compliment our regiment could bestow. His response was, "I will not leave you, my men, this day."

We then countermarched and passed under the foot of the hill on which the howitzer was planted, with McRae's and McNair's Regiments and Greer's Texas on the hillside. Rested a few minutes until heavy firing of small-arms was heard in front, and order came for us to march in the direction of the firing.

We had not preceeded far when we were fired upon by the enemy's infantry, who were posted in a thicket on our left. We instantly charged them, and drove them back, when we were fired on by a battery about two hundred yards distant on our right.

We charged the battery with McRae's and McNair's Regiments, gallantly *led* by Colonel Hebert, taking it and driving them from their guns. In this charge the three regiments became mixed. About this time Colonel Hebert and Major Tunnard were cut off and taken prisoners.

The enemy on our left opened a heavy fire on us. We charged and drove them off with a heavy loss to them. We then discovered the enemy's cavalry were flanking us on the right. Captain Gunnell, the senior officer in command, ordered us to take the fence, as a heavy body of the enemy's cavalry were flanking us on the right. We had scarcely taken the position when the cavalry made a bold and daring charge, and were repulsed with a heavy loss. At this time it was discovered that a large body of infantry were flanking us on the left. Captain Gilmore was immediately ordered to the left to meet the enemy in the thicket. Here a desperate fight ensued, the enemy having been thrown there in a large body. The Louisiana and Arkansas troops fought like bull-dogs, and drove them back with great slaughter.

This portion of the command then became separated from the balance. The men requested Captain Gilmore to take command, which he did. As he was forming the men in line, we were again flanked on the left. We charged, and drove the enemy back with heavy loss. Captain Gilmore then secured a flag, placed it front, and with the assistance of Lieutenants Gentles, Pelican Rifles, Morse, Pelicans No. 1, and Hobbs, of McRae's Regiment, succeeded in forming them in line. These young officers showed great bravery and coolness.

This command was from 300 to 500 strong, and was the left of McCulloch's Division. They secured a guide, and made for the point from which they first started, determined to cut their way out, but had but one slight skirmish with the enemy on their way out, and were the last to leave the field. This command picked up all the stragglers on the way out, and came out with 800 or 1,000 men. Generals McCulloch and McIntosh fell early in the action, and Colonel Hebert was taken prisoner, and Major Tunnard.

The regiments engaged withdrew to the opposite side of a large corn-field, and laid on their arms for the night. A number of regiments were not engaged, but were held in reserve. McCulloch's Division was ordered to General Price at 3 A.M. I will here mention the cool gallantry of Captain Gunnell in rallying the men through the whole engagement.

Arrived at General Price's camp near daylight. Soon after, our artillery and enemy's commenced a heavy duel. Churchill's Arkansas Regiment and Whitfield's Texas engaged their infantry on the right. Our regiment, McRae's, McNair's, Hill's, and Mitchell's regiments were on a hill on the left of the Telegraph road, within 250 yards of our batteries. The cannonading was said to be one of the grandest sights ever witnessed, and lasted for four hours, when General Van Dorn ordered the troops to be withdrawn, on account of a want of food and sleep. The Rangers fought bravely through the fight of the 7th, both officers and men. A great many of the regiments were completely exhausted for want of food and sleep, and wandered off on the night of the 7th in search of food, and were unable to rejoin their companies on the morning of the 8th. Our train was on the Elm Spring road to the Baston Mountain, and the army on the Frog Bayou road, falling back to this place. It would be impossible to picture the suffering of our army on this retreat.

When the army arrived at White River, our gallant little Captain J. B. Gilmore gave out; he was placed in a wagon, and soon after fainted, having eaten nothing for four days. The men were eating new corn; some would shoot a hog and eat the raw meat without salt.

The enemy lost in killed six to our one, and a greater number in proportion wounded. We turned two of their batteries, and came out of the fight with four guns more than we had when we went in. We have between 500 and 600 prisoners; having more than they have of ours. Have saved all our trains. The enemy burnt a large number of their wagons to prevent their falling into our hands. The army is now encamped seven miles from here, on the Frog Bayou road. The Louisiana Regiment stationed here for the present.

Casualties in Shreveport Rangers: Private John Craig supposed to be killed; Frank Cane wounded, not dangerously; M. F. Miller, L. J. Singer, J. F. Jus, D. S. Duval, and C. Wols, prisoners; J. Kimball, missing. All the rest are here, rather badly used up. If the Rangers have not seen hard service now, they never will. An exchange of prisoners will be made in a day or two.

Hoping, etc., etc.,

W. KINNEY.

CAPTAIN GILMORE'S REPORT

HEADQUARTERS SHREVEPORT RANGERS,
THIRD LOUISIANA VOLUNTEERS. }

Captain Gunnell, commanding Third Louisiana Volunteers:

SIR,—On the morning of the 4th of March, I left camp on Baston Mountain with my company, numbering sixty-three rank and file, and camped that night within three miles of Fayetteville.

Resumed the line of march with the regiment in the morning, camping that night at Elm Spring. The men very much fatigued, and many of them with their feet badly blistered. Resumed the line of march on the morning of the 6th, halting at Sugar Creek for a short time late that evening. Resumed the line of march that night, arriving three miles north of Camp McCulloch at about 2 o'clock on the morning of the 7th, remaining there until 7 A.M. The men were very much worn out, having had but little to eat since leaving Baston Mountain. The weather being very cold, and the men without blankets, they had but little sleep, and were, in consequence, in a poor condition to resume the march that morning. When the call was made to fall in, the Rangers fell in promptly. We marched within a short distance of the

Telegraph Road, when we were countermarched three miles. We turned off to the left, and while marching through the lane, we were fired on by a masked battery, about three hundred yards' distance on our right. The company was thrown into a little confusion, not expecting an attack from that quarter, but from which they soon recovered.

We were then marched a short distance up the lane, when we were fired on by a mountain howitzer stationed on a hill on our right. We then filed to the right, and marched upon the side of a hill, where we halted.

Soon heavy firing of small-arms was heard in front. The regiment was then moved forward, the company in its place, in line.

We had not proceeded far when we were fired on by a body of the enemy's infantry from a thicket on our left. We moved in the direction of the enemy, when heavy firing ensued on both sides. Owing to the thick undergrowth, we could not advance in regular line of battle, and became somewhat mixed up by other troops rushing through our ranks. After the enemy had been driven back we were fired on by a battery on the right.

We were then ordered and *led* by Colonel Hebert to charge the battery. Here the Rangers became mixed up with the other companies of the regiment and some Arkansas troops, and I was unable to get the entire company together again during the day.

After the battery was taken, we were fired on from the woods to the left of the battery. Here considerable confusion ensued in every company, caused by members of other companies and some Arkansas troops getting mixed up with them; but showed great bravery in driving the enemy back to the thicket.

I here made an effort to re-form the company, but had only partly succeeded, when it was discovered that a large body of the enemy's cavalry was flanking us on the right.

We moved in that direction to a fence. The cavalry made a charge on us at this point, but were repulsed with considerable loss. I was here ordered by Captain Gunnell, the senior officer in command, to go to his left into the thicket, to meet a large body of the enemy's infantry who were advancing upon us from that direction. I had not advanced far when a heavy fire of small-arms was opened upon us. Here a desperate fight ensued; but we succeeded in driving them back with great loss. Here the men showed the greatest bravery—the coolest and most determined fighting I ever witnessed.

At the flash of the enemy's guns the men would rush madly on them, routing them from behind logs, stumps and trees, shooting them at almost every step. In this fight were about 250 Louisiana and Arkansas troops engaged, and in the fight had become separated from the rest of the command.

I being the senior officer present, the men requested me to take command, which I did; and at once commenced to form a line, with the assistance of

Lieutenants Gentles, Pelican Rifles, Morse, Pelican Rangers No. 1, Hubbs, of McRae's Regiment, but had gotten but few of them in line when we were flanked by a body of infantry on the left. We instantly charged them, driving them back with considerable loss on their side and but little on ours—the above-named officers acting with great bravery and coolness. I particularly noticed the conduct of Lieutenant Henry Gentles. At times I saw him in the front ranks, using his gun with deadly effect upon the enemy, and at other times rallying the men and cheering them on. I then got a flag, and secured a guide—we having become lost in the thicket—and placing the flag in front, formed the men in line and started for the field we had left in the morning.

On our way out we had one slight skirmish with the enemy, picking up all our men who had become broken down in the fight.

When we reached the field, we numbered 500 or 700 men, composed of various regiments engaged in the fight that day.

Here I sent the men to their respective commands, taking the Louisianians who were with me. I joined the remainder of the regiment at the hospital on the road. My men at this time were badly used up—some were unable to go along with the regiment; others went in search of food, and could not get back to the company in the morning.

I never saw men so completely worn out from hunger and fatigue. We slept on our arms that night until 3 o'clock A.M., when we marched to General Price's headquarters on the Telegraph Road.

We were ordered on a hill to the left of the road, and remained there during a heavy cannonade between our batteries and the enemy's.

We were then ordered to march off the field, which we did in good order.

The missing of my company are as follows: Wounded—Frank Cane, severely (not dangerously); missing—M. F. Miller, James Kimball, Julos F. Jus, Charles Wols, John Craig, L. J. Singer and Daniel S. Duval.

I have the honor, Captain, to be your obedient servant,

Q. B. GILMORE,
Captain commanding Shreveport Rangers,
Third La. Vols.

WHO WAS CAPTAIN GILMORE'S
BODY SERVANT?

"Old Jeff" was a great favorite in the regiment. When his young master joined the company to go off to the war, Old Jeff was nearly "beside" himself, especially when he was informed he could go. He was an old campaigner, and it was amusing to listen to his tales, when he and "Ole Massa" fought the

Indians down in Florida. Of course he knew more about war, and how it should be conducted, than any darkey in the regiment. He was a splendid forager, and his mess never suffered for the need of "good things."

We had just eaten breakfast on the morning of the battle of Oak Hills; Jeff was putting away his dishes when the enemy opened fire on our camp. Of course everything was in commotion; the regiment was forming to take its position on that bloody field. The care of the company's (F) baggage devolved on Jeff, and most faithfully did he guard his charge, until the shells came crashing and exploding over the camp. He could not stand that, nor did he understand it. "They did not throw such things in the Indian fights." He forgot his charge, and hastened to discover some place of concealment; he ran and ran until he was completely exhausted; he knew not where to go. He laid down behind a log—a shell exploded near the spot—that was no safe place. He espied Reid's Battery busy at work handling their guns, and thought that would be a good place for protection. After reaching the spot he discovered that it was all but safe. In hunting about he found a place to hide in—glory! Alas! he found one of his fellow-servants stove into the hollow log so firmly, that he was unable to extricate himself. Poor Jeff! for six long weary hours he was running from place to place. Nowhere could he find a spot free from those awful bombs that followed him with such pertinacity. Everything must have an end—the battle closed—Old Jeff found himself safe and sound, and rendered a great deal of assistance to the wounded. He often afterwards remarked, "that if there were any more battles he would stay out of the way of the bombs."

Months rolled away; the army was once again on the eve of another battle, camped on the road near Elk Horn Tavern. On the morning of the battle of that name, while the army was manœuvering, Old Jeff, who had camped about six miles distant, rode up on a spirited horse with breakfast for his mess. He had two chickens nicely fried, about a dozen biscuits, some coffee, and a large coffee-pot strapped to his saddle. He rode into a large open field where the Texas cavalry were drawn up in line, and made inquiry where his command could be found. Scarcely had he spoken, when he was answered by the enemy (who had a masked battery about 300 yards distant) with a salute of four guns. Old Jeff, of course, was terribly frightened. Before the thunder of the guns had died away, General McIntosh ordered the cavalry to charge—the bugles sounded the charge—away they went as only Texans can ride. Where was Old Jeff? He tried his best to charge in the opposite direction; his horse, however, did not relish it, and took it into his head to follow his companions.

It was, indeed, a "grand spectacle" to see Old Jeff gallantly charging a four-gun battery, with an old coffee-pot and two chickens dangling from his saddle. It was nobly done—Old Jeff brought up between two guns—the bat-tery was captured. His blood was up; as soon as he got control of his horse he wheeled him about, put him in full gallop, and never pulled up until he arrived at the place where he camped the night before. He brags to this day of the gal-lant charge that he made. His mess, however, did not relish such gallantry, for they went through that long and tiresome day without eating, and had already been fasting three days previously.

CHAPTER XIX

THE RETREAT

At 9 o'clock, while the battle was still raging in all its fierceness, the order was given to retreat, when thousands of our men, eager to meet the foe, had not fired a shot. The troops were astounded. They left the field of battle, giving vent to their burning thoughts in bitter words and deep curses. *The infantry had not been whipped.* Wherefore the retreat? It is a mystery which has never been satisfactorily explained. Our dead and wounded were left behind, to the care of the enemy. The retreat was an acknowledgment on the part of our leaders of their inability to successfully cope with the foe, and to all intents and purposes we were whipped. During the whole battle General Van Dorn remained with General Price's wing of the army. His presence at the head of McCulloch's Division, to lead and direct the movements of these troops, would have enabled them to regain all the ground which they had lost. The loss of the Louisiana Regiment was 16 killed, 37 wounded, and 60 taken prisoners. The loss of the enemy in this desperately contested battle was computed at upwards of 3,000—800 more than covered the number of killed and wounded of the Confederate forces. The enemy precipitately left Arkansas the day after the battle, not attempting to pursue the Confederates, who were likewise rapidly retreating southward.

A review of the battle shows, perhaps, that more desperate fighting was never done during the whole campaign, than that of Hebert's Brigade. They charged and routed successively three brigades of the enemy; fought three and a half hours, unsupported, against a largely superior force, driving them back over a mile, and only desisted because completely exhausted and worn out. The battery charged and held so long belonged to Siegel's brigade, whose men were all armed with Colt's revolving rifles, every man having an extra cylinder loaded and prepared to replace the discharged one. We killed outright forty-seven of the enemy's cavalry, who charged into the open field, not wounding a man. The Ninth Iowa Regiment lost forty-seven men killed, and two hundred and thirty-seven wounded. Among the killed were four captains. One of the prisoners informed us that, when we first fired on their forces, out of a company sent forward as skirmishers, ten were killed and forty wounded. Such are a few of many facts demonstrating the desperate character of the fighting, and the unerring precision and deadly skill with which the Louisianians used their arms. This regiment emerged from the fight covered with new laurels. The foe could not be convinced that it was the only Louisiana regiment in the army, and frankly acknowledged the desperate valor with which they fought.

From the 8th of March the Confederates, scattered and disorganized, steadily retreated towards Van Buren. Every by-way and high-way, cottage, mansion, and cabin was filled with men seeking something to appease their starving and famished condition. They ate everything that they could obtain— raw corn, potatoes, turnips, etc. If one was fortunate enough to obtain a few morsels of ham or bacon, it was generously divided with his comrades, and ravenously devoured raw. The army reached Van Winkle's mills (where the lumber for winter-quarters was procured) to find the place deserted, and everything left behind. Every living biped and quadruped was immediately killed and eaten. At the door of the house stood a slop-barrel, nearly full of refuse provisions. It was upset, and the men scrambled for the decayed contents like a drove of hogs. From this statement some conception may be formed of the starving condition of the troops. The corn-bins along the road were seized by General Rains' cavalry to feed the stock, sentinels being placed around them to prevent their seizure by other forces. Such was the case at Van Winkle's. One of the captains of the Louisiana Regiment observing this, went among the men and said: "Boys, I am going to have something to eat, if I have to fight the whole d——d army. Who will go with me?" A number volunteering were ordered to get their guns and follow him. He marched the squad to the corn-bin, when the following colloquy took place: "Whose corn is this?" "General Rains'," replied the sentry. "What are you going to do with it?" "Feed the stock." "Well, by G—d," replied the captain, "I have had nothing to eat for four days, and I intend to have some of this corn. Stand aside, and let me pass." The sentry must have seen the ravenous hunger shining from the captain's glittering eyes, as well as known the desperation evinced by his manner and tone of voice. He permitted the captain to help himself, which he did, turning to the men and saying, "Here, boys, help yourselves. I have got my rations." The men did so, and quietly returned to their camping-place. One evening, Hart's Battery, with several of the Louisianians, halted on the roadside near a house and encamped. They were wild with hunger. Foraging parties went out to see what could be found that was eatable. They brought back a quarter of a yearling, some turnips and cabbage, piece of bacon, a turkey and a goose. Their success was the source of great rejoicing. The difficulty occurred to them, How could they cook these provisions without utensils? "Nil desperandum," they immediately instituted a search, resulting in the discovery of one of those large iron kettles so common in the country, used to boil clothes in on washing-days. Without troubling themselves with cleaning it, they carried it to camp, set it on stones, and built a huge fire under it, first nearly filling it with water. Into this was put beef, turkey, goose, bacon, turnips, and cabbage, all cut into small pieces. The men then each made a wooden spoon. The pot boiled, bubbled, and sputtered with its heterogeneous mass of meat and vegetables, while the men stood around it with eager gaze, watching the process of cooking. It was permitted to become thoroughly done, and when the signal was given, the scalding food was "bolted" down as only starving men can eat. Giving the experience of one of that party, we can bear testimony that it was considered one of the most delicious repasts ever eaten—sweeter, far, than the divine ambrosial of the immortal gods!

When the battle was lost, the train, left near the vicinity of Camp McCulloch, immediately returned by the same route which we advanced on. Hence the lack of provisions. It was well guarded by our cavalry, who repulsed several attempts of the enemy to capture it. To add to the horrors of the retreating army, tremendous rain-storms occurred, making Frog Bayou, along which the road ran and frequently crossed, a deep stream, which the men swam and waded innumerable times, many losing their guns in it, and sometimes almost their lives. The regiment arrived at Van Buren in straggling squads, tired, hatless, barefooted, hungry, dirty, and ragged. They had been in rain-storms, climbed steep mountains along narrow and rugged foot-paths, waded deep and cold mountain streams, starved, slept without tents or blankets on the wet and frosty ground; in fact, endured untold hardships and horrors. The retreat was more disastrous than a dozen battles. The Louisiana Regiment had only two hundred and seventy men in a body on the retreat; other regiments in the same proportion. Our physicians, wounded, and nurses were taken prisoners, and the ambulances sent for the wounded seized. The army reached Van Buren terribly demoralized, bringing with them five hundred Federals and eight pieces of artillery captured. When the army began its retreat Captain Goode, of the First Texas Battery, was not apprised of the movement, being in charge of a large number of guns. When he discovered the fact it was too late to follow the army. He immediately started for Missouri, with the long train of guns following him.

After traveling some distance, he left the main road, turning eastward towards White River. Down this stream he proceeded, following rough by-roads, reaching Van Buren in safety. Had the enemy been apprised of his retreat, unprotected as he was, they would have captured all these guns. As it was, Captain Goode's persevering energy and success in saving them immortalized his name in the army. On the 14th of March a flag of truce was sent to the enemy with two lieutenant-colonels, to be exchanged for Colonel Hebert and Major Tunnard. On the evening of March 24 these officers, accompanied by Captain Viglini, arrived at Fort Smith, where the army was encamped. Their return was greeted with heartfelt demonstrations of joy by all the regiment, indicative alike of the feelings of the officers and men, as well as the high estimation in which they were held. They all looked sadly debilitated and worn out, having been much exposed, as well as scantily fed during their stay among the enemy, who, like the Confederates, were short of provisions.

BATTLE OF ELK HORN

Official Report of General Earl Van Dorn.

HEADQUARTERS TRANS-MISS. DISTRICT, ⎱
JACKSONPORT, ARK., *March* 27, 1862. ⎰

COLONEL,—I have the honor to report that, while at Pocahontas, I received dispatches on the 22d February informing me that General Price had rapidly fallen back from Springfield before a superior force of the enemy, and was endeavoring to form a junction with the division of General McCulloch in Baston Mountain.

For reasons which seemed to me imperative, I resolved to go in person and take command of the combined forces of Price and McCulloch. I reached their headquarters on the 3d of March, and being satisfied that the enemy, who had halted on Sugar Creek, was only waiting large reinforcements before he would advance, I resolved to attack him at once. Accordingly I sent for General Pike to join me with the forces under his command, and on the morning of the 4th of March moved with the divisions of Price and McCulloch by way of Fayetteville and Bentonville to attack the enemy's main camp on Sugar Creek.

On the 6th we left Elm Spring for Bentonville, and from prisoners captured by our scouting parties on the 5th, I became convinced that, up to that time, no suspicions were entertained of our advance, and that there were strong hopes of our effecting a complete surprise and attacking the enemy before the large detachments encamped at the various points in the surrounding country could rejoin the main body. I therefore endeavored to reach Bentonville, eleven miles distant, by a rapid march; but the troops moved so very slowly that it was 11 A.M. before the head of the leading division (Price's) reached the village, and we had the mortification of seeing Siegel's Division, 7,000 strong, leaving it as we entered. Had we been one hour sooner we should have cut him off with his whole force, and certainly have beaten the enemy the next day.

We followed him, our advance skirmishing with his rear-guard, which was admirably handled, until we had gained a point on Sugar Creek, about seven miles beyond Bentonville, and within one or two miles of the strongly-intrenched camp of the enemy.

In conference with Generals McCulloch and McIntosh, who had accurate knowledge of this locality, I had ascertained that, by making a detour of eight miles, I could reach the Telegraph Road, leading from Springfield to Fayetteville, and be immediately in rear of the enemy and his intrenchments.

I had resolved to adopt this route, and therefore halted the head of the column near the point where the road by which I had proposed to move diverges, threw out my pickets, and bivouacked as if for the night. But soon after dark I marched again, with Price's Division in advance, and taking the road by which I hoped, before daylight, to gain the rear of the enemy. Some obstructions which he had hastily thrown in our way so impeded our march that we did not gain the Telegraph Road until nearly 10 A.M. of the 7th. From prisoners with forage-wagons, whom our cavalry pickets brought in, we were assured that we were not expected in that quarter, and that the promise was fair for a complete surprise.

I at once made dispositions for attack, and directing General Price to move forward cautiously, soon drew the fire of a few skirmishers, who were rapidly reinforced, so that before 11 o'clock we were fairly engaged, the enemy holding very good positions, and maintaining a heavy fire of artillery and small-arms upon the constantly advancing columns which were being pressed upon him.

I had directed General McCulloch to attack with his forces the enemy's left, and before 10 o'clock it was evident that, if his division could advance or even maintain its ground, I could at once throw forward Price's left, advance his whole line and end the battle. I sent him a dispatch to this effect, but it was never received by him. Before it was penned his brave spirit had winged its flight, and one of the most gallant leaders of the Confederacy had fought his last battle.

About 3 P.M. I received by aids-de-camp the information that Generals McCulloch and McIntosh and Colonel Hebert (incorrect) were killed, and that the division was without any head. I nevertheless pressed forward with the attack, and at sunset the enemy was flying before our victorious troops at every point in our front, and when night fell we had driven him entirely from the field of battle. Our troops slept upon their arms nearly a mile beyond the point where he made his last stand, and my headquarters for the night were at the Elk Horn Tavern. We had taken during the day seven cannon and about two hundred prisoners.

In the course of the night I ascertained that the ammunition was almost exhausted, and that the officer in charge of the ordnance supplies could not find his wagons, which, with the subsistence train, had been sent to Bentonville. Most of the troops had been without any food since the morning of the 6th, and the artillery horses were beaten out. It was therefore with no little anxiety that I awaited the dawn of day. When it came, it revealed the enemy in a new and strong position, offering battle.

I made my dispositions at once to accept the gage, and by 7 o'clock the cannonading was as heavy as that of the previous day. On the side of the enemy the fire was much better sustained; for being freed from the attack of my right wing, he could now concentrate his whole artillery. Finding that my right wing was much disorganized, and that the batteries, one after another, were retiring from the field, with every shot expended, I resolved to withdraw the army, and at once placed the ambulances, with all of the wounded they could bear, upon the Huntsville road, and a portion of McCulloch's division which had joined me during the night, in position to follow—while I so disposed of my remaining forces as best to deceive the enemy as to my intention, and to hold him in check while executing it.

About 10 o'clock I gave the order for the column to march, and soon afterwards for the troops engaged to fall back and cover the rear of the army. This was done very steadily; no attempt was made by the enemy to follow us, and we encamped, about 3 o'clock P.M., about ten miles from the field of battle. Some demonstrations were made by his cavalry upon my baggage trains and the batteries of artillery, which returned by different routes from that taken by the army; but they were instantly checked, and, thanks to the skill and courage of Colonel Stone and Major Wade, all the baggage and artillery joined the army in safety.

So far as I can ascertain, our losses amounted to six hundred killed and wounded and two hundred prisoners and one cannon, which, having become disabled, I ordered to be thrown into a ravine.

The best information I can procure of the enemy's loss places his killed at more than 700, with at least an equal number wounded. We captured about 300 prisoners, so that his total loss is nearly 2,000. We brought away four cannon and ten baggage-wagons, and we burnt upon the field three cannon taken by McIntosh in his brilliant charge. The horses having been killed, these guns could not be brought away.

The force with which I went into action was less than 14,000 men; that of the enemy variously estimated at from 17,000 to 24,000.

During the whole of this engagement I was with the Missouri Division under Price, and I have never seen better fighters than those Missouri troops, or more gallant leaders than General Price and his officers. From the first to the last shot they continually pushed on, and never yielded an inch they had won; and when at last they received the order to fall back, they retired steadily and with cheers. General Price received a severe wound early in the action; but would neither retire from the field nor cease to expose himself to danger. No successes can repair the loss of the gallant dead who fell upon this well-fought field. McCulloch was the first to fall. I had found him, in the frequent conferences I had with him, a sagacious, prudent counselor, and a bolder soldier never died for his country.

McIntosh had been very distinguished all through the operations which had taken place in this region; and during my advance from Baston Mountain I placed him in command of the cavalry brigade and in charge of the pickets. He was alert, daring, and devoted to his duty. His kindness of disposition, with his reckless bravery, had attached the troops strongly to him; so that, after McCulloch fell, had he remained to lead them, all would have been well with my right wing; but after leading a brilliant charge of cavalry and carrying the enemy's battery, he rushed into the thick of the fight again at the head of his old regiment and was shot through the heart. The value of these two officers was but proven by the effect of their fall upon the troops. So long as brave deeds are admired by our country, the names of McCulloch and McIntosh will be remembered and loved.

General Slack, after gallantly maintaining a continued and successful attack, was shot through the body; but I hope his distinguished services will be restored to his country. A noble boy, Churchill Clark, commanding a battery of artillery, and during the fierce actions of the 7th and 8th, was conspicuous for the daring and skill which he exhibited. He fell at the very close of the action. Colonel Rivers fell mortally wounded about the same time, and was a great loss to us. On a field where were many gallant gentlemen, I remember him as one of the most energetic and devoted of them all.

To Colonel Henry Little my especial thanks are due for the coolness, skill and devotion with which for two days he and his gallant brigade bore the brunt of the battle. Colonel Burbridge, Colonel Rosser, Colonel Gates, Major Lawther, Major Wade, Captain McDonald, and Captain Shaumberg, are some of those who attracted my special attention by their distinguished conduct.

In McCulloch's Division, the Louisiana Regiment, under Colonel Louis Hebert, and the Arkansas Regiment, under Colonel McRae, are especially mentioned for their good conduct. Major Montgomery, Captain Bradfute, Lieutenants Lomax, Kimmel, Dillon, and Frank Armstrong, A. A. G., were ever active and soldierly. After their services were no longer required with their own division, they joined my staff, and I am much indebted to them for the efficient aid they gave me during the engagement of the 8th. They are meritorious officers, whose value is lost to the service by their not receiving rank more accordant with their merit and experience than that they now hold. Being without my proper staff, I was much gratified by the offer of Colonel Shands and Captain Barret, of the Missouri Army, of their services as aids. They were of very great assistance to me by the courage and intelligence with which they bore my orders; also Colonel Lewis, of Missouri.

None of the gentlemen of my personal staff, with the exception of Colonel Maury, A. A. G., and Lieutenant C. Sullivan, my aid-de-camp, accompanied me from Jacksonport, the others having left on special duty. Colonel Maury was of invaluable service to me, both in preparing for and during the battle. There, as on other battle-fields where I have served with him, he proved to be a zealous patriot and true soldier. Cool and calm under all circumstances, he was always ready either with his sword or his pen. His services and Lieutenant Sullivan's are distinguished; the latter had his horse killed under him while leading a charge, the order for which he had just delivered.

You will perceive, Colonel, from this report, that although I did not capture, as I hoped, or destroy the enemy's army in Western Arkansas, I have inflicted upon it a heavy blow and compelled him to fall back into Missouri; this he did about the 16th inst. For further details concerning the action, and for more particular notices of the troops engaged, I refer you to the reports of the subordinate officers which accompany this report.

Very respectfully, sir, your obedient servant,

EARL VAN DORN, *Major-General.*

Col. W. W. Mackall, A. A. G.

BRIGADIER-GENERAL BEN M'CULLOCH

General Ben McCulloch arrived in Texas from his native State, Tennessee, just in time to command a portion of the artillery on the plains of San Jacinto, April 21st, 1836, over thirty years ago. He was then barely twenty-one years of age, but won general admiration from that band of heroes. That was the opening of his military career. For the ten succeeding years he resided upon the exposed Indian frontier of the infant republic, and so fully was his time give to the Indian wars that he followed no other business. His time passed in a succession of hardships and dangers such as few men have seen, in which he displayed undaunted courage, indomitable will, and the highest characteristics of the scout, the captain, the strategist, and iron-nerved fighter. He was never outwitted or defeated by the wily savage, which is saying a great deal. When the Mexican war broke out, McCulloch, refusing the command of a regiment, took the field as captain of General Taylor's spy company. In that capacity his services were of the most dangerous and important character; and we have General Taylor's authority for saying he performed every act well and thoroughly. He succeeded in every enterprise, and at Monterey gained unfading laurels, especially in storming the Bishop's Palace, where his friend Gillespie fell. He continued in the same arduous service until the close of the war, always enjoying the highest confidence of the veteran General, who intrusted enterprises to him that he would commit to no one else. McCulloch was the first to notify Taylor of the approach of Santa Anna with five times his number, and to advise him to fall back from Encarnacion to the stronger position at Buena Vista, in all of which none can deny he saved our army from surprise and consequent destruction. On that bloody field he received the public and official thanks of General Taylor for his heroic conduct and valuable services.

General McCulloch served in the Texan Congress of 1839, and the Legislature of 1845, the only political positions that he ever held. In 1846, when war was upon us, and he in Mexico, he was unanimously elected Major-General of all Western Texas. In 1849 he went to California, and was at once elected Sheriff of Sacramento. For the last eight years prior to secession he was United States Marshal for Texas, and in that time was sent as Commissioner to Utah, and next to Arizona. He was twice offered the governorship of territories, and was appointed Major of U.S. Cavalry, all of which he declined.

The moment Lincoln's election became known, McCulloch identified himself with Texas as an unconditional secessionist, and repaired to Texas to take part in any movement that might grow out of the presence of over 3,000 U.S. troops in that State. He was unanimously selected by the Committee of Public Safety to raise the men necessary to compel the surrender of San Antonio, with its arsenal and the neighboring forts, four or five in number.

Within four days he had traveled one hundred and fifty miles, and stood before San Antonio with eight hundred armed men, his old comrades and neighbors. His mission succeeded. Texas looked to him with confidence as one of her strong pillars in case of war. She sent him abroad to procure arms; but before he had fully succeeded the President appointed him Brigadier-General and assigned him to command of the Indian Territory, without men, money, arms, or munitions.

He reached Fort Smith late in May, his only companions being Major Montgomery and Colonel McIntosh. He immediately proceeded with his customary energy to organize an army, and, above all, secure the co-operation of the Indian tribes. Thus in June, 1861, he was on a mission among the Indians, resulting in laying the foundation of their final adherence to the Confederate cause. He next turns up the hero of the brilliant exploit at Neosho, Mo. Next we find him organizing that gallant little brigade composed of Arkansians, who so gallantly distinguished themselves at the battle of Oak Hills.

Disrobed of the Arkansas troops after this battle, and left with three or four reduced regiments, he took position at Camp Jackson, in order to recruit and drill an army, collect supplies and munitions, and endeavor to prepare for effective operations against the enemy. It was at this period that letter-writers, and great minds, who never saw an army, attacked his character as a General, knowing more about his resources and strength—when, where, and how he ought to move—all about his duties and responsibilities, than himself. Still he heeded not the clamor raised against him. Sickness ravaged his band to an astonishing degree (the Third Louisiana was a fair specimen of the conditon of the men at that period); recruits, for two months, did not come at all; the Arkansas River was very low; the Indians, in part, were surly and doubtful; the Jayhawkers of Kansas were tampering with them and menacing Northwestern Arkansas, and finally the splendid regiments that served to give him a goodly army arrived too late for a fall campaign.

The army started on an expedition against Kansas, but was turned back by the advance of the Federals under Fremont pursuing the forces under General Price. His plans were changed to meet this emergency, and his forces co-operated with those of General Price to check Fremont's advance. How assiduously General McCulloch labored to annoy the enemy it is needless to state. The blockaded roads, the expeditions of the cavalry, led by himself, attest his ceaseless activity, untiring energy, and sleepless vigilance. After Fremont's retreat, General McCulloch went to Richmond on a mission connected with his department.

While absent on this trip, an address, written by J. W. Tucker, in behalf of the Missourians, "To the people of the Confederate States," dated Springfield, Mo., December 24, 1861, was published in the *Arkansian,* a Fayetteville (Ark.) paper. In that address occurred the following passage: "With the exception of the battle of Springfield, not a sword has been drawn for the release of Missouri save by her own sons. At that memorable battle (Oak Hills) the Confederate commander was asked for the assistance of three regiments to pursue a defeated and disorganized foe, where 7,000 men and $1,000,000 worth of property were within our reach; but General Price asked in vain. So his requests were responded to when he went to fight the battles of Dry Wood and Lexington. Not aided, not supplied with a single percussion-cap, for the want of which latter article he was compelled to fall back two hundred miles with an army of 20,000 men. During this trying period, within which the State could have been disenthralled, our Confederate allies have maintained their camp on our Southern border in inglorious inactivity, not even protecting Missouri from Kansas Jayhawkers. We know these allied troops are as brave men as ever went to battle, and that they chafed like a caged lion to join the Missourians in their well-sustained resistance; but these troops had no orders to move. Can this be explained? There was no enemy to fight in Arkansas, and the army of Missouri was in every action and movement guarding the gates of Arkansas, Louisiana, and Texas."

To this attack on his motives, plans and movements, General McCulloch published the following reply in the Richmond *Whig:*

GENERAL M'CULLOCH'S REPLY

To the Editor of the Richmond Whig:

In your issue of yesterday there is a communication signed "J. W. Tucker," in answer to which I think proper to make the following reply, which you will please give a place in your paper:

Your correspondent says: "With the exception of the battle of Springfield not a sword has been drawn for the release of Missouri except by her own sons." On the 4th of July General Pearce, of Arkansas, and myself, with all the forces we could command, marched to aid the Governor of the State in cutting his way through his enemies, capturing over 100 of the enemy at Neosho, a point where we expected to attack Siegel with his whole command.

So much for his first assertion. He further says, speaking of the battle of Oak Hills: "The Confederate Commander was asked for the assistance of three regiments to pursue a defeated and disorganized foe, when 7,000 men and over $1,000,000 worth of property were within our reach; but General Price asked in vain."

Immediately after the battle was over, and, in truth, before all my forces had returned from the pursuit of the enemy, orders were issued for the wounded to be brought from the battle-field, the dead to be buried, and the army to be ready to march after the enemy that night. We did not march for the want of ammunition. Several of my officers informed me (when they heard the order) that some of their men had fired their last cartridge at the enemy, as we had only twenty-five rounds to the man before the battle began, and no more within hundreds of miles. After a conference with General Price, it was thought best to "let well enough alone." As to being asked for three regiments, I have no recollection of any such request.

So much for the second assertion.

Now for his third assertion, in which he wishes to convey the idea that I had not, nor would not aid Missouri with a man, a gun, or a percussion-cap, and that I would not even protect Missouri against the Arkansas Jayhawkers. At the time General Pearce, of Arkansas, and myself first entered Missouri on the 4th of July, we loaned General Price some six hundred and fifteen muskets. When our forces formed a junction at Cassville, Colonel Hebert, of Louisiana, at my request, loaned a Missouri officer about one hundred muskets. I have several times since given the Missourians the last cap I could spare from my own command. Let those officers say how many of their muskets were returned. General Pearce, I learned, recovered ten, while Colonel Hebert was only able to get a portion of those he loaned. Besides, it is a well-known fact that the arms of our dead and wounded were taken from the battle-field; nor did we get any of the small-arms left by the enemy.

As to the Kansas Jayhawkers and our inglorious idleness! My mounted men gave protection to the whole country on the borders of Missouri for one hundred miles north of the Arkansas line from immediately after the battle of Oak Hills until in October, when General Price retreated from Lexington to that section of the State.

So much for these charges.

It will be remembered that I was assigned to the command of the Indian Territory, with orders to defend it from invasion from any quarter; consequently, my participation in the battle at Oak Hills was upon my own responsibility, with a reliance of being sustained by my own Government.

As to my men chafing like a caged lion to join the Missourians, I must say this is new to me. It might be supposed that the Louisiana Regiment was exceedingly anxious to march, exposed to the sun and rain, with men covered with ninety-five tents taken from themselves by order of a Missouri general. These tents had the extra clothing of the men rolled in them, and were stored with a merchant in Cassville at the time we marched upon Springfield, and were taken out of his possession by order of Brigadier-General Parsons, conveyed on the same road with that regiment, and not a word of them or their contents mentioned to me afterwards by any Missourian.

If this was not enough to make the gallant Louisiana Regiment chafe like a caged lion to go with General Price, they only had to refer to his official report of the battle of Oak Hills to see how completely they had been deprived of the glory of taking Colonel Siegel's battery, which they did at the point of the bayonet.

As to the troops from Arkansas, they were likely to "chafe like a caged lion" because they were not permitted to go with their country rifles and shot guns, and see how they handled the muskets they borrowed and would not return.

Then there are the Texans! They "chafed like a caged lion" because they could not have the opportunity to capture another flag and piece of artillery to be appropriated by the Missourians, whilst they (the Texans) were continuing to pursue the enemy.

Perhaps all these gallant men were likely to chafe like a caged lion because they could not march with men who took possession of every mill and every blacksmith-shop in the surrounding country, and at the same time placed a guard over every store in Springfield, taking what they contained and applying it to their own use; thus depriving these men of the chance of obtaining a change of linen, a pound of breadstuffs, or a horse shod until after their wants were supplied.

I greatly fear the effort of J. W. Tucker to disparage the gallant soldiers of Arkansas, Louisiana, and Texas, and to deprive them of their share of the glory of the battle of Oak Hills, will add little to the good feeling which every true patriot should desire to see prevail among the soldiers of the different States at this time.

I have not thought proper, heretofore, to notice any of the misrepresentations going the rounds of the newspapers. First, because they had no responsible endorser, and secondly, because I hoped, for the sake of a common cause, that there should be no war of words among ourselves, when the enemy were to be met with the sword.

This hope has failed, and I am compelled to notice this publication lest my silence be construed as an admission of the truth of Mr. Tucker's statements— it being well known that I was in Richmond at the time his communication was published.

In conclusion, permit me to warn my countrymen, and to beg of them, not to put too much reliance in sensation articles written and published for effect. Up to the present time the country knows nothing of what has been done in Missouri.

I have the honor to be your obedient servant,

Richmond, January 17th, 1862.   BEN MCCULLOCH.

"General McCulloch," says a correspondent, writing from Camp Jackson, Arkansas, September 30th, 1861, "has been at his post all the time. He is as vigilant as a tiger. Every day at some time a man, dressed in dark clothes, wearing a brown hat, with thin flowing locks, may be seen galloping across the prairie. One evening last week, as we were out on regimental (Third Louisiana) drill, just before sun-down, a vast multitude of spectators belonging to the various companies, battalions, etc., having come out, a horseman was seen approaching at a fast gallop. Every person knew him. It was General McCulloch. He rode up to the left wing and spoke kindly and familiarly to Captain Viglini, and then said 'Good evening,' politely and cheerfully, to all. Lieutenant-Colonel

Hyams being busy making some remarks, the General rode up to the Adjutant, and remarked, 'Why are you not on duty, are you sick?' 'Yes,' was the reply. After conversing a few moments he said, 'I must go and see the Colonel.' The Colonel by this time had the line at a shoulder arms. As the General passed, 'present arms!' was the command. The General of course acknowledged it in his own unique and immortal style. Perhaps the character of none of our public men is so much misunderstood as that of General McCulloch. He is a Tennesseean by birth and Texan by adoption. He is a border man, an Indian fighter, and a ranger. Is this all? I had fancied him a perfect devil, a backwoodsman, a ruffian, an unpolished desperado.

"General McCulloch is a medium-sized man; perhaps he might be called a small man, with brown hair and whiskers. He doubtless has been handsome, and is still good-looking for a man of his age.

"A nice boot, well fitted to his foot; close, trim-made clothes, and, as before mentioned, a brown hat, neither high nor low, but of the planter style, with very clean, nice vest, short, sleek boots, gloves, and spurs, are the characteristics of his dress. His person is very neat and pleasant, slim, thin, and a small roundness of shoulders. He is as fine a horseman as ever sat in saddle. Age has left its mark on his countenance. His face is weather-beaten and brown from exposure; numerous crow-feet creep out from his somewhat sunken eyes. I think he would weigh about one hundred and forty pounds, and I would take him to be fifty years old, judging from his looks; and he is all that he has ever been represented—a bold, graceful rider, a desperate fighter, a reckless charger, a border man, and an Indian fighter of the highest type. Had he lived in the days of chivalry, he would have been a knight of the most superior class. More than this, General Ben McCulloch is a great man. Mentally he is of the sanguine-bilious temperment—a perfectly positive man. There is no half-way ground about him, no medium decision, no compromise, no guessing. It is, or it is not, with him. It can or it cannot be; and if the world should decide against him, or all the officers in his Division, I believe his own conscientiousness would prompt him to say, as would Jackson, 'I'll take the responsibility!' One of the strongest features in his mind is its precision, its clearness. Individuality is strongly marked. He is not a talkative man, and consequently not a very sociable one. He seems to be separate, self-existant, independent, original. I do not think any one ever knows his plans. He is an indefatigable student and thinker, and never loses any time. Of whatever subject his mind is directed to, he has very exalted ideas. He seems desirous of bringing his troops to the very highest point of discipline and military power. He detests stragglers and loafers. He loves order and decency. The first time the command was ever called out in line of battle at Crane Creek, about August 1st, as we were formed, the "long roll" beating vigorously, and our backs being toward a ravine, down which the enemy's cannon balls were expected, this command passed down the line, viz.: 'Steady, men, General McCulloch is loading the cannon himself.' On the next day General Rains attached the enemy, and as we were formed on a hillside to protect our battery, vast numbers of stragglers came in, thundering past us. Finally, Captain McIntosh, with one hundred and fifty scouts, came in, endeavoring to draw the enemy after them and to us on the hillside. It seemed as if the enemy would arrive immediately, but General McCulloch came in finally with two companies, the very last man. As he passed us he said, 'The enemy have stopped to take dinner, come on, boys, we will go and take dinner too.' He has a very fine rifle which he always carries. This is his only weapon or soldierly insignia. On the morning we left Crane Creek General McCulloch exhibited the greatest coolness. In person he would go three miles over the prairie with his staff in search of the enemy."

Such is a most perfect pen sketch by a Missourian (J. H. Robertson), of McCulloch as Confederate leader of the Western Army in 1861. It was his individuality, reliance on his own personal observations, regardless of extraneous assistance, which led him to needlessly expose himself at Elk Horn. Forbidding his staff to follow him, he departed to make personal observations and reconnoitre the enemy's position, ere ordering the mass of his troops into battle. Already the Louisianians were desperately engaged, and their fierce volleys and wild cheers told that they were accomplishing the work cut out for them. But McCulloch came not back. He was shot through the heart by a concealed marksman of the enemy, finally a victim to his fearless temerity. As a leader, McCulloch was idolized by his troops, and almost worshipped by the Louisianians, and his death was bitterly lamented as only lion-hearted, brave men can lament over the fall of an idolized chieftain. General McCulloch's body was conveyed to Little Rock and there interred, surrounded by a vast concourse of citizens and soldiers. Undoubtedly his death, so quickly followed by that of General McIntosh, occasioned the loss of the battle, as no more of his division were ordered to the support of those few regiments who fought so desperately and successfully on that blood-stained field.

Multiplied words can add nothing to his fame. It is as eternal as the granite hills. His body moulders in a soldier's grave. The Emerald sward, and doubtless sweet flowers, planted there by loving hands, cover his honored remains. Of all the martyr graves that dot Southern hill-sides and valleys, none contain the remains of a nobler soul, a more fearless and chivalric spirit, a more efficient commander, a more idolized chieftain, than that which holds the mortal portion of Brigadier-General Ben McCulloch.

BRIGADIER-GENERAL M'INTOSH

General James McIntosh was a native of Virginia. He graduated at West Point, and was Colonel in the United States service at the commencement of the war, commanding a regiment of cavalry on the Western frontier, at Fort Smith, when hostilities first began. With the secession of Virginia, and that chivalrous spirit worthy of his native State, he linked his fortunes to those of the Confederacy. He soon raised a fine regiment of cavalry in Arkansas, and joined McCulloch's little army; was appointed Adjutant-General of McCulloch's Brigade, and eventually received a commission as Brigadier-General of Cavalry a short period previous to the battle of Elk Horn. At the battle of Oak Hills he first met his old regiment. So much had he become endeared to this body of regulars that nearly a whole company deserted and linked their fortunes to the Confederate cause, becoming General McCulloch's body-guard—a company of stalwart, efficient and brave men. General McIntosh was a fearless rider, a reckless fighter, a dashing horseman. He was beloved by the whole army. In his death the Confederates lost one of their most gallant officers. The records written of him in this work are true criterions wherewith to judge his character and efficiency. His gallant charge at the head of his brigade at Elk Horn was one of the most brilliant incidents of the war. General McIntosh was a medium-sized man, with keen, black eyes, raven hair and whiskers. Without doubt, he was descended from Indian stock. Many claimed that he was a Cherokee by birth—an erroneous supposition. In his death the Confederate States lost an officer who would have made a brilliant record.

CHAPTER XX

THE MARCH EASTWARD

AFTER a short stay at Van Buren, when the different commands had become reorganized and recuperated somewhat from their exhaustion, the regiment left for Fort Smith. From this point they departed eastward in the latter part of March, their destination being Little Rock. On the march, Lieutenant F. R. Brunot, of Company K, died, and received a soldier's burial amid the wilds of Arkansas. Frank, generous to a fault, a lively companion and brave soldier, his loss was severely felt, especially by the members of the company to which he belonged. A lawyer by profession, he possessed talents of no ordinary character. Lieutenant O. J. Wells appointed A. S. C. of Regiment, March 21, 1862. The whole army was now on the move, concentrating toward the Mississippi Valley. Fort Smith and our Western border was being abandoned. To many this seemed an uncalled-for movement, and complaints loud and bitter were uttered. The movement was easily and satisfactorily explained. There was, then, no danger to be apprehended from an invading army. Why? Simply because Southwestern Missouri and Northwestern Arkansas were a desolate waste, having been stripped of nearly everything calculated to supply an army. Even with a friendly country in the rear, it was found impossible to supply the Confederate army with the necessary means of subsistence. Hence, it was argued, it would be impossible for the enemy to subsist an army so far removed from their base of operations as they would be by invading Arkansas, among a people too hostile to them, with destruction constantly threatening, not only their supply-trains, but also their pickets and foraging parties. The enemy were well aware of these facts, and hence moved rapidly northward after the battle of Elk Horn. They were nearly starved out while in the State, both before and after the battle.

Everything at this time indicated a terrible and desperate contest for the possession of the Mississippi Valley, and troops from both sides were rapidly concentrating for the fearful struggle. The regiment was now attached to the Second Brigade of General Price's army, under command of Colonel Hebert, who was reported as having received a commission as brigadier-general. Assuredly no officer was more worthy of such distinction than the brave and skillful Colonel of the Third Regiment.

The sick-list of the regiment was very large—the result of late hardships. They had, however, comfortable hospitals both for the sick and wounded at Little Rock, whose patriotic ladies were untiring in their endeavors to ameliorate the sufferings of the brave soldiers thus brought to their beautiful little city.

It is a mournful spectacle to see so many once strong and robust men wasting away 'neath the ravages of disease, far from home and friends, uncared for save by a few rough comrades. No soft hand soothes the fevered brow; no loving face bends over the attenuated features as the angel of death sets his seal there. The soldier can gaze unmoved on the fearful scenes of a battle-field; tread uncaringly over the dead and dying; remain untouched by the spectacle of mangled limbs and ghastly wounds; but the sight of a soldier dying from disease, with an accompanying thought of home and the loved ones there, will unnerve the stoutest heart. There will ever remain the remembrance of a scene witnessed on the Arkansas River.

A steamer on a bar fast aground, the ruddy glare of a pine-torch glittering, glistening, and dancing on the eddying stream, united with the hoarse whisper of the steam-engine mingling with the voices of men and the rattle of the capstan as the huge spar was made to perform its work. Silently two coffins were lowered into a yawl, followed by three or four soldiers. We watched it recede into the darkness. Soon a lantern's feeble rays, like the firefly's transient light, appeared on the shore, then vanished in the gloom and darkness of night.

Not long was it ere two rough boxes were lowered into new-made graves and fresh mounds of earth marked the spot where, on the banks of the lonely river, reposed two of the sons of liberty. These humble graves of patriots, buried in an unmarked spot, are still remembered.

> "By fairy hands their knell is rung;
> By forms unseen their dirge is sung;
> Their honor comes—a pilgrim gray—
> To bless the turf that wraps their clay.
> And Freedom shall awhile repair
> To dwell, a weeping, hermit there."

The regiment left Camp Poteau, Ark., on the 28th of April. A long, weary march was before them, notwithstanding their recent terrible sufferings and exhaustion. Day by day they toiled through the swamps. Oftentimes the wagons would not arrive. Heavy storms constantly arose; there were no tents or shelter; the mud was knee-deep; the streams swollen—often waded. Roads were repaired and bridges built; then they were water-bound. It seemed as if all the tortures and sufferings of years were being poured out in one huge vial of wrath upon these heroic spirits.

On the 13th most of the First Brigade arrived near the forks of Citron Creek, some distance above Little Rock. Here McDonald's celebrated Missouri battery was attached to the Third Louisiana. The regiment reached Little Rock on the 16th and were warmly welcomed. With five days' rations cooked, the regiment left Little Rock for Beauregard's army at Corinth, on board the steamers *Louisville* and *Kentucky*. The ladies of Little Rock gathered on the banks of the river, and there was the flutter of innumerable handkerchiefs as the boats steamed away down the stream. The men were in high spirits over the change in their mode of traveling.

Major Tunnard, on account of bodily infirmities resulting from the horrors and hardships encountered in Arkansas, obtained a furlough at Little Rock. Thus the regiment was left in command of a senior captain. Down the river—out once more upon the broad Mississippi—how the heart went out in warm throbs towards the loved ones; how the spirit yearned for a journey down the stream. But no! Up the river the boats proceeded, and the regiment was disembarked at Memphis on the 27th, and proceeded to encamp in the upper portion of the city, immediately on the river bank.

Reported to General Van Dorn.

The discipline enforced among the men here was very rigid. Dress parade twice daily, and roll-call five times, much to the annoyance of the troops. Memphis was alive with forces hastening towards Corinth, Miss., the threatened point of attack. Against Fort Pillow above, and Forts Jackson and St. Philip below, powerful fleets were in operation, and the dark gloom of disaster hung like a funeral-pall over the land.

On the 30th of April the regiment once more was on the move. They were in splendid spirits, and marched through the streets of Memphis with firm and regular tread. They attracted universal attention, and received a perfect ovation—the streets being crowded with men and fair ladies, who greeted them most enthusiastically. On their way to the depot of the Mississippi and Ohio Railroad they passed a seminary where a bevy of handsome young ladies had congregated—a rare bouquet of nature's most beautiful flowers. There was the fluttering of innumerable handkerchiefs, and each company returned the greeting in loud cheers as they passed this galaxy of beauty. Several of the ladies gave the men their delicate little cambric handkerchiefs as souveniers.

Left Memphis in company with five other trains, all loaded with troops, and reached Corinth on the first of May. The country around this place was low and marshy, the water impure and unhealthy.

CHAPTER XXI

EVENTS AT CORINTH

THE regiment now belonged to General G. T. Beauregard's Army of the West. A tremendous army was congregated here. Entrenchments thrown up on all sides, protected by heavy abattis of felled timber, and frowning with artillery of every description and calibre. Skirmishing with the enemy was a daily occurrence; but the Confederates felt hopeful and confident of success when the issue should be made.

On the 3d our pickets were driven in, and on the morning of Sunday, the 4th, the regiment left camp very early and proceeded to the intrenchments, where they remained until the afternoon, in a heavy rain, drenching all to the skin. The whole army was in motion this day, but nothing important transpired. The men were kept in a state of feverish excitement and anxious expectation, confronting, as they were, a powerful force of the foe, with whom we were daily skirmishing, and being under orders to move at a moment's notice.

On the 6th, news reached the army of the fall of New Orleans. It was astounding intelligence to the army, and caused intense excitement. Orders were issued for a reorganization of the regiment, by the election of field and company officers, as our term of service was about expiring. For many days the men had been discussing the question of their discharge, looking joyfully forward to a reunion with loved ones at home, and forming plans for the future. But they were in the power of strong military authority, and could not leave the army without being immediately seized and forced to return under the late Conscript Act of Congress. The excitement and dissatisfaction was intense. General Price issued an order promising furloughs to the regiment if victorious in the approaching battle, and closing his order with a fine tribute to the gallantry of the regiment. Outside of the question of their discharge, the men were in high spirits. Orders were read to move early in the morning. The men were under arms at 3 A.M. on the morning of the 7th, and at 8 o'clock in motion. They marched about six miles, and formed line of battle in a strip of woods immediately in the rear of an open field, on the right of the whole army.

The country was rolling ground. The road ran parallel to the position, and then abruptly turned off at a right angle leading between two large open fields skirted by a belt of timber. Beyond these fields were the enemy's pickets. Thus the outposts of the two huge armies confronted and watched each other's motions. The enemy were reported as only two miles distant. This might be the day before the great battle. The sun looked lovingly down upon this scene of spring beauty. The breeze sighed in murmuring, softened whispers amid the emerald foliage of the trees, while the subdued sound of voices and supressed laughter of the men died away on the morning air. O'er the soul swept memories of boyhood's years; the picture of a cottage home embowered in trees; the vision of a mother's and sister's loved forms. It was a day for reveries and dreamings, even amid all the surroundings of grim-visaged war. The next day the election for officers was ordered. The old excitement revived, and a large number of the men positively refused to have anything to do with the reorganization. In many instances officers were elected by a minority vote of the members of the companies. In the choice of officers there was almost an entire revolution in the regiment. The old officers were thrown aside and privates chosen to command the different companies—men who had shown themselves worthy of the confidence thus reposed in them. After the election of company officers, those chosen assembled to vote for field officers. While the voting was in progress, orders were received to move immediately, and soon the whole army was in motion. We marched about three miles and laid down on the ground without blankets or shelter, the roar of artillery being the music that lulled the men to sleep.

On Friday the 9th, Price's army was aroused early, and soon on the march. Under the direction of General Van Dorn the division pushed forward in a south-east direction from Corinth; and after crossing swamps, marching in line of battle through dense underbrush, over hill-tops, and across deep valleys, we halted to rest. At 12 M. four guns fired in rapid succession gave the signal to push forward. The object was to penetrate, in an easterly direction, to the north of Farmington, where the enemy were in force, and cut off their retreat towards Eastport on the Tennessee River, while the main body of the army attacked them in front. Company K was thrown out as skirmishers in front of the regiment. After a long and wearisome advance, we suddenly came upon the flank of the enemy, whom our forces had engaged in front, when they precipitately retreated to prevent being surrounded and captured. We took Farmington, the bridge they had constructed across the swamp, a large supply of clothing, etc. The bridge was destroyed, also a large gin containing cotton.

Farmington is situated in the centre of a succession of large, open fields. The fight lasted four hours, resulting in few casualties on our side. The regiment obtained a large number of letters, which furnished some information and a great deal of amusement to the boys. Some of these letters were rich specimens of orthography and penmanship, and not very flattering to the morals in certain portions of the North. This sharp engagement caused much enthusiasm among the troops, and the Third Regiment regained their old spirit and determination under the prospect of an early fight with the foe.

On the 10th the balloting for field officers was resumed, resulting finally in the selection of the following officers:

Roll of officers elected on the reorganization of the Regiment, May 8, 1862: Colonel, F. C. Armstrong; Lieutenant-Colonel, J. B. Gilmore; Major, S. D. Russell; Surgeon, P. F. Whitehead; Quartermaster, John Hanna; Commissary, F. Gallagher; Chaplain, A. Dicharry; Adjutant, J. H. Brigham.

Co. A.—J. Kinney, Captain; W. Babin, 1st Lieutenant; J. Ramouin, 2d Lieutenant; J. S. Randolph, 2d Junior Lieutenant.

Co. B.—D. C. Morgan, Captain; J. Davenport, 1st Lieutenant; W. P. Renwick, 2d Lieutenant; T. L. Beauchamp, 2d Lieut., Jr.

Co. C.—N. M. Middlebrook, Captain; A. Emanuel, 1st Lieutenant; A. W. McCain, 2d Lieutenant; W. T. Fagan, 2d Lieutenant, Jr.

Co. D.—W. E. Russell, Captain; S. M. Hyams, Jr., 1st Lieutenant; B. O. Morse, 2d Lieutenant; G. L. Frichel, 2d Lieutenant Jr.

Co. E.—O. Brashear, Captain; R. C. Holt, 1st Lieutenant; J. C. Turpin, 2d Lieutenant; ———, 2d Jr. Lieutenant.

Co. F.—W. Kinney, Captain; L. M. Dundon, 1st Lieutenant; J. O. Clark, J. Horn, 2d Lieutenants.

Co. G. —W. B. Butler, Captain; F. Gainirie, 1st Lieutenant; P. L. Prudhomme, J. Paul Bassier, 2d Lieutenants.

Co. H.—J. S. Richards, Captain; C. Hedrick, 1st Lieutenant; A. W. Carroll, J. M. Stuart, 2d Lieutenants.

Co. I.—J. E. Johnson, Captain; J. E. Hanna, 1st Lieutenant; T. McB. Meredith, 2d Lieutenant; J. R. Cottingham, 2d Jr. Lieut.

Co. K.—H. H. Gentles, Captain; J. B. Irwin, 1st Lieutenant; J. D. Williams, 2d Lieutenant; A. B. Payne, 2d Jr. Lieutenant.

Who does not remember the handsome, gay and dashing Frank Armstrong? The same gallant officer who afterwards, under General Forrest as Major-General of cavalry, gained an enviable name for bravery and efficiency in this arm of the service. Colonel Armstrong was an old army officer, hence a strict disciplinarian. Of fine personal appearance and commanding bearing, he looked what he really was, every inch a soldier. When the men were on duty he required and expected a strict observance of every military regulation and order. There must be no laxity in any particular. Yet when the men were free from duty they could approach Colonel Armstrong with the assurance that they would be treated as gentlemen and equals. He was always affable, kind, and courteous in his intercourse with the men. Colonel Armstrong appreciated the position of the early volunteers. He knew that a majority of them were men of refinement and education, of high social position previous to their becoming soldiers, hence in his intercourse with them there was no assumption of unapproachable superiority. Some idea may be formed of the estimation in which he was held when it is stated that the men, when speaking of him to each other, invariably called him Frank Armstrong. It was a rarity for any of them to prefix his title to his name. Such was the officer chosen to lead the regiment. One whom the men learned to honor for his soldierly qualities, and love with an idolatry second only to their devotion to the lamented McCulloch.

Lieutenant-Colonel Gilmore was born in Jefferson County, Kentucky, in 1827, and came to Shreveport in 1849. He was one of the first captains of the regiment; is a man of nervous excitability, with a temperment that flashed up like gunpowder when fire is applied to it. He was with all his excitability a fearless officer, always at his post in the hour of danger. The Major, S. D. Russell, a spare made man, with hair and whiskers slightly tinged with gray, was almost the opposite of Colonel Gilmore, being slow in motion, seldom losing command of his temper, or becoming unduly excited. He was calm and dignified in his bearing, firm, steady, and courageous in battle.

On Sunday, May 11th, Company K was sent out on picket, and afterwards relieved by Company A. Skirmishing was a daily occurrence, and the roar of artillery was such a common sound as to attract little attention. The camp of the Third Regiment at this time was in an open woods, rolling ground, outside of Corinth. While here they received a supply of tents. What shelters! They looked, when stretched, as if an army of rag-pickers had encamped there, and these tents were put up as signs of their occupation. In appearance, however, the men were little superior to their shelters. Almost constantly under arms or on duty, little time or opportunity was given them to attend to their apparel or cleanliness of their persons. Hence they were ragged and filthy. Their fare at this time was crackers and salt meat, not very wholesome diet assuredly. On the 12th our Adjutant, S. M. Hyams, Jr., left the regiment, having been appointed to the command of the Fifth Arkansas Regiment. On the 13th the regiment was still on picket in the position previously described. The morning was clear, the sun shining with pencilled rays through the o'erhanging branches of the trees, decked in their tender Spring foliage. Birds carolled their matin songs, while in the direction of Corinth arose the sound of the morning drum and the clarion voice of the bugle. A dash on the lines was momentarily expected, and the men were watchful and quiet. The drums and brass bands of the enemy could be distinctly heard from our position. Truly it was a strange spectacle. Two armies within sound of each other, the line of pickets on opposite sides of the same field, the men standing looking over the fence with eager, searching gaze, or leaning listlessly on their loaded pieces, watching for the foe, determined to take human life if an opportunity offered. Thus affairs remained until late in the afternoon, when an unexpected visitor in the form of a six-pound rifle shell dropped among the men. The scream and explosion of this missile were heard ere the report of the piece from which it was discharged echoed over the field. This missile was followed by others in rapid succession. Several men were wounded and bruised both by the shells and the falling limbs cut off from the trees overhead. The regiment was ordered to fall back into a ravine in the rear of their position. The order was misunderstood. Now occurred one of those scenes which cannot be accounted for, and which frequently happens among the bravest troops. There was a hurried rush by the whole regiment to the rear, resulting almost to a panic, many of the men running at the top of their speed across the adjacent hills. The pickets, however, stood their ground, owing to the determination of the captain, H. H. Gentles, commanding them. Through the strenuous exertions of the officers, the regiment was soon rallied and advanced to their original position. It was laughable then to hear the men blame each other, and saying they didn't run. Oh, no! Distinguished for gallantry and bravery they felt ashamed and mortified at their conduct, which after all was only the result of a misunderstanding of orders. Previous to the opening of the battery an old negro man attempted to pass the lines and was arrested and sent back to headquarters and released. He returned with a pass and was allowed to proceed towards the enemy's lines. In a very few moments he came back, and on being asked if he had seen any soldiers replied, "Lots of men coming on foot and on horses. They wasn't Yankees. Oh! no, but friends." The black scoundrel, it was afterwards believed, had betrayed our position, as the battery had fired with a precision of range conclusively showing that they were not shooting at random. Could the men have caught the dark hued rascal, there would have been a case of lynch-law, as their exasperation was very great. A large body of cavalry and infantry had approached our position, driving in the Confederate cavalry, who precipitately fled through the line, leaving the regiment alone to picket between the two huge armies. A portion of their cavalry made a dash on the line, but were driven back. One, however, was taken prisoner. He belonged to the First U.S. Regular cavalry, whom he abused as cowards in no very complimentary language. He refused to dismount when ordered, saying he "never had walked in his life, and he'd be d——d if he was going to now, for all the rebels in Christendom." He was speedily taught a lesson of obedience to orders by the men, not prescribed in Hardee's Tactics.

The regiment was relieved from picket on the 14th, and marched to a new camp in an open field, south-east of Corinth, near a spring of fine, cool, clear water. Tents sufficient to protect the men were furnished. There was a general cleansing of clothes and persons, and all felt better and refreshed after their continued duties, hardships and excitement. Here they once more received pay. Lieutenant J. Harvey Brigham, of Company B, was appointed Adjutant,★ Lieutenant J. Hanna, Company I, Regimental Quartermaster, and F. Gallagher, Commissary. One day succeeded another full of excitement and expectation of the great battle. On the 18th, nearly the whole army were outside of the fortifications around Corinth lying in line of battle in a huge semi-circle. The regiment was on the right of nearly the whole army. Far to the left was heard the sharp rattle of small-arms and the sullen roar of artillery, betokening heavy skirmishing, perhaps the prelude to a general engagement. The enemy were again repulsed with considerable loss. The next day was a repetition of the same scenes of desultory fighting by the skirmishers and out-posts. Yet amid the sound of spattering rifle shots and an occasional roar of field-piece, the regiment presented a strange appearance, characteristic of the reckless indifference of men accustomed to danger. There were groups playing poker, swearing and laughing over their cards, others were engaged in the interesting game of "mumble the peg." Some eating "hard-tack" and "salt junk." Others reading newspapers, engaged in discussions, telling jokes and yarns amid uproarious laughter, or lying in lazy attitudes 'neath the shade of the trees. There was suddenly the quick,

---

★After Lieutenant Washburn was captured at Elk Horn, Lieutenant J. Harvey Brigham was made Adjutant of the regiment, and continued to act as such until the re-organization, and was then *regularly appointed* as such and commissioned under Act of Congress, allowing the appointment of others than of line officers. At the beginning of the war this office was filled by some lieutenant appointed from the line officers. Lieutenant Brigham was second lieutenant of Company B. Adjutant Brigham lost the use of his right hand from a wound received at the battle of Iuka (September 19th) after which period Lieutenant A. W. Currie, Company H, was made Acting Adjutant, while Lieutenant Brigham was on detached service on general court-martial in Richmond, Va., but still holding his commission as Adjutant until he resigned (September 21st, 1864) in consequence of disability. After this no one was adjutant by commission, but only by appointment.

imperative command to "fall in," a rush and scramble for arms and equipments amid great excitement, showing the tension to which the nerves of the men were strung beneath all their apparent *indifference. They were only ordered to return to camp.*

The weather now became stormy, rain falling almost incessantly, yet orders were issued to cook three days' rations and be prepared to move. On the 21st the army was once more on the march, accompanied by trains of commissary stores. Proceeding cautiously eastward we halted about seven miles from Corinth on the Memphis and Charleston Railroad. Here the regiment was passed by Hardee's Division, composed almost entirely of Arkansas volunteers, a hardy, rough-looking body of men, full of fun and life. We were feeling the enemy's position, with the evident design of giving battle. The expedition was fruitless, as they could not be found. The army commenced moving back on the 22d. That night many of the troops, batteries, and trains remained in the swamps, the roads through them being impassable in the black darkness of a cloudy night. The situation was by no means an agreeable one. Major Tunnard reached the regiment on the 25th, and was once more warmly welcomed. Having procured a discharge from the service, he bade a final adieu to the regiment on the 26th of May, followed by the good wishes of the men who had served so efficiently under him.

On the 28th the trains of the whole army were in motion southward. The army made a feint on the enemy's position. There was some heavy skirmishing and artillery fighting. The Third Regiment was not engaged, and was among the last to leave Corinth. The army slowly fell back along high ridges covered with pine, then through swamps, boggy with mire and almost impassable. The men felt gloomy, sad, and dispirited at this abandonment of their stronghold. Not understanding or appreciating the consummate skill and strategy of General Beauregard in thus safely retreating in face of a powerful foe without losing arms, ammunition, guns or stores. They did not then know that great victories could be gained without fighting tremendous battles. On the 31st the regiment reached Baldwin, Miss., and encamped on a ridge among the pines, west of the N. O., J. and G. N. Railroad. Here the troops remained until the 6th, when the retrograde movement was continued. The railroad bridges and culverts were destroyed in the rear. The enemy's cavalry were very active in making raids on the road, attempting to destroy the track in front of our trains. But the splendid cavalry of Price's Division were equally energetic in foiling their attempts. Over hills and through gloomy swamps the regiment marched, sometimes knee deep in mud.

CHAPTER XXII

TUPELO

On Sunday, the 8th of June, a clear, beautiful Sabbath day, the regiment reached Tupelo and were marched about two miles east of this place and an eligible camp selected on a hill and near a small spring. The country here was rolling land covered with open woods. Here they remained encamped without incident worthy of note until the 16th, when the members of the regiment taken prisoners at Elk Horn arrived. They were greeted and welcomed as brothers meet after a long separation. They were surrounded by their comrades, all eager to learn something of life in Northern prisons, and the treatment of prisoners, overwhelming them with questions. Their statements were anything but flattering to our foes, and in some particulars horrible in their details.

General Hebert also arrived and established his headquarters on the ridge adjacent to the one occupied by the regiment. When the re-organization of the command was perfected at Corinth, the men were promised furloughs for sixty days. After their arrival at Tupelo, an application was made for the fulfilment of this promise. It was refused, and when the fact was announced to the regiment on the 16th of June, 1862, there was much excitement and dissatisfaction in camp. After long months of severe service, enduring untold hardships and trials, fighting several battles with a courage and bravery which had made their name everywhere distinguished, the only boon asked, the only favor which could have been conferred on them as a recompense for their deeds, was refused. Now they could look forward only to a life in the army until the termination of the struggle. The disappointment was most bitterly felt, and it is not surprising that it found expression in still more bitter words. The scarcity of water rendered it necessary to dig wells, and the men went to work with their customary energy at this new occupation. They soon had deep wells dug, neatly planked up to prevent their caving in, and water was found in abundance and very good. At this period camp discipline was very strict and daily drills very severe. Beside these duties there were heavy details for the purpose of cutting out and building roads through the swamps, labor which even to those accustomed to it is not considered light. Heavy timber was first cut, then carried by sheer physical strength to its proper place, as a foundation over swampy ground; this was filled in with brush and dirt. Such work was performed in mud and water knee deep—mentioned here only to show some of the duties of a volunteer.

On the 20th orders were read assigning General Van Dorn to the command of Eastern Louisiana and Southern Mississippi, and the Division was now under the supreme command of General Price.

On the 20th there was a review and general inspection, the occasion of unfurling a beautiful battle-flag presented to the regiment by Governor Jackson, of Missouri. This flag was made of the very finest material. It was red silk, with a strip of yellow silk around the edges. In the upper left hand corner was a crescent with "Third Louisiana" worked in it, surrounded by thirteen silvered stars. In the centre of the red ground was a scroll in blue, with the words "Oak Hills," and "Elk Horn," inscribed thereon, indicating that the regiment had distinguished themselves on those battle fields. This banner was one of the handsomest in the army, and, coming from such a distinguished source, was greatly admired by the men. They appreciated highly the compliment thus paid to their gallantry and heroism. On the 26th of June an order was read appointing the regiment as sharp-shooters for the brigade, a position which would place them in front in every battle, another tribute to their efficiency. They acknowledged the compliment, but did not much relish the situation.

The latter part of June was clear and hot. The camp was unusually quiet until the arrival of the news from Virginia, which was received with enthusiastic cheers by the troops amid much excitement. The official confirmation of the success of General Lee in defeating McClellan's army, was the occasion of firing salutes in every brigade of General Beauregard's army. As the guns pealed forth the tidings over the slumbering hills, the army grew wild with excitement and joy. Everywhere success seemed crowning our efforts. At Vicksburg the enemy in vain attempted to open the blockade of the Mississippi. The opposing forces were confronting each other at Chattanooga, and the news from Northern Mississippi and Arkansas encouraging. It seemed as if the day of success was once more breaking, after the gloom of a long night of disaster.

Colonel F. C. Armstrong received an appointment as Brigadier-General of Cavalry on the 6th of July. His loss to the regiment was a subject of general regret, although the men were glad to see their favorite commander thus elevated to a position for which he was eminently fitted and in which he would perform efficient service. In taking leave of the regiment he issued the following order:

HEADQUARTERS THIRD LOUISIANA INFANTRY, }
General Orders }   *Camp near Priceville, Miss., July 6th, 1862.* }
No. 7 }

Having been promoted and assigned to the command of a brigade of cavalry, the undersigned, with feelings of regret, relinquishes the command of
the Third Louisiana Infantry. Well tried Veterans! distinguished not only for
their daring gallantry on the battle-field, but for their soldierly and military
bearing on all occasions, and the alacrity and willingness with which they have
always borne the many privations and hardships they have had to undergo.
Fare-well! fellow soldiers! and remember that I will ever feel proud that I was
chosen to command the Veterans of Oak Hills and Elk Horn! the pride of the
Army of the West, the gallant Third Louisiana.

F. C. ARMSTRONG, *Brigadier-General.*

On the 15th of July about sixty privates left the regiment, being released
from military service under the provisions of the first Conscript Law of the
Confederate Congress. This was another serious blow to the regiment, as they
were deprived of the services of a number of their most steady, efficient and gallant men. About this period there was a general review of the division by General
Price. The old veteran looked as fine and pleasant as ever, the geniality of his
character shining forth in every lineament of his pleasant features. He saluted the
regiment in a marked manner as they marched by him with firm and solid tread.
A large number of ladies were present at this review, much to the astonishment,
as well as pleasure, of our men. They had not seen any ladies for many weeks,
and had begun to imagine that their existence was some strange phantasy of the
brain, or, perhaps, connected with some strange dream; or, as one remarked,
connected with their existence "when they were on earth before."

Reviews in July seemed the order of the day. A general one took place on
the 24th, at which were present Generals Bragg, Hardee, Price, Lyttle, Hebert,
Green, Maury, Phiffer, J. Perkins, Jr., and other distinguished personages.

Troops were continually departing for different points, until only the
Army of the West were left near Tupelo, under command of General Price,
who had charge of the department, comprising—North Alabama, West
Tennessee and Northern Mississippi. There was a fine bathing-place near our
camp, which furnished the men with a great amount of amusement. One
member of the regiment was drummed out for cowardice—the execution of
the sentence being witnessed by the men without regret, as they considered
the punishment deserved.

There was very little to occasion sport while in this camp, and hence they seized upon every little incident to indulge their witicisms and good humor.

After the departure of Colonel Armstrong, J. B. Gilmore became Colonel by promotion, S. D. Russell, Lieutenant-Colonel, and J. S. Richards, of Company H, Major. Colonel Gilmore was indefatigable—untiring in drilling the regiment. He usually rode on these occasions a small sorrel pony, which was very lazy. He would give an order for some manœuvre, and then "cluck" very energetically to his pony, using hands and heels in his endeavor to get him to the proper position as the men performed their evolutions. Hence, after these drills, you could hear all over camp many men shouting some order, followed by a sharp cluck! cluck! cluck! as they imitated the energetic manner of Colonel Gilmore. This pastime never failed to elicit shouts of laughter.

On the 29th the camp near Priceville was abandoned, the troops moving four miles above Tupelo to a position occupied previously by a portion of General Bragg's troops. From this camp the regiment moved in detachments to Saltillo., Miss., on the railroad, in close proximity to a spring, where General Andrew Jackson once camped with his troops during the second American war. As usual, the regiment was camped in an open field, skirted, and, in places, shaded with trees. This was a pleasant camp-ground, and water abundant, and fine for all purposes.

On the 4th of August orders were issued to be ready, at any moment, to move, in anticipation of the enemy's advance.

The brigade, commanded by General Hebert, was composed entirely of dismounted Texans, comprising the Third and Sixth Cavalry, and Whitfield's Legion, and the Third Louisiana. These Texans, gallant, brave, daring and dashing men, were devotedly attached to the Third Regiment in those ties which always bind brave men together.

At Saltillo the rations were very scant and the men in a starving condition, not because there were no supplies to be had, but because they had failed to reach the Commissary-General. The Texans refused to do further duty unless properly fed, and there was great dissatisfaction in the Louisianian Regiment. Feed and clothe a soldier and he is always ready for anything. These things so necessary to his health and comfort make up the sum of his existence. Deprive him of them and he is discontented, dissatisfied and prepared to commit any kind of insubordination. The days were unusually hot and clear, flies, mosquitos and gnats in myriads, which, added to hunger, made the life at Saltillo anything but agreeable. However, provisions soon arrived, removing the chief cause of dissatisfaction.

On the 9th General Armstrong visited the camp and was most enthusiastically welcomed. It seemed to rejoice the men exceedingly to once more see his familiar features and learn something concerning his numerous adventures as a cavalry officer.

Here a system was instituted of excusing from guard-duty two men of the detail who had the cleanest guns. The arms were thus kept in splendid order—burnished like a new silver dollar—without dirt enough about them to soil a clean cambric handkerchief. The arms of the guard every morning thus presented a splendid appearance.

The weather during the whole month of August was clear and intensely hot, much to the discomfiture of the troops. It was too warm for any kind of sport or fun. A revival occurred here among the Missouri troops, and preaching was a nightly occurrence. The scene at one of these gatherings was very impressive. A huge shelter protected the assembly from the night dews. Rough seats made of logs, covered the space beneath this shelter. Stands, on which were built fires from pine-knots, shed a lurid light over the vast concourse. The hymns sung would rise in rich cadences, floating away on the evening air in solemn, harmonious strains, followed by an earnest prayer and an impassioned, eloquent discourse. It was a strange spectacle to witness. These rough, bronzed soldiers, inured to danger and hardships, making bloodshed the chief aim of their lives, exposed to the evil influences of a soldier's dissipated and reckless existence, thus striving to seek a "home not made with hands, eternal in the heavens."

At Saltillo the "Owls" were very destructive, especially among the Arkansians, whose camps were but a short distance from the Louisianians. The usual morning greeting was—"Hillo! Arkansas, did the Owls catch any of you'ens last night. We'ens is all here." The reply generally showed that some one had disappeared. Every soldier knows what being caught by the "Owls" means; but for the information of the ignorant reader we state that this was a term applied to desertion.

Peaches were very abundant here, and the men enjoyed the treat exceedingly, becoming perfect gourmands in their appetites for this fine fruit. One day a mess, composed of four men, determined to have what soldiers termed a "square meal." They purchased a bushel of peaches, which were duly prepared for cooking. After a diligent search, they procured a huge oven. Having flour and lard they next made a crisp crust, with which the pot was lined. Into this was put all the peaches, overlaid with another crust of dough, and properly baked. In due course of time a fragrant, really delicious peach-cobler was ready to be devoured. Behold, then, these four men at their noon-day meal, with meat, bread and a bushel-cobler. It was devoured at a single sitting; but the gourmands were unfit for duty the remainder of the day. Verily, soldiers have delicate appetites.

THAT OWL

On the ever-memorable retreat from Corinth in 1862, we camped close by a mill not far from Baldwin, after a long and tedious day's march. Night set in, and with it a slight drizzling rain. The camp was gloomy indeed. Our poor fellows were tired after the day's toil, and, of course, wished a dry spot to lay their weary heads on. The Colonel had his tent stretched on the banks of the creek, and those who had not tents to shelter them from the inclemency of the night crowded into the Colonel's until it was "filled up." It was not many hours ere the whole camp was as still as death, save the solitary tramp of the sentinel as he marched back and forth on his beaten path, or changed the tiresome musket from shoulder to shoulder. About the "wee sma'" hours of the morning one of those hoary-headed owls settled himself on a tree opposite the Colonel's tent, across the creek, and poured forth one of his most melodious midnight hymns. Any kind of noise was, of course, prohibited in camp after tattoo.

The music of the big-eyed warbler disturbed the Colonel in his dreams, and, about half wake, he shouted: "Stop that noise, sir."

The owl, not understanding such a peremptory order, sung forth one of his sweetest refrains. Before the last note had died way, the Colonel, in a stentorian voice that aroused everybody from his slumbers, shouted, "Stop that noise *instantly,* sir."

Not being afraid of military law at midnight, the owl put forth his protest against the order of the Colonel in a higher key. By this time the Colonel was excited, and, in his loudest tones, called for the guard. The guard came rushing toward the tent. He was sitting straight up in bed. The guard rushed in almost out of breath—"What's the matter, Colonel." "Arrest that man immediately who is making that noise." The guard looked astounded. One of the boys who was sleeping in the tent with the Colonel understood the whole matter and quietly said: "Colonel, it is nothing but an owl."

The Colonel dismissed the guard, laid down and went to sleep. From that day to this he never said "owl." If any one is spoiling for a fight, let him go to Shreveport; go to the Colonel's store and say *owl* just once.

CHAPTER XXIII

THE ADVANCE

ON the last day of August there was a general review and muster of the troops. Before it was finished, orders were received to prepare to march on the enemy. Six tent flies and one wagon allotted to every hundred men. There was the usual bustle and confusion attendant on breaking up camp. Soon the army was in motion northward once more, and reached Baldwin, Miss., that night. This place, which we had left only a few days previously, had been visited by the enemy; the simoon-blast of war had swept over it and left only ruins behind.

THE COLONEL'S ARTILLERY

About two weeks previous to the battle of Iuka we encamped near Baldwin. Our regiment, with a section of artillery, was ordered on picket duty, about ten miles north of Baldwin, on the railroad. The regiment was under the command of Colonel Gilmore. The Colonel, on our arrival, ordered the regiment to camp in an old corn-field, and also stationed the section of artillery in the same corn-field. A little log-cabin across the road stood directly in range of these two guns. This little cabin was occupied by a widow lady and her three children. The widow was a beauty, and many of the regiment were lovers of the beautiful, and, of course, would hover around the cabin. Among those admirers was the Colonel. The fact was, the Colonel would rather have his right arm torn off at the shoulder than that any lady should suffer the least injury from any order of his. To prove this, the Colonel (the second or third morning after we arrived) went over to the cabin, when he explained the object of his mission in this wise: "Good morning, madam." "Good morning, sir." "Madam, I came over this morning to state to you that I am here with my regiment on picket duty; and also, madam, that my artillery is bearing directly on your front, and, if the enemy should come, I shall certainly bombard it." "Law me, Colonel, is there so much danger?" "There is, madam. My bombardments are terrible." "Sakes alive! I will leave right away." It is needless to state that the Colonel left.

Our advance-guard had a sharp skirmish with the enemy the day of our arrival at Baldwin, compelling them to fall back.

The next morning the regiment moved three miles up the road, and encamped with one section of King's battery. The object of this move was to protect workmen engaged in repairing the destroyed portions of the railroad previous to a general advance by the whole army. The men labored zealously at the new task assigned them. It seemed as if they were to learn every rough branch of industry while in the army. Dirt, roads, graves and welldigging, and now railroad building. At such labor they did not appreciate the old aphorism, "Variety is the spice of life."

On the 6th of September the regiment moved three miles farther up, camping in an open field near the railroad, five miles from Boonville. The enemy were but a short distance in front. The First Brigade arrived to strengthen our position. The enemy were within three-quarters of a mile, but the men were cool and camp very quiet. The weather still continued very warm, the roads ankle-deep with dust. The nights were beautiful, the soft moon-light bathing the earth with its flood of silvery rays. Yet the men failed to appreciate its loveliness, or feel the tender influences of its witching spell.

On the 10th, the regiment broke up camp and moved back to Baldwin, carrying once more their knapsacks. The next day the camp was rife with rumors of an active move against the enemy. The regiment took up the line of march very early, leading Hebert's brigade, which was in front of the army. After a hot, dusty march of fifteen miles, encamped in a valley watered by a babbling stream of clear, cool water. The army at this time were marching in an north-easterly direction from Baldwin. On the 12th, the army reached Bay Spring Mills; General Armstrong was in advance with his dashing brigade of cavalry, and in close pursuit of the retreating enemy. On the 13th, the regiment was in line at 3 A.M., and soon pushing rapidly forward, marching steadily until 5 P.M. The trains did not reach the regiment until very late at night. The tired and hungry soldiers had awaited their coming ere thinking of sleep. Having partaken of their meal of beef and corn-bread, they thought to rest. Vain delusion! Scarcely had they thrown themselves upon the ground, when, at 10½ o'clock at night, the drum beat the call to "fall in." Knapsacks were left behind, and another night-march commenced, with the expectation of soon meeting the foe. The men were in good spirits, notwithstanding tired limbs and hunger.

Amid the darkness of the night and the sombre shadows of the forest trees,

the army moved forward in the direction of Iuka, where it was known the
enemy were in force. When within one and a half miles of town, the army
was formed in column of brigades, and the Louisiana regiment sent forward.
General Hebert rode up to Colonel Gilmore and said: "Great things are
expected of you to-day."

About sunrise, as the army approached this place, the news came that the
foe had evacuated the town without a struggle, and General Armstrong was in
possession. The men marched eagerly and rapidly onward, reaching Iuka about
noon. The army captured about $200,000 worth of stores, consisting of arms,
ammunition, and commissary supplies of every description, including such luxuries as coffee, tea, sugar, condensed milk, cheese, mackerel, canned fruit and preserves, brandy, lager beer, whisky, Claret and Catawba wines, etc. The ragged
and half-starved soldiers feasted on "good things" for once, and had more than
a "square meal." Among other things, the regiment found some hand-cars,
which the men would push up the road, an up-hill grade, and, getting on them,
come down at break-neck speed. Iuka is situated in a valley, on the Memphis
and Charleston Railroad, and is quite a pretty place. It is noted for its fine min-
eral springs, and was a fashionable resort previous to the war. The people received
the Southern troops with every demonstration of joy; the ladies especially, of
which there were large numbers residing here, and handsome ones at that.

The soldiers feasted, frolicked and were in high glee and spirits at the sudden change in their condition. On the 15th they were on picket on the
Byrneville road north of Iuka. On the next day the brigade was in line of
battle on the Baldwin road south of Iuka, the first brigade occupying the position of the previous day. Rumors prevailed that the enemy had received
re-enforcements and were advancing to give battle. The regiment continued
in line of battle until the 19th, when they returned to camp, to remain only a
short time, being ordered out on the Byrneville road once more. While on this
road, Sept. 19th, news arrived that the enemy, under command of General
Rosecrans, was advancing on the Baldwin road. General Hebert received orders
to proceed with his brigade at a double-quick to meet them. The command,
at almost a full run for nearly three miles, hastened forward. Over the railroad,
through Iuka, and out on the Baldwin or Bay Springs road; when about a mile
from Iuka, the brigade was formed into line of battle. Immediately in their front
was a valley; in fact, the whole country was a succession of valleys and hills of
irregular formation, covered by a dense undergrowth. In a few moments the
battle opened. Although greatly outnumbered, this brigade steadily drove back
the enemy's line, and, gaining sight of a nine-gun battery from Cincinnati, O.,

charged it with desperate fury, notwithstanding it poured into their ranks a most destructive fire, the guns being heavily loaded with buck-shot. The fighting was of the most desperate character on both sides, the Confederates being opposed by the flower of Rosecrans's army, the early volunteers from the West, men accustomed to the use of arms, and of undoubted courage. For the third time during the war the Louisianians met the Fifth Iowa regiment, a stalwart body of men—heavy infantry. They were nearly cut to pieces in this battle. At times both lines would stand and pour destructive volleys into each other's ranks; then the Confederates would rush forward, with tremendous yells, invariably driving back the foe in their impetuous charge. The fight was mostly with small-arms. The battle continued until after dark, an incessant, prolonged roar of musketry. The captured guns were seized and run to the rear. The battle commenced a little after 4 o'clock P.M., and the stubbornness with which the Third Louisiana fought, is proven by the fact that, in less than three hours, out of two hundred and thirty-eight men who went into the fight, one hundred and fifteen were killed and wounded. Darkness put an end to the battle, and the men laid down on their arms in the full expectation of renewing it early in the morning. As the sable mantle of night fell upon the field of strife, thickly strewn with the dead, dying, and wounded of friend and foe, the First brigade arrived, with loud cheers. The loss in officers by the regiment was fearful. General Lyttle was killed, Colonel Whitfield wounded. Among the killed and wounded of the regiment were Colonel Gilmore, Adjutant Brigham, Captains Gentles, Kinney and Pierson, Lieutenants Irwin, Johnson, Trichel, Renwick, Hedrick and Ramora; prisoners, Lieutenants Babin and Washburne. The principal part of the fighting was done by the Second brigade of Lyttle's division of Price's army, and General Hebert received merited praise for the masterly skill and gallant manner in which he led his brigade into action. It is unnecessary to state that the Louisiana regiment fully sustained its blood-earned reputation; and this was by far the hardest-fought battle they had yet participated in, and the number of killed and wounded fully attest the truth of the statement, and the part they took in the affair.

The astonishment of the men was indescribable when, early the morning after the battle, orders were received to evacuate the place. Soon the long line of infantry was filing through the streets of Iuka, leaving the dead and wounded in the hands of the enemy. We carried off all our trains and artillery, including the greater portion of the captured stores of Iuka. The trains had all been prepared to leave previous to the battle. The night after the desperate struggle, the cars were heard all night bringing up re-enforcements, and probably General Price learned that the enemy were too strong to be successfully encountered.

The following interesting and additional account of the battle is from the pen of a member of the regiment:

"After General Herbert made disposition of his brigade for battle, the Third Louisiana being on the extreme left of the line, Colonel Gilmore ordered forward as skirmishers the left wing of his regiment. Company F, being on the right, came in contact with the enemy, and fired the first gun at Iuka. This little skirmish lasted about fifteen minutes, the enemy losing four or five men killed. I must state a circumstance that occurred during the affair. Two of the enemy took shelter behind a large tree directly in front of Company F. The tree, however, was not large enough to protect the two, one of whom was instantly killed by private Hudson; the other begged for his life most piteously, which would undoubtedly have been granted him had he relied on the word of a rebel. He was ordered several times to come to the company and his life should be spared, but he was afraid to expose his person. During the conversation between him and the captain, private J. Jus, it seems, became rather restless, left his position in the line, and slipped around until he came in view of the Yankee, then raised his gun and shot him through the head, at the same time remarking, "Damned if I don't fetch him." The Federal proved to be a lieutenant. The skirmishers were soon after recalled, and had scarcely taken their position in the regiment when we heard the enemy's order to advance, in loud tones, "Forward—guide centre, march!" Hardly had these words died away, when the same command, loud and clear, came ringing on our ears from our commanding officer. Colonel Gilmore immediately ordered forward Company K, Captain Gentles, as skirmishers. This company rapidly threw themselves in front of the regiment, and advanced double-quick up the hill, followed closely by the regiment. Directly in our front was one of those long, sloping hills peculiar to the country around Iuka. This hill-side was covered with large trees, with very little underbrush. The enemy's line soon appeared, and were immediately warmly received by the skirmishers, who nobly held their ground until the regiment came to their assistance. The fire immediately opened from both lines like a sudden clap of thunder, and continued without abatement for over two hours. At the commencement of the firing our boys dropped down on their knees, the best thing they could have done, as the greatest portion of the enemy's fire flew harmlessly over their heads, while their fire had telling effect on the enemy. The firing was fearful—the smoke enveloped both lines, so that they became invisible to each other. The lines could be distinguished only by the flash of guns. The evening was one of those damp, dull, cloudy ones, which caused the smoke to settle down about as high as a man's head. This terrible fire continued about half an hour, when the enemy were ordered to charge down the hill, but were so warmly received that they staggered. Instantly our boys received the order to charge, and, with their old battle-yell, they rushed upon the foe and drove them from the hill. On the hill the regiment suffered. A new line of the enemy opened fire on them. One of our regiments in our rear, by some mistake, threw their missiles of death in among us; this, indeed, was a terrible moment.

Major Russell rode to this regiment and stated that they were firing on their friends. About this time the Colonel's horse was shot under him, and he was wounded in the shoulder. The Colonel, now on foot, ordered a charge down the hill, and led it in person. Here the fighting was desperate; a number of our men were wounded, and a large number killed.

Night quickly set in, the flashes of the opposing guns almost met, prisoners were taken and retaken, no one could distinguish friend from foe, the leaden hail flew in every direction. Still our boys pressed on. Our Colonel was wounded; also Adjutant J. Harvey Brigham, and his horse killed. Major Russell came near losing his life by giving orders to a company of the enemy, mistaking them for one of our own. Sergeant White captured the enemy's flag; scarcely had he done so, when he was captured, was again re-captured, and finally captured. Our regiment was finally relieved by a Missouri brigade. We then marched back to where the battle first began, and slept on that bloody field that night. The Louisiana regiment never fought better, was well and easily handled, and were justly proud of the work so heroically performed in one of the hardest-fought battles of the war."

Dr. Luke P. Blackburn, aid to General Price, who was with him at Iuka, made the following statement:

"General Price was thrice ordered by General Bragg to move his army across the Tennessee River at Eastport or Iuka. On Thursday morning, the 11th, he moved his army of less than 14,000 men from Guntown toward Iuka. By rapid and forced marches he arrived within three miles of Iuka at daylight on Sunday morning. There he was informed by a courier from General Armstrong's command, whose cavalry had attacked the enemy on Saturday, that re-enforcements were being sent from Burnsville. The men, being very much fatigued, were ordered to rest and sleep in line thirty minutes. General Price knowing that Captain Saunders, with his company of one hundred and twenty men, had possession of the road between Iuka and Burnsville, and having implicit confidence in that officer, he had no fear of re-enforcements from Corinth until he should have captured the forces at Burnsville and Iuka. The column was put in motion; on reaching the edge of the town he was astonished to learn that the enemy, 2,000 strong, with 2,000 negroes, and a large train, had fled at 1 o'clock the night previous. He took possession of the place. The enemy came up again on Monday in small force, but soon retreated.

"Colonel Wirt Adams and Hieman's cavalry captured and burned a train of cars five miles from Iuka. There was no further demonstration until Friday, when Colonel Ord sent a flag demanding the unconditional surrender of General Price's army, stating that the army of General Lee had been destroyed in Virginia, Longstreet and Hill, with their entire divisions, captured, that the war was now virtually closed, and, as he wished to prevent the useless shedding of blood, he demanded an unconditional surrender. That he (General Price) was completely surrounded by an overwhelming force, and could not escape.

"General Price replied that whenever the independence of the Southern Confederacy was acknowledged, her rights respected, and the Vandal hordes of the North driven from her soil, that then, and then only, would he and his army be willing to lay down their arms.

"General Price, in obedience to orders from General Van Dorn, and being almost destitute of forage, unable to cross the Tennessee River, prevented from passing down toward Corinth by the unfavorable condition of the country, the enemy having possession of Yellow Creek, determined to fall back to Baldwin and there unite with General Van Dorn.

"The order to fall back was issued Friday morning, at 9 o'clock, when no one dreamed of an attack. On Friday evening, at 2 o'clock, the enemy, in line of battle, approached our outpost. Heavy skirmishing ensued. At 3 o'clock General Price ordered up the Fourth Brigade. When they reached their position, they found the enemy in line of battle, holding a good position on a hill. The order was given to charge them, which charge drove the enemy back two hundred yards, into a ditch formed by the road from Fulton to Eastport, and directly under their cannon, which were masked. General Price now reached the field. The firing had almost ceased. General Hebert and Colonel Martin, commanding brigade, with Whitfield's Legion, being all the force in line. General Price ordered up Gregg's and Green's Brigades, to form on the left, charge the enemy, and press them down on General Maury's Division, he being on the right. Before the arrival of their brigades, General Price ascertained that the enemy were lying in the road sheltered from our artillery. They were firing but one gun, and that on our right. The gallant and lamented General Lyttle suggested that, as they seemed to have but one gun in position, if the line would move forward the battle would soon be won. The order was given; our men emerged from the underbrush in line. They were then met by as terrific a fire from masked batteries and concealed musketry as was ever encountered. But the invincible Third Louisiana, Third Tennessee, and Thirty-seventh Alabama stood like statuary. When the order to charge was given, they rushed headlong through this sheet of fire and lead, and drove the enemy from their guns, Whitfield's Legion pressing on the right; the enemy would resist and fall back, until they were driven half a mile, losing nine guns.

"It was now dark. Generals Green and Gregg arrived, but too late to enter the fight. One hour of daylight, and the entire Yankee Division would have been captured. We held the field all night, brought in the wounded, and evacuated the place in accordance with the order issued in the morning. Our loss in killed, wounded, and missing, 482. That of the enemy, over 800. General Price brought off his entire train and captured stores. General Maury covered the retreat. General Lyttle fell while conversing with General Price."

INCIDENTS—GETTING THE TRAINS IN MOTION

As the enemy held the Baldwin road, the retreat was conducted on a road east of it, known as the Fulton road. There was some confusion in starting. General Price came riding up among the teamsters furious with anger. He was dressed in a many-colored shirt, well known by every soldier in the army as the dress he assumed when there was work to be done. A slouched hat covered his head, and a sabre was buckled around his portly person. We never remember to have heard General Price swear, only on this occasion, and he was not choice in his language at this time. He ordered the teamsters to drive on, adding, "If one of you stops, I'll hang you, by G——d." The trains went out of Iuka at a full run, the teams being urged to their utmost speed. When the loads became too heavy, clothing, tents, blankets, and bundles were thrown out on the roadside. If a wagon broke down, the mules were unhitched and a torch applied to the useless vehicle. There was no time or stop to think of saving the contents of these disabled wagons.

GENERAL S. PRICE

This incident of General Price was no true index to his character. An incident that occurred at Elk Horn was more indicative of his real disposition. When the retreat commenced, the Author, being sick, obtained a seat on the caisson of a battery. Immediately in the rear of this battery was General Price and staff, with a portion of General McCulloch's staff. As the retreating column passed along the road, it overtook a soldier badly wounded in the leg, who was limping along, regardless of his excruciating agony, in his endeavors to escape the foe. He was observed by General Price, who halted the battery, and thus addressed the man: "What is the matter, my good fellow?" "I am shot in the leg, General," was the reply. "Here, my man, get up on one of these guns. I'll lose every piece of artillery in the army but what I save my men." It was a noble action, showing General Price's true character, his love for the men of his army, and attention to their wants and comfort. His fatherly kindness and almost womanly tenderness of heart, evinced in just such incidents, were the foundation of the love which his soldiers felt for him.

THE PROXIMITY OF THE FORCES

So close were the lines to each other at the termination of the battle, that the opposing forces unknowingly walked into each other's lines and were forcibly seized and taken prisoners, in many instances resulting in hair-breadth escape, with the loss only of arms.

THE LOSS OF THE FLAG

In the battle of Iuka, Drum-major Patterson carried the colors of the regiment. During the progress of the battle he advanced in front of the regiment too far, discovering which, he began to fall back to his position in the line. The movement was observed by Lieutenant U. Babin, of Company A, who imagined R. Patterson was retreating with the colors. Rushing forward, the Lieutenant seized the colors, shouting, "Follow me, boys!" and ran rashly into the midst of the enemy's line. He was captured, with the colors, by the foe. It was one of those deeds of reckless bravery and rash daring which men often commit in the excitement of battle. No one ever questioned the drum-major's bravery, for he had exhibited already a strength of nerve beyond questioning. Lieutenant Babin exhibited a reckless disregard to danger, worthy a better fate than that which befell him. A story was told about this flag worthy of note. After its capture, an officer of the Federals gave it to an orderly, with instructions to convey it to General Rosecrans's headquarters. While attempting to execute this mission he was killed, and the next morning these beautiful colors were found on the field of battle, amid the dead and wounded, beside the cold and silent form of the Federal soldier. The regiment felt bitterly the loss of their flag, as only brave men can feel such a misfortune.

CHAPTER XXIV

THE RETREAT

ON the 20th of September, the army retreated twenty-seven miles, closely pursued by the Federals. In the early part of the day our forces in the rear were much harassed by the enemy's cavalry, but a well planned and executed ambush at the end of a lane, resulting in fearful slaughter, deterred them from pressing the pursuit, and by night it had ceased altogether. Early the next morning the army was back at Bay Springs. The bridge across the stream gave way as the last of the train was crossing it, causing the loss of one wagon, which was precipitated on the rocks below. The damage, however, was soon repaired. The retreat continued on the 21st and 22d, and on the 23d the regiment reached its old camping ground at Baldwin. Too much praise cannot be bestowed on Mrs. Belcher, an estimable lady of Baldwin, and other patriotic and kind countrywomen, for their attention to the wounded of the command. Colonel Whitfield, of the Texas Legion, Adjutant J. H. Brigham, and others, were received into her dwelling and nursed as if they were brothers and not strangers. It was but the manifestation of the patriotic devotion of our fair ladies for the cause which their friends and relatives had espoused. A devotion universal, as well as unparalleled in the annals of history. The Louisiana Regiment reached Baldwin with two hundred and seventy-five men, all told.

The troops rested but two days, when orders were issued to cook two days' rations and prepare to march.

On the 26th, a pleasant but cloudy morning, the army was once more in motion, this time proceeding westward. Owing to the roughness and hilly nature of the road, but eight miles were marched on the first day.

On the 27th the army marched fifteen miles, and encamped five miles from Ripley, Miss. The army was visited here by heavy rains, much to the discomfiture of the men.

On the 29th the regiment marched into Ripley and encamped. This is a small place, situated in a level plat of ground, and distinguished for no particular beauty, either of location or buildings.

On the 30th the march was resumed, the army proceeding thirteen miles, the weather being very warm, and encamped near a spring of fine water, which had been very scarce on the road. Passing through a small place called Ruttsville, a large number of ladies collected on the road-side to see the troops. A great many sharp witticisms passed between this fair assembly and the tired troops. Apples, grapes and peaches were abundant along the line of march—delicacies which the men made the most of, and greatly enjoyed.

On the 1st of October the regiment proceeded fifteen miles, and encamped within one mile of Pocahontas, forming a junction with the forces under Major-General Earl Van Dorn. The regiment encamped in an old corn-field, without shelter or protection of any kind.

The next day the army was once more in motion, leaving their trains behind, to camp between the Tuscumbia and Hatchie roads, prepared to move on either as circumstances might determine. A demonstration was made towards Bolivar, where the enemy were intrenched. They burned the bridge over the Hatchie, in front of our advancing troops. It was speedily rebuilt, and the army pushed rapidly forward toward Corinth, their true destination and point of attack. The men remembered the fortifications around this intrenched position, strengthened under the energetic labors of the enemy, and protected by heavy abattis of felled timber, and their hearts misgave then as to the final result when it was known where they were going into battle.

On the 3d of October, as the reveille sounded, the roar of artillery echoed over the land, disturbing the silence of the morning air, indicating that the advance-guard had commenced the attack on Corinth. It was not long before General Hebert's Brigade, led by the remnant of the Third Regiment, were in motion, making a forced march, reaching Corinth about 4 P.M. On every side were beheld evidences of the fierce conflict, in which the Southern troops had thus far been victorious. General Hebert's Brigade was held as a reserve. At night the men laid down on their arms, and soon the quietude and silence of the gloom brooded over the armed hosts of the two armies.

The troops had achieved wonders, charging the enemy's breast-works over the fallen timber with desperate valor, driving them from their intrenchments, and capturing several pieces of artillery. The success achieved was dearly bought, by the loss of many valuable officers and hundreds of brave men.

At daylight, on the morning of the 4th, the regiment was aroused from its slumber. The brigade was first marched to the right of the railroad, Company K, of Third Louisiana, being sent forward as skirmishers. After the lapse of an hour the brigade was marched back, and formed in line of battle to the left of

Corinth. A charge was made over a succession of small hills, defended with artillery, supported by infantry. The men gallantly rushed on the first line with loud cheers, under a scathing fire, and drove it back. By this time so many had fallen, that no further progress could be made against the overwhelming forces of the enemy. It would have been madness to have made the attempt, and the brigade was compelled to retreat. The regiment lost about thirty killed and wounded, being about one-third of the number in the fight. The right of the army succeeded in penetrating into Corinth, and even planted the Confederate flag on the Tishimingo Hotel. The depletion in the ranks of the different regiments was lamentable. The forced marches, the terrible hot weather, want of food, and need of rest, so completely exhausted the troops that large numbers of them did not enter the fight, having failed to reach their commands. As the regiment hastened from the field of battle, the remnant was formed into companies, and the retreat commenced, marching ten miles ere halting. Among the wounded were Colonel Russell, Lieutenant Williams, Company K, and Lieutenant B. Morse, Company D.

The army had fought with a desperation and valor unequaled — unprecedented in the annals of warfare—only to leave hundreds of brave men stiffening corpses on the field of battle, sleeping their long, last sleep beneath the frowning muzzles of the enemy's batteries.

The annexed official reports of Generals Van Dorn and Price furnish full accounts of the fearful struggle around and in this stronghold.

We saw, on the 4th, an instance of heroism seldom witnessed, even in the army. A lieutenant of the Thirty-seventh Alabama had his arm broken badly in the first day's fight, yet gallantly led his company all day with it in that condition. At night it was amputated. The next day, after marching twenty miles, he passed the spot where the trains were encamped, whistling "Dixie," and looking as calm and undisturbed as if nothing had occurred to ruffle his mind or cause bodily pain. The empty sleeve, hanging loosely by his side, united with his quiet exterior, spoke volumes for his fortitude in enduring the agony of excruciating physical torture.

Sunday, October 5th, the army was once more on the retreat. It was a bright and beautiful Sabbath-day, but its holy loveliness was marred by the bloody features of grim-visaged war. Guns were bellowing forth their hoarse thunder in front and rear—in front, where the enemy disputed the passage across the Hatchie; in the rear, where General Lovell's Division heroically held at bay the pursuing foe, gallantly covering and protecting the retreating army. A very sharp fight took place at Hatchie Bridge, demonstrating the fact that it would be impossible to retreat by the same route on which the army had advanced. The only avenue of escape lay in the direction of Bone Yard road. The sun sank beneath the horizon on the night of the 5th amid the thunder of guns on flank and rear. All night long, in the darkness and gloom, both of nature and spirit, the retreat continued, the army succeeding in crossing the Hatchie over a temporary bridge hastily constructed on an old dam at Crumb's Mills. The troops halted not until within five miles of Ripley, when they began to feel and realize that they had really escaped from a perilous position. They had marched twenty consecutive hours without halting, and were nearly famished with hunger.

On this retreat, lost thirteen wagons, which, overturning and breaking down, were destroyed. On the 6th and 7th the retreat still continued, the enemy continually pressing and harassing the rear. Large numbers of the men had straggled off in small squads, making their way toward Holly Springs, the destination of the army. They were worn out with fatigue, sadly depressed, almost demoralized. On the 8th, passed through Roxbury, marching rapidly on the Oxford road. A halt was made for a short time at a place called Hickory Flats, and then pushed on, camping late at night, and up long before daylight, only to resume the retreat. On the 9th, passed through Connersville, and across the Tallahatchie. Thus, day after day, the retreat continued, in sunshine and storm, heat and cold, until Holly Springs was reached on the 11th, where the scattered forces rapidly concentrated and were reorganized. The Third Regiment was in a terrible condition. Worn out with fatigue, sick, ragged, filthy, and covered with vermin, it was not strange that even their brave spirits should give way under the accumulated disasters, sufferings and hardships which had so rapidly befallen them. Human endurance is not composed of cast-steel, and they felt, as well they might, depressed in spirits, disheartened in mind, prostrated in body.

Hebert's Brigade was detached from Price's army at Holly Springs. The regiment was encamped in an open field east of the town, skirted by woods. The country is hilly, an alternate succession of ridges and valleys, near this place. Previous to the war, Holly Springs, Miss., must have been a beautiful city, but now sadly marred by the desolating scourge of war. Troops rapidly concentrated at this point for a last and final struggle.

Major Tunnard once more visited the regiment on the 12th. When he saw the deplorable, pitiable condition of the remnant of that gallant band of men whom he had left but a few months previously in high spirits and health, and strong in numbers, unbidden tears dimmed his eyes, and strong emotion filled his soul and choked his voice, as he returned the warm greeting of his old comrades.

REPORT OF MAJOR-GENERAL
EARL VAN DORN

HEADQUARTERS ARMY OF WEST TENNESSEE, }
Holly Springs, Miss., Oct. 20, 1862. }

GENERAL,—I have the honor to make the following report of the battle of Corinth:

Having established batteries at Port Hudson, secured the mouth of the Red River and navigation of the Mississippi River to Vicksburg, I turned my especial attention to affairs on the Northern portion of my district.

On the 30th day of August, I received a dispatch from General Bragg, informing me that he was about to march into Kentucky, and would leave to General Price and myself West Tennessee.

On the 4th day of September, I received a communication from General Price, in which was inclosed a copy of the dispatch from General Bragg, above named, making an offer to co-operate with me. At this time General Breckenridge was operating on the Mississippi River, between Baton Rouge and Port Hudson, with all the available force I had for the field, therefore I could not accept General Price's proposition. Upon the return, however, of General Breckenridge, I immediately addressed General Price, giving my views in full in regard to the campaign in West Tennessee, and stating that I was then ready to join him with all my troops.

In the meantime, orders were received by him from General Bragg to follow Rosecrans across the Tennessee River, into Middle Tennessee, whither it was then supposed he had gone. Upon the receipt of this intelligence, I felt at once that all my hopes of accomplishing anything in West Tennessee with my small force was marred. I nevertheless moved up to Davis's Mills, a few miles from Grand Junction, Tenn., with the intention of defending my district to the best of my ability, and to make a demonstration in favor of General Price, to which latter end, also, I marched my whole command, on the 20th day of September, to within seven miles of Bolivar, driving three brigades of the enemy back to that place, and forcing the return from Corinth of one division (Ross's) which had been sent there to strengthen Grant's army.

General Price, in obedience to his orders, marched in the direction of Iuka, to cross the Tennessee, but was not long in discovering that Rosecrans had not crossed that stream. This officer, in connection with Grant, attacked him on the 19th day of September, and compelled him to fall back to Baldwin, on the Mobile and Ohio Railroad. On the 25th day of the same month, I received a dispatch by courier, from General Price, stating that he was at Baldwin, and was then ready to join me with his forces in an attack on Corinth, as had been previously suggested by me. We met at Ripley on the

28th of September, according to agreement, and marched the next morning toward Pocahontas, which place we reached on the 1st of October. From all the information which I could obtain, the following was the "situation" of the Federal army at that time: Sherman at Memphis, with about 6,000 men; Hurlburt, afterward Ord, at Bolivar, with 8,000; Grant (headquarters at Jackson), with about 3,000; Rosecrans at Corinth, with about 15,000; together with the following outposts, viz.: Rienzi, 2,500; Burnsville, Jacinto and Iuka, about 6,000. At important bridges, and on garrison duty, about two or three thousand, making in the aggregate about 42,000 men in West Tennessee. Memphis, Jackson, Bolivar and Corinth are in the arc of a circle, the chord of which, from Memphis to Corinth, makes an angle with a due east line about fifteen degrees south. Bolivar is about equi-distant from Memphis, and Corinth somewhat nearer the latter, and is at the intersection of the Hatchie River, and the Mississippi Central and Ohio Railroad. Corinth is the strongest, but most salient point.

Surveying the whole field of operations before me calmly and dispassionately, the conclusion forced itself irresistibly upon my mind, that the taking of Corinth was a condition precedental to the accomplishment of anything in West Tennessee. To take Memphis would be to destroy an immense amount of property, without any adequate military advantage, even admitting that it could be held, without heavy guns, against the enemy's guns and mortar-boats. The line of fortifications around Bolivar is intersected by the Hatchie River, rendering it impossible to take the place by quick assault, and re-enforcements could be thrown in from Jackson by railroad; and, situated as it is, in the angle of the three fortified places, an advance upon it would expose both my flanks and rear to an attack from Memphis and Corinth.

It was clear to my mind that if a successful attack could be made upon Corinth from the west and north-west, the forces there driven back on the Tennessee and cut off, Bolivar and Jackson would easily fall, and then, upon the arrival of exchanged prisoners of war, West Tennessee would soon be in our possession, and communication with Bragg effected through Middle Tennessee. The attack on Corinth was a military necessity requiring prompt and vigorous action.

It was being strengthened daily under the astute soldier, General Rosecrans; convalescents were returning to fill his ranks; new levies were arriving to increase his brigades, and fortifications were being constructed at new points; and it was very evident that, unless a sudden and vigorous blow could be struck there at once, no hope could be entertained of driving the enemy from a base of operations so convenient; that in the event of misfortune to Bragg in Kentucky, the whole valley of the Mississippi would be lost to us before winter. To have awaited for the arrival, arming, clothing and organization of the exchanged prisoners, would have been to wait for the enemy to strengthen themselves more than we could possibly do. With these reflections, and after mature deliberation, I determined to attempt Corinth. I had a reasonable hope of success. Field returns at Ripley showed my strength to be about 22,000 men. Rosecrans, at Corinth, had about 15,000, with about 8,000 additional at outposts from twelve to fifteen miles distant. I might surprise him, and carry the place before these troops could be brought in. I therefore marched toward Pocahontas, threatening Bolivar, then turned suddenly across the Hatchie and Tuscumbia, and attacked Corinth without hesitation, and did surprise that place before the outpost garrisons were called in. It was necessary that this blow should be sudden and decisive, and, if unsuccessful, that I should withdraw rapidly from the position between the armies of Ord and Rosecrans. The troops were in fine spirits, and the whole Army of West Tennessee seemed eager to emulate the armies of the Potomac and of Kentucky. No army ever marched to battle with prouder steps, hopeful countenances, or with more courage, than marched the Army of Tennessee out of Ripley, on the morning of the 29th of September, on its way to Corinth.

Fully alive to the responsibility of my position as commander of the army, and after mature and deliberate reflection, the march was ordered. The ground was well-known to me, and required no study to determine where to make the attack. The bridge over the Hatchie was soon reconstructed, and the army crossed at 4 o'clock A.M. on the 2d of October. Adams's Brigade of cavalry was left to guard this approach to our rear, and to protect the train which was parked between the Hatchie and Tuscumbia. Colonel Hawkins's regiment of infantry, and Captain Dawson's battery of artillery, were also left in the Bone Yard road, in easy supporting distance of the bridge. The army bivouacked at Chewalla, after the driving in of some pickets from that vicinity by Armstrong's and Jackson's cavalry. This point is about ten miles from Corinth.

At daybreak on the 3d the march was resumed, the precaution having been taken to cut the railroad between Corinth and Jackson by a squadron of Armstrong's cavalry. Lovell's Division, in front, kept the south side of the Memphis and Charleston Railroad. Price, after marching on the same road about five miles, turned to the left and formed line of battle in front of the outer line of intrenchments, about three miles from Corinth. Lovell formed line of battle, after some heavy skirmishing (having to construct a passage across the dry bed of Indian Creek for his artillery, under fire), on the right and in front of the same line of intrenchments.

The following was the first order of battle: The three brigades of Lovell's Division, Villepegue's, Bowen's and Rust's in line, with reserve in rear of each; Jackson's cavalry brigade on the right, in echelon. The left flank of the division on the Charleston Railroad; Price's Corps on the left, with the right flank resting on the same road; Maury's Division on the right, with Moore's and Phiffer's Brigades in line; Hebert's Division on the left, with Gates's and

Martin's Brigades in line; Colbert's in reserve; Armstrong's Cavalry Brigades on the extreme left, somewhat detached and out of view. Hebert's left was masked behind a timbered ridge, with orders not to bring it into action until the last moment. This was done in hopes of inducing the enemy to weaken his right by re-enforcing his centre and left, where the attack was first to be made, that his right might be forced.

At 10 o'clock all skirmishers were driven into the intrenchments, and the two armies were in line of battle confronting each other in force. A belt of fallen timber, or abattis, about four hundred yards in width, extended along the whole line of intrenchments. This was to be crossed. The attack commenced on the right, by Lovell's Division, and extended gradually to the left; and by half-past 10 o'clock the whole line of outer works was carried, several pieces of artillery being taken. The enemy made several ineffectual efforts to hold their ground, forming line of battle at advantageous points, and resisting obstinately our advance to the second line of detached works. I had been in hopes that one day's operations would end the contest, and decide who should be the victors on this bloody field; but a ten miles' march over a parched country, on dusty roads, without water, getting into line of battle in forests with undergrowth, and the more than usual activity and determined courage displayed by the enemy, commanded by one of the ablest generals of the United States army, who threw all possible obstacles in our way that an active mind could suggest, prolonged the battle, until I saw, with regret, the sun sink behind the horizon as the last shot of our sharpshooters followed the retreating foe into their innermost lines. One hour more of daylight, and victory would have soothed our grief for the loss of the gallant dead who sleep on that lost but not dishonored field. The army slept on their arms, within six hundred yards of Corinth, victorious so far. During the night, three batteries were ordered to take position on the ridge overlooking the town from the West, just where the hills dip into the flat extending into the railroad depot, with instructions to open on the town at 4 o'clock A.M. Hebert, on the left, was ordered to mass a portion of his division on his left; to put Cabell's Brigade in echelon on the left; also (Cabell's Brigade being detached from Maury's Division for this purpose), to move Armstrong's Cavalry Brigade across the Mobile and Ohio Railroad, and, if possible, to get some of his artillery in position across the road. In this order of battle he was directed to attack at daybreak with his whole force, swinging his left flank in toward Corinth, and advance down the Purdy Ridge. Lovell, on the extreme right, with two of his brigades in line of battle and one in reserve, with Jackson's Cavalry on the extreme right on College Hill, his left resting on the Memphis and Charleston Railroad, was ordered to await in this order, or to feel his way along slowly with his sharpshooters, until Hebert was heavily engaged with the enemy on the left. He was then to move rapidly to the assault, and force his right inward across the low grounds south-west of the town. The centre, under Maury, was to move quickly at the same time to the front, and directly at Corinth. Jackson was directed to burn the railroad bridge over the Tuscumbia during the night. Daylight came, and there was no attack on the left. A staff officer was sent to Hebert to inquire the cause. That officer could not be found. Another messenger was sent, and a third, and, about 7 o'clock, Hebert came to my headquarters and reported sick. General Price then put General Green in command of the left wing, and it was 8 o'clock before the proper dispositions for the attack at this point were made. In the meantime the troops of Maury's left became engaged with the enemy's sharpshooters, and the battle was brought on and extended along the whole centre and left wing; and I regretted to observe that my whole plan of attack was, by this unfortunate delay, disarranged. One brigade after another went gallantly into action, and, pushing forward through direct and cross-fire, over every obstacle, reached Corinth and planted their colors on the last stronghold of the enemy. A hand-to-hand contest was being enacted in the very yard of General Rosecrans's headquarters, and in the streets of the town. The heavy guns were silenced, and all seemed about to be ended, when a heavy fire from fresh troops from Iuka, Burnsville and Rienzi, that had succeeded in reaching Corinth in time, poured into our thinned ranks. Exhausted from loss of sleep, wearied from hard marching and fighting, companies in regiments without officers, our troops (let no one censure them) gave way. The day was lost! Lovell's Division was at this time advancing, pursuant to orders, and was on the point of assaulting the works, when he received my orders to throw one of his brigades, Villepigue's, rapidly to the centre, to cover the broken ranks thrown back from Corinth, and to prevent a sortie.

He then moved his whole division to the left, and was soon afterwards ordered to move slowly back and take position on Indian Creek, and prevent the enemy from turning our flank. The centre and left were withdrawn on the same road on which they approached, and being somewhat in confusion on account of loss of officers, fatigue, thirst, want of sleep, thinned ranks, and the nature of the ground, Villepigue's Brigade was brought in opportunely, and covered the road to Chewalla.

Lovell came in the rear of the whole army, and all bivouacked again at Chewalla. No enemy disturbed the sleep of the weary troops. During the night I had a bridge constructed over the Tuscumbia, and sent Armstrong's and Jackson's cavalry, with a battery of artillery, to seize and hold Rienzi until the army came up, intending to march to and hold that point; but after consultation with General Price, who represented his troops to be somewhat disorganized, it was deemed advisable to return by the same road that we came, and fall back toward Ripley and Oxford. Anticipating that the Bolivar force would move out and dispute my passage across the Hatchie Bridge, I pushed rapidly on to that point, in hopes of reaching and securing the bridge before their arrival; but I soon learned, by couriers from Wirt Adams, that I would be too late. I nevertheless pushed on, with the intention of engaging the enemy until I could get my train and reserved artillery unparked on the Bone Yard road to the crossing at Crumb's Mills. (This road branches off south from the State-line road, about two and a half miles west of the Tuscumbia Bridge, running south, or up the Hatchie.) No contest of long duration could be made here, as it was evident that the army of Corinth would soon make its appearance on our right flank and rear. The trains and reserve artillery were therefore immediately ordered on the Bone Yard road, and orders were sent to Armstrong and Jackson to change their direction, and cover the front and flank of the trains until they crossed the Hatchie, and then to cover them in front until they were on the Ripley road. The enemy were then engaged beyond the Hatchie Bridge by small fragments of Maury's Division as they could be hastened up, and were kept in check sufficiently long to get everything off. General Ord commanded the forces of the enemy, and succeeded in getting into position before any number of our travel-worn troops could get into line of battle. It is not surprising, therefore, that they were driven back across the bridge; but they maintained their position on the hills overlooking it, under their gallant leader, General Price, until orders were sent to fall back, and take up their line of march on the Bone Yard road, in rear of the whole train. At one time, fearing that the enemy, superior in numbers to the whole force I had in advance of the train, would drive us back, I ordered General Lovell to leave one brigade to guard the reserve to Tuscumbia Bridge, and to push forward with the other two to the front. This order was quickly executed, and very soon the splendid brigades of Rust and Villepigue made their appearance close at hand.

The army corps of General Price was withdrawn, and Villepigue filed in and took position as rear-guard to the army against Ord's forces. Rust was ordered forward to report to General Price, who was directed to cross the Hatchie at Crumb's Mills and take position to cover the crossing of the teams and artillery. Bowen was left at Tuscumbia Bridge, as rear-guard against the advance of Rosecrans from Corinth, with orders to defend that bridge until the trains were embarked and on the road; then to cross the bridge and burn it, and to join Villepigue at the junction of the roads. In the execution of this order, and while in position near the bridge, the head of the Corinth army made its appearance and engaged him, but was repulsed with heavy loss, and in a manner that reflected great credit on General Bowen and his brigade. The army was not again molested on its retreat to Ripley, nor on its march to this place. The following was found to be our loss in the several conflicts with the enemy, and on the march to and from Corinth, viz.: killed, 594; wounded, 2,162; prisoners and missing, 2,102. One piece of artillery was driven in the night by a mistake into the enemy's lines and captured. Four pieces were taken at the Hatchie Bridge, the horses being shot. Nine wagons were upset and abandoned by the teamsters on the night's march to Crumb's Mills. Some baggage was thrown out of the wagons, not amounting to any serious loss.

Two pieces of artillery were captured from the enemy at Corinth by Lovell's Division, one of which was brought off. Five pieces were also taken by General Price's Corps, two of which were brought off. Thus making a loss to us of only two pieces. The enemy's loss in killed and wounded, by their own accounts, was over 3,000. We took over three hundred prisoners; most of the prisoners taken from us were the stragglers from the army on the retreat.

The retreat from Corinth was not a rout, as it has been industriously represented by the enemy, and by the cowardly deserters from the army. The Division of General Lovell formed line of battle, facing the rear, on several occasions, when it was reported the enemy was near; but not a gun was fired after the army retired from the Hatchie and Tuscumbia bridges. Nor did the enemy follow, except at a respectful distance. Although many officers and soldiers, who distinguished themselves in the battle of Corinth and in the affair of Hatchie Bridge, came under my personal observation, I will not mention them to the exclusion of others who may have been equally deserving, but who did not fall under my own eye; I have deemed it best to call on the different commanders to furnish me with a special report, and a list of the names of the officers and soldiers of their respective commands who deserve special mention. These lists and special reports I will take pleasure in forwarding, together with one of my own, when completed; and I respectfully request that they be appended as part of my report. I cannot refrain, however, from mentioning here the conspicuous gallantry of a noble Texan, whose deeds at Corinth are the constant theme of both friends and foes. As long as courage, manliness, fortitude, patriotism, and honor exist, the name of Rogers will be revered and honored among men. He fell in the front of the battle and died beneath the colors of his regiment, in the very centre of the enemy's stronghold. He sleeps, and glory is his sentence!

The attempt at Corinth has failed, and, in consequence, I am condemned, and have been superseded in my command. In my zeal for my country I have ventured too far with inadequate means, and I bow to the opinion of the people whom I serve. Yet I feel, if the spirits of the gallant dead who now lie beneath the batteries of Corinth could see and judge the motives of men, they do not rebuke me, for there is no sting in my conscience. Nor does retrospection admonish me of error, or of a disregard of their valued lives.

Very respectfully, sir, I am

Your obedient servant,

EARL VAN DORN, *Major-General.*

REPORT OF MAJOR-GENERAL PRICE
OF THE BATTLES OF CORINTH
AND DAVIS'S BRIDGE

HEAD-QUARTERS, ARMY OF THE WEST, }
Holly Springs, October 20th, 1862. }

MAJOR:—I have the honor to submit the following report of the operations of this army connected with the several engagements at Corinth and
Davis's bridge, of the 3d, 4th, and 5th instants. Having arranged with Major-
General Van Dorn to unite my forces with his for active operations, I joined
him at Ripley, on the 27th ult. My force at this time consisted of effective
infantry, 10,498; effective cavalry, 2,437; effective artillery, 928 men, and forty-
four guns, including two 24-pounder howitzers, and four rifled pieces of three
and five-eighths calibre. The infantry was divided into two Divisions, commanded by Brigadier-Generals Maury and Hebert. Maury's Division consisted
of three brigades, commanded by Brigadier-General Green and Colonels
Martin Gates and Colbert. The cavalry, except such companies as were on
detached service, was under command of Acting Brigadier-General Armstrong.
The artillery was appointed as follows: with Maury's Division, Hoxton's
Battery, Lieutenant Tobin, commanding; Bledsoe's Battery; McNally's Battery,
Lieutenant Moore, commanding; Lucas's Battery, and Songstack's Battery.
Hoxton's and Brown's Batteries, and Songstack's Battery were held as reserves,
under command of Lieutenant Burnett, Acting Chief of Artillery of the
Division. With Hebert's Division were Wade's, Landis's, Guibor's, Dawson's
and King's. The cavalry force under General Armstrong reported to the Major-
General commanding the combined forces, and afterward acted under direct
orders from him.

On the morning of the 30th ultimo, we took up the line of march in the
direction of Pocahontas, which place we reached on the 1st instant, and from
which we moved on the enemy at Corinth, bivouacking on the night of the
2d instant at a point nearly opposite to Chewalla, having left one regiment
of infantry and a section of artillery with the wagon-train as guard.

At 4 o'clock, on the morning of the 3d instant, we resumed the march,
my command moving on the main Pocahontas and Corinth road, in rear of
General Lovell's. At a point about a mile and a half from the enemy's outer
line of fortifications, my command made a detour to the left, with instructions
to occupy the ground between the Memphis and Charleston and Mobile and
Ohio Railroads. This done, my line—Maury occupying the right and Hebert
the left, with Coball's and Colbert's Brigades in reserve—fronted the enemy's
work in a south-easterly direction, the right resting upon the Memphis and
Charleston Railroad. While these dispositions were making, General Lovell
engaged the enemy upon our right. All being now ready for the attack, my

line was ordered forward at about 10 o'clock A.M. Almost simultaneously with
the movement, the opposed armies became engaged in desperate conflict along
the whole extent of my line. My command had scarcely cleared the position
of its first formation, when, entering an abattis of more than three hundred
yards, it became unmasked before a position naturally exceedingly formidable,
and rendered trebly so by the extent of felled timber through which it must
be approached, and the most approved and scientifically-constructed intrench-
ment, bristling with artillery of large calibre, and supported by heavy lines of
infantry. My troops charged the enemy's position with the most determined
courage, exposed to a murderous fire of musketry and artillery. Without faltering, they pressed forward over every obstacle, and, with shouts and cheers,
carried, in less than twenty minutes, the entire line of works—the enemy having fled, leaving in our hands many prisoners and two pieces of artillery —
one a 4-inch Parrott gun, the other a 24-pounder howitzer. Our loss in this
attack was comparatively small. This is attributable to the impetuosity with
which the charge was made and the works carried. It becomes my painful
duty, in this connection, to revert to the distinguished services of two gallant
officers who fell in this engagement—Colonel John D. Martin, commanding
a brigade of Mississippians, and Lieutenant Samuel Farrington, of Wade's
Battery. Colonel Martin fell mortally wounded while leading the charge
against an angle in the enemy's works, exposed to the fire of enfilading batteries. The gallant bearing of this officer on more than one bloody field had
won for him a place in the heart of every Mississippian, and the admiration
and confidence of his superior officers. Lieutenant Farrington was struck and
instantly killed by a shot from a rifled gun, while bringing one of the guns of
his battery into position. This gallant soldier, and courteous and chivalric gentleman, forgetful of personal interest, and mindful of the necessities of the service, resigned a lieutenant-colonelcy in the service of his State for a lieutenancy
in the Confederate service, and gave up his life, a glorious sacrifice upon the
altar of his country's honor, in the seventh of the battles in which he has been
conspicuous for cool, determined, and effective bravery. Though young, his
country mourns no more valiant defender, his command no abler commander,
his friends no worthier recipient of their affections. The outer works being in
our possession, my line moved forward in pursuit of the retreating enemy until
within one mile of Corinth, where the enemy was encountered in position
and in force. The necessary dispositions being made, my whole line again
moved forward to the attack about 3 o'clock P.M. Here the fighting was of
unparalleled fierceness along the whole extent of my line. The position of the
enemy along the whole extent of his lines was covered by fencing, heavy timber, or underbrush, while portions of my troops advanced through open fields
exposed to a deadly fire of batteries operating over the enemy's line of infantry.
Here, as in the assault upon the outer works, we had little artillery in action,
it being impossible to procure such positions for my batteries as would enable

them to co-operate effectively with the infantry. After continuous and most desperate fighting along the whole extent of my line, of nearly two hours' duration, the enemy, notwithstanding his lines had been trebled by reinforcements, was driven from his position, and forced to take refuge in his innermost works in and around the town.

The troops of my command, having nearly exhausted their ammunition in their heavy fighting through the day, were withheld from immediate pursuit, and the delay in procuring the necessary supply of ammunition forced me to close the fight for the day. My troops were withdrawn for cover, and laid on their arms during the night in the position from which the enemy had been driven.

About 4 o'clock on the morning of the 4th, three batteries of my command were placed in position, and opened fire upon the town, under the immediate orders of the Major-General commanding. About daylight, orders were received to advance my whole line. In the execution of the order, a delay was occasioned by the illness of Brigadier-General Hebert, commanding a division. He was necessarily relieved from duty. The command devolved upon Brigadier-General Green, who moved forward as soon as he could make the necessary disposition of his troops. It was after 9 o'clock when my line became generally and furiously engaged with the enemy in his innermost and most formidable works, from which his infantry and artillery could jointly operate against my troops. Here, as in the previous actions, my artillery could not be brought effectively into action, and but few of the guns were engaged. The fighting, by my command, was almost entirely confined to the infantry. My men pressed forward upon the enemy, and, with heavy loss, succeeded in getting into the works, having driven him from them, capturing more than forty pieces of artillery, and forcing him to take refuge in the houses of the town, and in every place that could afford protection from our galling fire. He was followed, and driven from house to house, with great slaughter. In the town were batteries in mask, supported by heavy reserves, behind which the retreating enemy took shelter, and which opened on our troops a most destructive fire at short range. My men held their positions most gallantly returning the fire of the enemy with great spirit, until a portion of them exhausted their ammunition and were compelled to retire. This necessitated the withdrawal of the whole line, which was done under a withering fire. The attack was not resumed, and we fell back to our supply-train, the men being almost exhausted from exertion and the want of food and water. General Villepigue's Brigade moved over to our assistance, but did not become engaged, as the enemy was too badly cut up to follow us. We fell back, in order to obtain water, some six miles from Corinth, where we bivouacked for the night, bringing off all our artillery and arms, save one rifle-piece, which had been inadvertently driven into the enemy's line while going into battle before daylight in the morning, and had been left. We brought off, also, the two guns captured at the outer line of fortifications on the 3d. It is impossible for me to do justice to the courage of my troops in these engagements, nor can I discriminate between officers and commands where all behaved so nobly. This is the less necessary, as the operations of my command were under the immediate observation of the Major-General commanding. For the minute details of the actions, especially of the artillery, of the 3d and 4th instants, I beg leave to refer the Major-General commanding to the reports of the commanding officers, herewith inclosed.

On the morning of the 5th instant we resumed the march in the direction of Pocahontas, my command moving by division, Maury's in front, each in rear of its ordnance and supply train, except Moore's Brigade, which constituted the advance-guard. After crossing the Tuscumbia, Moore's Brigade was hurried forward to protect Davis's bridge across the Hatchie, which was threatened by an advance of the enemy.

It being found that the enemy were in force, the remainder of Maury's Division was ordered forward, and finally I was ordered to move up my whole command. Moore's Brigade, with a section of the St. Louis Battery, and Songstack's Battery, were thrown across the Hatchie, but the enemy having possession of the heights commanding the crossing, as well as the position in which these troops were placed, and it being found that he was in very heavy force, it was deemed advisable to cross the Hatchie by another road, and these troops were withdrawn, after serious loss, to the east side of the Hatchie, where, being joined by Cabell's and Phiffer's Brigades, and assisted by the batteries of McNally, Hogg, Landis, and Tobin, they effectually checked the advance of the enemy. Green's Division, which had been delayed in passing the wagon train that had been unparked near the Tuscumbia, arriving on the ground, was formed in line of battle; but the enemy making no further effort to advance, the whole of my command was moved off by another route, General Lovell's command being in our rear.

This was our last engagement with the enemy. In this last engagement we lost four guns by the killing of horses. Our whole train came off without molestation or loss, except of a few wagons, that were broken down and had to be abandoned.

The history of the war contains no bloodier page, perhaps, than that which will record this fiercely-contested battle. The strongest expressions fall short of my admiration of the gallant conduct of the officers and men of my command. Words cannot add lustre to the fame they have acquired through deeds of noble daring, which, living through future time, will shed about every man, officer, and soldier, who stood to his arms through this struggle, a halo of glory as imperishable as it is brilliant.

They have won to their sisters and daughters the distinguished honor set before them by a General, of their love and admiration upon the event of an impending battle, upon the same fields, of the proud exclamation, "My brother, father, was at the great battle of Corinth!" The bloodiest record of this battle is yet to come. The long list of the gallant dead upon this field will carry sorrow to the hearth-stones of many a noble champion of our cause, as it does to the hearths of those who are to avenge them. A nation mourns their loss, while it cherishes the story of their glorious death, pointing out to their associate officers in this mighty struggle for liberty the pathway to victory and honor. They will live ever in the hearts of the admiring people of the government, for the establishment of which they have given their lives. Of the field officers killed were Colonels Rogers, Second Texas Infantry, who fell in the heart of the town, of eleven wounds; Johnson, of Twentieth Arkansas, and Daly, of Eighteenth Arkansas. Lieutenant-Colonels Maupin, First Missouri Cavalry, dismounted, and Leigh, Forty-third Mississippi. Majors Vaughan, Sixth Missouri Infantry, Doudell, Twenty-first Arkansas, and McDonald, Fortieth Mississippi. Many of my ablest and most gallant field-officers are wounded, several mortally. Of this number are Colonels Erwin, Sixth Missouri Infantry, Moore, Forty-third Mississippi, and McLean, Thirty-seventh Mississippi; Lieutenant-Colonels Pixley, Sixteenth Arkansas, Hedgespeth, Sixth Missouri Infantry, Serrell, Seventh Mississippi Battalion, Lanier, Forty-second Alabama, Hobson, Third Arkansas Cavalry, Mathews, Twenty-first Arkansas, Cambell, Fortieth Mississippi, and Boone; and Majors Senteny, Second Missouri Infantry, Keevir, Thirty-eighth Mississippi, Staton, Thirty-seventh Alabama, Timmins, Second Texas, Jones, Twenty-first Arkansas, Russell, Third Louisiana, and Yates and McQuiddy, Third Missouri Cavalry. For other casualties in officers and men, I beg leave to refer to lists inclosed. I cannot close this report without recognizing the eminent services and valuable assistance of Brigadier-Generals Maury, Hebert (whose services I regret to have lost on the morning of the 4th by reason of his illness), and Green, commanding divisions. I bear willing testimony to the admirable coolness, undaunted courage, and military skill of these officers, in disposing their respective commands, and in executing their orders. Through them I transmit to Brigadier-General Moore, and Acting Brigadier-Generals Cabell, Phiffer, Gates, and Colbert my high appreciation of their efficient services on the field.

Their skill in manœuvering their troops, and promptness and gallantry in leading them through the most desperate conflicts, elicit my highest admiration. And of my troops, as a body, I can say no juster or more complimentary words than that they have sustained, and deepened, and widened their reputation for exalted patriotism and determined valor. To my personal staff I return my thanks for their promptness in the delivery of my orders, and their gallant bearing on the field.

All of which is respectfully submitted.

STERLING PRICE, *Major-General.*

MAJOR M. M. KIMMALL,
Assistant Adjutant-General, Army of West Tennessee.

THE PRESENT APPEARANCE
OF THE BATTLE-FIELD

A recent explorer of this bloody battle-field thus speaks of its present appearance:

"Not the least memorable of the 'pitched battles' of the late war was that which was fought in front of this grand 'intrenched camp' that we call Corinth, on the 3d and 4th days of October, 1862.

"During the past two days, a portion of my sojourn here has been spent as a partial exploration of that part of the battle-field which lies in the north-western angle formed by the crossing of the Memphis and Charleston, and Mobile and Ohio Railroads. The sights that I saw of vast numbers of Confederate 'bones'—whole skeletons and parts of skeletons—lying exposed, and bleaching on the field, in the bushes, and on the hill-sides, under logs, and on stumps; of the neatly-inclosed and well-marked graves of the Federal soldiers, all buried at the proper depth; and of the forest trees in all directions rent and torn by shot and shell, and all the 'storm of the furious war,' and of many separate and distinct desperate conflicts, hand to hand and muzzle—all the 'sights,' I say, are well worthy of a brief record. Besides, I have another object in calling attention to the battle-field of Corinth apart from the gratification of public curiosity, and that is, to urge upon our people the propriety of collecting the bones of their dead brethren at some suitable spot near the place, and giving them a decent interment. It is estimated by an intelligent citizen of Corinth that, upon the two fields of 'Shiloh' and 'Corinth,' in the vicinity, there are not less that 12,000 'Confederate dead,' whose bones, for the most part, are bleaching above the ground.

"Of all the Confederate dead on this field, Colonel Rogers is, I am told, the only one who was properly buried deep enough to prevent the rains from washing the dirt away and exposing the bones. He, it is said, was buried under the immediate supervision of General Rosecrans.

"In the north-western angle, formed by the crossing of the railroads, from Corinth out to and beyond the outer works three and a half miles distant, the whole of this great battle-ground is dotted here and there—in some places thick as meadow mole-hills—with the graves of Federals and the exposed remains of Confederate dead. The Federal dead were all neatly interred in the usual way, with head and foot boards in every instance, and in most cases, I believe, were inclosed with wooden palings. The Confederate dead, it clearly appears, were merely covered on the ground where they fell. I saw but one Confederate *tumulus* where the bones—generally the skulls—were not more or less exposed, and scattered in all directions. At the outer line of intrenchments, where a portion of Maury's Division made the assault, I saw two human bones, one pelvis and two jaw-bones, lying on a stump, with no trace of a grave or *tumulus* nearer than fifty or a hundred yards. In front of the outer breastworks, not far from the same spot, were two *tumuli*, where six or eight Confederate dead had been covered up on the side of a hill. Here several skulls, and the feet of the most of the bodies, had been uncovered by the action of the elements, and were lying scattered on the ground, already bleached perfectly white, and, of course, rapidly crumbling to decay. The condition of these *tumuli* is a fair specimen of all the rest. In one place, the bodies of two or three Confederates were placed by the side of a log (to save labor) and a little dirt thrown upon them; the dirt had all washed away, and there the skeletons lie wholly exposed and uncared for, 'like the beasts that perish.'"

Little dreamed the gallant Price, when he wrote that the silent dead "would live ever in the hearts of the admiring people of the government for the establishment of which these heroic men gave their lives," that ere four years had elapsed from the date of that fearful struggle, such a record would be published as the above. Among those bleaching bones lie all that remains of those heroic spirits who, undaunted, battled against a powerful foe, who once stood in all the pride and glory of their fearless manhood among the gallant men of the Third Louisiana Infantry, as they stormed the enemy's batteries and intrenchments. By their side lie the sons from the far-off plains of Missouri, and the hills of Arkansas; from Mississippi, and the "Lone Star" state, martyrs in the same cause, animated by the same spirit in serving the country for which they sacrificed their lives.

CHAPTER XXV

CAMP ROGERS

WHILE encamped at Holly Springs, the days of October passed quietly away without incident worthy of note. It was weeks before the men fully recovered their old elasticity of spirits, and the regiment finally settled down into the old routine of a soldier's existence. On the 22d of October, orders were once more received to move, and early on the morning of the 23d the regiment was traveling southward. They were not overburdened with packs, as both clothing and blankets were scant. After proceeding a few miles from Holly Springs, the regiment was encamped at a spot known as Camp Rogers. Here a line of hills dip into the valley extending southward from Holly Springs. The camp was a pleasant one, on the hills, amid the shadows of large oak-trees. In front of it were wide extended fields, formerly cultivated in cotton, now covered with corn stubble. In the rear, westward, was a cotton-gin, and another uncultivated field, on the surface of the range of hills here quite level, and used as a drill ground. At this camp the regiment was assigned to the Third Brigade, Second Division, of General Maury's troops. The first night of their arrival was inaugurated by a heavy white frost, followed by bitter cold weather, and snow on the afternoon of the 25th. The men suffered very much, being scantily supplied with clothing, and insufficiently sheltered, their chief protection consisting of tent flies. Fortunately their propensity for foraging, together with large quantities of sweet potatoes brought into camp, in addition to their regular rations, kept them well supplied with provisions, an offset to their other wants. Hence they gathered in groups around their camp fires, roasted potatoes in the ashes, and amused themselves by indulging in soldiers' rough witticisms with the Thirty-sixth Mississippi, encamped on their left. This regiment was commanded by Colonel Witherspoon, whom the boys quickly nick-named "Pewterspoon," for reasons best known to themselves. There was the usual discipline here, drills, police, etc., varied by an occasional scout after "Bear," and chickens, resulting usually in complete success, or songs at night while gathered around the camp fires.

On the 1st day of November there was a division review, and the men were in high spirits once more. This was followed by a general review on the 3d, at which were present large numbers of ladies from Holly Springs and the surrounding country; also, Generals Van Dorn, Price, Maury, Bowen, Green and others. The day was clear and cold. The imposing array of men, with their guns glittering in the cold November sunlight, the assembly of fair ladies, the galaxy of dashing and distinguished officers, formed a brilliant and imposing spectacle. It was a combination of the beauty and chivalry of the country. Far away stretched the valley, hemmed in on one side by the undulating hills, and on the other by a dark line of forest, whose Autumn foliage had assumed the dark-brown hue of Winter's coloring. The occasion, display and scenery combined, made up a scene of warlike aspect, such as was seldom witnessed even in those days of bloodshed and strife.

On the 5th, the sun was obscured by heavy clouds; the atmosphere was hazy and cool. Orders were issued to cook three days' rations and be prepared to move. The men packed and shouldered their knapsacks, and loaded the wagons in anticipation of an early move. They were in uproarious good humor, pelting each other and the Mississippians with sweet potatoes, of which they had large quantities. The regiment was moved a short distance from the camp and halted. The valley was filled with long trains of wagons moving rapidly southward, and the whole army was in motion amid great excitement. The enemy were evidently on the advance, in too powerful force to be successfully resisted.

The Texans attached to our brigade had been promised the return of their horses, which were only a few miles distant; and, when there seemed a probability of moving without them, they positively and most determinedly refused to march. They were addressed by General Maury and Colonel Whitfield, in stirring speeches, all in vain. Have their rights they would, in spite of the whole army and all its commanders. The consequence was their horses were speedily hurried up and delivered to their owners. The scene that ensued beggared description. Mounting, they dashed off at full speed, in squads and singly, over ditches, fences and every obstacle, into the valley, yelling like demons released from the bottomless pit. In the saddle once more, these dashing Texans felt at home, and exhibited their joy in all manner of extravagant performances. Their ardor soon cooled down, and they formed and left for the rear to watch the foe. The Louisiana Regiment were sorry to lose these gallant comrades, who had fought with them through some of the bloodiest battles, exhibiting a dashing bravery as infantry worthy the laurels which they had gained in the cavalry service. Ere the day passed away, the wind rose almost to a gale, filling the air with dust and smoke, completely blinding and almost suffocating the troops. Heavy, dark and lowering clouds, like a funeral-pall, hung over the earth, which made the scene a gloomy and wintry one. That night the men slept in Camp Rogers, around the fires, and in pens built of brush and rails, on cotton procured from the gin near by. They suffered intensely, however, from the cold, being without blankets, which had been packed in the wagons and sent away.

The Mississippians had taken possession of the cotton-gin, and numbers of them were snugly ensconsed in these comfortable quarters amid the cotton. Some of the Third Regiment learned the fact, and a guard was formed, properly officered, apparently, who proceeded to the gin and authoritatively ordered the Mississippians out of the building, saying they had been sent there by the General to protect the cotton and place. The orders were obeyed. It is needless to say that a large number of the Louisianians enjoyed an excellent sleep that night, the guard being the suggestion of some sharp-witted privates, and a ruse to oust the Mississippians. So much for the experience of veterans.

The next day, November 6, the regiment were out on the parade-ground, fully armed and equipped, with their knapsacks on their backs, actually going through the evolutions of drill. Artillery and infantry were passing, and soon the slumbering echoes of the valley were awakened by the dull, heavy roar of artillery, far away toward Holly Springs. Still the drill went on as if no enemy was pressing the rear-guard of the army now in rapid retreat. It was, indeed, a strange spectacle. They were finally marched back to camp for inspection. Guns were cleaned out, and there was quite a fusillade as the men tested their cleanliness. This excited the ire of Colonel Witherspoon, who sent orders for it to be stopped. The Louisianians paid no attention to the order. They expected to fight soon, and were determined to be thoroughly and properly prepared. Soon an aid-de-camp arrived at regimental headquarters with the order that, if the firing was not stopped, Colonel Witherspoon would bring his regiment to the spot and fire into the men. This message spread like wild-fire through camp, the men tightened their belts, brought their cartouche and capboxes to their proper places for service, threw off their knapsacks, at the same time shouting all kinds of messages to the aid, such as "Tell Colonel Pewterspoon to send his regiment down here and we will give them a turn. Hav'n't got many cartridges, and just as leave expend them in fighting Mississippians as the Yankees." The men were actually exasperated, in the fullest signification of the word. They had been touched on their tenderest point—their *honor*. Whether Colonel Witherspoon actually sent this order was never clearly ascertained; but that one of his aids did, unthinkingly, deliver this message to Major Richards, then in command of the regiment, is an incontrovertible fact. This was an unfortunate circumstance, as it created an ill-feeling between the regiment and the remainder of the brigade which could never be eradicated. Colonel Witherspoon showed himself to be a chivalrous gentleman, an efficient and brave officer on numerous occasions.

On the retreat to Abbeville, General Hebert came into the camp, and was immediately surrounded by the men, who complained bitterly that they were put in a conscript brigade. The General replied: "Never mind, my men; never mind. You will soon make good soldiers of them all." The compliment thus delicately paid to the efficiency of the regiment did not soothe their irritated and discontented feelings.

The brigade, at this time, was composed of the Thirty-sixth, Thirty-seventh, Thirty-eighth, Fortieth and Forty-third Mississippi—regiments organized under the Conscript Act. The Third Louisianians did not take into consideration that, although volunteers and disciplined veterans, they had reorganized under the same act of the Confederate States.

These items are not pleasant records, yet adherence to truthfulness compels their insertion, as a portion of the actual occurrences connected with the regiment.

The army retreated steadily southward until it reached Abbeville, a short distance south of the Tallahatchie, on the Mississippi Central Railroad. Here the regiment encamped on a level plat of ground east of the railroad, between the Tallahatchie and Abbeville. The camp was beautifully shaded by oak-trees.

CHAPTER XXVI

ON the 14th of November, the regiment was suddenly ordered to the breastworks. These fortifications were solidly-constructed earth-works, on the north side of the Tallahatchie, near where the railroad crossed the stream, also, spanned by a rough bridge. They commanded a good view of the country; stretching away in front of them, a level plain of uncultivated cotton-fields. Confined in these works, the men passed the time as best they could. They were full of life and mischief. Their provisions were daily cooked in camp, and carried to them by details made for this purpose.

On the 16th a countryman came to the bridge with a drove of fine, fat hogs, which seemed adverse to crossing. *The kind and obliging* Louisianians eagerly volunteered to aid him. By some *unaccountable* means numbers of the swine were driven into the water, and, swimming down stream, never were found. Perhaps the boys did not relish a good supper of "bear" meat that night!

On the 17th, the regiment returned to camp, the weather being cold and stormy, continuing for two days, and then cleared off, with a biting wind from the north-west. The men frolicked, danced, sang and gambled at night, drilled during the day, and performed the duties of a regular camp-life while waiting for the appearance of the enemy. Lieutenant Washburn, taken prisoner at Iuka, returned again to the regiment at this place, and resumed his duties as Adjutant.

Major Tunnard once more visited the regiment at Abbeville on the 25th, and was joyfully welcomed. On this day there was a review of General Maury's Division, making a very creditable display. The days continued clear and cold, infusing an unusual quantity of activity and life into the men, who never grew weary in attempting some kind of mischief. The morning bugle was greeted with hoots, yells, and cries of every description, at last becoming so furious that a whole regiment was ordered on drill at daylight for indulging in this noisy pastime. The example had a salutary effect on the rest of the troops.

On the night of the 28th, at 10 o'clock P.M., the regiment was again suddenly ordered out to the breastworks.

The next day three days' rations were cooked, all extra baggage ordered to be sent off, and the trains prepared to move. The roar of artillery proclaimed the approach of the enemy and heavy skirmishing in the vicinity of Waterford. In the skirmish several men were wounded, a piece of artillery dismounted, but not lost, as the brave troops tied a rope around it, and, hitching in a team of horses, triumphantly dragged it from the field in safety. The army was compelled to abandon the intrenchments, and the first day of the winter months found them again retreating along the line of railroad, in a cold and drenching storm, and over roads knee-deep in mud and mire. The enemy pursued closely and persistently, making frequent dashes upon the rear-guard.

In Oxford, the scene almost beggared description. Long columns of troops, tired, wet and soiled, poured through the town, accompanied by carriages, buggies, and even carts, filled with terror-stricken, delicate ladies— whole families carrying with them their household goods and negroes. The scene was one of indescribable confusion and excitement—one of those gloomy pictures of war so distressing in all its circumstances.

The retreat was continued in the midst of a furious rain-storm, the roads being in a terrible condition, on through Water Valley, Spring Valley, Coffee-ville, and to Grenada.

On the 3d, as the trains were pushing rapidly forward, the thunder of artillery was heard directly west of the retreating army. It seems that the enemy were attempting to reach Grenada in advance of the Confederate army, by the way of the Mississippi and Tennessee Railroad, which forms a junction with the Mississippi Central at Grenada, in order to destroy the trains, and cut the railroad in the front of the retreating army. They were met, however, at Oakland by the fearless and gallant Texans, several regiments of whom dismounted and acted as infantry, much to the astonishment of the foe. This skirmish was a severe one, resulting in the enemy finally withdrawing their troops, with the loss of many men and two pieces of artillery. On the same day there was a brisk skirmish at Oxford, and a precipitate retreat from that place, many of the men having very narrow escapes from capture by the Yankees, who made a gallant dash into the town on the very heels of our army. Thus the retreating columns retrograded, day after day, in the drenching rain, amid the roar of artillery and unprecedented sufferings.

On the 5th, Rust's Brigade, formed and executed a well-planned ambuscade, by which the Federals were severely punished for their temerity in pushing too closely the retreating columns.

On the night of December 5, the regiment encamped at Grenada. The weather suddenly became intensely cold, and, the morning of the 6th, frost and ice were plentiful. Numbers of the men, exhausted and worn out with their constant marching, exposed to such inclement weather, were sick—some of them dangerously so, from typhoid fever and pneumonia. This retreat planted the seeds of disease in many a noble form, resulting in their sinking into early graves.

On the 7th, the regiment was encamped some distance west of Grenada, endeavoring to recuperate from their physical prostration.

On the 17th, moved camp once more to the vicinity of Grenada.

On the 23d, President Davis and General Johnston arrived at Grenada, creating many surmises and speculations as to the object of their visit at this time. Grenada was well fortified along the Tuscahoma and Yallabusha rivers, and a warm reception prepared for the foe.

On the 25th, there was a grand and imposing review at Grenada, at which were present President Davis, General Johnston, and other celebrities. News reached the army, also, of General Van Dorn's successful attack on Holly Springs, capturing 1,600 Federals, and $1,500,000 worth of stores of every description.

On the 28th, the regiment broke up camp, and left for Vicksburg. This had now become the great theatre of action, and desperate attempts were being made to capture this stronghold, in order to open the navigation of the Mississippi River. In December, the enemy made a landing, and stormed the breastworks commanding the Yazoo valley north of Vicksburg. They were terribly defeated by the Twenty-eighth Louisiana Regiment. Here Major Humble, formerly a lieutenant of Company I, Third Louisiana, lost his life. He was a fearless and gallant officer.

CHAPTER XXVII

SNYDER'S MILLS

THE regiment proceeded across the country to Yazoo City. Their reception at this place was very enthusiastic, especially by the ladies, who seemed untiring in their endeavors to supply the wants of the men. Here they embarked on boats, and proceeded to Snyder's Mills, on the Yazoo River. During this period the men were without their baggage, and very few had blankets, having left their knapsacks, tents, and bundles at Varden, thus enduring the weary march exposed, without shelter, to the sudden changes of the variable wintry weather.

After their first failure in the attempt to capture Vicksburg, the Federals had suddenly decamped, only to return once more in the latter part of January to renew the attack. From Vicksburg to Snyder's Mills is a line of abrupt hills, commanding the Yazoo valley, which had been fortified along the whole distance, some twelve miles. At Snyder's Mills the Yazoo strikes the bluff, and then turns almost abruptly westward for some distance, ere flowing southward. On this bluff were batteries of heavy guns in close proximity to the river, manned by the Twenty-second Louisiana. Just above these formidable and frowning batteries was a solidly-constructed raft of huge logs, completely blockading the stream. Thus this position, naturally formidable, was rendered doubly strong by the labor and ingenuity of man. The country back of this line of bluffs is a series of high hills, intersected by deep and narrow ravines, all covered with a dense undergrowth of cane, and heavily timbered, from whose huge branches drooped the pendent moss, and whose trunks were covered with clinging vines, all forming the luxuriant growth of nature peculiar only to a tropical clime. Almost immediately in the rear of the batteries commanding the Yazoo River, was the encampment of the regiment. In the absence of tents, the men excavated houses on the abrupt hill-sides, forming the roofs of rough shingles, firmly supported by posts—erecting, in fact, those rude shelters with a celerity truly astonishing, and for which soldiers are proverbially famed. The regiment had scarcely reached

Snyder's Bluff, ere they were ordered into the intrenchments, in anticipation of an expected attack. Defending, as they were, the most distant northern point of the fortification that protected Vicksburg, they were nerved to a determination which they had never before experienced, and, notwithstanding the need of many conveniences to make their position comfortable, were full of life and fun. The stake now being played for was a tremendous one, being the possession of the Mississippi River, involving the destiny of its whole valley, and the vital life and safety of the country. This occurred as another New Year began its cycle, the regiment reaching Snyder's Bluff on the 2d day of January, 1863.

The month of January passed away with little to attract attention or create any serious apprehension of an early attack from the foe, who seemed to have concentrated all their energy and ingenuity in an attempt to cut a canal across the elbow of land directly in front of Vicksburg, at which point the river makes an abrupt turn, flowing almost north-east until it strikes the bluff upon which Vicksburg is situated, and then turns abruptly south, inclining a little westward. The object of the enemy was to make the canal across the neck of land, formed by the peculiar course of the stream, large enough to float their steamers through, thus completely isolating Vicksburg, and obviating the necessity of running the gauntlet of the heavy batteries crowning the hill-sides and lining the banks.

On the 28th of January, the enemy's boats came into the Yazoo, but without approaching our point of defense. At this time, the heavy roar of guns in the direction of Vicksburg was a daily occurrence, the batteries either shelling the workmen on the canal, or engaging in a lively artillery duel with some formidable iron-clad, when venturing within range of the guns on a reconnoitering expedition. The regiment was almost constantly kept under orders, and thoroughly prepared to meet the foe at any moment.

On the 11th, there was a general review of the troops by Major-General Maury, and the regiment occupied a position in the line of intrenchments. General Maury had become a great favorite with the men, who had every confidence in his ability and power to successfully defend the point committed to his charge.

On the 13th, there was an election in the various companies to fill vacancies, occasioned by the resignations and deaths of several officers, resulting in the choice of the following 2d Junior Lieutenants: Thomas Gourrier, Company A; W. Middlebrook, Company C; ———Thomas, Company E.

On the 13th, Captain Charles A. Bruslé once more visited the regiment. He was appointed on General Hebert's staff, by the following general order:

General Orders, }   HEAD-QUARTERS, SNYDER'S MILLS, }
   No. 18   }   *February 24th, 1863.* }

"Extract."

II. Charles A. Bruslé, late a captain of the Third Regiment Louisiana Infantry, has been appointed Aid-de-camp, with the rank of first lieutenant, to date from February 7th, 1863. He will be obeyed and respected accordingly.

By the order of Brigadier-General Hebert.

W. D. HARDEMAN, A. A. G.

Thus, after having resigned from the Confederate service on account of physical inability to stand the severities of a soldier's existence, Captain Bruslé once more returned to the army, and the vicinity of his old company and regiment.

On the 18th, there was quite an excitement in the regiment, created by the report that a Yankee gun-boat had succeeded in reaching the Yazoo above, by coming through what is known as the "Pass." Volunteers were called for to go on a boat, protected with cotton, and capture the audacious visitor by boarding. Nearly the whole regiment volunteered, but only sixty were chosen, under the command of Captain H. H. Gentles, and Lieutenant Cy. Hedrick. Of this number only fourteen were finally selected for the expedition, in order to give other regiments a chance to share in the anticipated fight. The report proved false, and the whole expedition returned without having found the enemy. At this time the batteries were continually bellowing forth their hoarse thunder at Vicksburg, and events of thrilling interest and excitement were occurring.

On the 22d, a national salute was fired by the batteries in honor of the natal day of George Washington. The weather was very disagreeable, raining almost continually, and the rations were very poor; the men scantily clothed, after their numerous retreats and shortening baggage on the road.

On the 25th, the regiment was ordered out on a picket, in the midst of a heavy rain.

March, generally so stormy, opened with a bright and smiling sky, and an invigorating, refreshing atmosphere. The men were full of life, and passed their evenings in dancing, interspersed with music, both vocal and instrumental. Their new situation seemed to agree with them most wonderfully. On the 6th, the whole brigade attended the execution of a deserter from the First Louisiana Heavy Artillery, who had been captured in Federal uniform. His bearing was firm, and he met his death most courageously.

Some time in the middle of March, the enemy attempted to reach Yazoo

City from above, but were most signally repulsed at Fort Pemberton. On the 20th, heavy and rapid firing above our position drew numbers of the men to their eyries on the hill-tops commanding a view of the Yazoo valley. The cannonading, rapid and heavy, was in a north-westerly direction, and a cloud of white smoke could be distinctly seen to rise into the clear morning air, from the dark bosom of the trees. The enemy were attempting to force a passage into the Yazoo through the Sunflower, but were gallantly met and most signally repulsed by Featherstone's Brigade.

The regiment received a new uniform, which they were ordered to take, much against their expressed wishes. The material was very coarse, white jeans, "Nolens volens." The uniforms were distributed to the men, few of whom would wear them, unless under compulsion, by some special order. On the 22d, orders were issued to cook three days' rations, and be prepared to move ere daylight the succeeding morning. The weather was gloomy and rainy, the roads in a terrible condition. Some of the men suggested the propriety of wearing the new white uniforms on the approaching expedition, which, it was known, would be among the swamps of the Yazoo valley. The suggestion was almost universally adopted, affording a rare opportunity to give the new clothes a thorough initiation into the mysteries of a soldier's life. Thus the regiment assembled the next morning arrayed as if for a summer's day festival. The rain was falling steadily, and the roads were deep with mud, as they began the march towards Hayne's Bluff, a short distance above Snyder's Mills, and the points where the steamboats landed. This place was also fortified, and the river protected above by batteries of heavy siege-guns, commanded by Captain John Lumon. The men were in high spirits. The expedition was commanded by Brigadier-General S. D. Lee. On the night of the 23d, the regiment slept on board the steamer Peytona, and the next morning were transferred to a very small, side-wheel boat, called the Dew Drop, not a misnomer by any means. On arriving at the mouth of Deer Creek, the expedition was visited by a tremendous storm of wind and rain, compelling our little craft to seek shelter amid the over-hanging branches of the trees which drooped over the stream. The storm, with its accompanying hurricane, soon passed away, and the expedition proceeded on its way. The water was very high, and the flood covered the whole expanse of the country, with only here and there a patch of land visible, like some oasis in the great, sandy desert. What an expedition this was, comprising a perfect fleet of flats, flat-boats, skiffs, canoes, and every conceivable small floating craft. The men were wild with excitement and fun, and made the swamps re-echo with their shouts and laughter. They preceded the little steamer in their flotilla of small craft, cutting down trees, whose interpolated branches obstructed the passage. Arrived at Mr. Wilson's, on Deer Creek, at 12 o'clock P.M., on March 25th, where the regiment disembarked and sought rest on the low, marshy ground, in the fence corners, and on some old timbers of a defunct flat-boat.

The men were immediately detailed en masse to construct earthworks and obstruct the river. They labored with a hearty good-will and energy truly commendable, in the water and mud. General Lee was present in person to superintend the construction of the works, and was not afraid to share the severe toil. His actions and manner, so pleasant and affable, soon won for him the deep admiration and heartfelt esteem of the whole regiment. If he had orders to give, he delivered them in person. No neatly-dressed aids-de-camp, with their foppish airs and tones of authority, were deemed necessary to carry instructions. We distinctly remember the appearance of General Lee, as he stood conversing with Colonel Russell, on the deck of the Dew Drop, as the boat steamed slowly along Dear Creek. A huge, rough overcoat enveloped his form, below the knees, pants thrust carelessly into his high, military boot-tops, while his fine, manly features lighted up with smiles beneath his slouched hat as he watched the hilarity and mischief among the men in the boats, remarking as he did so, "Colonel, your men seem to be full of life." General Lee was always sincerely respected by all who served under him, as he was thoroughly practical in all he did, and never required what he would be unwilling to perform himself. The Twenty-second and Twenty-eighth Louisiana Infantry joined the Third Regiment in their labors and hardships. Details were daily made from the regiment, who proceeded to Snyder's Mills in skiffs, and transported all the provisions thence to the scene of operations. It was both a dangerous and laborious undertaking.

The boats of the detail generally proceeded across the country, through lanes and along roads, which considerably shorted the distance to camp. Often they were compelled to get out of the boats and push them by main strength along the rapid streams and over shallow places. On the 27th, one of these expeditions was proceeding up the Yazoo, with their boats loaded nearly to the gunnels with provisions. The wind was very high, almost a gale, and the river was very rough. In attempting to cross it, the boats shipped large quantities of water, threatening destruction to their loads and a thorough ducking to the crews. It was something amusing to witness the rapidity with which the men stripped off their clothing for a swim, although the situation was so perilous. The journey, fortunately, was made in safety. On one occasion the Commissary Sergeant was proceeding to the landing with a wagon load of provisions. General Hebert was standing, bareheaded, looking over the gate in front of his quarters, close to the roadside, when he observed the wagon. Calling the sergeant, the following colloquy occurred:

"What have you in that wagon?"

"Provisions, General, for the regiment."

"How many day's rations?"

"Two, sir."

"How are you going to get them there?"

"I have two skiffs at the landing."

"You cannot carry them in those. You'll sink the boats."

"Oh, no, General; I have made the trip before; besides—"

"Never mind; go along, my man; go along," and the sergeant was dismissed with a dignified wave of the hand, as the General pointed up the road, and resumed his journey, wondering what object the General had in view in his scrutinizing questioning. Suffice it to say that the sergeant's understanding was never enlightened.

The enemy abandoned their attempt to penetrate to the Yazoo by the way of Sunflower and Deer Creeks, doubtless considering it a perilous undertaking, in view of the stern and desperate resistance which they would meet in every foot of their advance.

On the 28th, the regiment was ordered to return to camp; so, boarding their numerous crafts, they once more moved down the creek, varying the monotony of the journey with numerous races, resulting in much amusement and excitement. As they passed General Hebert's quarters, at Snyder's Mills, each company saluted the General with loud and prolonged cheers, evincing their good feeling for their old commander. The compliment was pleasantly and gracefully acknowledged.

The regiment reached camp sadly soiled in their external appearance, only to find that some persons unknown had "out-Heroded Herod" himself, and their tents had taken legs and walked off during their absence. Verily there was much profane language used when the "situation" was fully comprehended.

Captain Butler, of Company G, Lieutenant Payne, of Company K, and several other officers were furloughed to obtain recruits for the regiment, whose depleted ranks proclaimed most forcibly the fearful desperation with which, up to this period, the command had served their country.

March went out, amid frost and very cold weather, without incident worthy of note. J. G. Perry, of Company K, and George Effner of Company F, were sent out to reconnoitre the country along Deer Creek, and discover whether the enemy had abandoned all intentions of reaching the Yazoo valley through this route. They departed on their hazardous enterprise in a small canoe, taking their arms with them.

The advent of the second Spring month was heralded by a genial atmosphere, and deep-blue skies overhead. These bounteous gifts of nature—blessings much enjoyed—were gratefully received by men who had lived through the recent stormy wintry months, scantily supplied with shelter, almost constantly in motion, and lately watching and waiting for an active and vigilant foe in their anticipated attack upon the long line of defenses which protected the city of hills—heroic Vicksburg.

The 1st day of April was marked with much excitement, breaking up the usual monotony of camp life, by the intelligence that the enemy were approaching. The troops were speedily under arms, and soon the deep roar of a signal-gun proclaimed the truth of the report, while the troops eagerly responded to its summons, and hastened to the line of defenses. Repairing to the brow of the hill commanding a view of the valley, many anxiously watched the manœuvres of the approaching foe. A cloud of black smoke, rolling above the tree-tops, marked the advance of the enemy's boats. Soon a transport, accompanied by three gun-boats, landed at Blake's plantation, a short distance below the bluff. The transport almost immediately returned down the river, while the iron-clads moved slowly up, and, sheltered by a strip of woods immediately in front of our position, commenced shelling the breast-works and hills. The missiles were badly aimed, and passed harmlessly over the men, exploding in the air, without injuring a single man. One boat, becoming embolded by the silence of our frowning batteries, and the apparent stillness of the whole place, steamed up toward our guns, in full view from the bluffs, but carefully screening herself behind the adjacent bend, was wise enough to keep out of sight of our huge guns.

After a short reconnoissance the gun-boats departed, having thrown about twenty shells without eliciting any reply. No clue could be obtained as to the purport of this sudden visit, terminating without any material design.

The enemy seemed very restless over their prolonged operations against Vicksburg, evidenced by innumerable expeditions into all the adjacent bayous, lagoons, creeks, and the expenditure of ammunition in shelling the silent woods and deserted, barren fields. At this period, they seemed to have abandoned all hopes of reaching the Yazoo *via* Deer Creek, as our scouts returned, after penetrating nearly to the Mississippi River, reporting not having seen or heard of a single enemy in the valley.

On the 3d, a large number of recruits arrived for Company G, and also Lieutenant-Colonel Russell.

On the 6th of April, the Yazoo began to rise very rapidly, being the effects of cutting the Grand Levee of the Mississippi by the Federals, for the purpose of flooding the Tallahtachie valley and driving our forces from the vicinity of Greenwood, to prevent their operating against the gun-boats and transports of the Yankees, as well as afford them better facilities for expeditions by water. This rise extended to the adjacent creeks and bayous, completely inundating the whole valley. With these apparent advantages, the increased flood actually placed a more efficient barrier to any land attack on the defenses protecting Vicksburg.

This new idea of the foe, together with a concentration of all their valuable means of attack, indicated an early, simultaneous and vigorous attack on some point of the line of defenses. Our troops were hastening up the Yazoo, to prevent the enemy's approach from the north.

On the 10th, Fort Pemberton was evacuated, after a most heroic defense. Several days passed away most quietly at Snyder's Mills, with little to relieve their monotony. Not a ripple of the waves of war, that thundered with such angry fury against the fortified hills of Vicksburg, disturbed the quietude of the lines. Several boats had succeeded in getting below Vicksburg in safety, notwithstanding the storm of iron hail poured upon them. It was the beginning of their final success. This occurred on the night of April 17. The terrific cannonading aroused the whole camp, and the flashes of the explosions could be distinctly seen.

After a pretended desertion of the siege, the enemy returned, only to increase their exertions for the capture of our stronghold. They imagined, perhaps, that their pretended abandonment of the siege would cause our troops to be withdrawn, and thus weaken our position, when, by a sudden return and an unexpected assault, he could gain possession of the place. This *ruse de guerre* failed most signally, and they returned only to find us still prepared, and his designs understood.

The days thus passed away, the roar of artillery at Vicksburg reverberating in sullen echoes over the adjacent valleys, and usually attracting little notice.

On the 16th of April, the raft which blockaded the Yazoo at Snyder's Mills gave way under the tremendous pressure of the accumulated flood of waters. This event was considered, at the time, a great misfortune. General Smith and other military celebrities soon assembled at the point of disaster, and held repeated consultations as to the best method of repairing the evil. The anxiety was intense. an unsuccessful attempt was made to recover the portions of the raft which had floated away, by sending the steamer Acadia below after them. The immense flood of water, and the rapid current, rendered the attempt of rebuilding the raft a fruitless one. Heavy siege-guns were immediately forwarded to this point, and placed in position as speedily as possible. Whatever human

ingenuity and skill could invent to strengthen the position, was immediately put
in practice. Thus the hill-sides commanding the river soon were thickly dotted
with frowning batteries of heavy siege-guns.

On the 19th, Major-General Maury left the division for a new post in
Tennessee. His departure was the subject of general regret. In his farewell address
to the officers and soldiers of his division, he said that to their chivalry and valor
did he owe much of the praise and honor bestowed upon him. Each officer and
soldier of his command felt that, to the efficiency, discipline, and gallantry of
their leader, they owed, in a great measure, all that had contributed to win them
a name for bravery and daring. To his new field of operations, General Maury
carried with him unanimous and heartfelt wishes for increased success, as well
as those deep, undying feelings of friendship and admiration which united the
soldiers of Napoleon to their idolized Emperor, and made them invincible in
battle. No soldier was there in General Maury's command too humble for his
notice, as well as the highest officer in his division. Understanding and appreciating the position and feelings of the Southern volunteers, his intercourse with
them was such as to gain their unbounded admiration, and entwine round each
soldier's heart those tendrils of affection and devotion which death only could
sever. Oftentimes have we seen General Maury dashing along the road, followed by his staff, when, meeting some soiled and uncouth-looking private,
wearily marching along the dusty road, he would bend forward gracefully in his
saddle, and, lifting his hat from his brow, salute the soldier with all the polished
ease and elegance of manner so indicative of the high-toned gentleman, and
with a soldierly politeness, worthy a superior, and not as if the object of his def-
erence and marked attention was the private soldier of his division. No wonder the men loved him and disliked to part with him.

> We had seen him on the fierce field of battle
> Firm as the granite, while the musket's sharp rattle,
> The cannon's deep roar, the charge of the foes,
> Told where thickest the fight, where fiercest the blows.
> We had seen him on march, long, toilsome, and dreary,
> Encourage the men, travel-worn, weak, and weary;
> Amid the quiet of camp, on the showy review,
> Always affable, kind, brave, courteous and true.
> Ever cherished, remembered, wherever thou mayst go,
> Brave Dabney H. Maury we bade thee adieu.

On the 21st, the whole regiment was armed with Confederate Mississippi
rifles, having sabre bayonets, making a fine appearance. These rifles were, however, almost worthless, as the sequel of their fate will show.

On the 23d, five transports and one gun-boat succeeded in getting safely past the batteries at Vicksburg, thus considerably augmenting the strength of the fleet below the city, and causing some anxiety to be felt as to the success of the designs of the enemy, which began to develop themselves. Thus success of the Federals in running the gauntlet of the heavy batteries caused considerable comment, and the press published some strange accounts of neglect and inattention on the part of the officers in charge at Vicksburg. Whether correct or not, certain was it, that the enemy had accomplished their object, despite the heavy fire poured into their steamers from the batteries. Their escape from destruction was assuredly miraculous. Thus, while these stirring scenes were daily transpiring at Vicksburg, the Third Louisiana Regiment was quietly encamped on the Yazoo, surrounding themselves with soldiers' comforts, and enjoying themselves in varied amusements. Summer-houses, built of cane closely entwined together, and covered with shingle roofs, occupied much attention, and gave the camp quite a picturesque appearance. These airy structures were very pleasant during the warm days, and afforded ample protection and shelter in stormy weather. The days of April, however, were usually clear and pleasant. The valley in front of the hills was mostly open fields, and where timber once stood was a heavy abattis of felled trees, intersected with lagoons and ditches. These were swarming with cray-fish, and the men not only found amusement in catching them, but also a very palatable article of food. They were caught in immense quantities, all the tackle necessary for their capture being confined to pieces of meat tied to strings. They could be drawn out of the water almost as rapidly as three or four of these simple lines could be pulled up, sometimes five and six cray-fish clinging to a single bit of meat. It required but a very few moments to fill a bushel bag with these ravenous shell-fish. Cray-fish soup was no rarity in camp. The Mississippians looked with great amazement and much disgust at the keen relish with which "them ere Cre-owl Louisianians" devoured this species of food. They could not appreciate such a peculiar taste.

On the 29th day of April, the long-anticipated attack on our position was commenced. The thundering echoes of war, which had so long disturbed the quiet of the Mississippi valley, at last found an answering echo from the emerald hills and peaceful valley of the Yazoo. Early on the morning of this day a huge cloud of smoke, rolling its dark volume over the valley below, admonished us that the foe were approaching in considerable force. Making Chickasaw Bayou (the scene of their first repulse in an attempt to reach Vicksburg by land from above) a rendezvous, they remained quietly in that vicinity all night. Our camps were filled with rumors that they were attempting to effect a second landing at this point. These rumors proved incorrect. About 9 o'clock A.M.,

April 30th, the fleet ascended the river and approached our position. The troops
were promptly in their places in the intrenchments. While the transports, some
eight in number, kept at a safe distance, three gun-boats ran up within range
of our batteries, and opened the fight. A terrific cannonading immediately followed. The iron-clad Choctaw ran up within easy range of our upper guns and
opened fire on them. They responded at once, and with a skill and accuracy in
handling the guns worthy of old cannoniers. The Choctaw was struck fifty-
three times during the engagement, which lasted nearly five hours. Her flag-
staff was shot away, and, as much hammering was heard on board of her after
the firing had ceased, it was thought that she was seriously crippled. The casualties at our batteries were two men badly wounded, and the cracking of a band
of one of the 32-pounder rifle guns. While the Choctaw was engaging the upper
batteries, the other gun-boats ran up within easy range of the whole line of
trenches, and opposite the lower batteries, and shelled the lines most furiously.
Although the bombardment was fierce and protracted (their shells exploding
in every direction), yet, strange as it may appear, no casualties occurred save
the killing of a horse in one of the light batteries. The bombardment ceased for
this day at 3¹/₂ P.M. Late in the afternoon, the fleet was augmented by the arrival
of more boats, so that it numbered fifteen transports, three mortar-boats, and
six gun-boats. During the progress of the first day's fight, the Third Louisiana
Infantry occupied a position near Blake's upper quarters, in the valley, near the
Yazoo, and later in the day in the marshy ground, directly in front of the fortifications at this point. Taking advantage of the sheltering protection of the
levee on the river bank, they obtained a position in close proximity to the
Choctaw, and fired into her port-holes whenever opened.

During the progress of the fight the enemy perpetrated one of those acts
of Vandalism, so common in war, by setting fire to Mr. Blake's deserted quarters. They supposed that the valley was free from Confederates, as they had seen
them apparently leaving this place. Retributive justice was summarily visited on
the perpetrators of this incendiarism. The left of the regiment was close at hand;
and, as the flames issued from the buildings, the sharp reports of their unerring
rifles caused several of the enemy to bite the dust, while the remainder incontinently "skedaddled" to their boats. One officer was shot while standing on the
deck of the iron-clad making observations. In the skirmish with the squad from
the gun-boats, who succeeded in effecting a landing without the knowledge of
the picket, Lieutenant J. R. Cottingham, of Company I, was thrice wounded,
and taken prisoner by the enemy. The whole picket narrowly escaped capture,
some of the men actually screening themselves from observation by jumping

into the river, and concealing themselves under the banks. There were no other casualties in the regiment. The scream of shells, the deep roar of heavy artillery, made Snyder's Mills a lively spot on the last day of April, and gave birth to numerous ridiculous incidents, notwithstanding the seriousness of the cause. During the night the trenches were occupied, and a line of pickets thrown out to watch the enemy's movements.

The morning of May 1st, 1863, the day usually devoted to scenes of festivity in honor of the Goddess of Flowers, dawned clear, bright, and beautiful, showing the Federal fleet lying opposite Blake's lower quarters, beyond the range of our batteries. In front of our lower battery was a large field under cultivation. Near its centre, between the line of fortifications and the Yazoo, is a depression in the surface of the lands extending down the valley, then covered with water.

Before the war, a large levee shut out the overflow arising from the freshets in the Yazoo. The enemy placed a picket on this levee, in full view and within easy range of our field-pieces. With perfect *sang froid* they paced to and fro along their elevated beat, regardless of the close proximity of our artillery. Operations commenced by a battery opening on this picket, resulting in no harm beyond driving them from the top, behind the sheltering protection of the embankment. Early in the day, a party of some forty or fifty, following the banks of the river, and sheltering themselves behind the levee and woods, suddenly appeared in close proximity to our upper batteries, where the river strikes the bluff, evidently bent on reconnoitering the raft. The heavy guns immediately opened on them with an unerring precision of aim, that compelled them to beat a precipitate retreat, with a loss of several of the party. Their next manœuvre was on the opposite side of the river, some distance below, in considerable force. As they were observed dodging among the trees and running across an old field, the gallant boys of the Twenty-second Louisiana gave them another lesson of their skill in managing siege-guns, and quickly drove them back once more. During these operations, the gun-boats remained quietly anchored in the stream. About half-past three o'clock P.M., they took position directly in front of our lower battery on Grave Yard Hill, and directed a concentrated fire on it from three of their boats, while two others shelled our headquarters; the mortar-boats sending their huge missiles into the valleys directly in rear of the intrenchments. The cannonading was terrific on both sides; the guns being handled with great skill. The ground in the vicinity of our lower battery was actually ploughed up by the heavy, plunging shot. The parapet was repeatedly struck, the shells often exploding within the works.

The firing continued incessantly for over four hours; yet, strange as it may appear, there was not a single casualty among our troops.

After the cessation of the fight, considerable hammering was heard in the direction of the enemy's boats, which, taken in connection with their refusal to engage our upper batteries, proves conclusively that they must have sustained considerable damage. During the night of the first, the Yankee fleet quietly departed, and the next morning not a boat was to be seen.

A DARING FEAT

About 4 o'clock P.M. on the first, while the gun-boats were firing on the lower batteries, a daring and successful feat of desertion occurred. The deserter belonged to an Illinois regiment, but was a Kentuckian, representing himself as General Sherman's orderly, and giving his name as William Hammond. He had been sent to the outposts with dispatches. Reaching these, he swam his horse around the cuts in the levee, and successfully passed the Federal pickets, emerging, in full view of both armies, from the bushes in the swamp land into the cultivated field. As his intentions became apparent, he was fired on, but spurring his horse into a headlong gallop, he turned towards the picket, fired his pistol in derision, and arrived safely in our lines, amid the loud cheers of the men. The boys were wild with excitement, jumping from the ditches upon the top of the breastworks, and along the hill-sides, regardless of the danger, in their eagerness to witness the race. As the deserter reached the lines, he threw his pistol from him, at the same time exclaiming, "Hurrah for old Kentuck."

He gave the information that the enemy were not strong enough to assault our works, and that the movement was a mere feint to keep our forces occupied, and to prevent their reinforcing the army at Grand Gulf, where a formidable demonstration was being made by General Grant to land his troops. The information was not credited at the time, although its correctness was clearly demonstrated by subsequent events.

FIRST VISIT FROM MORTAR SHELLS

Up to this period, amid all their experience in warlike missiles, the members of the regiment had never been under a visitation from mortar shells. Several of these huge visitors descended into the camp of the regiment, spoiling the appearance of the ground, and making *pi* generally of everything within their vicinity. The camp guard and details thought to find protection within the shelter of their houses in the hill-sides, but a view of the tremendous force and powers of destruction of the huge iron balls, soon drove them into the open air, as by far a greater shelter than caves, with the probability of a burial alive. The reserve artillery and infantry sought shelter from the flying shells, beneath the protection of an almost perpendicular hill. Imagine their surprise, when one of these shells, exploding over them, sent its fragments directly into their midst, considerably startling them from their dreams of security, doing, however, no damage beyond killing a horse attached to one of the batteries.

PREPARATIONS TO LEAVE SNYDER'S MILLS

On the 3d of May the regiment received orders to keep three day's rations cooked, and be ready to march at a moment's notice.

Stirring news began to reach us from below. During the attack on our position, the enemy had succeeded in effecting a landing at Grand Gulf. In consequence of the overwhelming numbers of the Federals, this place was evacuated after spiking the guns. The gallant Missourians of Bowen's Brigade fought most desperately, but were compelled to give way before the overwhelming numbers opposed to them. Our little army retreated to Port Gibson, where, being reinforced by Tracy's and Green's Brigades, another desperate conflict occurred, but again being outnumbered, were compelled to give way. Among the killed at Grand Gulf was Colonel Wade, of the Missouri Brigade, a man universally esteemed for his gallantry as a soldier, and his unvarying kindness toward all with whom he came in contact. At Port Gibson another able commander fell. Brigadier-General Tracy was one of the most efficient brigade commanders in the army, and his loss was irreparable. Disasters followed each other in rapid succession, the enemy successfully driving back our forces by their overwhelming numbers, unsuccessful attempts being made at Raymond and Big Black to check their steady advance. The threatening aspect of affairs east of Vicksburg filled our camp with innumerable conflicting rumors, and the men were full of excitement and enthusiasm. On the 16th, reports reached us of the capture of Jackson. On the 17th, the success of the enemy was confirmed by the sound of heavy guns east of our position, indicating severe fighting in the vicinity of Big Black. Kelton, formerly a private of Company E, Third Louisiana Infantry, but then attached to a battery, arrived in camp during the day, covered with dust and blackened with powder. He reported all the guns of his battery lost, except one. A portion of our troops precipitately retreated on the appearance of the enemy, without firing a gun, abandoning the artillery in their haste to place Big Black between themselves and the victorious foe. It is needless to record the fact that the gallant Missourians fought like tigers at bay, successfully withstanding the assaults of the Yankees, and escaping capture only by the most determined bravery, when the other troops gave way. They added new lustre to the laurel wreath which already adorned their names and fame, for distinguished valor and undaunted bravery. Thus the fierce storm of war, which had so long thundered in impotent fury against our young Gibraltar, was descending with fearful force upon our stronghold and its devoted defenders.

INCIDENTS OF LIFE AT SNYDER'S MILLS

The Third Regiment had never been more pleasantly situated than at Snyder's Mills, constantly subjected, as they were, to active service. With a skill, perseverance, and ingenuity truly commendable, they had erected comfortable quarters, and gathered about them all those little conveniences which become actual luxuries to the soldier. Within easy communication with all parts of the country, daily papers reached them, furnishing full particulars of the progress of the war throughout the land, while Vicksburg was sufficiently near to enable them to procure such necessaries as they needed, or were able to purchase.

SUPPLIES

Immense quantities of supplies of every description were transported down the Yazoo on steamers, and discharged at the landing above our camp. Thence they were carried in wagons to a depot commissary near at hand, or to Vicksburg. Thus a large amount of stores for subsistence accumulated at this point. Of course, the veterans of the regiment could not restrain their propensity for foraging, especially when the beef issued them was not only very poor, but actually, at times, offensive, the cattle often dying in the butcher-pens ere they could be slaughtered. The boys eagerly volunteered to load the supplies, and it was not an unusual occurrence for wagons to reach their destinations much lighter than when they started. It was unaccountable how fine hams would fall out of the wagons, along the road-side, and still more strange how squads following the train would find these hams, and carry them, not whence they were lost, but into camp. Eggs and chickens were plentiful, and a breakfast of broiled ham, fried eggs, and chickens, was no rarity. Yet about the quarters there was no appearance of a super-abundance of supplies; but, when the encampment was broken up, the mystery was explained, as every mess in the regiment uncovered underground store and smokehouses, most ingeniously constructed, with an eye both to concealment and the preservation of their contents. Verily, soldiers are queer bipeds. Major T. W. Scott, Brigade Commissary, and his clerks, Niolin and W. Johnson, could some wondrous tales unfold of the mysterious disappearance of their supplies, even when thoroughly guarded and watched by argus-eyed sentinels.

"THEM ERE MELITIA"

Near the regiment was an encampment of Mississippi militia, composed of men of good intentions, but most woefully ignorant of tactics and discipline. Their attempts at drilling and manœuvering gave rise to some rich, racy, and laughable scenes. Of course this afforded a never-ending source of amusement to the disciplined veterans of the regiment, and an opportunity for indulging their propensity for fun. Thus the drill of the militia was always the occasion for outbursts such as the following: "Now, men, mind you stand up straight, and form line like a ram's horn." "Now mind, I'm going to fling you into fours." "Into fours—git." "Into twos—git." "Now I'll swing you like a gate." "Swing like a gate—git." This new style of issuing orders was always received with uproarious mirth, and so confused the amateur soldiers as to completely incapacitate them for performing any evolutions. They were actually compelled to change their quarters to escape the sport made of them by "them ere cussed Cre-owl Louisianians."

A COMPROMISE WITH A COLONEL

Colonel Witherspoon, of the Thirty-sixth Mississippi, was often in command of the brigade, and whenever he passed the camp was almost certain to be made the subject of some rude joke, as the men had never forgotten the incident at Camp Rogers. On one occasion he detected two of the regiment in the very act of flaying a hog, which they had killed, a flagrant breach of military orders, and subjecting them to severe punishment. Here was an opportunity for the Colonel to repay some of the sport constantly made of him. Approaching the culprits, the following colloquy ensued: "Well, men, I have caught you in the very act of transgressing positive orders. There is no denying this fact."

"Yes, Colonel, we plead guilty, and have no excuses to make."

"I hardly know what to do with you. However, I will compromise with you. If you will agree to cease calling me 'Pewterspoon,' I'll promise to say nothing about this matter."

The boys eagerly made the agreement, shouldered their "game," and arrived safely in camp, and related their adventure. The story soon went the rounds, and the men showed their appreciation of the forbearance and general good-humor of the Colonel to their comrades by refraining from making him the subject of their fun. A simple act of kindness won immmediately their esteem and good will. Whether true or not, there are few of the regiment who do not remember this story as here related, and the cessation of all hostilities thereafter, toward Colonel Witherspoon.

PRIZE-FIGHTING

When the regiment first entered the service, there was, as is usual among a large number of men, numerous personal encounters. On such occasions the officers used their authority, and immediately prevented any serious collisions. The consequence was, that quarreling became almost a daily occurrence, the men seeming to feel satisfied that no serious consequences would result from it. At Snyder's Bluff a new order of proceeding was established, and by a tacit agreement whenever two men felt disposed to have a sparring-match they were permitted to do so, provided they went out of camp. On one occasion two fine-looking, stalwart members of Company A quarreled. The officer in command ordered them to cease wrangling, and go fight it out if they desired to. He was taken at his word, and the two men went up one of the narrow defiles, unattended by seconds or friends. None offered to follow them. In a few moments they returned to the company together, one having a badly-bruised face, and the other minus some of his front teeth. No explanations were vouchsafed, and the antagonists were friends, after having fought it out on their own line. This method of settling disputes made the men live harmoniously together, and almost entirely checked the propensity for indulging in personal encounters.

These are but a few of the numerous incidents of camp life at Snyder's Mills.

CHAPTER XXVIII

VICKSBURG

THE 17th of May dawned clear and warm. The bright, smiling skies seemed not as if they canopied events which would decide the destiny of a great nation. Yet beneath their azure clearness the fierce passions of man were at work, making fearful records for the historian's pen, and writing in letters of blood the instability of all earthly plans. The serene atmosphere was early disturbed by the dull, heavy reports of distant artillery. Orders were soon received to prepare to march toward the theatre of strife. Amid the most intense excitement, preparations to leave were begun. There was no transportation for clothing, stores, cooking-utensils, or camp-equipage. Provisions, accumulated for months, were brought from their hiding-places, and each man selected what he could conveniently carry. Knapsacks were filled to their utmost capacity with all the soldier's most valuable and treasured articles. Extra blankets, robes, clothing of all descriptions, tents, utensils, etc., were indiscriminately heaped together in the quarters and abandoned. The heavy siege-guns were either spiked, or loaded so as to burst them, a detail being left to accomplish this design, after the army had departed; also to blow up the magazines, and destroy the depot-commissary, containing an immense supply of provisions. The troops left Snyder's Bluffs for aye late at night, and proceeded toward Vicksburg, an intermingled line of wagons, artillery, and infantry. The night was very dark, yet the men pushed forward as rapidly as possible along the valley, wading streams and sloughs on the route. Notwithstanding the gloom which overshadowed their future, and the losses which they had sustained by their sudden abandonment of their recent position, as well as the proximity of the foe in such overwhelming force, they were in most excellent spirits, and very enthusiastic. They considered Vicksburg an impregnable stronghold, and experienced a peculiar pride in the prospect of defending it during the approaching struggle.

On the morning of May 18th, 1863, the regiment reached the Hill City, and were immediately placed in the intrenchments. These intrenchments were constructed on the crests of a line of hills, extending in a semicircle completely around the city, and about a mile in its rear. The whole country was a succession of abrupt hills, intersected by deep, narrow defiles. The regiment was placed near the centre of the line, on the left of the Jackson road, as it emerges from a deep cut through a hill. On the right of the road were the Twenty-first and Twenty-second Louisiana Regiments, consolidated, and on their left the Mississippi Regiments, comprising the remainder of Hebert's Brigade. General Hebert informed the men that they held the key to the city, on the most exposed portion of the line. The regiment responded that they would sustain their blood-earned reputation, justify the confidence reposed in their bravery, and perish to a man ere they would relinquish their position to a million foes. Perhaps no body of men were actuated by feelings of more determined courage, and a spirit of resistance even unto annihilation.

In the position which they occupied, the left of the regiment was very much exposed, no intrenchments being constructed on that portion of the line. Self-preservation, the first law of nature, admonished the men of their peril. Procuring spades and pickaxes, they went to work with a desperate energy, which rapidly constructed works on the gap in the line. Rumors and particulars of the disasters which had befallen our troops, poured in on our men as they took their respective positions along the lines. Numbers had fallen into the enemy's hands, and many pieces of artillery had been lost. Yet our brigades, fresh from camp, felt no despondency, and the shadow of defeat darkened not their brave spirits as they quietly waited for the foe. On the afternoon of the 18th the skirmishing began some distance outside of the line of works. Our forces were steadily driven back, until they reached the protection of our guns. The enemy hesitated as they reached the line of woods skirting the cleared ground in front of the breastworks. It was only momentary, however, and the spattering reports of the small-arms approached nearer and nearer. The next day was clear and warm. The enemy succeeded in establishing their position, and the siege commenced in earnest. About 1 o'clock P.M. the cannonading became terrific, the musketry deadly and heavy. The enemy charged the intrenchments on a portion of the lines, and were driven back with fearful slaughter, our own loss being very light. The Third Louisiana began to suffer from the enemy's sharpshooters at the very inception of the siege. Regardless of the unerring precision with which the enemy's sharpshooters used their splendid, long-range guns—fearless to a fault, they suffered severely for their temerity in their reckless exposure of their persons. Among the kiled and wounded of May 19th, were N. Schlade and L. D. Blanchard, of Company A. Noble soldiers of one of our best companies.

May 20th, at 1 A.M., the silence of the starlit night was broken by the roar of heavy guns. A huge iron-clad approached from below, and commenced a furious bombardment of the city, which was rapidly responded to by our heavy batteries. Below lay the fleet of the enemy, and above, the river was dotted with a huge fleet of transports and war vessels. On the peninsular the white tents of the enemy's encampment were plainly visible. Such was the panoramic view in front of Vicksburg on the third morning of the siege. At early dawn the mortar fleet of Commodore Porter opened fire on the beleaguered city, adding to the tremendous din their hoarse bellowing, accompanied with the fearful screams and tremendous concussions of their huge, exploding missiles. The place was a perfect pandemonium from early dawn. The hoarse bellowing of the mortars, the sharp report of rifled artillery, the scream and explosion of every variety of deadly missiles, intermingled with the incessant, sharp reports of small-arms, made up a combination of sounds not such as described by the poet as being a "sweet concord." A trip through Vicksburg exhibited some strange spectacles.

Huge caves were excavated out of the precipitous hill-sides, where families of women and children sheltered themselves from the hurtling shot and the descending fragments of exploding missiles. Fair ladies, in all the vigor and loveliness of youth, hurried with light tread along the torn up pavements, fearless of the storm of iron and lead, penetrating every portion of the city, as they attended to the necessities of their brave, wounded and dying protectors. The annals of history can furnish no more brilliant record than did the heroic women of Vicksburg during this fearful siege. Regardless of personal danger, they flitted about the hospitals or threaded the streets on their missions of love, utterly forgetful of self in their heroic efforts to relieve the sufferings of those who so gallantly defended their hearth-stones. Many, very many heroic spirits, bade farewell to earth amid the thunder and din of the siege, feeling the soothing pressure of soft hands upon their clammy brows, and the glance of tender, pitying eyes gazing into the failing light of their glazing orbs, as these ministering angels hovered about the lowly cots of the dying soldiers. No pen can describe in sufficiently glowing colors; no human language find words brilliant, forcible enough to do justice to the unwearying attentions, tender compassion, soul-felt sympathy, unvarying kindness, and unceasing labors of love, of the tender-hearted, heroic and fearless ladies of Vicksburg, toward their suffering countrymen. The Third Regiment suffered severely this day, losing nine men killed and wounded; yet, not for an instant failing in their spirits and enthusiasm.

May 21st. The firing continued rapid and heavy all day, the mortar-shells tearing the houses into fragments, and injuring several citizens, including one

lady. The enemy, in front of the Third Regiment, were slowly but surely contracting their lines, and the fire of their sharpshooters was particularly accurate
and deadly. Their batteries concentrated their fire on every one of our guns
that opened on their lines, and speedily dismounted them. A splendid piece of
ordnance, protected by cotton bales, was thus dismounted by the skillful fire
from the enemy's rifled pieces, their balls striking the bales, upsetting them on
the gun carriage, setting fire to them at the same time, and thus burning them
to the ground. It was a fool-hardy piece of business to expose the least portion
of the person above the breastworks, as a hundred rifles immediately directed
their missiles upon the man thus showing himself. No less than five cannoniers
were thus shot, in an attempt to apply a lighted fuse to the vent of a loaded gun.

The members of the Third Regiment suffered severely in their reckless
exposure of their persons to the fire of the enemy's sharpshooters, and the list
of casualties rapidly increased.

In conversation with the enemy (then a common occurrence, from the
proximity of the lines), a member of Company E, by the name of Masterton,
a Missourian, of huge dimension, and familiarly known in the regiment as
"Shanghai," found some acquaintances, and was invited into the enemy's lines,
with the assurance that he would be allowed to return. The invitation was
immediately accepted, and he trusted himself to the honor of the foe. He was
cordially welcomed, and all the delicacies and substantials, which the Federals
possessed in such profusion, were furnished him. After a feast, accompanied
with a sociable chat and several drinks, he was permitted to return, very favorably impressed with the generosity of the Yankees. The evening chats, after the
day's deadly sharpshooting, revealed the fact that there were members of both
armies who were personally acquainted, and, in one instance, two members of
the Third Regiment found a brother in the regiment opposed to them. Such
instances, not uncommon during the war, were not calculated to make persons
of the same family and blood feel over comfortable.

22d. The bombardment continued unabated from all sides of the beleaguered city, and was more rapid and furious than heretofore. Nearly all the
artillery along the lines was dismounted. The report of a single gun within the
breastworks was the signal for a concentrated fire of the enemy's batteries,
which poured a perfect storm of solid shot and shell upon the fated point,
resulting, usually, in the destruction of the battery, and killing and wounding
numbers of the artillerymen.

To the list of our killed and wounded were added the names of Leonard,
St. Amant, Guidici, Ellis, Chastant, Druett, Company A; Finley, Company B;

Murray and Arnaud, Company G; Duffy and Brandenstein, Company K. The fire was terrific, and the fearful list of casualties in the regiment much depressed the spirits of the men. The enemy made an assault on the right of the line, but were repulsed with terrible slaughter, and two hundred of them taken prisoners. This creditable affair was due to the unflinching bravery of the Second Texas Infantry—a gallant and noble regiment. About 10 o'clock A.M., four gunboats steamed up the river from below, and engaged our batteries. They were soon compelled to retire, badly damaged, with but few casualties among our skillful artillerists.

23d. The morning dawned cloudy and lowering; a light rain fell during the night, and summer showers during the day. The shadows of night, falling over the beleaguered city, brought with it no repose to the weary soldiers. Heavy details were made to rebuild and repair those portions of the works ploughed up and torn down by the heavy firing of the enemy's batteries during the day. It was no light task, after fighting all day beneath the rays of the summer's sun, thus, amid the shadows of night, to use pick-axe, spade, and shovel, carry heavy sand-bags, strengthen the torn-down breastworks with heavy timbers and cotton-bales, in order to be protected during the approaching day's combat. Rations, at this period, were plentiful, and were distributed to the men, already prepared, by details made for this purpose. General Grant sent in a flag of truce, asking permission to bury his dead, which were lying unburied in thick profusion outside of the intrenchments, where the enemy had assaulted the lines. General Pemberton refused to grant the request, replying that the battle was not yet decided. The Federal trains and troops were observed moving away from the camps, while rumors prevailed that Johnston was fighting their rear at Big Black. Yet no definite news of succor reached the besieged army.

Among the casualties in the regiment this day were: Lieutenant J. S. Randolph, S. Kohn, Company A; Corporal Scanlan, Company F; Aleck Garza, Lieutenant P. Bassier, Company G; J. McCowen, L. P. Simps, Lieutenant J. Stewart, Company H; J. Dunn, Corporal P. Lawson, W. A. McQuatters, M. V. Ray, Company I; S. P. Russ, Company K.

24th. Sunday dawned clear and beautiful, yet its holy quiet was disturbed by the fierce storm of war, which swept over the city of hills, and thundered in angry surges around its whole circumference. The houses of worship were deserted, and women and children sought shelter from the exploding shells in their underground habitations. The enemy had succeeded in establishing themselves directly beneath one of our parapets, above which stood the undaunted

and heroic men of the Third Regiment. They immediately commenced undermining this portion of the line, with the intention of blowing it up. As the sound
of their voices could be distinctly heard, our brave boys began to annoy them,
by hurling upon them every species of deadly missile which human ingenuity
coud invent. 12-pounder shells were dropped over the breastworks among
them, and kegs, filled with powder, shells, nails, and scraps of iron. A more
deadly, vindictive, and determined species of warfare was never waged. The
chief aim of both combatants seemed to be concentrated in the invention of
apparatus for taking human life.

25th. Another clear and hot day, and a continuation of the usual music
along the lines. In the afternoon, a flag of truce was sent into the lines, request-
ing a cessation of hostilities for the purpose of burying the dead. The effluvia
from the putrefying bodies had become almost unbearable to friend and foe,
and the request was granted, to continue for three hours.

Now commenced a strange spectacle in this thrilling drama of war. Flags
were displayed along both lines, and the troops thronged the breastworks, gaily
chatting with each other, discussing the issues of the war, disputing over differences of opinion, losses in the fight, etc. Numbers of the Confederates
accepted invitations to visit the enemy's lines, where they were hospitably entertained and warmly welcomed. They were abundantly supplied with provisions,
supplies of various kinds, and liquors. Of course, there were numerous laughable and interesting incidents resulting from these visits. The foe were exultant,
confident of success, and in high spirits; the Confederates defiant, undaunted
in soul, and equally well assured of a successful defense. The members of the
Third Regiment found numerous acquaintances and relatives among the Ohio,
Illinois, and Missouri regiments, and there were mutual regrets that the issues
of the war had made them antagonistic in a deadly struggle. As a general rule,
however, the Southerners were the least regretful, and relied, with firm confidence, on the justice of their cause.

Among the numerous incidents that occurred, none seemed to afford more
amusement than the one related of Captain F. Gallagher, the worthy commissary of the regiment. The Captain had been enjoying the hospitalities of a
Yankee officer, imbibing his fine liquors, and partaking of his choice viands.
As they shook hands, previous to separating, the Federal remarked: "Good day,
Captain; I trust we shall meet soon again in the Union of old." Captain G.,
with a peculiar expression on his pleasant face, and an extra side poise of his
head, quickly replied: "I cannot return your sentiment. The only union which
you and I will enjoy, I hope, will be in kingdom come. Good-bye, sir."

At the expiration of the appointed time, the men were all back in their places. The stillness which had superseded the fierce uproar of battle seemed strange and unnatural. The hours of peace had scarcely expired ere those who had so lately intermingled in friendly intercourse were once again engaged in the deadly struggle. Heavy mortars, artillery of every calibre, and small-arms, once more with thunder tones awakened the slumbering echoes of the hills surrounding the heroic city of Vicksburg. The casualties in the regiment were: Wounded, A. J. Powell, Company E, Sergeant E. Jolly, Company K.

26th. Clear and warm. The fight opened very early and kept up very steadily all day. In the city several ladies were killed and wounded by mortar shells. Sergeant W. W. Gandy mortally wounded.

27th. Clear and very warm. The firing was very brisk. About 11 o'clock A.M., the gun-boats approached our batteries, both from above and below, while all around the lines a tremendous, rapid cannonading began. The roar of artillery was terrific in its volume of sound. The Cincinnati, one of the finest iron-clads in the enemy's fleet, boldly approached our upper batteries, but was repeatedly struck, and compelled to return. As she turned in the stream a ball penetrated her hull, and she was only able to reach a sand bar in the bend, when she went down. This combat was witnessed by hundreds of ladies, who ascended on the summits of the most prominent hills in vicksburg. There were loud cheers, the waving of handkerchiefs, amid general exultation, as the vessel went down. Notwithstanding, positive orders prohibiting the fair ladies from needlessly exposing themselves to the flying missiles, they fearlessly sought some prominent position to witness combats whenever an opportunity presented itself. Many despondent soldiers gained renewed courage from the example thus given them by the heroic women of the Hill City.

This disastrous termination of the gun-boat fight seemed to satisfy the enemy in front, and they were quiet during the remainder of the day. The intention of this attack was for the gun-boats to engage and silence our upper batteries, while General Sherman assaulted the works on the extreme left of the line, from the direction of Snyder's Bluff. The whole plan failed most signally. A large number of articles from the sunken boat were picked up in the river, including hay, clothing, whisky, a medical chest, letters, photographs, etc. We often wonder if the surgeon of the Cincinnati, who so comfortably penned a letter to his affectionate wife as the boat neared our batteries, escaped unhurt. His missive never reached its intended destination, but fell into rebel hands to be perused and passed around. It was both well written and interesting. W. Smith, Company C, wounded to-day.

28th. Still clear and warm. A courier succeeded in reaching the city with 18,000 caps which were much needed. Heretofore, the Third Louisiana were armed with the Confederate Mississippi rifles furnished them at Snyder's Mills. These arms were almost worthless, often exploding, and so inefficient that the enemy boldly exposed themselves, and taunted the men for their unskillful shooting. On this day, however, the regiment was supplied with Enfield rifles, English manufacture, and Ely's cartridges, containing a peculiarly-shaped elongated ball, of the finest English rifle powder. These guns had evaded the blockade at Charleston, and had never been unboxed. Beside the rifles, every man was furnished with a musket loaded with buckshot, to be used in case of an assault and in close quarters. The men were so elated at the change in their weapons that they began a brisk fire in their eagerness to test their quality. The foe soon discovered the change, and there was a hasty retreat to the shelter of their rifle-pits, and the protection of their earthworks.

They wished to know where in the devil the men procured these guns, and were by no means choice in the language which they used against England and English manufacturers. Not a single casualty occurred in the regiment. As night approached there was the usual cessation of hostilities, and interchange of witticisms and general conversation between the belligerents. The mortars seldom ceased their work all day, and through the still hours of the night; spoke their thunder voices; and the concussions of their explosions shook the buildings to their very foundations. There was a strange fascination in watching these huge missiles at night, as they described their graceful curves through the darkness, exploding with a sudden glare, followed by the strange sounds of their descending fragments. The spectacle to the eyesight was quite agreeable, but to the other senses anything but pleasant. Casualties, wounded, T. D. Downey, Company E; P. L. Pennery, Company F. The day closed with a spring shower.

29th. Clear and warm. The cannonading was again very heavy and continuous. A gun-boat engaged the lower batteries without any material results. There were no casualties in the regiment.

30th. The day was clear and unusually warm. The constant daily fighting, night work, and disturbed rest began to exhibit their effects on the men. They were physically worn out and much reduced in flesh. Rations began to be shortened, and for the first time a mixture of ground peas and meal was issued. This food was very unhealthy, as it was almost impossible to thoroughly bake the mixture so that both pea flour and meal would be fit for consumption. Yet these deficiences were heroicly endured, and the men succeeded by an ingenious application of the culinary art in rendering this unwholesome food palatable, calling the dish "Cush-cush." Another messenger arrived with despatches and a supply of percussion-caps. While the news from without seemed cheering, not an item of intended succor reached the undaunted soldiers who so heroically defended Vicksburg against the overwhelming forces of the enemy. J. N. Hewitt, killed, Company B. Wounded, R. Quinn, Company E.

31st. The last day of May, the month of smiling skies and budding flowers. There was a clear blue sky overhead, the usual struggle around the works. Sunday brought with it no cessation of hostilities. Fourteen long days and wearisome nights had passed away and still no prospects of relief to the defiant troops. The mortar fleet concentrated their fire on the court-house, near the central portion of the city. The building was occupied by a company of Mississippi militia. One of the huge bombshells finally penetrated into the building, and exploded with tremendous force, killing two men and wounding several others. The militia incontinently "skedaddled" from such hot quarters to a more secure position.

The wreck of the Cincinnati was boarded by a daring party of Confederates, who set fire to the exposed portion of the boat. This gallant exploit was accomplished without any loss. Wounded, S. Allain, Company A; D. Shoemaker, Company B. Up to this date the killed and wounded of the regiment numbered fifty.

June 1st was a clear and unusually warm day. The men sought shelter from the sun's scorching rays beneath the shade of outstretched blankets, and in small excavations and huts in the hill-sides. It seemed wonderful that their powers of physical endurance did not succumb to the accumulated horrors and hardships to which they were exposed. But they faltered not, either in spirit or determination. A deadly shell exploded in the midst of Company F, killing Sergeant J. Roberts, and wounding L. J. Singer, P. Sheridan, J. Charlton, and F. A. Davis.

2d. Dawned clear and warm. Last night a large fire occurred in the city, the result of incendiarism, destroying several buildings. The sky was overcast with dull, leaden clouds, the glare of the conflagration, the bombs' meteoric course through the air, the heavy concussions of the mortars, the sharp reports of rifled-guns, and the shrill scream of the shells, made up a grand and gloomy scene of warfare, during a siege such as is seldom witnessed. Captain J. Beggs, appointed Chief of the Fire Brigade, was promptly on hand directing the operations which soon stayed the progress of the flames. There was the usual heavy cannonading at early dawn, and dusk. During the hottest portion of the day the enemy seemed content to seek shelter from the sun's scorching rays, but in the morning they exercised their skill by pouring a rapid and heavy fire into the breastworks.

Killed: A. Carro, F. Escobeda, Company G; wounded: J. O. McCormick, Company I.

3d. The day opened with the usual music and sharpshooting and cannonading. Seventeen days and nights the fierce conflict had continued, and still no definite news of succor reached the undaunted troops who held at bay the powerful forces of the foe. True reports reached the besieged, that General J. Johnston was concentrating troops at Clinton, with a view of succoring the heroic garrison of Vicksburg, yet it seemed a slender thread of hope. The Third Regiment was becoming sadly decimated in numbers, yet the survivors fought with the same determined, unconquerable, valorous spirit that had always distinguished them. They had promised to hold that portion of the lines intrusted to them, and accumulating disasters unnerved not a single brave spirit or filled a single soul with despair. The tremendous storm of iron and lead continually poured upon them, was received with an indifference to danger worthy of heroic self-sacrificing devotion that distinguished the Spartans at Thermopolae. Though their thinned ranks required an increased amount of exertion and labor, and consequently augmented the burden of their accumulated hardships, there were no complaints, a reckless disregard to peril, and a spirit of heroism manifesting itself by the men composing and singing, with harmonious voices and enthusiastic chorus, songs regarding their situation. What a strange spectacle! These unsheltered, half-fed men, amid the din and uproar of a furious siege, thus manifesting a spirit of reckless disregard for their perilous surroundings. The sweetest strains of the poet's song, the most brilliant record of the historian's pen, the most forcible and elegant language ever coined from the English vocabulary could in no wise do justice to the spirit that animated the souls of this gallant body of Louisianians. From the plains of Missouri to the dashing waves of the Gulf, from the mountain ranges of Virginia to the broad prairies of Texas, their fame had gone over the land, and they were determined that no stain should now mar the fair escutcheon of their bravery. The day was cloudy, and the sun sank below the western horizon behind a bank of clouds.

Wounded: J. W. Blankenship, Company B.

4th. Heavy firing, as customary. Day clear, and very warm. The ration furnished each man was: peas, one-third of a pound; meal, two-thirds of five-sixths of a pound; beef, one-half of a pound, including in the weight bones and shanks; sugar, lard, soup, and salt in like proportions. On this day all surplus provisions in the city were seized, and rations issued to citizens and soldiers alike. To the perils of the siege began now to be added the prospect of famine. The gaunt skeleton of starvation commenced to appear among the ranks of the brave defenders.

It seemed wonderful that human endurance could withstand the accumulated horrors of the situation. Living on this slender allowance, fighting all day in the hot summer sun, and at night, with pick-axe and spade, repairing the destroyed portions of the line, it passed all comprehension how the men endured the trying ordeal.

Wounded: A. Wrinkles, Company G.

5th. Warm and clear. The day passed as usual. A citizen and a little girl killed in the city by a Parrott shell from the breastworks. The gun-boats above and below remained quietly anchored in the stream, evidently indisposed to make any demonstrations after the warm receptions which they had already received. Not a rumor was afloat, for a wonder.

Wounded: C. Castex, Company G.

6th. The morning dawned quite clear. A few summer clouds floated lazily across the azure sky, and the day eventually became one of the hottest yet experienced. The city was rife with rumors, among which was the report of Johnston approaching with succor. The story almost gained full credence by the report of cannon being heard toward Big Black. The welcome sounds were received with shouts along the whole line. Long, anxiously, eagerly had the men been listening for the welcome signal, and now felt as if relief had assuredly come. Ah! on what a slender thread does an expectant soul hang its feeble hopes. There was much stir among the enemy's troops, and large numbers began to move toward their rear, plainly indicating that danger menaced them at some point. The Federals appeared in numbers on the opposite side of the river, firing into the city with long-range rifles, and also with several Parrott guns planted behind the levee. This addition to the means of annoyance by the enemy, made it a very dangerous undertaking for the pedestrian to travel along the streets. Our river batteries immediately opened on the foe, shelling in turn the woods and embankment on the opposite side, everywhere in range of the guns. The Yankees were thus compelled to become very wary in exposing themselves. The artillerymen armed themselves with Enfield rifles, and, repairing to the river bank, kept up a sharp fight with them across the turbid waters of the stream. There were no casualties resulting from this harmless long-range amusement.

The casualties in the regiment up to this date numbered sixty-five.

Wounded: M. Bossac, Company A; T. N. Dill, Company F; J. Connor, Company A.

7th. Very hot, and clear. The mortars, after several hours' silence, opened fire again, very live. This Sabbath-day finished the third week of the siege, and still no hopes of relief. The men did not lose heart, but still kept in fine spirits. The members of the regiment fought to-day with renewed vigor, and a reckless exposure of their persons, killing and wounding a large number of the enemy. Heavy firing was heard west of the Mississippi, afterward ascertained to have been an attack on the Yankee forces at Milliken's Bend by the troops of the Trans-Mississippi Department.

Wounded: N. Mora, Company G.

8th. Clear and warm. The struggle raged with unabated fury. The enemy's lines were slowly but surely approaching nearer to our own breastworks, and the struggle was daily becoming more fierce and deadly. The Federals procured a car-frame, which they placed on wheels, loading it with cotton-bales. They pushed this along the Jackson road in front of the breastworks held by the Third Regiment. Protected by this novel, movable shelter, they constructed their works with impunity, and with almost the certainty of eventually reaching our intrenchments. Rifles had no effect on the cotton-bales, and there was not a single piece of artillery to batter them down. They were not a hundred yards from the regiment, and the men could only quietly watch their operations, and anxiously await the approaching hand-to-hand struggle. There was no shrinking or quailing. Danger had long since ceased to cause any fear, and fighting was a recreation and pastime with the majority of the men. Exploding shells and whistling bullets attracted but little notice. Even death had become so familiar, that the fall of a comrade was looked upon with almost stoical indifference; eliciting, perhaps, a monosyllabic expression of pity, and most generally the remark, "I wonder who will be the next one." Men are not naturally indifferent to danger, nor do their hearts usually exhibit such stoical indifference to human agony and suffering; yet the occurrence of daily scenes of horror and bloodshed, through which they passed, the shadow of the angel of death constantly hovering over them, made them undisturbed spectators of every occurrence; making the most of to-day, heedless of the morrow. Though constantly threatened with death, they pursued with eagerness limited occasions for amusement. The song and jest went around, fun actually being coined from the danger which some comrade escaped, or attempted to nimbly dodge.

Wounded seriously, J. M. Burke, Company B.

9th. Clear and pleasant. All night long the fight was kept up. The movable breastwork in front of the intrenchments of the Third Louisiana, became a perfect annoyance to the regiment, and various plans were proposed for its destruction, only to be declared unavailable. Some of the men actually proposed to make a raid on it, and set it on fire, a plan which would have been the height of madness.

Finally, a happy invention suggested itself to the mind of Lieutenant W. M. Washburn, of Company B. He thought that if he could fill the cavity in the butt of the Enfield rifle balls with some inflammable material which would ignite by being fired from the rifle, the great *desideratum* would be obtained. Thus, procuring turpentine and cotton, he filled the ball with the latter, thoroughly saturated by the former. A rifle was loaded, and, amid the utmost curiosity and interest, fired at the hated object. The sharp report was followed by the glittering ball, as it sped from the breastworks straight to the dark mass of cotton-bales, like the rapid flight of a fire-fly. Another and another blazing missile was sent on the mission of destruction, with apparently no satisfactory results, and the attempt was abandoned amid a general disappointment. The men, save those on guard, sought repose, and all the line became comparatively quiet. Suddenly some one exclaimed, "I'll be d——d if that thing isn't on fire!" The whole regiment was soon stirring about, like a hive of disturbed bees. Sure enough, smoke was seen issuing from the dark mass. The inventive genius of Lieutenant Washburn had proved a complete success, and the fire, which had smouldered in the dense mass of cotton, was about bursting forth. The men seized their rifles, and five companies were immediately detailed to keep up a constant and rapid fire over the top and at each end of the blazing mass, to prevent the enemy from extinguishing the flames. They discovered the destruction which threatened their shelter, and made impotent attempts to extinguish the fire with dirt and water. But as the light increased, the least exposure of their persons made the unwary foe the target for a dozen rifles, handled by skillful marksmen.

The regiment were in darkness, while the blazing pile brought into bold outline every man of the enemy who thoughtlessly exposed himself within the radius of the light.

The rifles of the regiment sang a merry tune, as the brave boys poured a constant shower of bullets above and around the great point of attraction, which was soon reduced to ashes and a mass of smouldering embers. How the men cheered and taunted the foe, can better be imagined than described. The achievement was a source of general satisfaction and rejoicing. The Yankees could not understand how their movable breastwork was thus given to destruction, under their very eyes.

Edmonson, Company D; T. McFee, Company B, and F. J. Benton, Company K, were killed during the day. The night was unusually warm and cloudy.

10th. Ere the gray dawn it began to rain, and soon poured down in torrents. There was no cessation of the rapid and heavy firing around the lines.

Sunshine and storm were alike impotent to stay the progress of the fight, or prevent the hail of deadly missiles from being poured upon the heoic defenders of the besieged city. All day long the rain fell, filling the trenches with water, and thoroughly wetting the exposed, unsheltered troops. The scenes at the breastworks beggared description. In the mud and water the men fought on, as if Heaven did not add to their sufferings the inconvenience and horrors of their situation. As usual, they made sport of each other's sufferings. At night the storm culminated into a terrific and concentrated fury. The long weeks of heat, and the constant and heavy cannonading, had impregnated the whole atmosphere with electricity, which now burst forth with tenfold fury. Lightning, with its jagged edges and forked tongues, darted from the dark masses of clouds upon the city, followed by the deep, sullen and heavy roll of Heaven's sublime artillery, mingling its volume of sound with the scarcely less voluminous and heavy thunder which rolled its incessant waves around the fortifications. A scene of such sublime and soul-stirring grandeur, linking together man's fierce passions and Heaven's dark frowns, could scarcely be imagined, much less described. The Yankees added to the many rumors afloat, by shouting to our men the following information, "You had to get England to assist you after all. The mouth of the Mississippi is blockaded, and Price is in possession of Helena, Ark. We have enough men at Milliken's Bend to keep Kirby Smith in check, and after we capture Vicksburg, we will soon drive Price out of his comfortable quarters." The men only hoped the half of the information was correct, while they defiantly scoffed at the idea of Vicksburg ever surrendering, as thus proclaimed so confidently by the enemy. A number of the regiment visited Vicksburg and the camps, to obtain stove-pipes and tin-gutters to sharpshoot through, by planting them in the intrenchments.

Wounded—P. Grillet, slightly; Company D.

11th. Morning dawned cloudy. The day cleared off cool and pleasant. Below the city two gun-boats floated lazily at anchor, while above not a vessel was in sight. In front of the Third Louisiana the enemy planted two ten-inch Columbiads, scarcely a hundred yards distant from the lines. These terrible missiles, with their heavy scream and tremendous explosion, somewhat startled the boys, being a new and unexpected feature in the siege, and necessarily increasing the already accumulated dangers of their situation. After knocking the breastworks to pieces, and exhibiting their force and power, the enemy commenced a systematic method of practice, so as to make the shells deadly missiles of destruction.

So skillful and expert did they soon become in handling these huge siege-pieces, that they loaded them with powder, producing force sufficient to only propel the shells over the breastworks, and they rolled among the men, producing a general scramble to escape the force and danger of their explosion. Frequently they rolled some distance down the hill-side ere exploding. One of these shells entered one of the shelters excavated in the hill-side, where a group was assembled, composed of Colonel Russell, Lieutenants Davenport and Washburn, and several members of Company B. Ere the party could escape, the terrible missile exploded. Strange as it may appear, but one of the party was killed outright, while all the remainder were wounded and bruised, with but one single exception. Several were severely burned by the large grains of powder with which the shell was loaded, making torturing but not dangerous wounds. The mere idea of forcing powder into a fresh burn will afford some conception of the agonizing, excruciting pain of this species of wounds.

Among the casualties this day were—Killed: Sergeant B. Brice, Sergeant T. Howell, Company B. Wounded: Lieutenant-Colonel S. D. Russell, Lieutenants J. Davenport, W. M. Washburn, J. M. Sharp, Company B; A. Girod, Company I; ——— Cole, Company F. Seventy-five killed and wounded to this date.

12th. Clear and plesant. The siege-guns were particularly destructive, especially among the right companies of the regiment. To-day, our troops succeeded in getting a mortar in position, in a ravine in the rear of the line of fortifications, but did not use it then. No prospects of assistance, and provisions were becoming very scarce. Fresh beef had long since been used up, and, also, a large number of sheep, and the troops were now living on rations of bacon. The labor of keeping the works repaired was increased by ther tremendous power and destructive force of the shot from the siege-guns. Yet the brave men did not despair, or give way in spirit, under these trying circumstances.

Wounded: Captain N. M. Middlebrook, Lieutenant Fagan, Company C; ——— Hubbard and C. Quinelty, Company G.

13th. Clear and pleasant. We give the following synopsis of rumors daily circulated, as a fair specimen of the means used to buoy up the spirits of those inclined to despair in the midst of the gloom, horrors, and hardships of the siege: Generals Forrest and Featherstone destroy nine transports in the river loaded with provisions; General Price captures two gun-boats above, three transports, and had crossed the Mississippi River; General Johnston was at Clinton, Miss., with 25,000 troops, and positively asserted that he was approaching to succor the garrison. Such were the reports constantly circulated, and usually received, with a large margin of the allowance for their falsity. One mortar opened on the Yankees late in the evening. As the shell marked its graceful curve in the air, and suddenly fell into the enemy's lines, the troops cheered most vociferously. They enjoyed, to the fullest extent, the astonishment and consternation of the Yankees. But a few shells, however, were fired ere the enemy concentrated upon the point whence came the dangerous missiles, the fire of every gun within easy range pouring such a storm of shell upon the offending mortar as caused its speedy abandonment. It was almost certain death to remain in its vicinity. This mortar was used only a short time, and then the attempt to render it effective given up. A heavy siege-gun, planted near the extreme point of the peninsula, above the mortarfleet, opened fire on Vicksburg, but with inaccurate range, rendering its missiles harmless visitors. Nine transports came down the river loaded with troops.

No casualties in the regiment.

CHAPTER XXIX

SIEGE CONTINUED

JUNE 14th. Clear and warm. The cannonading and musketry continued unabated. Another courier reached the city with a large supply of percussion-caps. The enemy were daily reinforcing their already tremendous army, thus increasing their available strength, while every man disabled inside of the lines added to the weakness of the defenders. General Grant's facilities for prosecuting the siege to a successful termination were thus increased to an almost certainty, and he could afford to prolong the contest, and accomplish, by starvation and a lengthened attack, what he could not obtain by either stratagem, skill, or brute force. A successful general he certainly was; yet the accomplishment of his plans was purely the result of having at his command all the available means and strength of the most powerful nation on the face of the globe. Not a circumstance transpired within our lines that the foe did not know, and they were informed of the true condition of affairs, knowing full well, and confidently expecting, that the gaunt skeleton of famine, then seizing the besieged forces, would ultimately prove the conqueror. They needed but to wait, while they kept up, with unabated fury, their daily and nightly attack on the place. All around the city the firing was very lively and continuous, even from the sharp-shooters on the opposite side of the river. Thus closed the twenty-eighth day of the siege, adding to our list of wounded and killed the names of William McGuinness, Company A; S. W. Sanders, Company B; and W. Burns, Company H.

Our upper river batteries exhibited some excellent skill in firing on the wreck of the Cincinnati, to prevent the enemy from working on it and moving the guns, which they were attempting to accomplish.

W. McGuinness, mentioned among the wounded to-day, was shot through the right eye as he was looking through one of the pipes planted in the earth-works to observe the effects of his shooting. He was seen by one of the enemy, who fired at him with deadly aim. This incident is given to show how close the combatants were to each other, and with what certainty each party used their rifles upon the smallest-sized object exposed to their aim. McGuinness recovered, but lost his eyesight and a piece of the bone from the side of his face. The escape from death was miraculous.

15th. Day cloudy and threatened rain. The firing was very rapid, and shot and shells flew into and over the place in every direction. The enemy seemed to feel in a particularly lively humor. They made a charge on the breastworks held by the Twenty-seventh Louisiana Infantry, on the left of the position occupied by the Third Louisianians, in a mass, four columns deep. They were repulsed, and terribly slaughtered. A small rifle-gun, planted on the side hill, immediately in the rear of the Third Regiment, enfiladed their advancing columns, making great gaps in the ranks—as the balls literally ploughed a passage through their dense array of men. This episode, in the usual monotony of the siege, infused new life and spirit into the Confederates. They felt in the humor for a desperate hand-to-hand conflict, knowing that they would have an opportunity of effectively returning some of the blows dealt them. But the daily loss of friends and comrades, whose fall they were powerless to avenge, rendered their feelings and situation anything but agreeable.

Heavy cannonading was heard toward Snyder's Mills and outside of the lines, thus once more arousing a general hope of speedy relief.

Killed: Silas Crane, Company E; Edward Douglas, Company I.

The close of the day threatened rain, which was not a desirable visitor to the men.

June 16th. Dawned pleasant, light summer clouds floating gently across the empyrean. The firing had continued all night, and there was no diminution in its rapidity and volume. The place, as usual, was full of rumors of succor. The rations furnished the men were still good; sufficient to keep away actual starvation, but not to satisfy the voracious appetites of the troops. How the other troops felt, we know not, but the boys of the Third Regiment were *always hungry*. They had always possessed somewhat fastidious tastes, and were quite epicurean in their appetites, which they had heretofore indulged to their fullest extent. Imagine, then, the deprivation which they suffered, the great self-denial practiced by them in thus receiving the scant rations daily dealt out to them, without murmuring over their condition. True, there was yearning after the forbidden flesh-pots of "Egypt," but no possibility or probability of their desire after forbidden meats being satisfied.

17th. Morning cloudy, but did not indicate rain. Cannonading brisk and very rapid, in fact, terrific in the afternoon. The day was unusually sultry. Another columbiad opened on the regiment at close range, and the enemy's lines were now so near, that scraps of paper could be thrown by the combatants into each other's ranks. Thus, a Yankee threw a "hard-tack" biscuit among the men of the regiment, having written on it "starvation." The visitor was immediately returned, indorsed as follows, "Forty days rations, and no thanks to you."

Despair held no rule in the brave spirits who defended this portion of the work, and the tremendous mass of iron poured upon them no terrors for their unflinching souls. Another building was destroyed by fire, caused by the explosion of a shell.

Killed: Tom Cobb, Company D.

Wounded: L. Flores, Company G.

18th. Cloudy and very warm. The "Vicksburg Whig" published an extra, containing a few items concerning the siege of Port Hudson. This paper, published at intervals, was printed on one side of wall paper, taken from the sides of rooms. It was very small, and a great curiosity in the way of a relic. It was decidedly an "illustrated" sheet, not exactly after the style of "Frank Leslie" and "Harper" pictorials. The river began to rise, and the boats below had disappeared. At this time the enemy became imbued with the mania for setting fire to the city, and, as the shells exploded, a stream of liquid fire descended from them. At night they presented a beautiful spectacle, notwithstanding their destructive mission. No serious consequences resulted from this new species of warfare.

Wounded: J. Brenning, Company F; J. Gueton, Company G.

19th. Clear and warm. The firing was comparatively light. The rations issued at this time were: flour, one-quarter of a pound; rice flour, one-quarter of a pound; peas one-quarter of a pound; rice, sugar and salt, in equally small proportions. Tobacco and bacon, one-quarter of a pound. It was a small allowance for men to sustain life with, exposed to the horrors of the siege, and almost constantly occupied. Yet the troops were unusually healthy. The Parrott guns kept up an annoying fire on the city, from the opposite side of the river. Our batteries opened on them with little effect, as they were concealed and well-protected by the levee. One of these guns produced no smoke nor report, and the only intimation of danger would be the shrill scream of an ugly shell. It was generally believed to have been fired with gun-cotton. No serious injury resulted from this annoyance, save to brick walls and frame buildings, few of which escaped the missiles so constantly showered upon the place.

20th. Clear and warm. At early dawn every gun along the line suddenly opened, keeping up a rapid and continuous fire. All concurred in the opinion that such a tremendous cannonading had never been equaled in their experience, and the volume of sound surpassed anything yet heard. It seemed as if heaven and earth were meeting in a fearful shock, and the earth trembled under the heavy concussions. The gun-boats approached from below, but ere reaching the range of our batteries, retired with their flags at half-mast, causing much speculation as to the meaning of this manœuvre. The cannonading was kept up steadily all day. The men were in unusually fine humor. They seemed to care little that a powerful enemy was within arms-length of them, and that their flag was flaunting its folds in their very faces.

A glance over the breastworks would exhibit a panoramic view of a large portion of the adjacent works, the puffs of smoke curling upward from the guns, used with such dexterous skill, or the light, vapory cloud arising from the discharged rifles of the sharpshooters. Such a glance must be taken very hastily, as the whiz of a Minie-ball, or the shrill scream of a shell, admonished the spectator that he was seen and already made a target of. The view, under such circumstances, was perhaps more pleasant to the eye than comfortable to the other senses.

During the day, one of the enemy climbed up to the parapet of the Third Louisiana works, and boldly looked over, no doubt with the very laudable intention of having a good view of affairs within the forbidden ground. He paid a fearful forfeit for his temerity, being shot and instantly killed by one of the regiment standing near the spot where he exposed himself. The attempt was considered an unusually bold and fool-hardy one. The combatants watched for each other with the keen-sightedness of an eagle, and the ferocity and vigilance of a tiger seeking prey. Consequently, the least exposure was instantly discovered, and as quickly brought a bullet to the spot. Perhaps volumes could be filled with the incidents of this siege; its grotesque and mournful scenes. On this day J. Lee, of Company B, received his death wound, being shot through the head with a Minie-ball. He was carried down the hill-side, and laid upon the ground, near the spring where the men came for water. Comrades were passing to and from the lines, laughing, talking and joking with each other, all unmindful of the dying soldier. Bullets whistled by, and huge shells screamed his requiem, or thundered his dirge in their fearul explosions, as his spirit departed amid the din of the fierce conflict. Yet, such a scene was a common occurrence, and men whose souls once thrilled with all the finer sensibilities of the human nature, looked on with stolid, stoical indifference. With a blanket for a winding-sheet, and in his soiled and battle-stained garments, the brave soldier was placed in the hastily-dug grave, and left to rest in peace.

No useless coffin inclosed his breast;
    Nor in sheet nor in shroud we bound him;
But he lay like a warrior taking his rest,
    With his tattered blanket around him.

Killed: J. Lee, F. M. Howell, Company B; J. W. Naff, Company G.

21st. Cloudy and warm. The day's observations resulted in discovering little apparent change in the situation. On the right hand bank, up the river, the enemy's trains were seen on a sand-bar. At a distance they looked like a hive of busy bees, and were doubtless engaged in conveying stores to their troops.

The Parrott guns still annoyed the city, and were heavily fired on by our batteries. The wreck of the Cincinnati was again shelled, the enemy being discovered at work on it, but were speedily driven away by our skillful gunners. Lieutenant Holt, of Company E, lying in a tent sick in the commissary camp, was shot in the leg, and badly wounded by a ball shot from a Belgian rifle, nearly a mile distant. A courier arrived with dispatches and caps. He had floated down the Yazoo, through the fleet, on a plank, and was taken out of the water completely exhausted. His name, unfortunately unknown, assuredly deserves a place in the history of these daily events for his daring and determination in reaching the beleaguered city. The day passed without any unusual occurrence, and no light, as yet, glimmered through the dark cloud which hung like a funeral pall over the heroic defenders of the Hill City.

Killed: L. Stewart, Company I; Corporal Martin, Company H; wounded: Lieutenant U. Babin, Company A; Lieutenant R. C. Holt, Company E; Sergeant George Miller, Company E.

22d. Clear and warm. The sharpshooting very lively. Artillery comparatively quiet. No special change in the aspect of affairs. Two regiments on the right, Texans, we believe, charged upon the enemy outside the lines, capturing a colonel, a lieutenant-colonel, a captain, and eight privates, one hundred and fifty stand of arms, spades, shovels, etc.; killed and wounded forty, losing only eight men. This little episode of the siege caused much excitement and enthusiasm along the whole line. The day closed clear and cool.

Killed: Charles Dupuy, Company A.

23d. Cool, clear and pleasant. The activity of the enemy increased. They opened fire on the city from a 100-pounder Parrott gun, planted on the peninsula, upward of three miles distant. Between this gun and our lower batteries a fierce duel occurred, exhibiting some splendid skill in handling heavy artillery.

A feverish excitement and expectation prevailed of hearing something definite from General Johnston, and, as day after day passed without any reliable information of succor, the anxiety became intense. The constantly decreasing rations admonished the men that the siege must terminate disastrously if succor did not soon reach them.

Wounded: S. Kohn, Company A; Alexander Garza, Company G.

24th. Commenced raining in the night. A dark and lowering morning. About 12 M. at night a heavy skirmish commenced on the right. The mortars bellowed forth their hoarse thunder, and four rifled batteries kept up a continual fire on the city from the front. On the lower river batteries a heavy concentrated attack was made, resulting harmlessly. The enemy across the river were very busily engaged at their usual sport. The balls from their long-range rifles penetrated to Washington Street, killing one, and wounding two men. The evening was beautiful, and the moon shed its soft effulgence over the embattlements of the beleaguered city. The wearied mind of the soldier, with all the surroundings of grim-visaged war, could not but yield to the witching influence of the spell, and dream of home and the loved ones, and speculate on the probable destiny that awaited him. Of the inward soul-struggle of these heroic soldiers the world will never know. The hours of dark despair, succeeded by the presence of bright-winged hope, the treasured thoughts and pleasant dreams of the future, the bitter agony of perishing expectations, all the inward struggles of light and darkness, are as a sealed book to the probing gaze of the world. But one mission was theirs; to defend to the last extremity the city wherein centred all their pride. Whether they did so, let History record, and the world determine.

25th. Warm and hazy. The heavy Parrott gun on the peninsula kept up a destructive fire on the lower portion of the city, doing terrible execution on the buildings. Along the lines it was comparatively quiet early in the day. Poor Amidé Hebert, of Company A, was brought to the hospital early in the morning, terribly mangled by a rifled 24-pounder shell. He was conversing with some friends in the Twenty-second Louisiana Regiment, when the ball struck him. It took off one leg at the hip joint, and stripped the bone of the other of all flesh to the knee, where it was torn away. Horribly mangled as he was, he conversed in cheerful tones with his friends. As he was carried into the hospital, he said to Dr. Whitehead, the regimental physician, "Wouldn't it surprise you, Doctor, if I should recover?" Brave fellow, the terrible shock to his nervous system rendered him oblivious to all pain. He lived for more than an hour, and then fell asleep, from which there is no waking, adding one more to the list of noble comrades who had sacrificed their lives in defense of cherished principles. A more shocking spectacle of war's butchery was never witnessed than the mangled living body of Amidé Hebert presented.

Just after noon the enemy sprung the mine beneath the Third Regiment, which they had been so long preparing. Six Mississippians, working in the counter-mine, were buried alive in the earth. This counter-mine counteracted the force of the explosion. The enemy immediately charged in heavy columns the gap made in the works, when a fierce hand-to-hand struggle ensued. The heroic and brave men of the regiment, sadly depleted in numbers as they were, undauntedly faced the foe, using their muskets and rifles with deadly effect upon the close columns of the Yankees.

While desperately fighting the fearful odds opposed to them, succor arrived. The Sixth Missouri Regiment, of Bowen's Brigade, led by Colonel Erwin, suddenly reinforced the regiment. Well the Louisianians knew their old comrades. Shoulder to shoulder had they stood together on many hard-fought fields, unmoved, unconquerable. These heroic spirits from Louisiana and Missouri loved each other as brothers, for they were united in bonds cemented by a fierce baptism of blood. They rushed into the desperate melee unfalteringly, and after a short struggle succeeded in repulsing the enemy with terrible loss. Colonel Erwin needlessly and rashly exposed himself by jumping on the top of the intrenchments, and calling to his men, "Come on, my brave boys, don't let the Third Regiment get ahead of you!" They were his last words, for he was killed almost instantly by the deadly aim of the enemy's sharpshooters. Colonel Erwin was a grandson of Henry Clay, and a more noble, gallant, or braver man never led a regiment. He was universally beloved, especially by the heroic troops whom he commanded, and his death was bitterly mourned. Hand-grenades were freely used in this fierce struggle. These missiles weigh about a pound, are an oval-shaped iron shell, a little larger than a hen egg, and filled with powder. In one end is a small cylinder, at the bottom of which is a gun tube, on which is placed a common percussion cap. Into this cylinder is inserted a small rod, having a flat piece of circular iron on the end, about the size of a half dollar. This rod is drawn out to its full length, and held in its place by a light spring pressing on it. The reverse end of the shell has a wooden rod inserted in it, about six inches long, and feathered. This guides the shell. When thrown, the grenade usually falls on the bottom attached to the rod, which is forced on the cap, exploding the missile. These shells were thrown in immense quantities, and with considerable effect. Many were caught or picked up when not exploding, and hurled back upon the foe. Numbers struck the men, exploding and making frightful wounds.

This struggle was a severe test upon the courage of the Third Regiment, but they met the Federals with their usual determined valor, aided by the gallant Missourians, whom they loved and honored as fit compeers to stand by their side in the deadly breach. The loss of the regiment in this brief struggle summed up thirty men, of which the following is an imperfect list:

Wounded: Major D. Pierson.

Killed: B. Berry, Co. A.; J. Breaux, Co. A; Sergeant J. T. Sharp, Co. B; J. C. May, Co. B; —————— Masterton, Co. E; F. Ray, Co. I; Corporal A. Kelly, J. L. Vaughan, Co. I.

Wounded: P. C. Wills, Co. A; Lieutenant W. P. Renwich, J. M. Smith, G. Vaughan, Co. B; G. C. Spillman, R. Cole, Co. C; J. Merritt, R. C. Hammett, Co. D; J. Myers, Co. E; George Effner, W. Hudson, Co. F; E. Escobeda, Lieutenant Paul Bossier, Co. G; Corporal J. C. Rice, Corporal G. P. Mouran, H. C. Hough, J. Haines, G. T. McFarland, M. P. Cartwright, M. Sandridge, Co. I.

A large number of the wounded were injured by the hand-grenades. While this encounter was raging, the enemy's batteries in front and rear kept up a fierce cannonading. The day was very warm, and the sun sank below the horizon looking like a great ball of fire through the bluish haze—as if ashamed to shine bright and clear upon such a scene of butchery and bloodshed.

26th. Clear and warm. The firing was kept up very lively, as usual. During the night the members of the regiment repaired the damage to Fort Beauregard, and were ready for the foe once more, with spirits as determined and undaunted as ever. The enemy succeeded in enfilading the ditches, and compelled the men to leave a portion of the works, while they fired into them. The Fifth and Sixth Missouri Infantry were close at hand, held as a reserve in case of another attack. The Louisianians needed no better assistants. In front, the Parrott guns were used with some effect, killing and wounding several gentlemen and ladies in the city.

Wounded: Captain W. E. Russell and W. Badt, Company D.

27th. Cloudy and very warm, and the place full of rumors. At this period, the fortieth day of the siege, Vicksburg presented a fearful spectacle, having the appearance of being visited with a terrible scourge. Signs wrenched from their fastenings; houses dilapidated and in ruins, rent and torn by shot and shell; the streets barricaded with earth-works, and defended by artillery, over which lonely sentinels kept guard. The avenues were almost deserted, save by hunger-pinched, starving and wounded soldiers, or guards lying on the banquettes, indifferent to the screaming and exploding shells. The stores, the few that were open, looked like the ghost of more prosperous times, with their empty shelves and scant stock of goods, held at ruinous prices. "Ginger beer," "sweet cider," "beer for sale," glared out in huge letters upon placards or the ends of barrels, seeming the only relief to the general starvation. It would have puzzled a scientific druggist to have determined what were the ingredients of this decoction called "beer." Palatial residences were crumbling into ruins, the walks torn up by mortar-shells, the flower-beds, once blooming in all the regal beauty of spring loveliness, trodden down, the shrubbery neglected. No fair hands were there to trim their wanton growth; no light footsteps to wander amid nature's blooming exotics, or lovely forms seen leaning confidingly on some manly arm, while rosy lips breathed soft words of affection and trust. Ah! no; such scenes were the hallowed memories of halcyon days gone by. Fences were torn down, and houses pulled to pieces for fire-wood. Even the enclosures around the remains of the revered dead, were destroyed, while wagons were parked around the grave-yard, horses tramping down the graves, and men using the tombstones as convenient tables for their scanty meals, or a couch for an uncertain slumber. Dogs howled through the streets at night; cats screamed forth their hideous cries; an army of rats, seeking food, would scamper around your very feet, and across the streets, and over the pavements. Lice and filth covered the bodies of the soldiers. Delicate women, and little children, with pale, care-worn and hunger-pinched features, peered at the passer-by with wistful eyes, from the caves in the hill-sides. Add to all these horrors, so faintly portrayed, the deep-toned thunder of mortars and heavy guns, the shrill whistle of rifle-shot, or the duller sound of flying mortar-shells; the crash of buildings torn into fragments; the fearful detonation of the explosions shaking heaven and earth; the hurtling masses of iron continually descending, and you may form some conception of the condition of the city. Human language is impotent to portray the true situation of affairs. Yet such in reality were some of the scenes of the siege. At the breast-works were the tried heroes. Without flinching or faltering, our brave troops confronted the foe, swearing, with unquailing spirit, never to surrender, and rather to die among the ruins of the devoted city than give up the place. Such a spirit, defiant from first to last, was worthier a better fate than that which eventually befell the heroic garrison.

The brave men, growing daily weaker under their increasing labors and starvation, began to complain at the long delayed succor, so frequently announced as near at hand. They would not stop to reason on the subject. Their courageous souls could perceive no brilliant sun of hope breaking through the dark clouds of disaster which canopied them. They dreamed not of the difficulties which environed the young Confederacy, and that an all-powerful enemy was contracting the cordon of its strength around it on all sides, threatening it with speedy annihilation. Even with such a leader as General Joe Johnston, it required time; long weeks of constant, unwearying labor to organize an army sufficiently powerful to successfully attack the enemy, securely posted within strong intrenchments. Already, six weeks of unceasing battle had passed away—six weeks of such fighting as the world had seldom witnessed; yet the enemy, with all their material and appliances for conducting the siege to a speedy and successful termination, had most signally failed in every attempt. The Spartan band of Southern heroes held their position, utterly regardless of the furious storm of grape, canister, shell and shot poured upon them by the overwhelming forces of the Federals. With the demon of famine gnawing at their heart-strings, they still daily shouted their defiance to the assailants, and their rifles were as actively handled, as skillfully aimed, as if nearly half their number were not disabled, and many sleeping peacefully beneath the green turf, above which rose the scream of shell, all the horrid din and saturnalia of the fierce conflict. The undaunted soul would ask, Ought we not to succeed? Are all these horrors, sufferings and fearful sacrifices to bring forth no fruit, no strength and hope for coming days? Ah! a mysterious fate had issued its decree, and mortal vision could not see the result of its decision.

Wounded: F. Hargrove, Company H.

28th. Another Sabbath morn. The golden sunlight mellowed with its brilliant light the hill-tops and the dark-green foliage of the trees. Birds caroled their matin songs, as if war was not holding its high carnival within and around the besieged city. The mind would forget the unceasing din of battle, and soar away into the realms of fancy. The hill-sides have a soft carpeting of emerald sward, upon which the soldier casts his wearied body. He has forgotten his surroundings, is oblivious to the screaming shells and singing bullets. A smile flits across his bronzed features, as memory exhibits one of the beautiful pictures of the past. The light of lustrous blue eyes is beaming upon him with a soft tenderness beyond portrayal. Look, weary soldier, into the liquid depths; gaze once more upon the exquisite loveliness of the fair face so beautifully shaded by a profusion of glossy, dark curls. See again those coral lips breaking into a loving smile, rippling in laughing wavelets over the whole face; recall again their soft pressure upon your own lips; drink in with deep inspiration all the beauty of the picture which imagination now paints from the realities of the past. Dream on, oh heroic spirit, for ere the sun shall have reached the Western horizon, thou shalt fill a hero's honored grave; while her you have been dreaming about shall weep with uncontrollable anguish over thy fate, or, perchance, in days hereafter, come with flowers and strew them over thy humble tomb, or plant them there to flourish as a token of her remembrance and constancy, their rich fragrance filling the air with sweetness, above the lowly mound where reposes thy earthly remains!

The brilliant morn soon settled into a noon of unusual warmth. One of the lower batteries in front succeeded in silencing a Parrott gun across the river, and a lively shelling in the woods compelled the sharpshooters to beat a hasty retreat.

The Catholics of the city held services in their Cathedral, notwithstanding the danger of such a proceeding. As the congregation was emerging from the building, the Argus-eyed enemy across the river discovered the unusual number of people in the streets, and instantly opened on them with a Parrott gun. As the shells came screaming wickedly through the streets, exploding or entering the building, men, women and children hastily sought shelter to escape the danger. Several persons were struck by fragments of shells, but, fortunately, no one killed. Such an unheard-of, ruthless and barbarous method of warfare as training a battery of rifled cannon upon an assembly of unarmed men and worshiping women, is unparalleled in the annals of history.

Meat at this period became exhausted, and orders were issued to select the finest and fattest mules within the lines, and slaughter them, for the purpose of issuing their flesh as food to the troops; a half pound per man was the ration of this new species of flesh. Several Spaniards belonging to the Texas regiments were also busily occupied in jerking this meat for future consumption.

This meat was also supplied to the citizens from the market, and sold for fifty cents a pound. The first meal which we remember to have eaten of mule-flesh was at the house of Mrs. Robert Henderson, whose husband commanded one of the heavy batteries on the river. We assure the ignorant reader that the food was consumed with a keen relish worthy the appetite of a gourmand, or an epicure over the most dainty repast. Mule-flesh, if the animal is in good condition, is coarse-grained and darker than beef, but really delicious, sweet and juicy; at least such has experience in testing its quality proven it to be. Besides this meat, traps were set for rats, which were consumed in such numbers that, ere the termination of the siege, they actually became a scarcity. Hunger will demoralize the most fastidious tastes, and quantity, not quality of food, becomes the great desideratum.

Mortally wounded: L. J. Benton, Co. K. Severely wounded: Sergeant J. A. Derboune, Co. G.

29th. Very warm; floating clouds overhead. The author made a hearty breakfast on fried rats, whose flesh he found very good, and fully equal to that of squirrels. The thought of such food may be actually nauseating to many of the readers of this record, yet, let starvation with its skeleton form visit them, and all qualms would speedily vanish, and any food, to satisfy hunger, be voraciously devoured, and considered as sweet manna. It is a difficult matter for persons surrounded with abundance to realize the feeling produced by extreme hunger; no pen-picture, no grouping of words in all their forcibleness and power, can convey to those who have not experienced the sensation produced by this gaunt visitor. It must be felt to be realized; and if once felt, the idea of eating dogs, cats, rats, or even human flesh, would contain nothing repulsive or repugnant to the feelings.

The firing on the lines was not so brisk as usual. The enemy were once more undermining the works held by the Third Louisiana Infantry, and the men went spiritedly at work digging a counter-mine. The laborers were so near each other that the strokes of the pickaxes could be distinctly heard, as well as the sound of the voices. Thus the deadly struggle went on, the brave boys never once dreaming of despairing or giving up, although fighting over a volcano which at any moment might burst forth and ingulf them in a general ruin. The men of the regiment knew not what fear meant, and would not relinquish their position or falter in their defence of this place intrusted to them, though the whole earth beneath was a huge powder-magazine, requiring only a spark of fire to hurl them into eternity. Theirs was a spirit of unfaltering bravery, which no terrors could for an instant make quail. Dauntless, their spirits soared towering above the accidents, the uncertainties of their existence. What more could be required of mere men, subject to all the chances and changes of mortality, calmly slumbering on the verge of a fearful precipice of destruction?

A large number of skiffs were constructed and conveyed to the lower portion of the town. Speculation became rife as to the meaning of this new movement. What could it possibly mean? The conviction seemed finally to settle on every mind that a desperate attempt would soon be made to cross the river with the army, and escape into the Trans-Mississippi Department. Whatever may have been the intention in building these boats, it was never divulged, and the accomplishment of such a design never carried into effect, or even attempted. It would have been an insane enterprise in the presence of the enemy's gun-boats and troops.

The Federal sharpshooters very impudently wished to know how we liked mule-meat, proving conclusively that they were constantly informed of every event which occurred within the lines. Their question, however, was responded to in not very flattering or complimentary language. Thus affairs daily grew darker, and the men actually raved at the idea of surrendering, after their long, gallant, and heroic defence. Their spirits were unconquered—unconquerable. The nights were brilliantly beautiful, with their flood of moonlight silvering the embattlements and hill-sides—such nights as the poets make immortal, and kindred spirits meet to whisper fond words of love. Yet here how different! The silvery radiance only rendered more fatal the rifle's deadly aim, or darkened the flitting light of the huge bombs, as they described their graceful curves through the air on the mission of death and destruction.

Mortally wounded: D. Echols, Company K. Slightly wounded: H. Finlay, Company K.

30th. The last day of June. The sun shone brightly, while groups of summer-clouds floated gently across the heavens. The sharpshooting was slow but constant—unceasing all day. The gun-boats approached the terminus of the lines below, and poured a concentrated fire of shells into the intrenchments, doing little damage or injury. Across the river, the peninsula looked lonely and deserted. The general apathy in fighting appeared ominous, and a dull, leaden weight unaccountably oppressed the mind, and gave a gloomy hue to every object. The hospitals were sad scenes of agony, suffering, and death, with their numerous occupants. Ah! how the heart grew mournful with heavy feelings; how the soul filled with tears as the spectator wandered slowly through the rows of rough cots, and gazed upon the suffering, dying occupants! Misery, such as one cares seldom to witness, was seen on all sides—these heroic men, slowly wasting away under disease, the agony of torturing wounds, augmented by the need of proper nourishment and medicines. In a tent, on the outskirts of the hospital grounds, lay a dying soldier. His brother had passed away to the unseen shores of eternity but a few days previously. An unconsolable grief filled the heart of the survivor, and the fatal shell which struck him knelled his own death-doom. Sympathizing friends gathered around him, and with soft words soothed his dying hours, as he incessantly talked of the brother gone before him. Ah! those touching scenes in hospitals! What pen shall fitly portray them? Who shall give life by words to the groups of sorrowing faces, gathered near some dying soldier, as they conversed about the agony of the gray-haired father and mother far away, or the wild grief of some doting sister? Then the humble burial! A rough pine coffin, made of boards, torn from some old building or fence, wherein the remains are placed. Some comrade gently severs a lock of hair from the tangled mass, saying, as he places it in the bosom of his soiled, gray jacket, "I will carry this home to the loved ones there; it will be a treasured relic for the grieving relatives." After long months that relic reaches its destination—a memento of a comrade's faithfulness to his feelings when he stood over the silent form of his fellow-soldier.

The humble grave is dug; the coffin reverently placed therein by comrades, with uncovered heads; then filled up, the hurtling shot, screaming shells, and booming guns being the only service for the dead. A plain board, roughly lettered, is placed at the end of the freshly-made mound, to mark the spot where, "after life's fitful fever," sleeps one of the heroes of Vicksburg. Ah! how many such scenes have we witnessed! How vividly do they return in all their mournfulness and distinctness, with the accompanying dirge of war's fearful requiem!

July 1st. The month made famous in the annals of American history. In the present century, rendered still more noted by some of the most glorious, as well as most mournful, events connected with the late desperate struggle. Could the framers of the Constitution of the Western Republic have gazed upon the scenes transpiring in the land, their hearts would have despaired of the final success of their patriotic endeavors. But the end is not yet. This dawning of a new month still found the billows of angry strife thundering in foaming crests around the heroic city. A clear sky was overhead, and the sun poured down a golden flood of intense, suffocating heat upon the combatants. Again the gun-boats below opened a lively cannonading upon the intrenchments. Elsewhere around the lines everything was comparatively quiet. At 2 P.M. the enemy exploded the mine beneath the works occupied by the Third Louisiana Infantry. A huge mass of earth suddenly, and with tremendous force and a terrible explosion, flew upwards, and descended with mighty power upon the gallant defenders, burying numbers beneath its falling fragments, bruising and mangling them most horribly. It seemed as if all hell had suddenly yawned upon the devoted band, and vomited forth its suphurous fire and smoke upon them. The regiment, at this time, was supported by the First, Fifth, and Sixth Missouri Infantry, and upwards of a hundred were killed and wounded. Numbers were shocked and bruised, but not sufficiently to more than paralyze them for a few moments. The scene that followed beggared description. At first there was a general rush to escape the huge mass of descending earth. Then the survivors, without halting to inquire who had fallen, hastened to the immense gap in the works to repel the anticipated assault. The enemy, taught by a dearly-bought experience, made no attempt to enter the opening, not daring to assault the intrepid defenders. An immense number of 12-pounder shells, thrown from wooden mortars, descended among the troops, doing fearful execution. The fire was tremendous, rapid, and concentrated, yet there was no flinching among those brave

Southerners. The undaunted Missourians stood shoulder to shoulder with the intrepid Louisianians. These heroes of Oak Hills, Elk Horn, and Corinth could not flinch under the most scathing fire. They had already been tried in the refining crucible of danger, and found composed of the purest metal of bravery. Steel hearts and avenging arms knew no fear.

The wounded and dying were speedily conveyed to the hospitals for attendance. The spectacle was horrible in the extreme. Stretched out on the greensward, with no shelter save the overshadowing trees, with the bright sunlight peering in tremulous rays through the intervening foliage, lay these men, suffering from every conceivable wound known in war. Some writhing in the agonies of death, others bruised, torn, mangled, and lacerated by shell and shot, while others were blackened and burned from the effects of the explosion. Gazing upon this scene of human agony and suffering, the emerald trees, greensward, smiling skies, and golden sunlight seemed a fearful mockery. Surgeons, with sleeves rolled up to their elbows, hands, arms, and shirts red with human gore, hastened hither and thither, or were using their keen-edged instruments in amputating some shattered limb, extracting balls and fragments of shells from the lacerated bodies, or probing some ghastly wound of the sufferers. Men, fearfully mangled in body and limbs, groaning with agony, some clutching the green-sward in their death-struggles, others with crushed, bruised bodies lingering in speechless torment! Such were the scenes of war on this hot July afternoon. It seemed as if some avenging Nemesis must descend and curse the land where such scenes were enacted, saving an heroic people from the relentless pursuit of the avenging hand of fate. Yet the end was not yet. What a record for the opening of a new month! The sun sank in the west in a cloudless sky, and quiet reigned over the besieged city. The moon rose majestically in the eastern horizon, tinging the turbid waters of the Mississippi with its bright, silvery sheen, while the taunts of the foe echoed across its eddying surface, as Night once again spread her dark mantle over the earth.

Killed: Robert Hammett, Co. D; B. F. Hickman, Co. K; John Reese, Joe Bird, Co. H; L. Flores, Co. G.

Wounded: Captain J. Kinney, M. O'Brien, Co. A; H. Kelly, J. H. Johnson, J. Totle, F. M. Worley, M. Higginbotham, A. Williams, Co. B; J. M. McBride, W. J. Carson, W. Evans, J. Tedley, N. Moody, Co. C; H. Duke, J. McDaniel, J. Fonteneau, Co. D; ——— Movin, Co. G; Captain Joe Johnson, P. Smith, D. Bliss, Co. I.

2d. The morning dawned clear amid the roar of guns, the explosion of shells, and the angry scream of solid shot. The enemy opened very briskly from mortars, columbiads, and Parrott guns, and kept up a hot fire on the city and lines. Provisions were very scarce, and murmurs of discontent began to be heard, but only among a few, whose patriotism and devotion gave way under the accumulating horrors and the gnawings of hunger. The majority of the troops were as eager, undaunted, and unconquered as when the enemy first appeared, expressing a willingness and determination to hold the place as long as a mouthful of anything eatable remained to sustain life. It was the hour that tried the souls of men. The dark cloud of disaster hovered over the devoted garrison, and fanned their courageous souls with the shadow of its sable, restless pinions. Would it envelop them in its gloomy folds, and surrender become a reality, became a painful question. A few fleeting days must determine for succor and freedom, or defeat and capture. Provisions were becoming a rarity, and mule-flesh was freely issued, and ravenously devoured. The approaching national anniversary was looked forward to as a day of fearful strife. The boys laughingly inquired, "We wonder who will be best satisfied with the grand celebration?"

The guns on the peninsula poured a rapid fire on the city; the 100-pounder Parrotts doing terrible execution on the buildings, about sunset. Our batteries were very quiet. The question was frequently propounded, in view of an expected surrender, "Why not expend our large supply of ammunition in firing upon the enemy, rather than permit it to pass into their hands, to swell the list of their captures?" Echo questioned "Why?"

The sun dipped beneath the western horizon amid the thunder of guns. Storm-clouds hung low in the heavens, athwart whose darkness the forked lightning played in fitful gleams. A fierce southeast wind swept shrieking by; not a star or gleam of blue sky was visible through the leaden canopy of clouds. The scene was gloomy in the extreme. It seemed as if the spirits of those who had fallen along the lines were visiting the doomed garrison, warning them, amid gloom and darkness, of their coming doom. We laid down to sleep, while the mortars still fired rapidly upon the city, and soon forgot all care in the land of dreams, regardless of the exploding bombs, red glare, and the hum of their descending fragments. Thus passed another day.

Killed: Lieutenant J. Horn, Co. F; F. J. Brosi, Co. F, wounded.

3d. The morning was clear. The cannonading was terrific, and a storm of iron hail was poured upon the city, and the hospitals seemed a special mark for the enemy's shot and shell. In the afternoon a heavy storm-cloud gathered in the north and northeast, hanging like a funeral pall over the city. A flag of truce went out to the enemy's lines, and rumors began to prevail that the place was about to be surrendered. The brave garrison indignantly denied such a contingency, yet scarcely knew what to believe. Affairs looked very gloomy. The night was clear and quiet, and the spirit of disaster once more fanned the air with its sable pinions ere a final descent upon the city. Out on the realms of mind soared swift-winged thought, reviewing the events of the past forty-eight days—days of such suffering, horror, and carnage as the soul shuddered to contemplate. Then the soul would be filled with sad memories of the spirits gone, the mouldering bodies, sleeping in peaceful quiet beneath the newly-made mounds of earth. Yet amid all the zephyrous-winged thoughts the glittering stars looked smilingly down upon the quiet city and its slumbering hosts.

CHAPTER XXX

THE SURRENDER

JULY 4th, a day memorable in the annals of American history, was destined once again to be made memorable as a day both of rejoicing and humiliation to those who had besieged and defended Vicksburg. Early in the day it became known that negotiations were pending for the surrender of the Southern stronghold. A perfect storm of indignation burst forth among the troops. What, surrender, and that, too, on the 4th of July, above all other days? Impossible! Alas, it became too true! The following order was early promulgated:

HEADQUARTERS, FORNEY'S DIVISION, ⎫
July 4th, 1863. ⎭

I am directed by the Lieutenant-General commanding to inform you, that the terms for the capitulation of Vicksburg and garrison have been completed, and are as follows:

The officers and men will be paroled at once, retaining their private baggage; commissioned officers their side-arms, and mounted officers one horse each.

At 10 o'clock, A.M., to-day, each brigade will be marched out in front of its respective position, stacking arms; it will then return, and bivouac in rear of the trenches until the necessary rolls can be completed.

You will please state to your troops that these terms are concurred in by the general officers, and you will caution your men not to avoid being paroled, as it is to their advantage to have their papers properly made out.

So soon as the order is received you will cause white flags to be displayed along your lines.

I am, General, very respectfully, your obedient servant,

Official: J. H. FORNEY, *Major-General Commanding.*
W. D. HARDIMAN, *A. A. G.*

The receipt of this order was the signal for a fearful outburst of anger and indignation, seldom witnessed. The members of the Third Louisiana Infantry expressed their feelings in curses loud and deep. Many broke their trusty rifles against the trees, scattered the ammunition over the ground where they had so long stood battling bravely and unflinchingly against overwhelming odds. In many instances, the battle-worn flags were torn into shreds, and distributed among the men as a precious and sacred memento, that they were no party to the surrender.

When the appointed hour, 10 A.M., arrived, the surrender was effected in conformity with the published order. The troops were marched outside the trenches, along whose line fluttered white pennants, arms were stacked, and, in sullen silence, they returned within the lines, and sought convenient camps in the rear of the intrenchments, where they might give free expression to their pent-up feelings. Soon along the entire line Federal soldiers paced where so recently arose the sulphurous smoke and deafening din of fierce battle.

The siege of Vicksburg was at last ended. Thus, forty-eight long days and nights, twenty thousand Southerners, decreased finally to a mere handful, had successfully resisted the combined assault of 120,000 Federals.★ Such a siege was unparalleled in the annals of American history for duration, and not surpassed in any land for violent assault, and the number of missiles hurled at the assailed. The Federals who marched into the place had more the appearance of being vanquished than the unarmed Confederates, who gazed upon them with folded arms, and in stern silence, a fierce defiance on their bronzed features, and the old battle fire gleaming in their glittering eyes. This was when the Federals first appeared. During all the events of the surrender, not one had been seen, and afterward no word of exultation was uttered to irritate the feelings of the prisoners. On the contrary, every sentinel who came upon post brought haversacks filled with provisions, which he would give to some famished Southerner, with the remark, "Here, reb, I know you are starved nearly to death." They knew that nothing but this gaunt skeleton had compelled their opponents to capitulate, and even then the honors of war claimed had been granted them. Moreover, the terms of capitulation were as favorable as could have been expected. The officers expressed great astonishment at the place being held so long behind such feeble, illy-constructed works as those around Vicksburg—works that were a sad commentary on the skill of any engineer calling himself such.

At noon on the day of surrender the fleet approached the city, decked with innumerable flags, and the thunder of artillery proclaimed the exultation of the conquerors. It was a sad spectacle for the ragged, emaciated, yet heroic Confederates, who had so stubbornly endeavored to retain possession of this stronghold.

★A fact stated by General Herron, U. S. A., to Lieutenant Fowler, of General Forney's staff.

SCENES AFTER THE SURRENDER

During the siege of Vicksburg, there was a class of non-combatants who distinguished themselves in a marked manner. These were the speculators, embracing nearly every merchant within the limits of the city, without distinction of nationality. These bloodsuckers had the audacity to hold their goods at such prices that it was an utter impossibility to obtain anything from them. Four hundred dollars was the price of a barrel of flour; coffee was ten dollars per pound, and everything else in like proportion. Some of these, worse than villains, refused to sell to the soldiers at any price, and, consequently, were not objects of special love by the brave men.

When the Federal soldiers entered the city they mingled freely with the Confederates, and expressed their sympathy with their deplorable situation by every possible means in their power. They were now no longer deadly combatants, but mortals of similar feelings. A retributive justice speedily descended upon the speculators, as the Federals broke open their stores, completely plundering them. The Southerners looked on this work of destruction with feelings akin to satisfaction, and felt as if a portion of their wrongs were avenged. Wines, for which the sick had pined in vain, were brought to light; luxuries of various kinds were found in profusion. The Federals brought them into the streets, and throwing them down, would shout, "Here, rebs, help yourselves, you are naked and starving and need them." What a strange spectacle of war between those who were so recently deadly foes! Such generosity was no rarity, and softened down much of the deadly animosity and bitter feeling experienced by the vanquished for their foes. Many found friends and relatives, and the Third Regiment had more than its share among the Federal troops. They met with cordial greetings; yet each adhered most tenaciously to their political sentiments and discussions; furious and warm were the special order of the day.

Aside from the speculators was a class of citizens in Vicksburg, who did their duty nobly. Let it be known, everywhere written in ineffaceable characters upon the pages of history; traced with golden letters upon the scroll of Time; stamped with an indelible impression upon every manly Southern heart, that the LADIES OF VICKSBURG were as true as steel, charitable to a fault upon every occasion, when their services were needed. Flittering like ministering angels about the hospitals, giving aid and comfort to the sick and wounded; hovering with tearful eyes over the dying soldier; threading their way along the torn-up streets amid the scream of shot and shell, and the storm of descending iron on missions of love and mercy, they exhibited a heroism and devotion beyond portrayal by human language.

The rememberance of her deeds there come back to us now with a force which mere words can give no expression to. Devoted women of Vicksburg! to-day, when the storm of war has passsed away and bright-winged peace once again smilingly sits on the thresholds of our homes, the heroes of thy city still remember thee with an imperishable love, eternal, undying as the soul itself.

Could human language furnish expressions sufficiently strong and beautiful, then would thought soar amidst its intricacies, and pluck therefrom its choicest words and transcribe them on these pages, that they might shine with radiant splendor here, a feeble tribute to thy kindness, love, and patriotism.

THE HOSPITALS

To the diary of Captain Charles A. Bruslé, an officer on General Hebert's staff, we are indebted for the substance of the following records:

"There were two classes of hospitals in Vicksburg: those for the sick, and those for the wounded. A week after the siege, Washington Hospital contained three hundred sick; the average deaths daily being from five to eight. During the siege the number of patients reached nearly eight hundred, and the deaths were proportionately greater, footing up eighteen or twenty daily. In this hospital very few wounded were admitted, so that, although much suffering was depicted upon the countenances of the poor inmates, yet were the scenes not so heart-rending as those exhibited by a visit to the hospitals containing the wounded. In the latter could be seen men with both legs off; some with an eye out, others without arms, and again, some who could once boast of manly beauty and personal attractions, rendered hideous by the loss of the nose or a portion of the face, so as to be unrecognizable by their nearest and dearest kindred. If one wishes to view the *havoc* of war next to the battle-field, this is the place to witness it. So fearful, so horrible are the scenes, that, long after you have left the place, perhaps haunting you to the verge of life, the screams of the wounded, the groans of the dying, or some form cold and stiff in death's icy embrace will ring in your ears and be present to your mental vision. One more picture and the tableau is complete—the burial of the dead. During the siege, trenches fifty feet long and three feet wide were dug, to receive the bodies of the brave men and officers. They usually contained about eight bodies. It was seldom a coffin could be procured, and the brave defender of his country had to be wrapped in his blanket and lowered into the cold earth which was hastily heaped above his mortal remains."

THE "CONTRABANDS"

Of course, large numbers of the officers had their negro servants with them, and the disposition to be made of them became a matter of great anxiety.

The following order from Major-General James B. McPherson, to Lieutenant-General John C. Pemberton, relative to negroes belonging to officers, was first received:

HEADQUARTERS, PAROLED PRISONERS, ⎱
Vicksburg, July 6, 1863. ⎰

Circular:—The following is published for the information of all concerned:

HEADQUARTERS 17TH ARMY CORPS, ⎱
Vicksburg, July 6, 1863. ⎰

Lt.-General Pemberton, Commanding C. S. A. Forces, Vicksburg,

GENERAL:—In relation to the question of servants, I am authorized to say that each commissioned officer can send in the *boy* whom he wishes to take with him with a *pass*, stating the fact to my Provost Marshal, Lieutenant-Colonel Wilson, who will question him as to his willingness to go, at the same time stating to the boy that he is free to do as he likes. If the boy or servant says he wishes to go, a pass will then be issued to him.

General officers will not be permitted to take with them mounted men for couriers. Major-General Grant furthermore directs me to say that he cannot permit you to send a courier with dispatches to your Government to-day, but will do so as soon as the public interest will permit.

Two teams will be allowed for your headquarters; one team for Division Headquarters; one four mule-team for Brigade Headquarters; one four-mule team for each regiment; one team for Major Orme, Chief Quartermaster. Very respecfully your obedient servant,

JAMES B. McPHERSON, Major General.

By order Lieutenant-General PEMBERTON. ⎱
R. W. MEMMINGER, *A. A. G.* ⎰

Official: S. CROM, *A. A. G., to Brigadier-General* HEBERT,
Commanding Brigade.

In conformity with the above order, large numbers of negroes immediately sought Lieutenant-Colonel Wilson's quarters, and seemed so eager to leave Vicksburg with their former masters and employers, that Major-General McPherson thought best to send the following letter to General Pemberton:

GENERAL:—I am constrained, in consequence of the abuse of the privilege which was granted to officers to take out one private servant each (colored), to withdraw it altogether, except in cases of families, and sick and disabled officers.

The abuses which I speak of are, *first,* officers coming with their servants here, and intimidating them instead of sending them by themselves to be questioned; *second,* citizens have been seen and heard in the streets urging negroes, who are evidently not servants, to go with the officers; *third,* negroes have also been brought here who have been at work on the fortifications.

Very respectfully your obedient servant,

J. B. McPHERSON, *Major-General.*

These letters need no comment at the present time. They are inserted here as connected with events transpiring at Vicksburg, and as forming an important portion of the history of the late unnatural war.

Numbers of the negroes attached to the Third Louisiana Infantry stayed with it, and attempted to leave with their former employers, but were detained. The parting between them at the lines often exhibited very affecting scenes.

COMMENTS ON THE FALL OF VICKSBURG

When the city fell, and was surrendered on the 4th of July, the men broke forth in bitter denunciation of Lieutenant-General Pemberton, boldly proclaiming that they had been sold to the enemy. Surrender on the 4th of July! Why should that day, of all others, be chosen for their humiliation? They preferred dying—a thousand times more preferable—than making the National Anniversary a thrice memorable natal day, and give to the United States a new impulse for prosecuting the war. Would it not be received as a good omen, and infuse a new spirit into the efforts of the foe for their subjugation? Such were some of the fierce denunciations used, whether justly or not the world has never discovered. Yet it seems scarcely probable or possible that General Pemberton could have been actuated by such perfidious motives.

That General Pemberton was not altogether blameless, is a fact known to the public generally; yet that he should be made to bear the whole of that disaster is wrong. We resume, in connection with this subject, extracts from the diary already mentioned. Lieutenant-General Pemberton was guilty of gross neglect of duty in two ways:

1. In not fortifying Vicksburg so as to resist an attack from the rear with the least possible loss of life.

2. In not procuring supplies for the garrison sufficient to make a protracted defence in case of a siege.

This is the great and chief cause of complaint. Notwithstanding public and private opinion regarding this subject, starvation was the actual cause of the surrender, as the records of these pages plainly demonstrate. Communications were received from the Yazoo Valley giving information that immense supplies could be obtained from this source. Yet no efforts were made to obtain these supplies or transport them to Vicksburg, although it was known that General Grant was making strenuous exertions to cross the river and attack Vicksburg from the rear, and might succeed at any moment. Again, the large quantity of supplies which accumulated at Snyder's Mills were allowed to remain there, and were eventually destroyed for the want of transportation, which should have been furnished at all hazards, regardless of the loss of camp equipage and clothing.

These are indisputable facts, and are placed on record as necessary to the completeness of the history concerning the siege and fall of Vicksburg, and not with a view of casting undue reflections upon the course pursued by Lieutenant-General Pemberton, who afterwards nobly served the Confederacy as a colonel of artillery.

AFTER THE SURRENDER

July 5th. Rations for five days were issued to the Confederates from the Commissariat of the Federals. These rations consisted of bacon, hominy, peas, coffee, sugar, soap, salt, candles and bread. How the famished troops enjoyed such bounteous supplies it is needless to state. For once the brave boys were the objects of their enemy's charity. They grew jovial and hilarious over the change in their condition. The Yankees came freely among them, and were unusually kind. They asked innumerable questions, and were horrified at the fact of the men eating mules and rats, and openly expressed their admiration for the unfaltering bravery of the Confederates. The men of the Third discussed the events of the siege, and the probability of soon being paroled. Visions of home and the loved ones there rose in rainbow tints before their imaginations, and many plans were formed for the period of their freedom from military service until their exchange. Rained very hard during the afternoon.

7th. Clear, and very warm. Vicksburg presented a strange yet animated scene. Immense numbers of steamers crowded the landings. The streets were thronged with crowds of citizens and soldiers, the Yankees eager to inspect the effects of the siege—the Confederates equally as curious to view the gun-boats, steamers—whatever was new and strange to them. On this day the work of paroling was commenced.

The men were paroled separately, and subscribed to the following oath:

Vicksburg, Miss., July 7, 1863.

To all whom it may concern:

Know ye, that I, ———, a private, Company —, — Regiment — Volunteers, C. S. A., being a prisoner of war in the hands of the United States forces, in virtue of the capitulation of the City of Vicksburg and its garrison by Lieutenant-General John C. Pemberton, C. S. A., commanding on the 4th day of July, 1863, do, in pursuance of the terms of said capitulation, give this my solemn parole, under oath:

That I will not take up arms again against the United States, nor serve in any military police or constabulary force in any fort, garrison or field-work held by the Confederate States of America, against the United States of America, nor a guard of prisons, depots or stores, nor discharge any duties usually performed by officers or soldiers, against the United States of America, until duly exchanged by the proper authorities.

Sworn to and subscribed before me, at Vicksburg, Miss., this 7th day of July, 1863.

JOHN O. DUER,
Captain 40th Illinois Regiment, and Paroling Officer.

A new spectacle to the brave boys of the Third Louisiana was to-day witnessed in Vicksburg, which was the free intermingling between the Yankees and negroes on terms of equality. The author saw a United States officer walking through the streets with a negro woman leaning on his arm. He carried an umbrella, doubtless to shelter his lady from the sun, and prevent the bright light from *tanning her ebony complexion.* How such a scene affected a Southerner then can better be imagined than described. Now, it would scarce elicit a passing glance.

Thus affairs progressed from day to day, with little change. The Confederates crossed the river in numbers, being permitted to do so by the Federals, who well knew that it was a most effectual method of demoralizing and destroying the efficiency of the army.

On the 11th the army was formed in proximity to the road leading to Jackson, preparatory to having their baggage examined, and bidding a final adieu to the scene of their heroic valor. The Third Regiment were alone honored with a row of sentries completely encircling them. None were allowed to enter or pass beyond this line, unless by special permission. Whether the Yankees still feared some outbreak from the brave Lousianians, who had fought them with such desperation and courage, or whether it was a precaution adopted by the officers to keep the men together, was not discovered. At this time it was well known that the attempt was about to be made to march the entire army to some point in the Confederacy, and keep them in camp until finally exchanged. They were determined to see their homes and relatives. Expostulations, threats and commands were words wasted, and a child might as well have endeavored to move a mountain with its puny arm, as for any officer to change their fixed purpose.

At 11½ o'clock A.M., July 11th, the army bade a final adieu to Vicksburg. They marched out of their stronghold with a proud step, and a stern defiance on their faces. The roadsides and embankments were crowded with Federals, to take a farewell glance at the troops who had fought them so stubbornly and desperately. Not a word of exultation or an outburst of any feeling was manifested by the foe. Honoring the heroic garrison for their bravery, they would not add to the humiliation of their surrender, by a single taunt. As the Third Regiment passed out of the works which they had defended with such obstinate bravery, they saw a large detail actively engaged in filling up the approaches which they had dug to the intrenchments occupied by the regiment. The old spirit of definace broke forth in words, as they witnessed the scene.

"Oh! yes," said one, "shovel dirt, d———n you. It is all you are good for. You can do that better than fighting."

"Dry up," retorted a Federal; "you rebels have grown wonderful sassy on Uncle Sam's grub."

It was a home-thrust, and the boys journeyed by in silence.

The day was a scorching hot one, and the men yet weak and all unaccustomed to marching. Yet, under these disadvantages, they tramped steadily forward, making fourteen miles, and encamping on the east side of Big Black. Their whole line of march was through the United States forces, who gathered in large numbers along the road to see the captured army. The Confederates, during this first day's march, began to exhibit a terrible state of demoralization. There was no regular organization of either companies, regiments or brigades, and large numbers of the men were constantly leaving for home. The Third Regiment had only a handful of men left, comprised mostly of those whose homes were within the enemy's lines. On the 12th we reached Raymond, marching a distance of twenty-one miles. At this place the ladies stood on the streets with refreshments for the wearied, weak troops, whom they welcomed with every demonstration of joy, and many kind, encouraging words.

The next day, at 12 M., the troops arrived at Pearl River, where they met the outposts of the Confederate army. An attempt was made at this stream to prevent the men from crossing, except in organized bodies. It most signally failed, as they constructed rafts, above and below the regular crossing, and ferried each other over. The troops proceeded about twelve miles east of Pearl River, ere they halted. General Pemberton rode in advance, and endeavored in vain to halt those who had left the main body. They either paid no attention to his commands, or left the highway for some less public road. That night a large number of the Third Regiment encamped near a corn-field, some distance from the main road. They had but a single frying-pan, as cooking utensil for the whole body. It was used in succession by squads of three and four, and then passed on. Corn was prepared and devoured on this occasion in its simplest form, yet with keen relish and in quantities sufficiently large to have killed men with the usual digestive organs. A Georgian did actually die from eating too much of this new food, finishing nearly two dozen ears. He was buried near the road-side, and a large placard pasted on a tree, giving his name and regiment, and setting forth the fact that he died from "the effects of eating too much green corn." No one, however, heeded the warning contained in this singular obituary notice.

How strange the contrast between their present situation and that of a few days previously! Then they were living amid the uproar and excitement of a fierce and deadly conflict; now they were unarmed wanderers over the land. Regular sentinels watched, while the remainder of the party slept soundly, most sweetly, with no screaming shells or thundering explosions to rudely disturb their slumbers.

The night was dark and cloudy, and the sentinel on guard must be his own time-keeper, for no stars shone in the sky to guide his judgment. All around was the silent woods, dark and gloomy, disturbed save by the chirrup of insects and the katydid's not unmusical voice. How strange seemed the situation!

The next morning, the 14th, at 3 A.M., started once more on the journey, reaching Brandon at 12 M., a travel of twenty miles in a half day. There were fifty of the Third Regiment left as a nucleus. They were hungry, tired and sore, and, although praised as being the brave defenders of Vicksburg, could not then appreciate the compliment, as it did not satisfy their wants. The roar of artillery was heard all day, indicating fighting between the forces of General Johnston and the Federals at Jackson.

Succeeded in drawing some rations on the 15th. At this point General Pemberton ordered Adjutant Curry to make a detail from the regiment, to guard some commissary stores on the railroad. Captain Gentles, of Company K, was detailed, with several men, who all most positively refused to do such duty, as being in violation of the provisions of their paroles. Captain Gentles was ordered under arrest, and here the matter remained for the time being. This episode created great excitement, and resulted in some queer discussions as to the full meaning and extent of the parole. At this period the men, however, exhibited a disposition to interpret it in its literal and closest signification.

On the 16th, the party started on the road leading back to Pearl River, to endeavor to find the regimental wagon. After proceeding nearly three miles, they were halted and turned back, now marching on the road to Enterprise. Meeting a few of the regiment, they reported this organization as having melted into a myth, the wagons in the woods almost deserted. A very few of the regiment reached Enterprise, and were immediately furnished with the following furloughs, for thirty days:

Special Orders,⎱   HEADQUARTERS THIRD LA. INFANTRY, ⎱
  No. — ⎰   *Enterprise, Miss., July 21, 1863.* ⎰

In compliance with Division Circular Order of this date, to me directed, I hereby furlough—— for (30) thirty days, to take effect from the 23d July. Members of companies raised on the east bank of the Mississippi River will rendezvous at Demopolis, Ala., or such other places as may be hereafter designated by the War Department. Members of those companies raised on the west bank of the Mississippi will rendezvous at Alexandria, La., to march to Demopolis, Ala., or to such other point as may be hereafter desginated by the Secretary of War.

Transportation will be furnished to ———, to and from his home, to the place of rendezvous.

SAMUEL D. RUSSELL,
Lieutenant-Colonel Commanding Third Louisiana Infantry.

Previous to this period the mass of the regiment had already left the army, and, crossing the Mississippi River wherever this object could be successfully accomplished, had made their way homeward in small squads. The greater portion of the command resided in parishes west of the Mississippi River. The receipt of furloughs by the few who reached Enterprise was the signal for a general scattering of the men over the different States, wherever they had friends and relatives. The conduct of the Third Regiment in thus voluntarily disbanding was not the exception, but the general rule in the army. The men who had fought so long and bravely, and who had suffered so severely, felt, after their capture and paroling, as if they were not only exempt from all military duty, but privileged to go where they pleased, and do as they pleased, until exchanged. They sadly needed rest and recreation, and sought their homes, as being the most favorable places to obtain these most desirable objects. Thus melted away the gallant army of Vicksburg, and the Confederacy lost the services of some of her bravest, most heroic, and truest defenders. General Grant could not have employed a more efficient method of disbanding and disorganizing an army than the very course he pursued. It was as effective as if a scourge had swept them from his path. How joyfully the bronzed and weather-beaten veterans of the Third Regiment were welcomed home by friends and relatives after years of absence and peril, we leave to the reader to imagine. Yet in many homes there were aching, sorrowful hearts, and tearful eyes for the loved one who came not back, whose voice was hushed forever, whose mouldering body quietly rested beneath the hill-side sod of the fallen city, leaving behind a name for heroic devotion and undaunted bravery, which would be inscribed on the scroll of time, and live in song and story.

INCIDENTS—THE COB-WAGON
AND THE MORTAR-SHELL

In the early part of the siege, all the negroes belonging to the regiment were used as cooks to prepare food for the men in the trenches, under the superintendence of the Commissary Sergeant and proper details. They had a perfect horror of shot and shell, and the proximity of one of these missiles would stampede the whole band from the vicinity of the fires and utensils, to seek some shelter beneath the hills. The first cooking camp was in the rear of Vicksburg, almost in direct range of the shells from Commodore Porter's mortar fleet. The place eventually became so warm that it was an utter impossibility to keep the cooks about the fires. Hence a move was rendered necessary. A spot was chosen south of Vicksburg, in a deep valley. There was not a sign of any unwelcome visitors having reached the sequestered vale. Fires were speedily built, and the negroes were hilarious over their work, feeling secure in their new position. A small one-horse wagon was sent to the grist-mill near at hand to procure a load of cobs to facilitate the process of baking. It was driven up near the fire. Rude jokes and uproarious laughter arose on all sides as the ebony-hued cooks indulged in their coarse witticisms. One of the detail was unhitching the horse, while a young fellow by the name of Stephens, a member of Company I, had just taken out the hind gate of the wagon, and was standing about three feet from the end of the vehicle. The sullen roar of a mortar had been heard but a moment before. No notice was taken of the accustomed miniature thunder. Suddenly the ominous scream of the huge missile was heard as it cleft a swift passage through the air. Every one intuitively ceased laughing and talking, and intently listened to the increasing voice of its approach. Nearer, yet nearer! the mad rush of the iron mass. Shriller, more hideous its fearful scream. The negroes stood with trembling limbs, and dilated, distended eyes, as if fascinated, spell-bound. "Look out, boys," shouted one accustomed to the sound, "it's coming among us." The voice roused some few, who started off at full speed. "What's the use of running?" said a young fellow standing near Stephens; "you will probably only rush into danger." It took but a few seconds for all this to occur, while the shell was still descending. With a scream like the concentrated shout of a thousand demons, down, down it came, into the very centre of the camp, just missing the end of the wagon, and descending with temendous force into the earth. Stephens was seen to fly backward through the air, performing a feat of gymnastics not usually a part of any programme. "Hurt any, Stephens?" shouted one of the boys. Stephens sprang nimbly to his feet, replying, "Not much; bruised some; but I'll be ——, boys, if that wasn't what I call a narrow escape." A loud burst of laughter greeted the response. Six inches variation in the descent of the missile would have caused his instantaneous death. The shell, fortunately for all, failed to explode, but made a hole in the ground fully fifteen feet deep, and sufficiently large for a man to crawl into. It was used for many days afterward as a receptacle for trash, although the boys jocularly remarked, that they preferred digging holes themselves, as being far preferable to Porter's very *striking* and *forcible* method. The tremendous power and force of a mortar-shell must be seen to be apppreciated. It is almost incredible how far one of these missiles will penetrate into the solid earth.

THE RULES OF CIVILIZED WARFARE

All History teaches us that during modern times, no matter how fierce and deadly the struggle between nations appealing to arms for a settlement of differences and difficulties, the hospitals for the sick and wounded were considered as sacred spots. Where fluttered the yellow ensign, insignia of the purpose for which a building was used, it was regarded as an emblem of safety, and unapproached by the storm of war. Yet in this nineteenth century, and to the American race, was reserved the spectacle of disregarding every law which should govern a people engaged in a deadly struggle. The siege of Vicksburg furnished no more terrible commentary upon the inhuman warfare waged during the recent strife, than the fact that the Confederate hospitals were selected as the special targets for the Federal guns. There the flag furnished no protection to the mangled and helpless inmates. The city hospital was a large building, standing in a prominent position, and visible for miles. Yet day after day the fire of Commodore Porter's mortars was directed upon the spot. The building itself was crowded with wounded, while the grounds around it were filled with tents, containing the maimed soldiers. To the physical agony of their wounds was added the constant mental dread of the missiles which fell among and around them, or, bursting in the air overhead with thundering detonations, descended in hoarsely screaming fragments among them. What mattered it that there were congregated there hundreds of maimed, suffering men! What mattered it that they were helpless bodies, animated by heroic spirits! Was not the avenger abroad, and a malignant spirit of warfare which gave no heed to their fears or complainings? Oh! the terrible picture of that hospital, with its brave sufferers, and the exploding shells above the spot. It is painted ineffaceably upon the tables of memory as then often seen, and the horrors of the picture mar now, as then, all the serene beauty of the Summer sky. Several shells penetrated the building, injuring many of the occupants, already crippled and wounded. One huge shell descended through the roof in an oblique direction, to the ground floor, exploding almost within the surgeons' room. The hoarded and scanty supply of medicines were almost totally destroyed, and the chief surgeon lost a leg. In the centre of the city the Washington Hotel was used for hospital purposes. Yet the enemy's Parrott guns were directed, by what malignant spirit God knows, upon the spot, although the hospital flag floated above it. In the southern portion of the city was another large building used for a similar purpose. This place became the particular target for the columbiads planted on the peninsula opposite the city. These are not imaginary statements, but stern facts, unimpeachable, and able to be substantiated by reliable, valid authority. Whether the wrongs thus perpetrated were intentional, cannot be known, but the fact of their existence is sufficient, and properly belong to a truthful record of events, that transpired during that memorable siege. Comment is considered unnecessary.

WOUNDED, BADLY

A member of Company F was severely wounded, being shot through the body. After recovering somewhat from the first shock of the wound, he broke forth in bitter invectives against the Yankees, completely exhausting the whole English vocabulary of vituperation in his denunciations.

"What in all creation is the matter, George?" asked a friend.

"Don't you see, I have just put on a clean, new shirt, the last one I have, and that d——d Yankee has shot it full of holes? My skin will get well, but the apertures in this garment never will heal up."

This comical idea of the wounded veteran caused a general laugh. The very thought of so much solicitation about a shirt, regardless of the wounded body, was something ridiculous beyond what had yet occurred.

"I WANT TO GO HOME"

One day, toward the close of the siege, a Mississippian, a tall, awkward specimen of the country regions of that State, suddenly broke forth in loud lamentations, the tears actually streaming down his face as he incoherently sobbed, "Boo-hoo! boo-hoo! I wish they would—boo-hoo!—stop fighting, or surrender, or something else, I want ter go home and see my ma! boo-hoo!" "Stop your d——d blubbering, you ninny-hammer," said one of the Third. Then "I want ter go home" was shouted down the line amid uproarious mirth. It became a bye-word for the remainder of the siege.

"SIMEON, WIGGLE WAGGLE"

Just on the slope of the hill-side, behind the intrenchments, one afternoon, sat one of the men on a stump. A natural wit, he was amusing his comrades lying around him, by a perfect fusillade of "small talk" and sharp witticisms. The right hand lay negligently across his lap, the other grasped the stump. Phiz! zip! "Boys, some d——d Yankee is making a target of me. But let him go ahead, if he thinks there is no hereafter." The words were scarcely uttered, ere a Minié ball struck him, carrying away the thumb of the right hand, and entering the fleshy part of the thigh. Groaning with pain, he was helped away, and sent to the hospital. A friend soon called to see him: "Well, Dave, how do you feel? I am sorry to see you here. Not seriously wounded, are you?"

"No; I guess not. Only a flesh-wound."

He was calm and seemingly unconcerned now. Suddenly he remarked:

"Look here, Will, there is one thing that troubles me terribly. I don't know what to do," looking troubled.

"Well, what is it? Anything I can do for you?"

"You see that thumb?" holding up the hand minus such a portion. "No you don't, for it is gone as clean as a whistle. Well, I have been thinking for some time of a very serious matter."

"What is it?"

"How shall I play Simeon, wiggle waggle? Simeon says up, Simeon says down. Can't come it with this hand. Ha! ha! ha!"

His love of fun overcame his physical agony, and he indulged the propensity at the expense of his own sufferings. He never recovered, but now fills a soldier's grave on the hills of Vicksburg; the last man of the regiment buried there ere the troops left the place. Rest in peace, friend Echols, till the last reveille summon you forth from the tomb.

THE LAST MEAL

The provisions had all been distributed. The meagre meal of bread and meat was voraciously consumed at once by some, while others ate but sparingly, carefully laying away the remainder for some other time. A soldier sat amid his comrades, who were laughing and chatting over their food in high spirits. Jovial, light-hearted, fond of a good joke and sport in any form, he was always creating mirth. Moroseness and ill-humor could not linger where he was. Consequently, he was a great favorite among his comrades. On this occasion it was noticed that he did not eat his food. Looking at the scanty store with a comical expression on his manly face, he remarked:

"I say, boys, isn't this *some* for a hearty, strong *man?* General John C——— is training us like thorough-bred racers, knowing that too much food is not good for the wholesome. I am nearly reduced to the proper fighting weight, and think I can toe the mark about right. What do you think of it, boys? Let's put up a sign, 'Prize Ring! Training done in the most thorough and scientific manner.' But I am devilish hungry. But I believe I'll save my food until morning." Hesitating a moment, he resumed, "No; I'll be hanged if I do. Suppose I get shot, then I'll lose all the pleasure of eating my meal. So here goes." The food disappeared, when the soldier jumped to his feet and seized his rifle, remarking: "I'll have a little sport sharp-shooting." In less than five minutes he was a corpse, a bullet having penetrated his brain. Poor Ed. Benton, we wonder if some spirit did whisper his doom to him, as he resolved to eat that last meal! We know not, yet this is an authentic record.

HOW A COMMISSARY WAS "DONE FOR"

One gloomy evening, several forms could have been seen stealing away from the intrenchments occupied by the Third Regiment, as if bent on some mysterious mission. Not far distant, a commissary of one of the other regiments had snugly ensconced himself in a secure position near some deserted cabins. Some of the Argus-eyed boys discovered that his quarters contained more provisions than the "regulations" allowed. It required only a few moments for the discoverer of this fact to gather a few choice friends from the groups of hungry men, to make a raid on the hoarded treasure. Like a spirit, we follow their footsteps as they approached the victim of their wiles. They soon surrounded his quarters, and watched his movements. He was preparing his supper. Savory bacon, and, *actually, "slip-jacks" made of flour,* with molasses to give them an additional flavor. Had he peered into the darkness, while thus cooking his fine meal, he would have seen eyes, glittering in the darkness like a fierce tiger's, glaring at him—eyes brilliant with the fires of starvation and hunger. All unconsciously, he completed his cooking, ate a portion of his food, then carefully placed the remainder safely away for his morning meal. Alas! for the uncertainty of human expectations. After arranging everything to his entire satisfaction, the occupant of the tent laid down on his humble couch, to seek repose. Without no one was astir, and only an occasional shot along the lines broke the silence. Hark! was that distant thunder? No; for bright constellations of stars glittered in the clear sky over-head, with no storm-cloud to mar their clear brilliancy. Again that sound swells upon the air. What does it mean? Watchers near recognized in it the deep voice from the land of slumber. *The sleeper was snoring!* Dark forms, like spirits of evil, arose from the earth where they had so long lain motionless, and with noiseless footsteps glided toward the tent, entering its opening front. Soon they emerged, laden with the spoils, which were found quite abundant and of great variety. Assembling in a dark group, one at last broke the silence, saying, "By George, boys, what a breakfast we will have! But I am devilish hungry; let's go back and finish the Captain's supper." A general assent was given, and they returned, and, seating themselves coolly, ate the remaining cakes and fried meat, without rousing the unconscious sleeper from his slumbers. The last sweetened morsel disappeared within the hungry jaws of one of the party, who, wiping the molasses from his lips with the sleeve of his gray jacket, remarked, "There'll be h—l to play in the morning about this affair; but mum's the word, boys. Let's be going."

Imagine the surprise of some of the Mississippians the next morning, when they beheld the Louisianians bountifully supplied with delicious biscuits and bacon. Their astonishment found vent in bitter words of complaint, that "them ere Louisianians had plenty to eat, while they were nearly starved to death." The boys of the Third Regiment had not become veterans in the service to be starved as long as anything eatable could be obtained, and had learned some accomplishments, which their less experienced comrades of the Mississippi regiments never dreamed of.

HOW THEY DID IT

The teachings of moral philosophy have no potency over the human mind under certain contingencies. If a man is actually suffering for the need of some particular object, yet is assured in his own mind that the perpetration of a wrong will supply his necessity, he seldom lingers to moralize over the nice points raised by his own conscience. Hunger, gaunt famine, with its pallid, sunken eyeballs, is perhaps, the very worst demon with which the human will can contend. Innumerable facts, with all their horrid and thrilling details, attest the truth of this assertion. A starving soldier is the very worst of all moralists, and it is as useless to expect the habitual robber to desist from plundering, when gold is placed in his way, as to anticipate that a hungry soldier will not steal food when other resources fail him.

At Vicksburg, every one knew that the depot contained a large supply of breadstuffs, meal, rice, flour, etc., put up in bags. These supplies were guarded day and night by faithful sentinels, whom neither persuasion, threats nor gain could make false to their duty. The southern end of the building was securely barred by heavy oak timbers, nailed over the windows and doorway. In this end of the building was a room used as a stable, probably for some quartermaster's or commissary's horse. A single doorway led out of this room into that portion of the bulding used as a store-room for the supplies. This doorway was blockaded with a sugar hogshead. Such were the means used to prevent access to the treasure from the rear, while in front stood the Argus-eyed sentinels, with loaded guns and fixed bayonets, ready to give any intrude a warm reception. One stormy night, five members of the regiment quietly came into the camp where the food was cooked, and aroused two slumberers from their repose. A hurried, low-toned explanation was given in answer to the inquiries as to what was wanted, and the whole party moved out of the camp toward the river. Up the adjacent hill-side, past the hospital, where the maimed and dying soldiers lay, through a deep cut in the road, until they reached the railroad, like flitting shadows passed the hurrying forms. Boldly proceeding down the road, they soon reached the depot. Without hesitation—with a skill and rapidity which would have shamed a scientific burglar, the heavy timbers were removed from one of the windows, until a sufficiently large aperture for the purpose was made. Into this clambered a portion of the party, using a comrade's shoulder as a stepping-stone. Where was the guard, did you say? Innocent questioner! What little noise that was made was lost amid the storm and the roar of guns. Those who entered the room as noiselessly and successfully, removed the only obstacle that intervened between them and the coveted prize. It required extreme caution to remove the heavy bags; yet it was accomplished. A form appeared at the opening and lifted out a huge, white bundle. It was instantly seized and shouldered by one of the party, who staggered away with his burden. A second, third and fourth performed the same task, until only a single man remained. He likewise obtained his load, but stirred not. The mystery was soon explained. Receiving two more bags, he aided his comrades within to descend, when they all hurried from the scene of their exploit. Meeting at an agreed rendezvous, the party, with great demonstrations of joy, exulted over their success. A portion of the precious burdens was deposited in a secure place, while the remainder was conveyed to the intrenchments—a distance of over two miles. It seemed incredible that weakened, starving men could thus carry a load averaging from one hundred to one hundred and fifty pounds. Yet so it was. The very desperation of their hunger gave them an unnatural strength, just as a physically weak man becomes endowed with supernatural muscular powers under circumstances of imminent peril. A successful "foraging" party was always welcomed with great demonstrations of joy, for supplies thus procured were generously distributed among the comrades. Liberality toward each other was one of the features that marked the conduct of the Louisianians, and a mean, niggardly man among them was as heartily depised and as rare as a cowardly one.

Such incidents are, perhaps, not very flattering to the morality of the regiment, but they are none the less matters of fact, and will serve to explain how the "boys," at times, had an abundance, while their less venturesome and wondering comrades of the Mississippi regiments suffered the pangs of extreme hunger.

STEALING VEGETABLES

One Sunday evening two of the non-commissioned staff of the regiment were returning to camp from the intrenchments when the following colloquy occurred:

"Sergeant," says one to the other, "wouldn't you like some vegetables, especially some good cabbage?"

"Major," was the reply, "as a Yankee would say, I rayther reckon as how I would. Vegetables! what a luxury! Where can they be found, and what *do* you mean?"

"Aisy, now, as the Irishman would say. I have been reconnoitering lately, and have found a large garden of cabbages; but the owner of the place is very watchful, and swears that he will shoot the first soldier he catches in his garden. I have discovered a picket loose at the bottom. It is on our route, and suppose we make a raid and 'cabbage' a mess of something green."

"Agreed, with all my heart. But, Major, what shall be the *modus operandi?*"

"Well, you watch at the opening in the fence, and I will go inside. If anything suspicious should happen, whistle and I will know what it means."

The two plotters were soon arrived at the scene of operations. It was a large garden, extending eastward down a gentle slope to a small rivulet, or rather ditch, running north and south. The opening was soon found. Major instantly entered, and proceeded in a course directly westward, and then his form disappeared in the murky gloom of the night. Sergeant sat down by the fence, and thrusting his head into the opening made by shoving aside the bottom of the picket, became all ears and eyes in his watchfulness. Out toward the breastworks came the sound of the sharpshooters' rifle-shots, with the occasional roar of a piece of artillery. Lights glimmered in some of the houses. Mortar-shells, with blazing fuses, described graceful curves through the air in their flight into the besieged city. The atmosphere was calm, the stars looking out from the clear sky overhead as if angel eyes gazing upon the din, uproar and carnage of battle below. What wonder that the soldier fell into a reverie, and lived once more amid scenes far away. What wonder that ———. Phiz! Zip! What was it? Only a stray Minié-ball, that made a close passage to his scalp, cutting the hair from his head. A rude awakening from his pleasant thoughts; yet still he changed not his position. He was on guard, and could not desert his post. The minutes seemed ages. What could Major be doing? Assuredly not going to carry off the whole cabbage-bed! Yet he was gone sufficiently long to accomplish such an undertaking. He'd be hanged if ———. The shrill scream of an approaching shell from a rifled gun this time cut short his new train of thought. Knowing, from the peculiar sound, that he was nearly in range, he looked in vain for some sheltering protection. The ground was smooth and level, not a single indenture to protect the smallest object. Action must be instantaneous, and he threw himself close alongside of the bottom board of the fence. With an exultant scream the shell tipped the pickets above his prostrate form, and descended into the garden in the exact direction taken by the Major. The sergeant jumped to his feet, and a shrill whistle broke upon the air. Breathlessly, intently he listened. No answering signal penetrated the darkness and disturbed the reigning silence. Again and again the signal was given. Still no response. Running rapidly along the fence a few yards, he was about to climb over when Major came hastily to the spot, a mountain of perambulating cabbage.

The tension to which the nerves of the sergeant had been strung relaxed in invectives.

"Why in the devil, Major, didn't you answer my signal? I thought that shell had killed you, and one of the Third Regiment would be found dead in a citizen's garden, slain in the very act of stealing. What a disgrace for a veteran to be *caught* stealing! People would have proclaimed 'retributive justice,' and 'served him right.'"

"By the way what were you doing when that last customer so unceremoniously and uninvited visited us?"

"Well, you see, sergeant, the ground is very hard, and the cabbage strongrooted, and I was stooping down, with a good hold on the stalk with both hands. You can imagine the position: about to give it a 'strong pull, a long pull, and a pull altogether,' when I heard that ———— shell coming, and immediately threw myself upon the ground."

"How close did it strike, Major?"

"It went into the ground, about a foot from my head, and nearly buried me alive."

"I should judge so, from your personal appearance, covered as you are with dirt, from your head to your heels. Why, you look like an Irish gravedigger. Let's leave this place, as the Lord has warned us both that 'thou shalt not steal,' more forcibly that pleasantly."

The two men traveled off at a "double-quick," carrying their "greens" with them. Arriving in camp, they soon forgot their narrow escape, as they laughed and talked over a huge dish of boiled cabbage, which was consumed with a voraciousness and keen relish commensurate with the danger in procuring it.

RUNNING THE GAUNTLET

The history of the manners and customs of the aborigines of America furnishes some thrilling narratives of the practice of treating prisoners in accordance with the heading of this article. It was reserved to a later and more civilized people to furnish an ordeal more trying to the nerves than the one instituted among the savages. Every evening the provision detail went from the camp south of Vicksburg to the intrenchments, a distance of over two miles. The provisions prepared during the day were placed in a four-mule wagon, and proceeded to the regiment every evening about sun-down, accompanied, usually, by a man from each company, the commissary-sergeant and several negroes. The road through Vicksburg was comparatively safe, but on arriving at the upper portion of the city, where it branched off in a north-easterly direction, the party were in direct range of the mortar-shells. As soon as the danger became imminent, they would halt, listen for the dull roar of the mortars, and wait for the passage of the terrible missiles. Their descent or explosion was the signal for a hot race, ere the next messenger of death was launched upon the city. Men, mules and wagon stampeded in a hot race along the road, for life and death was probably the issue of their speed. There were no spare moments for shouting or laughter then. Arriving about half way to the trenches, the party would take a good breathing spell, ere again proceeding to confront a new danger, from which there could be no escape. Yet there was no shrinking, as they faced the flying bullets and rifle-shells from beyond the line of works. The rifle-balls would cut up the dirt in the road, or shrilly whistle through the air, in their rapid flight. Accustomed as men may become in braving danger during moments of intense excitement, it required a steadiness of nerve and firm resolution to quietly proceed along a road, into which bullets were constantly dipping, or over which they were flying from an enfilading fire. Such, however, was the case with the provision detail of the Third Louisiana Infantry. There were innumerable hair-breadth escapes and laughable occurrences attending their daily journey to and from the intrenchments; yet, during the whole siege, not a man among them received the slightest injury. The long races from flying shells and descending bombs in those hot June days are indelibly impressed upon the memories of all of that band. They braved the dangers of the siege without any of the excitement that buoyed up the dashing bravery of those who occupied the intrenchments. Though often with flying feet spurring the dust of the road to escape threatening death, no one would question their courage. Theirs was a cool, dispassionate courage, worthy the fame and heroism which made the regiment notorious. As non-combatants it was somewhat laughable to observe with what earnestness and care they selected the safest route to escape the line of fire. Boys, do you remember it all now without the aid of this notice? *We do, distinctly and most emphatically.*

CHAPTER XXXI

SONGS

THE men often indulged their propensity for song-writing, and if their productions did not exhibit splendid poetical talent, the sentiments of these songs manifested the spirit which animated them, their reckless disregard to danger, and their propensity to make mirth out of their sufferings. It was no unusual occurrence to hear, amid the battle's fierce din, the choruses of these songs shouted forth with stentorian voices, or their strains at night softly floating away over the intrenchments on the quiet air.

OUR FLAG

BY W. M. WASHBURN, CO. B.
Air: "Her bright smile haunts me still."

I.

There is freedom on each fold,
  And each star is freedom's throne,
And the free, the brave, the bold,
  Guard thine honor as their own.
    Every danger hast thou known,
      That the battle's storm can fill;
    Thy glory hath not flown;
      We proudly wave thee still.

II.

Floating in the morning light,
  Freedom's star will shine afar
Floating in the murky night,
  All shall see thee, freedom's star.
    For *"sic semper"* thy refrain;

And thy motto e'er shall be,
 Let tyrants wear the chain;
  I am, I will be free.

III.

O'er the land and o'er the seas,
 Where the howling waves are torn;
In the calm, the storm, the breeze,
 Be thy standard proudly borne.
  For there's freedom on each fold,
   And each star is freedom's throne;
  The free, the brave, the bold;
   Thy glory is their own.

A LIFE ON THE VICKSBURG HILLS

By A. Dalsheimer, Co. K.
Air: "Life on the Ocean Wave."

A life on the Vicksburg hills,
 A home in the trenches deep,
A dodge from the Yankee shells,
 And the old pea-bread won't keep.
  The bread—the bread—
 And the old pea-bread won't keep.

Like a rebel caged, I pine,
 And I dodge when the cannons roar;
But give me corn-dodger and swine,
 And I'll stay for evermore.

Once more in the trench I stand,
 With my own far-ranging gun;
Should the fray come hand to hand,
 I'll wager my rations I run.

The trench is no longer in view;
 The shells have begun to fall;
'Tis a sound I hate—don't you?
 Into my rat-hole I'll crawl.

The bullets may whistle by,
    The terrible bombs come down;
But give me full rations, and I
        Will stay in my hole in the ground.
            Oh! a life on the Vicksburg hills,
                A home in the trenches deep,
            A dodge from the Yankee shells,
                And the old pea-bread won't keep.

DO THEY MISS ME IN THE TRENCH

By J. W. NAFF.*
Air: "Do they miss me at home."

Do they miss me in the trench, do they miss me?
    When the shells fly so thickly around?
Do they know that I've run down the hill-side
    To look for my hole in the ground?
But the shells exploded so near me,
    It seemed best for me to run;
And though some laughed as I cray-fished,
    I could not discover the fun.

I often get up in the trenches,
    When some Yankee is near out of sight,
And fire a round or two at him,
    To make the boys think that I'll fight.
But when the Yanks commence shelling,
    I run to my home down the hill,
I swear my legs never will stay there,
    Though all may stay there who will.

I'll save myself through the dread struggle,
    And when the great battle is o'er
I'll claim my full rations of laurels,
    As always I've done heretofore.

---

*Killed the day after writing this song.

I'll say that I've fought them as bravely
    As the best of my comrades who fell,
And swear most roundly to all others
    That I never had fears of a shell.

THE RAINBOW OF HOPE

By W. M. WASHBURN, Co. B.
Air: "Life on the Wave."

There's the rainbow of Hope in the moonlit sky,
    Man the works—fling trembling away, my boys,
The breeze is soft, our God is on high,
    He will shield us, if we are still true, my boys.
We have slept in the calm, we have laughed in the storm,
    We will sing by the bomb's red glare, my boys;
Should the foe come on, with a strong heart and arm,
    And a keen blade, we'll send him away, my boys.

And the rainbow of Hope, while it lingers still,
    We will strike for the dear ones of home, my boys.
We will trust to our blades, and to God's good will,
    And fling ever fear to the winds, my boys.
We will bear every hardship, or peril, or pain,
    For our loved ones are trusting to us, my boys,
And we'll proudly return to greet them again,
    Or as proudly fill a soldier's grave, my boys.

Light hearts we bring to rescue our land,
    Though a shadow has hung o'er her of late, my boys.
We will strike for our homes with a steady hand,
    And a smile for whate'er be our fate, my boys.
Though some may sleep 'neath the hill-side sod,
    Though none go back to their homes, my boys,
Yet the hearts that are true to their country and God,
    Will all meet at the last reveille, my boys.

The following letter needs no comment:

HEADQUARTERS, ARMSTRONG'S BRIGADE, ⎫
Athens, East Tennessee, July 22d, 1863. ⎰

SIR—General Armstrong desires to know the casualties in the Third
Louisiana Infantry in the campaign from Grand Gulf to the capitulation of
Vicksburg, and the part taken by that regiment in heroic defence of that place.
He feels confident that they have sustained their former blood-earned rep-
utation, and, as a source of gratification, he desires to know its conduct and
its losses.

He offers his sincere congratulations upon its prospect of soon resuming
the field, and, notwithstanding its depleted numbers, hopes the war-cry of
the "Bloody Third" will be heard loudest in the battle-din soon again.

He tenders his respects to his many friends in the regiment.

I have the honor to be, very respectfully,

Your obedient servant,

A. BURWELL, *A. A. G.*
Officer commanding Third Louisiana Infantry.

P. S.—Let the memory of Ben McCulloch nerve them to even more
heroic deeds in future.   F. C. ARMSTRONG.

OUR SURGEONS

Dr. Moss, who was appointed surgeon of the regiment, was a private in
the ranks of Company I. He was born in Wilkinson County, Miss., March 19,
1837. He graduated in the Medical Department of the University of Louisiana
in March, 1861, with great credit to himself and his class. He was among the
first to answer his country's call. The absence of all official documents and dates
makes it impossible to give the exact period of his appointment as assistant surgeon, and finally as surgeon of the regiment. He endeared himself to every
member of the regiment by his unvarying kindness and attention to the sick
and general affability. His was a heart as tender as a woman's. He was surgeon
of the regiment at its final dissolution in Shreveport in 1865. Returning home,
full of bright hope and youthful vigor, skilled in all the branches of his profession, he found an early grave. He died August 3, 1865, aged 28 years and 4
months. He needs no eulogy from the author's pen, as he lives fresh and green
in the heart of every brave soldier of the Third Louisianians.

Dr. P. F. Whitehead is a native of Kentucky, and had been a resident of the State of Missouri a year previous to the war. He was appointed surgeon of the First Regiment, Missouri State Guard, that was organized.

Continuing with Price's army, he was eventually appointed surgeon of the Third Louisiana Infantry shortly after its reorganization.

He remained with the regiment all through its long, wearisome marches and desperate battles, until it was eventually confined within the intrenchments of Vicksburg.

Dr. Whitehead was most thoroughly skilled in every branch of his profession. He soon endeared himself to the men by his untiring efforts to relieve their sufferings, and his unvarying politeness of manner and genial affability. Of fine personal appearance, refined and polished in manners, it is not surprising that the men learned both to admire and respect him. No higher compliment can be paid to his skill as a surgeon—no statement attest the confidence placed in that skill—than the mention of the fact that, at Vicksburg, every member of the regiment requiring the amputation of a limb, or some delicate surgical operation, would allow no other physician to operate on them except Dr. P. F. Whitehead. Innumerable scientific and skillful operations have we witnessed performed by him. All through the eventful siege he was untiring, unceasingly occupied.

After the fall of that place he became Senior Surgeon of Scott's Louisiana Brigade, which position he retained until the commencement of General Johnston's famous Georgia campaign, when he was assigned to duty as chief surgeon of Loring's Division. He occupied this situation until the close of the war, and was surrendered with the army at Greensboro, N.C., April 26, 1865. Dr. P. F. Whitehead is now practicing his profession in Vicksburg—the scene of some of his most arduous labors during the war.

CHAPTER XXXII

EAST OF THE MISSISSIPPI

WHO of the war-worn veterans of the Third Regiment, Louisiana Infantry, does not remember the first return home from the army, since the inception of the war, after that memorable siege of Vicksburg? How the heart throbbed quick and strong, as the soldier approached the well-known homestead! His footsteps, though spurning the earth in quick strides beneath his hastening feet, kept not pace with his eager spirit. Very often he unexpectedly reached his hearth-stone. What a welcome does he receive! The clasp of loving arms around his form, and the imprint of warm lips, again and again upon his own browned and bearded face. Then there were innumerable questions showered upon him, and the thrilling recital of the siege rehearsed, with all its horrors and heroism. Then he must needs have his long hair shorn, and his face subjected to the tonsorial art; change his faded and soiled gray uniform for the garments of a quiet citizen at home; and behold the rough veteran metamorphosed into the good-looking, respectable gentleman at home. Who would ever dream that this pleasant, sociable man was, but a few days previously, the reckless soldier, standing where bullets filled the air like drops of summer rain, ready for any species of danger or rascality? Truly the changes of life are wonderfully strange! How unnatural did it seem to be free once more; free in the full meaning and acceptation of the word; no more prompt obedience to military orders; no more following the beck and nod of some officer! Is it a dream? Free! to go and come as he pleases! It is incomprehensible. Wake up! shake yourself, man, for it is a reality. Those halcyon days at home! They were the golden sunbeams that shed a flood of soft radiance over the whole soul of the paroled soldier. Now commenced a life of enjoyment, while the days of probation existed, for it was uncertain when they would again be summoned to take up arms. Social gatherings, balls, parties, fishing and hunting were freely indulged in, as the inclination or situation of the soldier made necessary. They were scattered over the State in city, town, hamlet and country, and made the best possible use of their freedom.

CHAPTER XXXIII

DEMOPOLIS, ALA.

THE halcyon days of the furlough have expired, and the men once more begin to congregate at this point, in obedience to published orders.

In the latter part of August, 1863, a few members of the Third Regiment were assembled in camp. These were men whose homes generally were within the enemy's lines, and who were too true in their devotion to the Southern cause, too uncompromising in their spirit of hostility to seek their homes, thus situated, only, perhaps, to subject themselves to restrictions on their freedom of word and action.

The camp at Demopolis was in an old, uncultivated field, beneath the shelter of some huge oak-trees. The Confederates were without tents or cooking utensils. They constructed some rude bunks and shelters beneath the overshadowing branches of the trees, and accepted the "situation" with a truly commendable spirit. The whole command did not number twenty-five men. Near the spot selected were the quarters of General Hebert. Of course, he was always to be found near the Third Louisiana Infantry, whom he had so often led in battle, and who respected and honored him for his soldierly qualities. Without the shadow of a doubt, the men and the General mutually admired and respected each other, although the one would frequently complain, in not very choice language, of the strict discipline enforced by the other, or his seeming spirit of opposition to their wishes and denial of their frequent requests. The men had nothing to do at Demopolis save eat, drink, sleep, read and make merry over their haps and mishaps. "Idleness," we are told, "is the devil's workshop,"—a saying often verified by these veterans. They wandered over the country around Demopolis on all kinds of expeditions. Not a house, or highway or by-way but was explored and well known. The Tombigbee River, close at hand, was very convenient for bathing and expeditions in boats, both of which were frequent occurrences. The evening was usually the signal for a general gathering at the camp, and an indulgence in scenes of uproarious mirth and frolics—dancing and singing being the chief amusements. No one interfered with their hilarity, and they were allowed to make as much noise as they wished. No one was near to be disturbed by it.

One day four members of the regiment started out on an exploring expedition, and to visit a distillery some miles from camp. They traveled nearly all day without accomplishing their object, and finally became lost in the swamp. Here was a predicament. Spreading out, at short distances, like a line of skirmishers, they pushed forward in expectation of discovering some road. They were eventually successful, and finally reached the Tombigbee, many long miles above camp. There was a crossing at the place, where they struck the river; but the boats were on the opposite side. What was to be done? After a short consultation two of the party stripped, plunged into the broad stream and boldly swam across. It required but a few moments to unmoor a boat, obtain the remainder of the party, and row rapidly down the stream. They were now in high spirits, and awoke the slumbering echoes along the shores with shouts and songs. As they descended, they stopped at several landings and purchased watermelons, until they had a full cargo on board. The party arrived in camp during the "wee sma'" hours of the night, completely worn out with fatigue. The melons were sold the next day, netting a profit of seventeen dollars in Confederate money.

On the 30th of August a flag reached camp, being the gift of General Maury, our old division commander. This token of esteem and remembrance on the part of a general whom the men had learned to love and respect was highly appreciated. The flag was a Beauregard battle-flag, having inscribed on it—Oak Hills, Elk Horn, Iuka, Corinth and Vicksburg. It was soon gayly floating on the breeze, above the quarters of the regiment.

On the 2d September camp was transferred from Demopolis, Ala., to Enterprise, Miss. The detachment had a lively trip to the latter place. The encampment selected at Enterprise was in the pine woods, about a mile from the town. Some system was observed here, and each regiment had its own quarters in regular succession. About twenty-five of the Third Regiment and four hundred of the brigade were in camp on the 14th of September.

On the 15th it was reported that 15,000 of the Vicksburg prisoners were exchanged, and that the Louisiana regiments were to report to General H. W. Allen, at Shreveport. Of course, such a statement created great excitement, especially among the band of the Third Louisiana Infantry represented at Enterprise. Many of them were eager to unite their fates with the fortunes of the regiment, while others talked of joining the cavalry. Yet no permissions were granted for the men east of the Mississippi to join their comrades in the

Trans-Mississippi Department. It was an idle, lazy life which the paroled troops led in camp, with no duties to perform, or anything to occupy their time and attention. Of course, they must have some excitement.

One night very late several of the regiment came into camp very noisy, from having imbibed, what they termed, too much "torch-light procession." The occupants of the various bunks were unceremoniously roused from their slumbers and pulled out of bed. A tall, droll member of Company K (J. Barrat), who looked much like an Indian, concluded he would have a menagerie performance out of a certain member of Company H. Every one remembers J. R. Nash. He was a strong, stout-built man, hailed from the mountain regions of Tennessee, and was as good-natured as he was powerful. The Company K man went to Nash's bunk, rudely shook him, and shouted:

"Get up, Nash, and paw like a goat, and I'll give you a drink." Nash obeyed; a ring was formed; he pawed up the ground with one foot, spit and spluttered like a goat, ending the performance with a "Baa-a-aa" that would have shamed the veritable king of the tribe. It is needless to state that the ridiculous performance was received with loud shouts and laughter by the crowd of witnesses, and the promised reward instantly handed to him. The next morning an order was received from General Hebert, whose headquarters were near by, that there must be less noise in camp. Was it obeyed? Nearly all the pines in and around camp were blazed, and the resinous substance which oozed from the wood would burn readily and fiercely. That night, suddenly, every pine-tree broke into a brilliant blaze, while all the sheds and shelters as unaccountably caught fire. "Fire! Fire!" was shouted, with the full power of stentorian lungs, when a voice would shout, "Stop that nose. It's against orders. No noise in camp. General Hebert will arrest you all." It is quite needless to state that no notice was taken of this *strict obedience* to orders, while General Hebert is reported to have remarked, "It is useless to notice the boys; they will have their fun, despite military rules and regulations."

On the 22d General Allen arrived at Enterprise, and was eagerly sought by many of the members of the regiment, who wished to cross the river. He gave them no definite encouragement, but said that he would like to have them with him, and thought that no harm would result from their joining their commands, provided they could get through the lines. Ah, there was the rub! Major H. F. Springer, formerly a member of Company G, was running the blockade of the Mississippi with Government dispatches and ammunition. He needed teamsters, and wished to obtain them from the regiment. His request was refused. However, several volunteered to go at 7 P.M. On the night of the

26th, five men left camp with their knapsacks on their backs, bidding their comrades good-bye, who jocularly remarked, "We expect to see you back, in charge of the cavalry, in three to four days." The next morning , at 8 A.M., this same party reached Shubuta, after marching all night, and making thirty-five miles. They were soon in charge of Major Springer's teams and wagons, bound for the Trans-Mississippi. Captains Richards and Middlebrooks succeeded in obtaining permits to join their companies, and had left some days previously. Captain Gentles, held under arrest by General Pemberton's orders, had tendered his resignation to the War Department, but it was not then accepted. He eventually became the leader of a party of mounted scouts. The regiment could not boast of a braver, more daring or efficient officer than H. H. Gentles. The officers eventually remaining in camp were Captain Brashear and Lieutenant Thomas, Company E; Lieutenant A. B. Payne, Company K; W. T. Fagan, Company E.

Some time in December, 1863, the paroled prisoners were declared exchanged, and were armed and equipped, the detachment of the Third Regiment doing some duty in Enterprise. After General Polk superseded General Hardee in command of the paroled troops, he issued an order for the consolidation into one regiment the men of the Third, Seventeenth, Twenty-first, Twenty-second, Twenty-sixth, Twenty-seventh, Twenty-eighth and Thirty-first Louisiana Infantry, who were on the east side of the river. They were divided into companies, the men being allowed the privilege of selecting their company officers from any of the officers of these regiments, not absent without leave. The Third Regiment formed one company, designated as Company H, with the following officers: Captain, C. H. Brashear; First Lieutenant, J. P. Parsons, (Seventeenth Louisiana); Second Lieutenant, W. T. Fagan; Second Jr. Lieutenant, A. J. Thomas. First Sergeant, C. Hurley; Second do., A. B. Booth; Third do., J. Roddy; Fourth do., T. Williams. First Corporal, W. E. Walker; Second do., J. F. Chambers; Third do., W. B. Sheffield; Fourth do., R. J. Galloway. The members of the Twenty-seventh, Twenty-eighth, and Thirty-first selected Lieutenant A. B. Payne as Second Sr. Lieutenant of their Company F. The officers retained the same rank in the Twenty-second Louisiana Infantry as in their old regiments. The company officers selected the following field officers: Colonel, J. W. Patton; Lieutenant-Colonel, —— Landry; Major, Washington Marks. Early in January, 1864, this organization, known as the Twenty-second Louisiana Heavy Artillery (the greatest number of men being from that regiment), was ordered to Mobile, and stationed in the redoubts and forts around the city. "The little squad comprising Company H," says an officer, "was recognized as the Third Louisiana Infantry, from the Secretary of War down to the particular friend of the regiment, General Louis Hebert." "The remainder of the regiment were always reported as absent without leave." Until the consolidation, orders were always addressed to Captain —— —— or Lieutenant ————, Commanding Third Louisiana. A few officers and men remained on the east side, because it was in exact conformity to orders, and because they believed that their services were more needed there than in the Trans-Mississippi Department. Many, perhaps a majority, were influenced by mixed motives, their homes and friends being on the east side of the Mississippi. There "was always a deep longing for a reunion with their old comrades, with whom they had shared so many dangers and privations." It was this same magnet of homes and friends that led the mass of the regiment across the Mississippi River, afterwards followed by those who wished to link their fate with the final fortunes of the regiment. Of the organization of the regiment and its final destiny, this work will give full particulars.

In the spring of 1864, nearly all the troops at Mobile were sent to reinforce General Johnston's army. The Twenty-second Regiment was sent across the bay to Pollard, a station on the railroad, from a point opposite Mobile to Montgomery. The summer passed away very quietly. Only on one occasion were the enthusiasm and hopes of the men excited; by the regiment being sent across the line into Florida, to repel a raid of the enemy from Pensacola. The object of the expedition was accomplished without fighting, save by the cavalry. When Farragut attacked the forts below Mobile, the regiment was ordered to Fort Gaines. The steamboat which was first sent broke some of her machinery. Another was sent, and the command arrived in the lower bay, just in time to witness the close of the naval engagement. An hour earlier, and the regiment would have been in the fort, thus narrowly escaping capture by making a hasty retreat to Mobile. Soon after, Company H was ordered to Battery Tracy, in the bay; Companies A, D and F, to Spanish Fort. Here, during the fall and winter, all the men were sick with chills and fever, Lieutenant Thomas being the only exception to the general rule.

In February, 1865, Canby, with 70,000 men, attacked Spanish Fort and Blakely. At Tracy and other batteries in the bay, there were from one to three companies of heavy artillery, of the First and Second Louisiana, etc., in all about 5,000 men. A stubborn fight ensued, continuing for two weeks. The soldiers, who so desperately fought the foe behind the intrenchments of Vicksburg, did not quail or tremble under the heavy fire poured upon them. 'Twas only a rehearsal of an already familiar drama.

On the 7th of April the fort fell, most of the garrison escaping to Tracy and Blakely. The next day this place also fell, and Tracy was evacuated a few days afterwards. The evacuation and surrender of Mobile quickly followed the fall of the forts. When the boat, on board of which was Company H, backed out from the landing, the Federals were seen in the streets of the city. M. C. Aldrich, Frank Goodwin (a member of Company D, shot in the ankle) and Lieutenant A. B. Payne, were the only members of the old Third Regiment in Spanish Fort, the remainder being at Tracy. During the most of the fight, they were under a severe fire from the enemy's guns, firing over Spanish Fort, and also from the vessels in the harbor. How did these bronzed, yet youthful heroes of Vicksburg and other hard-fought engagements, stand the trying ordeal? As only brave men will, with an unflinching bravery, a heroic devotion and patient endurance, such as only noble, unconquerable spirits can exhibit in times of danger. The roll of this company, annexed, contains the names of some of the best and truest soldiers of the Third Regiment. After the evacuation of Mobile, the regiment proceeded to Meridian, and remained at that point and its vicinity until the final surrender of the troops under General Taylor to General Canby. Like their comrades in the Trans-Mississippi, they were among the very last to leave the waning star of the Confederacy, sinking into the gloom of a long night.

AN INCIDENT

On Monday, May 25, during the flag of truce, following the general charge upon our lines, while the troops of each army were out on neutral ground, W. B. McGinness, of the Iberville Grays, met an old Dutch friend from Missouri who belonged to a Missouri (Federal) regiment. After exchanging compliments, etc., the Federal politely invited McGinness to his camp to take supper, get some papers, and last, but not least, to join him in a social drink. McGinness was too modest to refuse the kind and liberal invitation of his Dutch friend, and not selfish enough to partake of the luxuries which arose before his mental vision (a rarity to a rebel appetite) by himself; so he kindly extends the invitation to several of his friends. Octave Bevin, of Iberville Grays, Company A; Sergeant C. Hurley, of the Pelican Rifles, Company K; and Louis Eddons, of Monticello Rifles, Company H, who willingly acceded to McGinness's request to accompany him, went to the Dutch friend's camp, were kindly received by the Yankees who belonged to regiments that had fought ours (Third Louisiana) at Oak Hills. Met

John Nagle, who had deserted from the regiment at Camp Creek and joined the Northern Army. The party imbibed several drinks, and then sat down to supper, which was unceremoniously interrupted by the appearance of a lieutenant and guard, with orders to arrest the party for being within the Yankee lines. They were marched to General Quimby's headquarters. The General was perplexed what to do with them, whether to retain them as prisoners of war or to send them back to their command. While here, McGinness entered into conversation with Captain Barton, of New York, A. D. C. to the General, and soon discovered that he (McGinness) knew a number of the Captain's friends in California. The Captain became interested and sympathetic—proposed to the General to permit him to take the "rebels" to Major-General McPherson's headquarters and let him dispose of them. The General consented. Captain Barton relieved the guard and took the men to McPherson's headquarters. He informed the General of the circumstances of the party coming into their lines. The General considerately consented to send them back. He ordered Captain Barton and the lieutenant to escort them to their lines.

These boys of the Third Louisiana were particularly indebted to Captain Barton for their release. He informed them that, if they were detained as prisoners, he would write to their command, stating that they were prisoners and had not deserted, and he would have the letter endorsed by the General and sent over by flag of truce.

After their release, the Captain gave the men coffee, all the late papers, and a canteen of whisky each. The captain and the lieutenant then accompanied them to the lines, which they reached about 8 o'clock at night, some two hours after the flag of truce had people then residing at that place. They finally obtained lodging and expired. Before parting, they emptied the canteens of the captain and lieutenant, by drinking each other's health. The consequence was, all were somewhat "elevated." They parted the best of friends, to endeavor to kill each other, if possible, the next day.

Morning came. Hurley was considerably demoralized; Eddons very sick; Bevin and McGinness feeling as if they had pillowed their heads upon a ten-inch Columbia when it was fired.

Such are the outlines of an incident which was a frequent occurrence during the war. The "rebels" never met their foes thus that they were not the recipients of great kindness and many polite attentions. Yet, after this interchange of courtesies, they would fight each other as fiercely and stubbornly as if they had never met. The haps and mishaps of war are often very strange, exciting and interesting.

CHAPTER XXXIV

WEST OF THE MISSISSIPPI

ON the morning of October 21, a small party of men appeared on the banks of the Mississippi River, about equidistant from Waterloo, La., and Rodney, Miss. The party had two wagons, heavily loaded, and a skiff. The evening previous they had bivouacked in the grounds around Oakland College. This party consisted of Captains B. W. Clark and Fontleroy, Majors Springer and Lasalle, and the following members of the Third Louisiana Infantry: J. Webb, Company C; J. R. Nash, Company H; A. J. Perry, Company I; F. D. Tunnard and W. H. Tunnard, Company K. A heavy fog hung, like a cloud, over the stream, completely shutting out a view of the river. The boat was launched with a celerity and dispatch perfectly marvelous, baggage and dispatches hastily loaded into it, and swiftly rowed across the river. An ambulance, mules and horses were soon ferried across, and hastily left the dangerous vicinity. The blockade was successfully evaded. Major Springer drove rapidly away from the river, leaving behind him the squad of Louisianians, with their heavy knapsacks. Behold them on this October day, wearily traveling along an unknown road, in close proximity to posts of the enemy, and hiding behind the embankment, to prevent being discovered by the enemy's gun-boats patrolling the river. They were already travel-worn and completely exhausted for want of rest; yet many long miles must be footed ere they reached their destination (Alexandria). Two of the party were quite sick.

The next day they passed through Tensas Swamp, along Choctaw Bayou; crossed the Tensas and Bayou Louie; also, the Ouachita River. They were cordially welcomed and hospitably entertained by the residents on Sicily Island. That night they reached Harrisonburg, after marching twenty-six miles, and were actually refused permission to sleep on the galleries of the houses by the *very patriotic* in the cabin of a very poor man, about three miles from Harrisonburg. This hospitable man was named Daly. The cabin was a very rough structure, with only a single room; yet here slept the man and his wife, another woman, a young girl, three children, and the five Louisianians.

The next morning they bade their warm-hearted host adieu, after tendering compensation for their accommodations, which was refused. A cold, drizzling rain was falling, yet the road through the dreary pine-forest was good, and the party traveled twenty miles. That night they stopped at Mr. Baker's, and were kindly treated.

The next morning was very cold, yet the party traveled merrily along through the silent and gloomy pine-woods, entertaining each other with jokes and all manner of witty fusilades. Crossed Little River, and stopped at a lady's house by the road-side, having traveled twenty-four miles. Learned to-day that the Third Louisiana Infantry were ordered to assemble at Grand Ecore, November 10.

The next day (25th) reached Alexandria, and obtained transportation to Natchitoches; but, ere continuing on their journey, they met Colonel Crow, of the Twenty-sixth Louisiana Infantry, who informed them that he was authorized to establish a parole-camp near Alexandria, and had already selected a deserted plantation, a short distance above the town, for this purpose. During their short stay in the place they were hospitably entertained by the Rev. W. E. M. Linfield and lady. Mr. Linfield was, at that time, the Methodist minister at Alexandria. He kindly allowed the party of wandering and homeless Louisianians the use of his unfinished study between the church and parsonage.

It is needless to relate how the rough boys enjoyed their comfortable quarters. To Mrs. Linfield's kind-heartedness were they indebted for many little luxuries, to which they had long been strangers. Everything in and around Alexandria was in a state of confusion. Families gathered up their household goods, and rapidly departed, in anticipation of an early advance of the enemy.

CHAPTER XXXV

ON the 30th, the nucleus for the future Third Louisiana procured requisitions for cooking utensils, provisions and transportation. After innumerable difficulties, they finally succeeded in procuring two skillets, one without handle or lid. They next turned their attention to transportation. Proceeding to the Government stables, they found a number of "frames," once, doubtless, properly called mules. The harness was in pieces, but was soon tied together with innumerable pieces of string. Asking for the wagon, they were pointed to one of those veritable plantation cane-carts, which made its own music when driven. Three mules were speedily selected and hitched to this original vehicle. The men mounted into the cart, two seized the lines, and the rest plied the moving skeletons of animals with blows from heavy rods. Away they went, in high glee, through the centre of Alexandria, bound for Camp Crow, two and a half miles above the town. Arriving at the plantation, they selected the most comfortable building in the long rows of negro cabins, and prepared to live as best they could. The mules were put in a stable near by, benches and bunks soon constructed, and camp formally established. Such was Camp Crow, on the first day of November.

South of these quarters was a large field of waving cane, standing untouched, on the broad and cultivated acres, a sad commentary on the desolation and destruction produced by war. It was almost a daily task for the party to go into this field with their cart and fill it with cane, and driving it back to their quarters, unload it into one of the rooms. For the remainder of the day they contentedly sat upon the gallery and ate sugar-cane. It was a somewhat strange spectacle, to see these Louisianians out in the cane-field, a small, solitary band of reckless, indifferent soldiers, cutting cane only to gratify their own fondness for the nutritious juice. Not in days gone by were such laborers wont to work on those broad acres. Theirs was a more sable hue of complexion, and their hearts were light and gladsome, breaking forth upon the evening air in strains of that rude yet exquisite melody peculiar to negro voices and songs, and which the Southern planter loved to hear. It was a lazy and lonely life which the men led on this place, as no more troops reported at

Camp Crow. Their rations were very indifferent, their utensils consisting of two skillets, one broken, one tin cup, two tin plates, no knives or forks. Their situation became unbearable, and a scout was projected in order to better their condition. One dark night two of the party left the quarters, and returned about 12 M., bringing with them a skillet, broom, bucket, musket and ammunition. They grew hilarious over their success, as usual. To add to their privations and annoyances, rats were innumerable, and flies and mosquitoes troublesome beyond description.

On the 3d of November, General H. W. Allen's orderly was about to leave for Natchitoches, with the General's ambulance horses. He asked one of the Louisianians to accompany him, and ride the spare horse. It was readily agreed to. Neither saddle nor bridle could be procured. The soldier was not to be deterred from the journey by such disadvantages, so boldly mounting, bare-back, he started on his travels. Ere he had completed the journey to Natchitoches, a distance of some eighty miles, he was most thoroughly impressed with the fact that a ride of fifty miles a day, on a horse without saddle or stirrups, was a much more trying ordeal than fighting a battle. The remainder of the party reached Grand Ecore some time near the middle of November, and found very comfortable and pleasant quarters. The residence of Colonel Russell was in this place, and the men were the recipients of innumerable kindnesses from the Colonel and his estimable lady.

On the 17th there was an informal meeting of the regiment at Grand Ecore. Quite a number reported, of whom a list was taken, and the men were permitted to return home, with instructions to report every two weeks.

The squad who had been in camp at Alexandria still formed a nucleus for the regiment, being without any homes or friends. Soon, however, two of the party, F. D. Tunnard and brother, discovered friends, and eventually found a home, Mrs. L. L. McLauren's. This lady's residence was on the banks of Red River, four miles east of Natchitoches, on an island known as Tiger Island; Red River, during its high stages of water, completely surrounding it, flowing through what was formerly the channel of the river, and known as Old River. L. L. McLauren was Colonel of the Twenty-seventh Louisiana Infantry, and fell at the memorable siege of Vicksburg. A man of undaunted bravery, and a gallant officer, he was idolized by his men, a fit leader for that noble and heroic organization. Mrs. McLauren's residence was a general rendezvous for numbers of the paroled soldiers. They always found a cordial welcome. She was generous to a fault, a lady of unswerving devotion to the Southern cause, unusually fond of having young people about her, and making them feel perfectly at home and enjoy themselves to the full bent of their inclinations. Consequently, her house was constantly thronged with gay soldier lads and beautiful, lively, entertaining lassies, the fairest flowers among Louisiana's lovely exotics. A short residence in this mansion entirely obliterated all formality, and Mrs. McL. was known by no other name than "Auntie." "Auntie" became endeared to many a manly heart by those associations which are an indestructible part of the human soul, and lives yet fresh and green in numbers of strong hearts and brave spirits. Every expedient known to social gatherings was here resorted to in order to make the time pass pleasantly, and such scenes of hilarity as here occurred, crowded one upon the other in rapid succession, are seldom witnessed and experienced. Hunting, fishing expeditions into the woods, quilting parties, cards, practical jokes of every description, music and romps were some of the amusements indulged in. Such was Tiger Island during the fall and winter of 1863, and such the home the wandering Louisianians found. Truly their "lines had fallen in pleasant places." Those were halcyon days, whose memory is ineradicable. Freed from the conventionalities which clog society in social circles, the time sped away, bringing on its golden pinions joy, fun and life in its brightest colors.

On the first of December there was another gathering of the Third Regiment at Grand Ecore, about twenty-five being present, mostly members of companies D and G, and another adjournment for a week. Many pleasant days were spent at Dr. Butler's, the father of Captain W. B. Butler, of Company G. The people on Red River never flagged in their efforts to make the paroled prisoners happy and contented. There was quite a party of the Third at Dr. Butler's on the occasion of Captain Butler's birth-day, December 6th, among whom were Lieutenant-Colonel Pierson, Lieutenant Emanuel, Company C; Captain Haley, Twenty-seventh Louisiana, and several unobtrusive privates. That was more than a square meal. "Turkey, fresh pork, sausage, turnips, lettuce, salad, chicken salad, peas, hominy, roast eggs, sauces, bread, butter, milk, pies, preserves, pound cake, egg-nog, claret, champagne cider, etc., formed a regal feast for those terrible war times."

Thus day by day slipped away into the irrevocable past days spent in the quiet social circle; trips into the country in pursuit of pleasure, or to the camp at Grand Ecore; days of cold and sleet, then mild and balmy, alternate succession of clouds and sunshine. December 11th was such an one. Early the rain fell rapidly, then there was a lull in the storm. The sun shone bright and golden through the rifted clouds, whose dark and jagged edges looked threatening and strong. How emblematical of a soldier's varied existence! Life with him then was but a storm-cloud, through whose gathered gloom, occasionally shone the sun of hope and happiness. To some it was almost a nonentity, creatures of circumstances; at times it was a quiet calm full of remembrances of the Past, uninfluenced by the Present, looking not for aught from the Future. Again it was a storm, upon whose surging billows he tossed amid a sea of excitement. Then the glimmer of some uncertain hope would shine mellow and golden upon his heart, making, with its uncertain light, dancing pictures of future joy and happiness.

On the 15th, General H. W. Allen addressed the people of Natchitoches in one of those noble, stirring appeals, so characteristic of the man. The building was crowded to its utmost capacity to listen to the idolized and revered chieftain and statesman. Perhaps, no man has ever been so deeply enshrined in the hearts of Louisianians as is Governor Allen; the true and tried soldier, the uncompromising patriot; the kind and affable Governor; the soldier's and widow's friend. His memory will be kept bright and green in thousands of warm and loving hearts long after the war and its incidents have been forgotten, or only recalled as some strange dream of the past.

On the 16th of December an order was issued for the regiment to assemble permanently in camp at Grand Ecore on the 5th of January, 1864.

The holidays passed away without incident worthy of note. In camp, the boys had a merry time quaffing rich and royal egg-nog, and partaking of a regal repast, the munificent gift of Mrs. Colonel S. D. Russell. On Tiger Island were assembled a large party of lively spirits at the hospitable mansion of Mrs. McLauren. The assembly consisted of Widows E. Sleade and Cole, Misses Frank Penny, Allie Tucker, M. J. Barlow, Captain F. Avery, aid-de-camp to General Hays, Sergeant-Major O. Penny, J. Macey, Lieutenant Dunkermann, 27th Louisiana, and the two members of the Third Louisiana. There were card parties, mock marriages, attended with a regular *chevarri* from all the children on the plantation, both white and black. The scenes were rich and racy indeed, and attended with uproarious mirth.

The year '63 went out amid a blustering storm. The wind blew almost a hurricane, shrieking forth a wrathful requiem over the dying year, while snowflakes, descending thick and fast, filled all the wintry, biting air. The gloom was indicative of the dark storm-cloud of war, that hung like a funeral-pall over the land, bringing sorrow and woe to thousands of once happy households. The mind involuntarily winged a thought towards the coming year, and sadly questioned, "Will 1864 still find the land the scene of bloodshed and fierce strife?" It trusted not, and looked forward to the day-spring of a brighter hope. The Confederate soldiers, the patriot sons of the South, were thought of amid their terrible sufferings in Tennessee and Virginia, as they nobly endeavored to roll back the swift tide of invasion.

CHAPTER XXXVI

THE new year opened bitter cold, the mercury in the thermometer indicating six degrees above zero at six o'clock A.M. It froze all day.

On the 5th of January, the two Louisianians, after a warm parting with their hospitable friends, were once more on the road with their knapsacks strapped to their shoulders, *en route* for Grand Ecore and the rough experiences of camp life. As they journeyed on, they were overtaken by a carriage containing two ladies and acquaintances, who insisted on their riding. Of course no objection was made to such a proposition. Arriving at the landing opposite Grand Ecore, the soldiers parted from their kind-hearted friends, after pressing warm kisses upon their soft, rosy lips. As one of the men turned his back upon the carriage, a sweet-toned voice called to him, "Will, come back, I want to tell you something." Approaching the carriage, a lovely face bent close down to the lowered window of the door, a pair of fascinating blue eyes gazed into his own as he inquired, "Well, what is it?" He was under a mystic spell, as that same musical voice uttered in low tones, "Oh! nothing, only I want to kiss you again." There was a long, lingering pressure of lips upon each other, and then—the carriage disappeared around a bend in the road; and the soldier trod light-hearted over the sands on the river's shore.

About thirty men assembled on the 5th, and proceeded at once to establish themselves in the comfortable quarters. The weather was very cold, and the men poorly supplied with blankets, yet they were in high spirits. It seemed as if no change of circumstances could ever break the brave spirits of the members of the regiment, who easily and quietly adapted themselves to every phase of a soldier's life. On the 6th, Company C arrived. W. H. Tunnard was appointed and acted as Commissary and Quartermaster. Wagons and rations were procured in Natchitoches, and Grand Ecore became a regularly established camp. The days slipped away with little worthy of note. The weather was usually stormy, and the road to Natchitoches terribly muddy, almost impassable; making the daily trip of five miles and back anything but agreeable.

On the 19th of January there was a dress parade of the regiment; about seventy-five men present. Orders were issued strictly prohibiting the men from leaving camp more than half a mile, without a written permit. The days of January passed away pleasantly with mild, balmy spring weather. The men enjoyed themselves as best they could, and were continually engaged in mischief of some kind. On the 6th of February, a large party properly mounted, went to Winn Parish, a distance of fifteen miles, to a frolic. It consisted of Adjutant Currie, Lieutenants Clark, Company F, and Meredith, Company I, Sergeants Derbonne and J. Norris, Company G, the Commissary Sergeant and J. Sompeyrac, 27th Louisiana. Arriving at the appointed place, they found a large number of beautiful girls present. The dancing commenced as the sun was dipping 'neath the western horizon, continuing without intermission until six A.M. the next morning, when the last sett left the floor. During the night the house was surrounded by cavalry, who stationed armed men at every outlet. The Captain came to the doorway and demanded the papers from the men. Not one among the party had any. Lieutenants Clark and Currie said they could vouch for the men, who belonged to the Third Louisiana Infantry, and had only left camp for the purpose of enjoying the frolic. He was not satisfied. Some warm words ensued, when the Captain was informed that the boys "would see him and his buttermilk cavalry d——d before they would have their fun interrupted." Arms were drawn; the old fighting spirit of the Third Regiment was aroused, and affairs began to look serious. The ladies screamed, or sat in pale groups around the room. After some cool reasoning the matter was finally adjusted by the men being formed in line and duly inspected by the Captain, who remarked, as he finished his task, "I have been looking for a deserter, and expected to find him here; I do not wish to interfere with your amusement. Good-evening, gentlemen"; bowing himself out of the room. For once in his life, he had found men who were neither afraid of leveled rifles, nor to be intimidated by a game of "bluff."

On the 8th, Major Lasalle, Department Paymaster, visited Grand Ecore, and paid off all men to whom the Government was indebted, up to September, 1863. Now ensued the usual scenes of gambling, to which the soldiers were so much addicted. On the 14th, all the men in camp were furloughed for fifteen days, to be renewed every two weeks until they were exchanged. The boys were in high spirits over this good luck, while the officers were furious with anger, declaring that the whole proceeding was a scheme, concocted to destroy the organization of the regiment.

On the 15th of February, Grand Ecore was lonely and deserted, and parole camp a myth, the soldiers having eagerly and rapidly left for their homes. Thus, with the furloughing of the men, the bright star of reorganization that had risen and shone so brilliantly upon the gathering members of the regiment, went out once again in the gloom of the uncertain future. Growing restless under their protracted inactivity, numbers joined scouting parties in the Mississippi Valley, others formed bands and hovered within and around General Banks' army. Many remained quietly at home enjoying the society of friends, while still others, who were homeless wanderers, aided the planters in saving their stock, household goods and negroes from the approaching desolation of war. Thus, for a period of five months, the curtain of oblivion conceals the regiment.

CHAPTER XXXVII

CAMP NEAR PINEVILLE

JULY 4th, 1864, the curtain rises upon a new scene in the drama of war. A year has elapsed since the fall of Vicksburg. The fierce and protracted struggle around the stronghold, ending at last in disaster, had spread a gloom over the whole South. The brave and patriotic Confederates who had struggled so tenaciously, so fiercely for its preservation, who endured the tortures of hunger, the constant fatigue, unrelieved in the trenches, the burning summer sun during the day, the heavy, penetrating dews at night, the drenching storms, standing undismayed, unbroken in spirit amid the storm of bullets, hurtling shot and hissing shells, exhibited a spirit similar to that which animated the Spartans at Thermpoylae. Going forth on parole after the fall of their stronghold, they had scattered to their homes and friends, over the length and breadth of the Confederacy. At this period, numbers had already been exchanged and were once again confronting the foe, exhibiting their devotion to their country by deeds of heroic valor amid the thunder roar of battle. The majority of the Louisianians captured at Vicksburg were still, however, up to this period, unexchanged. They comprised the following regiments: Third Detachment of Twelfth, Seventeenth, Twenty-sixth, Twenty-seventh, Twenty-eighth, Thirty-first, and a portion of Miles's Legion, forming a brigade, under the command of Brigadier-General Allen Thomas, formerly Colonel of the Twenty-eighth Regiment. Under the pressure of stringent orders then promulgated, the men rapidly assembled in camp near Pineville, preparatory to being exchanged, thoroughly organized, equipped, and put once more into active service. The *morale* of the troops of this brigade was such that it was anticipated on future battle-fields they would obtain a glory bright and untarnished, a fame wide-spread and imperishable, adding new laurel-wreaths of patriotism, devotion, and valor to the chaplets already encircling the brow of Louisiana.

The summer days, hot, hotter, hottest, fleeted rapidly away, while the men employed the time as best they could lying 'neath the shadows of the pines, indulging in speculative fancies, yet interested spectators of the fierce struggle for supremacy between the contending hosts. Notwithstanding their bitter experiences, they desired to plunge once again into the whirling vortex of strife, and aid their patriot brethren in their struggles for homes, country and freedom. Not an event of interest occurred to vary the monotony of their idle existence. Exchange was the theme of speculation, the chief topic of conversation, yet, like a "Jack-o'-lantern," was an unapproachable, uncertain reality, a doubtful question of the still more doubtful future. Thus unchanged, the days passed away, while the solemn pines, in whispering voices like the far-off murmuring of the ocean waves on a sanded shore, hymned the requiem of their passing hopes and lost opportunities. It was not always thus, however. The gentle summer air would swell into thunder-toned voices, borne from the mountains and valleys from Virginia and Georgia, mingled with triumphant shouts of victory. Aye, victory, radiant, triumphant, would poise like the incarnation of beauty upon the Southern banner, a point to the obscurity which shrouded the future as if it contained the germs of white-winged peace and final success. The rainbow of Hope, with every tint of its exquisite coloring, would stand out in bold relief against the dark war-cloud that hung over the land, and was fast sinking into the horizon of the past; its dark setting rendering all the more beautiful the soft hues. It seemed then as if the sun of peace was tinging with its parting beams, the jagged edges of the storm-cloud as with a silver lining. Thus it seemed as if the Southern hosts were striding forward towards the goal of their hopes, the prize for which they contended so stubbornly, and gave so freely the priceless treasure of their rich, red blood.

Thus, while the men indulged in their speculations, they were actually suffering both for want of provisions and shelter. The rations consisted chiefly of corn-meal and beef, and not in large quantities. They were without tents, and usually slept on rough beds built in the open air, protected from the night-dews only by shelters of brush. They generally congregated around some rough log-cabins in the woods, whose shelter they sought in rainy weather, but found the fleas more intolerable than a good drenching.

On the 23d of July the following order was read to the troops:

General Orders }   HEADQUARTERS TRANS-MISS. DEPT. }
   No. 56 }   *Shreveport, La., July* 21, 1864. }

All officers and men captured at Vicksburg, who have reported at Enterprise, Demopolis, Vienna, Natchitoches, Shreveport and Alexandria, at any time prior to April 1st, 1864, have been declared exchanged by the Commissioner of Exchange.

All those in this Department who are embraced in this list will *immediately* rejoin their commands in the field.

By command of
GEN. E. KIRBY SMITH.

S. S. ANDERSON, A. A. G.

Such was the order which finally proclaimed the exchange of the Vicksburg prisoners. This notice of exchange was read to the troops on the 23d day of July. Once more they belonged to the Confederate army, to become active participators in its future fields of operations. This notice of exchange created much excitement in camp. The reality of the situation was, however, acknowledged and realized by the men being once more put into active service. The Third Regiment was rapidly approaching a complete organization. Its existence as a regiment was acknowledged by the War Department, commissioning Lieutenant-Colonel Russell as Colonel, Major Pierson as Lieutenant-Colonel, and Captain J. S. Richards, of Company H, as Major.

Thus, notwithstanding Company H, of the 22d, claimed to be the only true representatives of this organization, reporting the majority of the members thereof as absent without leave, it here exhibited a wonderful vitality, and stood in the brigade of gallant Louisianians as one of its most gallant regiments. At this time, Companies B, C, D, E, F, G, H, I and K, had representatives in the camp. The period had now arrived when absentees must report to their several commands. Stringent orders and measures were promulgated and adopted to compel their attendance. As patriot sons of Louisiana, as true soldiers desiring once more to confront the foe side by side with the comrades with whom they had fought upon many hard-contested and bloody battlefields the majority of the absentees came willingly and voluntarily into the camp near Pineville.

More than a year of inactivity! a year surrounded by the comforts and blessings of home in the companionship of its dear and loved ones! The memory of this year nerved anew each strong arm and stout heart, especially when such marks of war's desolation as Red River Valley, Alexandria, Compté, Grand Ecore, and other places exhibited, proclaimed the vindictive barbarity and fiendish malignity of a foe, rivaling in cruelty the ancient Goths and Vandals of Europe.

Unusual activity and energy, displayed in every department, proclaimed a determination to organize, arm and equip the brigade as speedily as possible. The name and fame of these Louisianians, as being among the most heroic defenders of Vicksburg, gave great hopes that they would soon win more brilliant and imperishable laurels upon future battle-fields.

About this period two members of the 27th Louisiana were shot for desertion. This necessity for taking human life to compel obedience to orders was sadly deplored by all. Yet such a necessity often existed during the war. The first duty of every soldier is obedience to orders. If right, it is just; if wrong, the blame rests where it properly belongs—with those promulgating them. This instance is mentioned to exhibit the determination of those in authority to compel obedience to orders, which was but right, if calmly and dispassionately considered.

On Sunday, the 24th instant, 1,100 troops belonging to the department arrived from New Orleans, in exchange for Federal prisoners recently sent below. They arrived filled with admiration and enthusiasm, for the ladies of the Crescent City, unconquerable in spirit, enthusiastic worshipers at the shrine of the Confederate cause, undismayed by the presence of implacable foes—these fair patriots, with untiring zeal and energy, ministered to the wants and necessities of every Confederate soldier who reached New Orleans during the war. Fame can wreath no brighter chaplet; history contains no fairer page; memory retain no more beautiful impression than was furnished by the devotion and patriotism of Southern women during the recent fierce, internecine struggle. To them should be reared a monument more durable than brass, more pure and polished than the finest Parian marble. They will live ever unforgotten in the hearts of the South's braves sons.

On the last day of July General Polignac's Division arrived and encamped a short distance from the regiment, but the next morning were gone. These troops were like the shadow of some fleecy summer cloud, lingering but an instant, to flit by and then disappear. At this period there was an unprecedented lull in the storm of war. The paroled, or rather exchanged prisoners, arrived rapidly in camp, and the brigade was growing in numbers. At this time, many of the men were nearly entirely destitute of clothing, going in rags, and barefooted. There were some such cases in the Third Regiment. This state of affairs was unavoidable. Many men in the regiment were long miles from their homes, perhaps in the hands of the enemy, and were dependent on the charities of friends both for clothing and food. The ladies, however, were ever foremost in supplying the wants of the destitute and suffering, and many a noble soldier treasured, and still retains in his patriot heart, memories ineffaceable of the daughters of the Sunny South. Words were but feeble instruments to express all the debt of gratitude, manly affection and admiration felt by the Southern soldier for the fair ladies. In history is now transcribed, inscribed on every page in bright and glowing characters, their deeds of devotion, patriotism, suffering, heroic endurance and daring.

On the 8th of August, Captains Gallagher and Bruslé arrived in camp, and were most cordially greeted by the men. Captain Gallagher had always been a favorite with the regiment, being considered the best commissary who had ever catered to the ravenous appetites of soldiers. Most assuredly, Captain Gallagher took advantage of every favorable opportunity for supplying the men with, not only everything eatable which the Commissary Department furnished, but also many articles not properly belonging to a soldier's rations. He never took advantage of his position to appropriate any luxuries or delicacies that happened to fall into his hands, but divided them with an honesty and exactness among the men, which was known and highly appreciated by the recipients of his favors. The same statement could not be made concerning the majority of the Commissaries in the army. The peculiar side-pose of Captain Gallagher's head on his shoulders, and the twinkle of his eyes, his abrupt manner, and, when excited, stammering method of speech, gave rise to innumerable jokes and witticisms at his expense. Brave, fearless, always present during times of danger, Captain Gallagher discharged his duties most faithful, and was universally esteemed by the organization with which he was connected.

CHAPTER XXXVIII

HO! FOR SHREVEPORT

ON Tuesday evening, the 9th instant, orders were received in camp, near Alexandria, for a portion of the Third Louisiana Infantry to be prepared to move early the next morning for Shreveport, to relieve the Crescent Regiment, then doing post duty at that place. After numerous delays incident to the leisurely embarkation of troops, at noon on the 10th instant the first detachment of the regiment, numbering 110 officers and men, exclusive of 18 Yankee prisoners, were snugly packed on board the small steamer "Lelia," bound for a new destination. Reader, have you ever traveled up Red River on board one of these "kick-up-behind" crafts in low water? If not, you have missed one of *the pleasures of navigation*. Just imagine one of these small boats, indiscriminately crowded with horses, mules, negroes, soldiers, officers, white men, *gentlemen at large,* baggage and wagons, and you may form some conception of the freight on board the "Lelia."

During the passage storms daily arose; and if the boat had been built of sieves, it could not have leaked worse. However, a ducking is one of the least of soldiers' mishaps. On the 12th instant the boat arrived at Grand Ecore, amid lowering clouds and driving rain. Yet here numbers of ladies from Natchitoches and the surrounding country, assembled to welcome the regiment. Mysterious bundles, containing clothes and comforts for the outer and inner man, found their way aboard the boat. Vociferous cheers attested the heartfelt farewell of the boys as the steamer departed, while amid general hilarity and good-humor, the "good things" were opened and freely partaken of. What mattered it that the boat ran "kerchug" against a sand-bank! It only brought forth a full chorus of cheers.

A member of the regiment was sitting on a barrel-head, with a sympathizing companion by his side, conversing in low tones. They were hundreds of miles from friends and relatives, and the scenes which they witnessed at Grand Ecore and on the boat, after its departure, made them feel lonely and homesick. They bewailed the fate which separated them from homes far away, as they glanced at the happy groups scattered about the deck discussing the contents of numerous freshly received packages. Suddenly a voice broke in upon the conversation, exclaiming, "Come, boys, and eat some cakes." Forgotten was home; finished all reverie, and conversation laid aside—memory of friends. Shades of corn-meal, defend us! *Cakes! Simon-pure flour cakes!!* They quickly descended from the elevation of their observatory, and were soon discussing the excellences of some fair lady's culinary skill. Thanks to the generous kindness of Prue Hyams, the homeless were not forgotten.

Nothing occurred of special interest on the way up, until arriving at Colonel S. M. Hyams's plantation, Lac des Mures. Here the boat stopped to land a passenger. Imagine the general surprise when Captain Isaacson, the kind, obliging and gentlemanly commander of the boat, was invited on shore, and no sooner arrived at the Colonel's residence than he was forcibly seized and detained by the colonel in the following manner: The Colonel appealed to the men, his old command, to sustain his authority, while he proclaimed a feast in preparation for the whole regiment. Of course, he was upheld in his summary proceeding. The Captain was indiscriminately stuffed with a bushel of peaches, washed down with some excellent "fire-water" from a Confederate distillery; then followed a cart-load of melons, grapes *ad infinitum,* milk, fine gumbo, barbecued pork, beef, mutton, etc.—the men being likewise provided for. They bowed most *gracefully* to the *exacting* demands of the Colonel, and a scene of hilarity, joy and freedom from restraint ensued such as was seldom witnessed during the late warlike times.

Lieutenant-Colonel S. M. Hyams was formerly an officer of the Third Louisiana Infantry, disabled by disease from following and participating in the fortunes of his old command. Yet he remembered his former companions-in-arms with not less warmth and generous hospitality than they cherished for one of their first field-officers, and appreciated this token of his kindness and remembrance. His welcome to them was as the oasis in the desert to the fainting traveler—a golden sunbeam descending from a rift in dark storm-clouds. Veteran troops of the Confederacy, the regiment never experienced a more genial welcome, a more hospitable reception, than that given them by Lieutenant-Colonel S. M. Hyams, his estimable lady, fair daughter, and near relatives, on the 13th day of August, 1864. Sufferer from the inroads of a Vandal foe, he appreciated the protecting power of the troops, and out of the abundance of his generous impulses welcomed them, and bade them God-speed on their way, feeling thrice blessed by his kindness. With many regrets, the men bade adieu to their kind-hearted host and hostess, making the shores and woods re-echo to their vociferous cheers, as the boat proceeded up the river. Nightly the men disembarked. With bundles of blankets thrown over their shoulders, they would frantically rush from the boat, over a single plank, as if spirits loosed from Pandemonium, and seeking the contiguity of some sheltering bush, tree, or shade, build fires, and soon, amid oblivious slumber, forget all life's cares, harrowing thoughts, etc., *red bugs, ticks and mosquitoes* permitting. Thus, with an occasional thug into the bank, stoppage on a sandbar or some hidden snag, the detachment arrived in Shreveport, without serious accident, at 9 o'clock A.M., August 16, after a trip of six days.

CHAPTER XXXIX

CAMP BOGGS

ON the arrival of the regiment at Shreveport, they immediately disembarked, and proceeded to the camping-ground previously occupied by the Crescent Regiment, about one and a half miles south of Shreveport. This camp was situated in an open field, regularly laid off in avenues and cross-streets, along which the tents were ranged in lines, or rows, parallel with each other. The ground slopes gradually away on every side, being a knoll or rolling ground. On the west and north was a small stream, half encircling the camp, where springs furnished an abundant and refreshing supply of cool water. To the south and east were woodlands, a growth of huge pines, red and white oaks, and an undergrowth of every variety. Almost an unobstructed view northward was furnished by the cleared space outside the line of fortifications which circumvented Shreveport to the hills which overlook the valley, formed by the junction of Red River and Twelve-Mile Bayou, where nestles the city, with its daily life and activity; the throbbing heart, that sent its pulsations, its life-giving power through every artery of the Trans-Mississippi Department. Fortifications! How the sight of earth works recalled Vicksburg, with its scenes of horrors, suffering and starvation, making even the veteran soldier shrink from their contiguity!

One unacquainted with Shreveport at this period, as the great central point, the nucleus of all military operations, could scarcely imagine the activity which prevailed there; the influx and egress of all grades of military officials; the arrival and departure of steamers and trains, shipment and receipt of stores, etc. Yet outside of military circles there was nothing enticing or attractive about the place, and the mere drone of society would soon tire of its monotony—seek in vain for some amusement to while away the listless hours.

Thus, through all the days of August, time sped on in its noiseless flight, while the nations of earth were working out their appointed destinies—nations as varied in their forms of government, as there are differences in human language, color and races. To the careful peruser of history, it would be a difficult task to determine which is the best adapted form of government—

conduces most to the happiness, prosperity and security of the governed. Not an example adorns the record of the past and present of a nation which has not seen revolution, crime and bloodshed; many, indeed, having disappeared in the gloom of an Egyptian night, never again to gain a position among the nations of the earth. At this period, it seemed as if the republican form of government was a failure. The history of Rome, Sparta, Athens, Switzerland and Poland, all down the vista of years, proclaimed this system a failure. The American Republic, the last and latest of the earth, seemed about to disappear amid such convulsions as the world had never witnessed. Yet this disproved not the perfection of a free government—its claims to pre-eminence among civilized nations. Fanaticism, with its deadly poison, pervaded every branch of the National Capitol, and ignoring the provisions and safeguards of the Constitution, upon which rested the whole strength of the American Government—the sovereignty of States; freedom of thought, speech, and action had plunged the land into the vortex of civil strife. After nearly four years of a fearful struggle, every valley and hill-side were dotted with the graves of its victims—Northmen and Southmen slept together in calm repose. Yet the struggle continued undiminished, while the patriot sons of the South still heroically battled for the preservation of their rights and independence. Alas! how fallen seemed this once proud and powerful nation!

Shortly after the arrival of the Third Regiment at Shreveport, the men were furnished with good shoes, hats, a few blankets, and were promised, ere long, a substantial uniform.

Strange as it seemed, up to this period this veteran regiment had been furnished with but little clothing in two years, and not a single substantial uniform by the Confederate Government. The State furnished a handsome uniform while the regiment was at Camp Jackson, Ark., under Brigadier-General Ben McCulloch, during the first year of the war. Now, however, the men seemed hopeful of better treatment.

As a matter of some interest, the following list of the prices of vegetables and fruit are given for reference: Butter, $5 per pound; eggs, $5 per dozen; beans, $2.50 per quart; apples, 25 to 50 cents each; melons, $1 to $5 each. It was a great mystery how poor people managed to live.

On the last day of August the regiment in camp numbered 150 men. On this day a provost guard was also sent to town, and heavy details made for the different departments, Government workshops, arsenals, etc. thus reducing the number of men in camp, and making duty very onerous. Besides the several guard details in town, a heavy guard was employed at the Yankee prison, near camp. This prison was an inclosure, formed by heavy oaken timbers, firmly nailed together, and set some distance in the ground. This inclosure was square in form, and covered an acre or two of ground. Here both Southern delinquents and Northern prisoners were alike confined.

On the 3d of September the second detachment arrived in camp, increasing the available strength of the regiment to about 300 men. This detachment was composed chiefly of members of the Eighth Battalion Louisiana Heavy Artillery and Twelfth Louisiana Infantry. Besides these men, the regiment was rapidly being filled with recruits, making it stronger in numbers than in efficiency. The arrival of a squad of conscripts in camp was the signal for a general assemblage of the veterans, who were not at all choice or backward in pouring forth a perfect fusilade of jokes. "Give me the little man with the big, two-story hat." "I want the man with the wooden leg." "Get out; he's my choice." "I wonder if they have any marks about their legs," etc., were some of the expressions used.

Thus, through all the hot days of September, the regiment remained at Camp Boggs, regularly and monotonously performing their duties of guardmounting, morning drill, policing camp, and evening parade. Such were the days. A roseate hue would tinge all the western horizon, or light clouds flit lazily across the sky overhead, and camp-fires glittered among the long rows of snow-white tents; shouts, laughter, the hum of voices, mingled with songs, sentimental and religious, would float away on the still evening air. Such were some of the employments and duties of this veteran regiment at this period.

Thus the days slipped away into the irrevocable past. The fierce stormcloud swept in its fury over Virginia, Georgia and Missouri. The result of the elections in several Northern States proclaimed the probability of no change in the political status of the land.

On the night of the 8th of October the first frost visited the country, while the flight of migratory birds southward, proclaimed the approaching advent of cold weather. The men were, however, in high spirits, having a good supply of tents and neatly constructed log-houses, with good fireplaces and chimneys. Thus prepared to meet the coming winter months, they laughed in derision at approaching cold.

On Saturday night, the 15th, a grand vocal and instrumental concert was given by the Shreveport Glee Club, at the request of Governor H. W. Allen, for the benefit of the Missourians serving in the Trans-Mississippi Department. This club had but recently been organized, and was composed of gentlemen residing in Shreveport, officers belonging to the army, several members of the regiment, in all seventeen persons, possessing more than the ordinary musical talent of amateurs. The concert was complete, both as to its success and the entertainment. The music was excellent, and the large theatre hall crowded. The proceeds resulted in the handsome amount of $5,000.

After the performance, the audience was addressed by a Missouri officer present, who paid a glowing tribute to the sympathy of Louisianians for their sister State, in which the Third Louisiana Infantry was warmly eulogized for past services in the State of Missouri. Governor Allen, in behalf of the performers, made a few appropriate remarks in reply. This incident is worth recording, as furnishing a pleasant episode to warlike scenes, and exhibiting the feeling which animated Louisianians, always ready to extend the hand of fellowship to her suffering sister States. The latter part of October went out amid storm, frost and ice. The forests changed their emerald hue for the manifold coloring of autumn. Icy winter, with his chilling breath and hoary locks, was upon us. The majority of Southern soldiers were at this time still in the field doing their duty nobly, unflinchingly, notwithstanding the wintry season added greatly to their hardships and suffering. They needed warm clothing, especially socks and gloves. It seemed as if the old days of Valley Forge, with its horrors, would be re-enacted. The Third Louisiana Infantry, but recently returned from firesides and homes, were perhaps better supplied than most regiments, yet were actually in need of warm clothing. The Government, up to this period, had furnished nothing save a few blankets and shoes. Fortunately, they had plenty of shelter—both tents and cabins. Louisiana's noble and warm-hearted Governor, H. W. Allen, one who knew a soldier's wants from personal experience, furnished the men of the regiment with a number of suits of clothes, comprising pants and shirts, homespun, and entirely cotton. Inadequate though it might be to keep out the chilling, wintry air, heartfelt expressions of gratitude were bestowed on him, for his remembrance of one of Louisiana's veteran volunteer regiments. Strange as it seemed, this old regiment, with its scarred veterans and depleted ranks, its wide-spread reputation, had never been properly clothed since its organization, save by the State. The mother is always most solicitous for the welfare and safety of her children.

Nearly the whole month of November was cold, stormy and gloomy, and consequently the men suffered in proportion. The Northern election gave rise to fierce political discussion among the Confederates, who seemed to anticipate some species of relief from the election of McClellan. Lincoln's return to office by a large and increased vote put an end to the discussion which agitated the Southern mind. Reconstruction, and General McClellan's peace measures founded thereon, all disappeared. The general sentiment among the soldiers was satisfaction at the result of the Presidential contest. Lincoln's plans and purposes were known, and the only hope of defeating them seemed in a persistent and determined armed resistance. Yet there were numbers greatly dissatisfied, and openly proclaimed their sentiments. It mattered little to them that the South had resolved to succeed or perish amid the ruins of the magnificent temple she was endeavoring to rear amid a baptism of the richest blood of the people. They were disappointed and suffering. Forbearance against existing abuses and patriotism were ceasing to be virtues; hence constant and frequent cases of desertion occurred. Thus dissatisfaction and demoralization pervaded the army, while among the people at home speculation and extortion ruled affairs. Letters from the army said: "It is no wonder men desert, for scarcely a letter comes from their homes that does not tell of grim want and pinching hunger standing at their thresholds. Those at home, whose duty it should be to protect and provide for poor families of men who are in the army, are deaf to the calls of duty." The Third Regiment was not exempt from the prevailing contagion, and numerous desertions occurred, principally among the recruits.

It was a hard matter for a man to know that his wife and little ones were suffering at home, and he not permitted to relieve their wants. Every fierce blast of the wintry wind that shrieked around his tent or log-hut brought vividly before him his own home circle, a picture of squalidness, suffering and want. The voice of nature would be heard as it tugged at his heart-strings. Around that home, centered and clustered all the bright hopes and aims of his life. What wonder, then, that duties were forgotten, and only the warm and loving impulse of his own nature followed!

CHAPTER XL

THE monotony of camp was seldom disturbed during the winter months, save by some practical joke or foray at the expense of the poor conscript. The weather was unusually rainy and stormy, yet happy, very many happy hours were spent in those rough log-huts, despite storms without. Christmas Day, 1864, was a cloudy, raw, disagreeable one, yet the boys were early astir, and seemed disposed to enjoy the occasion to the full bent of their inclinations and means. Egg-nog seemed a prevailing beverage, while towards the dinner hour, various and sundry savory and unusual dishes were to be found in course of preparation.

At one tent, a party consisting of Major Richards, Lieutenants Emanuel, Company "C," and Washburn, Company "B," Sergeant F. D. Tunnard, Company "K," Sergeant R. Brennan, Company "F," Sergeant W. H. Tunnard, A. C. S. Department and Corporal J. R. Nash, Company "H," sat down most cozily to dinner, consisting of a fine roast turkey, light bread and butter, potatoes, pies, cake and coffee. They enjoyed the repast most royally, laughing and chatting over their dinner, eaten from tinware, as if it had been a regal feast, daintily prepared and partaken of from dishes of the most costly and exquisite porcelain. It was undoubtedly enjoyed as if such had really been the case.

The new year dawned clear and pleasant, with the thunder of war echoing over the land. The year 1865 witnessed one of the most fierce desperate and bloody struggles that the world ever saw. The holidays passed away with little of interest transpiring. Of course Shreveport was the theatre of many gay and festive scenes among the post officers. To the private soldier they differed little from other days. He had the same round of duties to perform, without relaxation or relief. Ah! how he missed the joyous scenes and festivities of more peaceful times, when he mingled in gay throngs, or participated in the pleasant reunions around the home altar! Such memories were of the past, while the present was full of clouded realities, and the future seemed to contain no olive-branch of peace for the land.

On the 8th of January the regiment received a complete outfit of clothing, consisting of hats, shirts, drawers, shoes, socks, blankets, and a fine suit of

Confederate gray cloth. Of course the excitement and rejoicing were great over such good fortune, and Captain Hanna's Acting Quartermaster's tent was encircled by a perfect dense wall of living, jostling, boisterous and rude men. It was an unusually pleasant and agreeable scene. During the past week there had been an unusual advent of military celebrities in Shreveport, consisting of Generals Price, Buckner, Forney and Polignac. Men began to speculate as to whether it did not portend early active operations. On the 11th troops were moving through Shreveport, going below.

January was very rainy, and contained little of interest beyond the agitation of the question of peace. Constant and accumulated disasters falling upon Southern arms, made the hearts of the people as sad and gloomy as the dark stormy days.

On the 15th of February, notices were published, tendering an ovation to General Forney's Division by the citizens of Bossier and Caddo Parishes. General Forney remembered the gallant regiment which once served so heroically under him, and sent an invitation to the veterans of the Third Louisiana Infantry, proposing to pay them marked and special honors. Upon this distinguished occasion the invitation was most cordially accepted. Now began active preparations for this important event. All the veterans of the regiment were daily drilled, arms, equipments, and clothing duly inspected. The number of old members present was 150. It seemed something like former times to witness the evolutions, firm, even tread, erect carriage of this battalion of stalwart, bronzed veterans.

In accordance with previously published notice, the grand festival and barbecue occurred on Saturday, February 18th, 1865. The day was one of peculiar loveliness—a bright blue sky, golden sunlight, and a fresh, balmy spring atmosphere. It seemed as if Providence was smiling with lavish bounty upon the scene. At 9 o'clock A.M., the detachment of the Third, preceded by General Forney's Division band, proceeded to the place for the review. At 10 o'clock the division was drawn up in line of battle in a large open old field, west of Colonel Watson's residence, facing and parallel with the Marshall road, about two miles from Shreveport. They were first inspected by Lieutenant-General E. Kirby Smith, attended by Major-Generals Magruder and Forney, followed by their respective staff-officers.

At an early hour an immense concourse of fair ladies from far and near, together with citizens, soldiers and negroes, had assembled upon the ground, giving to the scene an appearance of great festivity. After the inspection, the regiments wheeled into columns by companies, and marched in review before the general officers, posted in front and centre of the line. As far as the eye could reach was this moving mass of men, their arms glittering like burnished silver in the morning sunbeams, while in front, along the whole line, was the assembly of Louisiana's fair daughters and gray-haired men, gracing with their presence the warlike scene. The review being finished, the lines were formed, advancing in columns of attack, preceded by a line of skirmishers, and then retreating in double-quick, the regiments formed into columns of companies, making two opposing lines of battle after breaking to the rear. They then changed front to the rear on the left of the first line, advancing to the attack. First was heard the scattering fire of the skirmishers, seen the small puffs of white smoke of the rifles extending from left to right far into the woods skirting the field. This was soon followed by the roar of a piece of artillery, then another and another, mingled with volleys of musketry as the line advanced.

A battery in front belched forth its thunder, and clouds of sulphurous smoke mounted into the air, and rolled away on the morning breeze. This was answered by a fierce volley of musketry and a charge by the line, who with fierce yells rushed on the guns, gallantly led by the color-bearers. The whole scene was a fine representation of one of those bloody dramas which had so frequently deluged Southern soil with a crimson stain, and sent a thrill of joy or woe from the centre to circumference of a struggling people. Yet this was devoid of the horrors attending an actual battle. Still, so exciting and impressive was the scene, that some fair ladies fainted, others screamed, while down the blanched yet handsome features of others coursed the tears caused by some sad memory thus vividly brought to light of similar scenes of stern reality, where, far away on bloody battle-fields, fell the loved ones.

The division now formed in columns of regiments near the reviewing officers, for the purpose of being presented to that gallant band; the veterans of the Third Louisiana Infantry, who were present by special invitation, and as the honored guests of the occasion. This organization, preceded by a strong field-band, was now marched on the ground, making a fine appearance in their new uniforms, burnished rifles, and a beautiful banner floating above them. They were inspected by General Forney, who then rode to their front and saluted them, which was responded to by three hearty cheers from the men.

Marching close to the division, General Forney then introduced them as follows:

"I have the honor of introducing to you that gallant band, the veterans of the Third Louisiana. They are birds of the same feather as yourselves. I do not speak unadvisedly when I tell you they are true and tried soldiers. For forty-eight consecutive days did this gallant band stand amid shot and shell as thick as hail. Though thinned in ranks, and few, yet, like yourselves, does each one feel as if he was a host in himself. I propose three cheers for the veterans of the Third Louisiana Infantry."

The cheers were given with a wild enthusiasm, exhibiting the high appreciation in which the "veterans" were held by their fellow-soldiers. The division presented arms, banners were waved amid strains of music from the band. This compliment was returned by the regiment. The arms were then stacked, and, mingling together, the troops attended the speaking. This was the first ovation to this Veteran Louisiana Regiment, and as such, to-day forms the brightest chapter in their history, and is remembered with feelings of deep gratitude, and added yet greater incentive to the high respect entertained by them for their old commander, Major-General Forney. Addresses, concise, pointed and stirring, were now delivered to the vast concourse of people by Colonel Louis Bush, Colonel George Flournoy, and Colonel R. R. Hubbard. Governor H. W. Allen, though absent, sent a letter of welcome to the hospitalities of Louisiana to this war-worn division of Texans. After the addresses were finished, all repaired to the tables, where a bountiful and substantial repast sufficient for all was spread. Here, the Louisianians were again specially honored by having tables exclusively set apart for them. The utmost harmony, cordiality and good feeling prevailed, and not an incident occurred to mar the festivities. The regiment made a fine appearance. The banner, it was stated, was a new one, very beautiful. It attracted great attention, and was constantly surrounded by crowds of admirers.

It was a red field bordered with yellow, with a deep, heavy gold fringe. In its centre are two blue scrolls, almost in the form of an X, having embroidered on them, with yellow floss silk, the mottoes: "Oak Hills," "Elk Horn," "Iuka," and "Corinth." In the upper right-hand corner is a cross of white silk, with twelve stars set thereon of yellow gold thread, bordered with black velvet cord. The flag is of fine silk the trimmings being of the finest and costliest materials. It was manufactured by Mrs. T. L. Maxwell in South Carolina, previous to the fall of Vicksburg. It was presented to the regiment by Captain T. L. Maxwell, formerly regimental A. C. S., at that time post A. C. S. at Jackson, Mississippi. It escaped the misfortune of ever entering Vicksburg by mere accident, and reached the regiment when they began to assemble in Parole Camp at Enterprise. This flag was successfully carried across the river by Captain M. Middlebrook, Company C, and was exhibited for the first and last time on this occasion of distinguished honor paid the Veteran Louisiana

Regiment. The 18th of February will not soon be forgotten by the immense concourse assembled near Shreveport. Upwards of 15,000 people were present on this occasion.

This incident seemed to be the ending of any excitement, until towards the first of April, when depredations and robberies began to be so prevalent in and around Shreveport, that a special patrol under commissioned officers, mostly picked men, guarded the city. It became dangerous for even General Smith or any staff officers to be caught in the streets at night. Consequently, some ridiculous scenes occurred between the veteran patrols and the post officers. One night the guard was inspected and drilled in the streets by an officer duly belted with sabre and sash. Another night an old Captain was arrested for not allowing a staff officer to interfere with his instructions, which he assumed he knew better than the Captain. These episodes caused much sport as well as indignation among the men. At this period much excitement existed over the constant reverses befalling the Confederate armies. Sherman's successful march through Georgia and the Carolinas and the final surrender of General Lee, caused a culmination in the excitement. Commissioners from General Canby to General E. Kirby Smith, reached Shreveport early in May. Confusion, worse confounded reigned everywhere among troops and citizens. On the 10th of May Camp Boggs presented a strange spectacle. The men were gathered in groups everywhere, discussing the approaching surrender. Curses deep and bitter fell from lips not accustomed to use such language, while numbers, both officers and men, swore fearful oaths never to surrender. It was such a scene as one seldom cares to witness. The depth of feeling exhibited by compressed lips, pale faces, and blazing eyes, told a fearful story of how bitter was this hopeless surrender of the cause for which they had fought, toiled, suffered for long years. The humiliation was unbearable. Paper money became worthless; rations were issued in large quantities; such as coffee, and other delicacies. The weather kept clear and pleasant, as if in mockery to the general gloom and despondency. Sunday the 13th, Shreveport was quiet. Troops began to leave for home, openly and unmolested; yet the Third remained. The 15th was cloudy and rainy. Shreveport was crowded with citizens. Ammunition was loaded into wagons and sent away.

On the 16th, rumors were in circulation in camp that Shreveport would be set on fire that night and plundered. This reported implicated members of the Third Regiment, but to their honor it was subsequently discovered that this report was false. That night some one stole the drum and beat it in camp. No one could be found who knew anything of the matter. Doubtless it was a practical joke played by some fun-loving member of the regiment on the strength of the general excitement. Be this as it may, the whole camp was aroused and orders issued for the regiment to promptly fall in. The order was quickly obeyed. Colonel Pierson, in command, made a few stirring remarks, telling the men "that Shreveport was about to be plundered and destroyed; that he expected every man to do his duty as a soldier, and the people of the town were looking to them for protection. They must not, should not be disappointed. He hoped the men would uphold their former honor and reputation, and be as firm and true as steel." Ammunition was issued to the regiment, then came the commands, "Right face, forward by file left—march," delivered in clear, deep-ringing tones; and the regiment was off for Shreveport. That night they bivouacked in the Court-House yard; and the city remained quiet and undisturbed, save by the patrols firm footsteps in their rounds.

The next day was the 17th of May. For four long years had the Third Louisiana Infantry battled for the South, homes and freedom; four long years of horrors, suffering, toil and bloodshed. They had trod the soil of Arkansas, Missouri, Tennessee, Mississippi, and left their heroic dead upon the hills and plains of those States; and, now once more in their native State, were to witness the final overthrow of the Confederacy. They must relinquish arms and see their proud banner trailed in the dust, never more to be raised by mortal hands. What a torturing reality for their brave and noble spirits! This day camp was formally established in the Court-House yard. A division of Missourians arrived also.

On the 18th they were informed that the Missourians had come to relieve them. They became indignant and furious, and threatened to leave *en masse*. A delegation of prominent citizens besought them to remain. Governor Allen addressed them most feelingly. All in vain. That day a Missouri Colonel addressed his regiment, and informed the men that they had been sent there to guard the Louisiana Regiment. Such, at least, was reported to them. That afternoon they were relieved, and sentinels placed around them, who officiously told the men they were stationed there to guard them. Injured in feeling, wounded in pride and spirit, the brave boys carried out their threat.

The morning of the 19th found the majority of the regiment gone, or preparing to leave. They were allowed to take Government horses, mules and wagons, and leave the place. Clothes, linen, cotton, thread, buttons, leather, etc., from the Quartermaster's Department, were issued to them in such quantities that they were unable to carry them away or dispose of them. The condition of affairs was terrible, awful, heart-rending.

On the 20th the men were all furloughed by the Confederate authorities, or, more properly speaking, formally discharged from the Confederate army. Numbers left, declaring they would take neither furlough, discharge nor parole. Many went down the river in pontoons. The officers staid with the men until the finale. Major Richards left on the 20th, and Lieutenant-Colonel Pierson on the 21st. The parting among the veterans was most affecting. Many put their arms around each other and sobbed like children; others gave the strong grasp of the hand, and silently went away with hearts too full for utterance, while still others would mutter a huskily spoken "good-bye" or deep oath. Such were some of the farewell scenes. Together in battle or camp, in sunshine and storm, in suffering and pleasure, in sorrow and joy, on the weary and toilsome march! No wonder that their hearts were linked together in bands of steel, with ties unspeakable, inexpressible. No wonder the parting, perhaps for years, perhaps forever, wrung their souls with torturing agony.

Sunday, the 21st, was hot. The streets were thronged with people. All the Government stores were thrown open. Then began a scene which beggared description. Government stores, of every imaginable description, were seized, the streets filled with goods, official papers, etc., scattered everywhere. It was awful, terrible beyond portrayal. Large quantities of these goods were eagerly bought for silver by rapacious speculators. To the honor of the Missourians be it recorded, that they soon restored order, seized the goods from the speculators, and stored them in the Court-House.

At this period Confederate officers disappeared very suddenly; the stars and bars mysteriously departed, but citizens in fine apparel became quite numerous. Passing strange!

This same evening, as the sun sank below the western horizon, tinging the waters of Red River with a roseate hue, two pontoons left the wharf at Shreveport, and went down the river. Those pontoons contained the last departing members of the regiment. In one were Captain N. M. Middlebrook, Company C; Captain W. B. Butler, Company G; Captain Curry, Company H; Sergeant F. D. Tunnard, Company K; Sergeant W. H. Tunnard; —— Trichel, Company D, and one private of Company C. The other pontoon contained Captain T. Gourrier, Company A, and six privates of the same company.

Such was the finale of the regiment, whose members had done their duty nobly from their first organization to the period of their dissolution. Their name for deeds of daring and heroic sacrifices was proverbial, and was known from the hills of Virginia to the plains of Texas. For patient endurance, silent suffering and sacrifice, unconquerable bravery and stubborn, desperate fighting, they had no superior among the many gallant regiments of the Confederacy. Let the veil of obscurity fall over the deeds of those who often were misled during moments of excitement, or blindly followed their own wishes in preference to military orders. The curtain falls upon the bloody drama of war; the foot-lights have been extinguished; the actors have all departed; the audience of the world's wondering nations turned to other scenes. The pen which has dotted these reminiscences through long and weary months is laid aside, as white-winged Peace, all radiant with joy, settles down once more upon the land of Columbia.

CHAPTER XLI

SCENES FROM CAMP LIFE AT CAMP BOGGS

THAT MUSIC

"Oh, were you ne'er a school-boy!
And did you never train?"

THESE lines were forcibly brought to mind by an unusual sound being heard in our camp this Sunday evening, October 2, A.D. 1864; being no less than the music of a full band, bass and tenor drums and fife. So unusual an occurrence soon brought together a large circle of admiring spectators, who interspersed the performance with remarks both polite and profane. What mattered it that novices, yea! verily, the greenest of amateurs, essayed their first efforts! Was it not music? Did not the heart expand under its revivifying influence? The forms of some drew up to their full height, as with martial tread they marched off with firm military step. The great spirit of Shakespeare haunted not the hearts of the musicians, proclaiming from his mouldering dust these forcible words:

"He that hath not music in himself, and whose soul is not moved by sweet concord of sounds, is fit for treason, stratagem and spoils."

Soldiers naturally love music, yet have we heard them curse, "long, loud and deep," at the roll of a tenor drum, calling them from morning sleep or to daily drill. The introduction of so much *musical material* into the Third Louisiana Regiment, however, is a novelty, even to the veterans, and well worth recording.

PREACHING IN CAMP

Preaching to soldiers in these times of war and bloodshed is oftener the exception than the general rule; especially had such been the case during our experience of nearly four years' campaigning. Perhaps other commands have been more blessed in this respect than the one to which I am attached; true is it, however, that the rank growth of vice and sin has been permitted to spring up and flourish unchecked in our midst, under the demoralizing influence of war's fierce blast. An occasional warning voice has been heard in our midst, yet Christianity has few supporters, and very seldom is the heartfelt hymn or prayer heard. Yet the expounder of truth always finds a respectable and attentive audience in the regiment.

But a few days since a preacher came into our midst and exercised the peculiar privilege of his vocation. 'Twas night. The pale crescent moon wrapped the earth in an uncertain light. The stars looked down from the far-off realms of space like the sleepless eye of Omnipotence. Gathered in one of the avenues of the camp were a number of the men, quietly, attentively listening to words which fell from the lips of a speaker standing in their midst; a dim candle lighted the scene; its feeble flame flickering in the evening air and making dancing shadows around the group. It was the picture for the pencil of a Rembrandt, or the pen of a Goethe. The speaker, with his gray locks and wrinkled brow, showing the footprints of time, standing in the midst of that group of eager listeners—men just entering the threshold of life, yet whose vocations placed their feet upon the verge of the grave—the rows of tents, the black groupings of adjacent shelters, all made an impressive scene. Occasionally, mingling with the speaker's words, came laughter from some group assembled around a camp-fire near by, a shout of some unthinking, free-hearted stroller about camp. Words, rich with eloquent meaning, rolled from that aged speaker's lips, like rippling waves of ocean, successively, rapidly breaking upon a sanded shore; the light of a hidden power burned in his eyes, as he pleaded, warned and urged his hearers of the life to come, and the consequences of an unprepared condition for its hidden realities. The exhortation finished, a closing hymn was sung, rolling its waves of pure melody out upon the night's still air, over the adjacent hills and valleys, the benediction pronounced and the audience dispersed to discuss, some in serious, others in jocular vein, the subject-matter of the discourse.

Such is one of the occasional, more impressive scenes from our camp life.

THE STORM

On the morning of Novembers 1st clouds gathered in heavy masses, shutting out the light of the sun's golden rays, obscuring all the heavens. Northward they sped, with their fleecy vapors, flitting by with arrowy speed, towards the distant north. Anon they discharged their gathered moisture, with steady fall upon the dying earth. The drops fell with regular rapidity upon the canvas roofs of our sheltering tents like the pattering footsteps of many feet. Snugly ensconced beneath their several tents, the soldiers whiled away the tedious hours of their confinement with song, story and anecdote.

There came a lull in the storm, a stray gleam of sunlight fell across the earth from a rift in the clouds o'erhead. 'Twas but a momentary delusive lull. Soon in the north and west gathered a long line of inky blackness athwart, which gleamed with vivid light the lightning's brilliant flash, followed by the deep and muttered roll of the jarring thunder. Gleam followed gleam in rapid succession, accompanied by deeper, louder roar of the crashing roll of heaven's artillery. Nearer, yet nearer, came the black shadow of the storm-king; Boreas, in all the fierceness of wrathful power preceded his approach. In all its fury it burst upon our exposed encampment. Fiercely descended the wind in powerful, fitful gusts, accompanied by a deluge of descending rain. What a scene was there—a hurrying to and fro! Loud shouts and laughter of the imprisoned men rising high above the storm's deep-toned roar. Tents, released from their fastenings fell in ruins upon their occupants. Flies flew upward like a huge white-winged bird, their ropes and tackle streaming out from their sides. Luckless victims to the storm-king's sport emerged like drowned rats from the shrouds of their tents amid the shouts and laughter of their more fortunate comrades. No respecter of persons is the storm in its wrath, and officers suffered equally with privates. Tent after tent, shelters and sheds bowed before the inexorable monarch, until the camp presented a woeful picture of desolation and disaster. The sergeant-major assisted by the adjutant, each convulsively clutched the poles of their local habitation, and tenaciously clung to them with the desperation of despair, yet convulsed with laughter as the storm swayed them to and fro like the steps of a drunken man. Our surgeon, in fiery haste arrived from Shreveport to escape the threatened storm, and hurriedly darted beneath the shelter of his tent, and inwardly congratulated himself on his fortunate escape from a ducking. Alas! for the imaginary security of frail mortality. The first blast of the storm brought his tent around his ears, completely burying him beneath its ample folds, from which, after various struggles and contortions, he emerged, a veritable water-fowl. The commissary sergeant fared little better; with naked feet and bared shoulders, and long hair streaming in the air, he emerged from his reeling tent, like a veritable spirit of the storm. The fly blew loose, the tent-pins pulled up. Ably assisted by aid within, he convulsively clutched a corner rope of the fly, braced his feet in the sandy soil, and held on with the energy of despair. Finally releasing his hold, with axe in hand, he flitted around the tent here, there, everywhere, driving down pins, tightening the loosened cords, etc. He saved his tent, but received a complete baptizing from the cold, chilling northern storm. Such are some of the incidents of this stormy November day. Cries and shouts of all kinds helped to fill up the measure of the confusion worse confounded. "Hoop! hoop! hurrah!" "Bring on your whisky." "Here's your mule!" "Quarter less twain." "Knee deep—*no bottom!*" "Farewell, my sheltering snow-bird; fare ye well forever." "Hoorah! Doc., got plenty of diluted medicines for the ailing of humanity?" "Just a-going, a-going; how much for a tent, gentlemen? Just a-going—*gone,* by Jupiter!" Language, however, fails to do justice to such a scene. On all sides there is fun and laughter at the haps and mishaps, and scarcely a single word of complaint, such is the stoical indifference with which such casualties are met by the soldier. The more fortunate, dry and comfortably sheltered, find an inexhaustible fund of merriment in the mishaps of their comrades, and enjoy their unenviable condition in many sly jokes and witticisms which are received as given with great humor.

"HERE'S YOUR HONEY"

'Twas one of those beautiful autumnal days when a quiet hush seems to pervade all nature; the sun looked down bright and golden from the deep azure sky; the air, balmy and pleasant, disturbed not a whispering leaf on the autumnal-clothed trees; even camp, so usually the scene of constant activity and bustle, was almost death-like in its quietude. The sun was sinking to its repose in the west, casting long shadows athwart the earth, when a strange life and activity arose in camp. The men emerged from their tents like a nest of hornets aroused by some invader of their domains, all attracted towards a central point, which seemed a seething volcano of cries, rude jokes, a laughter high above all, where there arose the cry of "Here's your honey." We followed the bent of a natural curiosity, and soon discovered the cause of the uproar to be a "little old man," with a cap on his head and stick in hand, under the escort of one of the valiant captains of the regiment, earnestly and eagerly searching the camp for some stolen honey. As he proceeded from tent to tent, ransacking old boxes, pulling nicely-arranged beds into heaps of disorder, the uproar and crowd increased. Unmercifully they made the intruder the subject of witticisms and sly jokes, making honey the theme of it all, until he could stand the assault no longer. Turning upon his persecutors with a lugubrious expression of features, laughable to behold, and raising his stick aloft, he exclaimed: "Gentlemen, some one took a basket containing three bottles of honey from my place. I care not for the honey, only give me back my basket! Men, that basket belonged to my brother. He's in the army, and I hate to lose it. Give me my basket." "No you don't, old fel," said a voice; "you want some one to bring back the basket and then take him up for stealing your honey. No *yer* don't. 'Lasses is sweet, but honey am sweeter."

Stooping to enter a tent, he was assaulted by a full dose of flour from the mischievous occupant. As he suddenly emerged, sputtering and blowing the white powder from mouth and nostrils, a serio-comic spectacle, a new uproar greeted him. "Take him out," said one; "hunting honey is a pretence; he is trying to steal some one's flour." Thus this seeker after lost sweetness was assailed on all sides with a thousand absurd suggestions how to find his honey, until, almost crazed, he fled from the camp, followed, as long as visible, by the loud vociferations of the men, "Here's your honey."

OUR QUARTERS

We have read descriptions of palaces, with their marble colonnades, tessel-ated floors, ceilings frescoed and embellished with carved and curious figures, adorned, ornamented and furnished with all the richness and elegance which art and genius could devise, or the skill of man produce; yet no such picture intrudes its glare and glitter upon us this cold, wintry day. The heart, wearied with long years of suffering, danger and hardship, amid the stirring and event-ful scenes of our struggle for national independence, naturally turns to an hum-bler scene, with its fond associations. "Home, sweet home," is a theme which melts the heart of the sternest of our scarred veterans. Many times have we seen the tears steal down the bronzed cheeks of those who have passed unmoved amid the horrors of the battle-field, as the strains of this cherished refrain came from some saddened heart, gushing its melody from a sweet-toned voice or instrument. We remember the cottage home embowered in trees, with the rose and honeysuckle clambering over the trellis at the ends of the porch, and the jessamine, with its sweet-scented flowers, perfuming all the summer air. We remember, too, with intense yearning, the social family gathering in the evening, the fondly-loved sister and brothers, the adored mother and revered father, now exiled from that cottage home, or battling in the ranks of our coun-try's patriots. Ah! how these memories throng to the mind and bring forth long-dormant reminiscences of the past! But what have these thoughts to do with "Our Quarters?" Nothing, dear reader, save as a reverie of camp-life.

The winter wind is whispering a sighing requiem through the pine-boughs which form a shelter near my present home. Its breath is sharp and biting. What matters? Does a tent, with its canvas roof, and its sides closely pinned and sodded down, keep old Boreas at bay? Moreover, there is a comfortable fireplace at one end, with its mud chimney outside, where the fire crackles and the ruddy flame leaps joyfully upward, as if denying all old Winter's fierce attacks. We sit (my companions and self, I mean,) around this cozy fire, and laugh and chat away the laggard hours as if stern war was not a bitter reality, and life had no aim save the enjoyment of its flitting hours. Soldiers are proverbial for their light-heartedness and reckless joviality under the most trying circumstances. The tent-poles at either end are ornamented with knapsacks, the relics of many campaigns and long marches, while from a pole, which is swinging overhead, hangs our scanty wardrobe of soiled, tattered, and threadbare garments. On one side of the tent is a broad bed, tastefully made up, with perhaps, knapsacks or some bundles for pillows. At its head is a shelf, upon which is ranged our tinware and cutlery, a small box of sugar and a jar of molasses; at its foot is a table, on which is a portfolio containing the treasures and writing materials of "Beta Omega," an inkstand, brushes, combs, rules, box of tacks, books in the shape of a history of the French Revolution, Hardee's Tactics and a Bible, an old tin cup full of corn-meal, with a piece of candle rising from its midst, and a simple camp candlestick; on the opposite side is a single bedstead, minus an occupant, a barrel of meal, saddle and bridle. Under each bed can be found mess-boxes containing our daily sustenance, old boots and shoes, a bag of potatoes, skillets and pots for cooking, tin pans, etc. The floor is covered with boards, making it appear neat and comfortable, almost home-like; several stools are scattered about in negligent disorder, while, to finish the picture, a small black and somewhat savage and decidedly ugly terrier is playing about the floor, or lazily sleeping before the fire.

Such is the picture of our quarters this windy winter's day, where we pass our idle hours, regardless of sunshine or storm, contentedly smoking our pipes, or discussing the latest news items. A soldier's tent is parlor, kitchen and bedroom, and contains within its small and circumscribed limits all the conveniences of his existence. How seldom do we imagine what man can endure and still continue hopeful, healthy and joyous! Such is a soldier's life.

OUR NOBLE WOMEN

No published record or portion of the history of the war could possibly be complete without some tribute to the fair ladies of our land. The gallant men of the Third Regiment have cause to remember them on innumerable occasions.

President Davis, in one of his appeals to the people of the Confederate States, closes with these sentiments: "I conjure my countrywomen—the wives, mothers, sisters and daughters of the Confederacy—to use their all-powerful influence in aid of this call; to add one crowning sacrifice to those which their patriotism has so freely and constantly offered on their country's altar; and take care no one who owes service in the field be sheltered at home from the disgrace of having deserted their duty to their families, to their country, and to their God."

In these days of civilization and Christian enlightenment, woman's influence is not only acknowledged, but properly appreciated, by man—not only in the quiet home-circle, but also bearing upon the destinies of nations. The above appeal from the model statesman, the chief executive of the infant Confederacy, is a most glorious tribute to the influence of our fair women. What a record for the pages of its history! President Davis acknowledged it as controlling the destiny of a convulsed people, even as it moulds, forms man's individual character and aspirations. Truly woman's influence over the destiny of a nation was never more earnestly proclaimed, or sincerely acknowledged and felt, than during the late struggle.

As the thirsty and tired wayfarer gains renewed strength and freshness at the fountain where the cool and glistening waters, with their diamond spray, form rainbow hues in the sparkling sunlight, so man draws new hope, inspiration and vigor from woman's encouraging smile, and gentle, loving words. From time immemorial—when Mary watched before the tomb of a Divine Saviour; through the stormy scenes of the ancient republics; in the midst of the exciting events of the Crusade; through every great era in the world's changing history, down to the late eventful struggle—women have occupied prominent positions where works of love, kindness and tenderness were to be performed, or sacrifices made for the weal of mankind. Steadfast has she ever proven herself in hours of danger and toil, ever ready to meet, with heroic fortitude and cheerful hope, the rough storms of life, and, with cheering words of encouragement, rouse the desponding spirit of man's stronger, yet frequently less hopeful, nature. Hers has been a proud station in the midst of the late revolution—sending forth the loved and dear ones of her household to meet the ruthless invader; laying these precious jewels on the altar of her country; hiding the torn and bleeding tendrils of her affections by unwearying labors for the welfare and comfort of the absent one; enduring privations at home little dreamed of; with words of hope and encouragement for the desponding, sometimes despairing soldiers; waiting and watching by the wayside and public thoroughfares with comforts for the sick and wounded as they were sent from the scene of active strife; visiting hospitals; giving aide and necessaries to captive friends amid insolent foes; facing the horrors of the battle-field; ever on her mission of love and mercy within the walls of besieged cities; at home, abroad, everywhere exhibiting a devotion and unwavering constancy for the country's good, which should have caused a blush of shame to mantle the cheeks of many who called themselves *men—men,* forsooth, who, with ashen lips and trembling knees, prated of the dangers they *dared* not encounter.

Oh! glorious the record of the noble women of the Sunny South! Not a Southern soldier but has cause to remember thee. The recollection of thy deeds of love, thy gentle words of hope, strengthened anew their brave hearts and strong arms to strike new blows in thy defence.

The image of some bright face, the music-tones of some voice in a far-distant home, implanted in the Southron's heart a new aspiration for deeds of daring and valor, with an influence beyond the power of expression. Southern chivalry is gathering up the broken fragments of the temple of their perished hope, and will yet erect a mausoleum glorious and beautiful, with its colonnades, dome and arch. It will be the Mecca which they will come to worship. Inscribed on its highest pinnacle, in letters of living light, shall be thy names, oh! daughters of the South! proclaiming to the world thy sacrifices buried 'neath this glorious edifice, the shadow of that more beautiful temple, for which thy sons, fathers, husbands and brothers so fearfully toiled, so lavishing and freely sacrificed and poured out their lives, treasure and blood.

Amid the overshadowing gloom of the country's peril, thy all-powerful aid was invoked to illume, with its bright influence, its dark hours; to strengthen its weakness, and bring success out of disaster. Nobly was it answered, but all in vain. What a glorious mission was thine! *Gentle woman! the bulwark of a nation's success, a nations' freedom!* Worthy art thou of our smiling skies, the South's broad and fertile valleys, its beautiful mountain scenery and great streams! Heroic women, worthy daughters of a land of flowers, sunshine and brave men. How her sons worship at the shrine of thy beauty and worth, and proudly proclaim thy heroic deeds of self-sacrificing devotion, when no light gleamed through the jagged clouds of war, as the storm swept over the land like a besom of destruction!

All-glorious, all-radiant are these records; worthy the poet's sweetest strain, the painter's most beautiful conception, the musicians most glorious symphony, the orator's loftiest flights of eloquence, the historian's most brilliant records, every Southerner's deepest homage and love.

UNMARKED GRAVES

DEDICATED TO THE WOMEN OF THE SOUTH

I.

Bring flowers, sweet flowers, from the South's sunny plain;
Plant their rich beauty o'er the graves of the slain—
Let their fragrance so pure, like incense of old,
Perfume the soft air, as some censer of gold,
Swung to and fro in cathedral dim and lofty,
Where strains of rich music floating out softly,
Fill the soul with emotions so calm and so deep,
Where worshipers kneel in adoration so sweet.

II.

Let Beauty's soft tears, like the dews of the night,
Or the diamond's bright rays, reflecting the light,
Fall on these lonely graves; love's tokens so pure,
Which memory green keeps, while Time shall endure.
While Fame shall proclaim, with his deep, brazen voice,
Names of heroes, who, in the land of their choice,
Fell in the strife on the field of their glory—
Their lives an offering to song and to story.

III.

In hearts true and tender, monuments shall stand,
More polished in beauty than aught in the land;
Than e'er Greek Demetrius, with his skill wondrous,
Chiseled from marble so rough and so pond'rous.
Monuments pure and rare, deep watered with tears,
Time cannot destroy with the long lapse of years;
Or memory true from its tablets efface
A glory and beauty in patriot blood traced.

IV.

Laid 'neath the droop of the lone weeping willows,
Laid where the surge of the ocean's dark billows

Thunder their requiem on the bright sanded shore,
Nature's fit anthem of mystical power.
Unmarked graves, in shadowy vale and dense wood,
where, fiercely fighting, patriot soldiers once stood,
Ling'ring falls the light on each emerald mound,
With a halo of Beauty, golden, profound.

Natchitoches, Louisiana, January 24th, 1865.

THE "PERSONNEL" OF THE REGIMENT AND HOW THEY ACCEPT THE "SITUATION"

In events of unusually startling nature, the mind naturally investigates causes, reasoning from these to the effect produced. Thus in reading the history of this gallant organization, the peruser inquires, "Who and what were these men?" Let us answer. The members of the Third Louisiana Infantry were principally men of high social standing at home; intelligent, refined, young, the fires of youth glowing in their stalwart forms. Voluntarily offering their services to their country, they were actuated by a firm conviction of the justice of their cause. From workshop and counter, from cottage and mansion, from the lordly plantation and the crowded city, they came, standing side by side in defence of a common cause. Look at them; the fire of a fixed determination glowing in their clear, bright eyes, the strength of a settled purpose evinced in their firm tread and upright carriage.

No wonder that they distinguished themselves on the battle-field, covering themselves with an imperishable glory. There is not to-day a man living who ever doubted the courage and gallantry of the whole regiment. Thus they fought through the stirring scenes of the whole war, and when the inevitable decrees of fate decided against them, they accepted the issue as brave men only could.

If they were gallant soldiers, now are they good citizens, and can be implicitly trusted in their fealty to the Government. They feel that they have been overpowered, and accept the situation as brave and honorable men. Such men as the Gourriers, C. D. Craighead, F. Roth and brother, Landry and brother, William Johnson, Pierre Richard, Alexander Hebert, C. Nicholls, H. Le Blanc and brother, J. Richard, A. Jolly, N. Gayard, H. Guidici, P. Slaven, M. Coughlan, N. Richard, and many others of Iberville; Major W. F. Tunnard, F. D. Tunnard, Bentons, Waddell, Gentles, Bells, Jolly, Booth, Alexander, Aldrich, Hardy, Heroman, Knox, Hackett, etc., of Baton Rouge; Brighams,

Washburn, Davenport, Evans, Hinson, Whitstone, Holt, Brashear, Harris, Carters, Quipin, etc., of Morehouse; Hyams, Breazeales, Blair, Russells, Walmsleys, Airey, Morse, Espy, Levasson, Trichels, Butler, Prudhommes, Derbonne, Bossiers, Charlevillis, Cloutiers, Hallers, Murphy, Norris, etc., of Natchitoches; Lacy, Wells, Kinney, Gilmore, Kendall, Robson, Clark, Cole, Effner, etc., of Shreveport; Pierson, Emanuel, Middlebrook, etc., of Winn; Hedricks, Richards, Guy, Young, Tompkins, Currie, Page, Bradley, Eddins, etc., of Carroll; Gunnells, Evans, Humbles, Broadway, Smith, Moffits, Fluetts, Dunns, Hannas, Cottinghams, Grays, Johnsons, Killeys, Masons, McFarlands, Merediths, Moss, Sandridge, etc., of Caldwell, are considered the most trust-worthy of citizens. Yet were they the first to answer to the bugle-call. These are all true men. In financial and commercial circles, in workshops, at the bench and counter and in the fields, are they striving to rebuild their fallen fortunes, striving to regain the loss inflicted by war. They are neither despondent nor despairing, but work with alacrity and cheerfulness to repair the many ravages of the conflict. Such are the positions of men who gave fortunes, staked their lives on the issue of war. The heroism displayed in accepting their defeat is not less praise-worthy than their undaunted bearing in the deadly battle-field.

ROLLS OF THE COMPANIES

THE following rolls of the Companies composing the 3d Regiment La. Infantry are necessarily incomplete, being compiled from notes, without the aid of any official documents. All the records of the Regiment were destroyed; first, when Vicksburg was surrendered, and again when the army was finally disbanded. This statement is considered necessary, in order that no complaints may be made for any errors which may occur in these lists:

ROLL OF COMPANY A, IBERVILLE GREYS

Captain Charles A. Bruslé. Wounded, Vicksburg, May, 1863.

Pritchard, J. A., 1st Lieutenant. Resigned, May 3d, 1861.

Brown, T. C., 2d Lieutenant. Promoted May 3rd. Resigned, June, 1861.

Verbois, T. R., 2d Junior Lieutenant. Promoted 2d Lieutenant, June, 1861. Wounded at Oak Hills, August 10, 1861.

Goodwin, F. W., 1st Sergeant.

Ramoin, J. B., 2d Sergeant. Elected 2d Lieutenant, May 8, 1862. Killed at Iuka, September, 19, 1862.

Babin, U., 3rd Sergeant. Elected 1st Lieutenant, May 8, 1862. Wounded at Vicksburg.

Chastant, J. M., 4th Sergeant. Killed at Vicksburg, June 22, 1863.

Terrel O., 1st Corporal.

Bevin, O., 2nd Corporal.

Browne, H. S., 3rd Corporal. Discharged, N. O., May 3, 1861.

Arceneaux, E. A., 4th Corporal. Discharged, N. O., May 3, 1861.

Arceneau, M. Private.

Allain, S., Private. Wounded at Vicksburg, May 31, 1863.

Amoin, T., Private.

Allsbach, J., Private. Discharged, Sept., 1861.

Aucoin, S., Private. Discharged, June 28th, 1861.

Brawn, C. H., Private.

Breand, S., Private. Discharged, 1861.

Breaux, J. H., Private. Died of wounds, Vicksburg, June 25, 1863.

Bridges, D. F., Private. Killed at Iuka, Sept. 19, 1862.

Boissac, E. M., Private. Wounded at Vicksburg, June 6, 1863.

Broussard, M., Private. Wounded at Iuka, and died at Jackson, Miss., Sept., 1862.

Blanchard, N., Private.

Blanchard, L. D., Private. Wounded at Vicksburg, May 19, 1863.

Babin, A., Private. Discharged, N. O., May 3, 1861.

Bellfield, E. C., Private.

Barlow, E. D., Private.

Beard, N., Private. Wounded at Oak Hills, August 10, 1861.

Bell, J., Private.

Berry, B., Private. Died of wounds, Vicksburg, June 26, 1863.

Breaux, E. L., Private. Wounded at Iuka, Sept. 19, 1862.

Crowell, James, Private.

Coughlan, M., Private. Discharged, 1861. Wounded at Oak Hills, August 10, 1861.

Connor, James, Private. Wounded at Vicksburg, June 6, 1863.

Craighead, C. D., Private.

Davis, S. D., Private. Killed at Iuka, Sept. 19, 1862.

Dupuy, C., Private. Killed at Vicksburg, June 22, 1863.

Dennis, J., Private.

Ellis, J. A., Private.

Guidici, H. E., Private. Appointed Sergeant, February, 1862. Wounded at Vicksburg, May 29, 1863.

Gayard, N., Private. Wounded at Iuka, Sept. 19, 1862.

Gourrier, E., Private. Elected 2d Junior Lieutenant, Ft. Smith, June, 1861.

Gourrier, E., Private. Elected 2d Junior Lieutenant, May 8, 1862 at Corinth. Wounded at Iuka.

Gourrier, S., Private. Killed at Iuka, Sept. 19, 1862.

Gleason, P., Private. Died at Jackson, Miss.

Hebert., J. L., Private.

Hebert, V. A., Private. Appointed Orderly to General L. Hebert.

Hebert, Alexander O., Private.

Hebert, Amidi, Private. Killed at Vicksburg, June 25, 1863.

Hebert, G. S., Private. Appointed Assistant-Surgeon.

Hersch, B., Private. Killed at Iuka, Sept. 19, 1862.

Hall, W., Private.

Johnson, W., Private.

Johns, A. J., Private.

Johns, W. H., Private.

Joly, A. J., Private. Wounded at Iuka, Sept. 19, 1862.

Kahn, S., Private. Wounded at Vicksburg, June 23, 1863.

Kenney, John, Private. Elected Captain, May 8, 1862. Wounded at Iuka, Sept. 19, 1862. Killed at Vicksburg, July 1, 1863.

Le Blanc, E., Private. Wounded at Oak Hills. Killed accidentally, Aug., 1861.

Le Blanc, H., Private.

Leonard, F., Private. Killed at Vicksburg, May 19, 1863.

Landry, M., Private. Wounded at Iuka.

Landry, J. A., Private. Appointed Brigade Quartermaster, 2 M. at Tupelo, Miss., 1862.

Le Blanc, M., Private.

Lanoux, F., Private. Discharged, 1861.

McManus, J., Private. Wounded at Oak Hills, Aug. 16, 1861.

McGueri, Private.

Macready, J., Private.

McGinnis, W. B., Private. Wounded at Vicksburg, June 14, 1863.

Mintor, N. Private.

Nichols, C., Private.

Norton, C., Private.

O'Brien, M., Private. Wounded at Vicksburg.

Nicholas ———, Private.

Pruett, C., Private. Wounded at Vicksburg, May 22, 1863.

Polson, W. H., Private.

Richard, B., Private. Appointed Sergeant, Feb., 1862.

Richard, N., Private. Discharged, 1861.

Richard, J., Private. Taken prisoner at Iuka, Sept. 19, 1862.

Richard, E., Private.

Roth, F., Private.

Randolph, S. A., Private. Elected 2d Lieutenant, May, 1862. Killed at Vicksburg, May 23, 1863.

Schade, N., Private. Killed at Vicksburg, May 19, 1863.

Sanders, W., Private. Wounded at Iuka, Miss., and Corinth, Miss.

St. Amant, B. T., Private. Wounded at Vicksburg, May 22, 1863.

Slaven, P., Private.

Scheirer, J., Private.

Springer, ———, Private. Elected 2d Lieutenant, May 7th, 1861.

Terrell, G., Private. Discharged, Sept. 1861.

Terrell, O., Private.

Verbois, O., Private. Discharged, 1861.

Willis, P. C., Private. Wounded at Vicksburg, June 23, 1863.

White, P., Private.

Willhardt, W., Private.

ROLL OF COMPANY B, THIRD LOUISIANA

R. M. S. Hinson, Captain. Killed August 10th, 1861, at Oak Hills, Mo.

W. T. Hall, 1st Lieutenant. Resigned May 1, 1862, Memphis, Tenn.

D. C. Morgan, 2d Lieutenant.

J. H. Brigham, 2 Juionr Lieutenant. Appointed Adjutant of the Regiment, May 8, 1862, Corinth, Miss.

W. L. McMurtry, 1st Sergeant. Discharged April 23, 1862, Little Rock.

C. Adamson, 2d Sergeant. Discharged August, 1861, Maysville, Arkansas.

W. P. Douglas, 3d Sergeant. Discharged October 6, 1861.

J. W. Petitt★, 4th Sergeant. Died, September 9, 1861, at Springfield, Mo.

J. C. Williams, 5th Sergeant. Transferred July 1, 1861, Fort Smith, Ark.

E. J. Wright, 1st Corporal. Discharged December 8, 1864, Winter-quarters, Ark.

W. J. Buford, 2d Corporal. Transferred January 15, 1865, Shreveport, La.

Shelton, D., 3d Corporal.

Traylor, W. P., 4th Corporal. Died September 19, 1861, at Springfield, Mo.

Alford, Thomas R., Private. Killed May 19, 1863, at Vicksburg, Miss.

Armstrong, P. D., Private.

Aldridge, F. J., Private. Discharged April 17, 1862, Little Rock, Arkansas.

Brown, T. J.★, Private. Died October 2, 1862, at Iuka, Miss.

Briscoe, James M., Private. Died June 3, 1864, at Morehouse Parish, La.

Boyer, ———, Private. Died June, 1861, at Vicksburg, Miss.

Brice, John W., Private. Died April 12, 1862, at Dardanelle, Ark.

Beauchamp, T. L., Private. Died May 17, 1862, at Corinth, Miss.

Blankenship, John,★ Private. Died July 17, 1863, at Morehouse Par., La.

Blankenship, William, Private. Remained east of Mississippi River after fall of Vicksburg.

Brigham, D. L., Private. Discharged November, 1861, Benton County, Ark.

Bass, E. A., Private. Drowned September 6, in Red River.

Bussey, A. L., Private.

Buckmaster, D., Private.

Boatner, E. J., Private.

Benk, James, Private. Disabled at Vicksburg.

Collier, Thomas, Private. Discharged June 6, 1861, Little Rock, Arkansas.

Cole, L. J., Private.

Cooper, J. H., Private.

Cooper, W. T., Private.

★Died of wounds.

Cravens, T., Private. Disabled at Iuka.

Darwin, J., Private. Discharged October 7, 1861, Maysville, Ark.

Davis, William, Private. Discharged December 8, 1861, Winterquarters, Ark.

Davenport, Joe, Private.

Evans, E. M., Private. Discharged August 9, 1861, Wilson's Creek, Missouri.

Evans, D. M., Private.

Frazier, C., Private. Died April 3, 1862, at Van Buren, Ark.

Fenley, W. F., Private. Killed May 22, 1863, at Vicksburg, Miss.

Felton, J. G., Private.

Fogerty, James, Private. Discharged July 16, 1862, Tupelo, Miss.

Hughes, P., Private. Died May, 1861, at New Orleans, La.

Hewitt, M., Private. Died September 13, 1861, at Springfield, Mo.

Hewitt, J. N., Private. Killed May 30, 1863, at Vicksburg, Miss.

Higginbotham, T. C., Private.

Higginbotham, J. N., Private. Died August 28, 1861, at Springfield, Mo.

Higginbotham, C. W., Private. Discharged June 30, 1861, Fort Smith, Ark.

Howell, W. H., Private. Killed June 11, 1863, at Vicksburg, Miss.

Howell, J. M., Private.

Hubbard, F., Private. Transferred February, 1863, Snyder's Bluff, Miss.

Harrison, B., Private. Discharged July 16th, 1862, Tupelo, Miss.

Henderson, R., Private. Captured at "Elk Horn," Ark., March 8, 1862. Refused exchange.

Handy, H. F., Private.

Hall, B., Private.

Jones, John, Private. Transferred June 6, 1861, Little Rock, Ark.

Jones, G. W., Private. Discharged July 16, 1862, Tupelo, Miss.

Gelks, J. F., Private.

Kelley, William, Private. Died August 30, 1861, at Springfield, Missouri.

Lee, John W., Private. Killed June 20, 1861, at Vicksburg, Miss.

Land, Thomas, Private. Discharged May 30, 1861, N. Orleans, La.

Lawhead, William, Private.

Meaders, H., Private. Died October 1862, Oakalona, Miss.

McCluskey, Thomas, Private. Discharged October 4, 1862, Little Rock, Ark.

McCallaghan, William, Private.

May, James C., Private. Killed June 26, 1863, at Vicksburg, Miss.

McIntosh, W. B., Private. Discharged April 18, 1862, Little Rock, Arkansas.

McFee, A. L., Private. Transferred March, 1863, Snyder's Bluff, Miss.

McFee, Eugene, Private.

McGrane, John, Private. Discharged July 16, 1862, Tupelo, Miss.

Newton, J. B., Private. Died September 11, 1861, at Springfield, Missouri.

Norton, B., Private.

O'Brien, Jerry, Private. Discharged April 18, 1862, Little Rock, Ark.

Pickett, D., Private.

Potts, T. J., Private. Discharged September 24, 1861, Bentonville, Ark.

Quinn, G. B., Private.

Renwick, J. P., Private. Killed August 10th, 1861, Oak Hills, Mo.

Renwick, W. P., Private.

Risor, William, Private. Discharged July 16, 1862, Tupelo, Miss.

Roland, ———, Private. Transferred July 20, 1861, Bentonville, Ark.

Raidt, F., Private. Discharged August 10, 1862, Baldwin, Miss.

Robard, G. W., Private. Discharged October, 1861.

Smith, S. D., Private. Killed May 20, 1863, at Vicksburg, Miss.

Steward, James, Private. Killed September 19, 1862, at Iuka, Miss.

Small, John, Private. Discharged September 8, 1861, Winterquarters, Ark.

Sullivan, Con, Private. Discharged September 8, 1861, Winterquarters, Ark.

Sharp, J. T., Private. Killed June 25, 1863, at Vicksburg, Miss.

Silbernagel, B., Private.

Saunders, J. N., Private.

Sparks, T. H., Private.

Sharp, James M., Private.

Taylor, Joseph, Private. Killed August 10, 1861, at Oak Hills, Mo.

Tubberville, A. H., Private. Discharged September 10, 1861, Maysville, Ark.

Turner, Joseph, Private. Discharged July 16, 1862, Tupelo, Miss.

Vaughan, G. B., Private.

Whitley, J. B., Private. Died June, 1861, at Vicksburg, Miss.

Whittaker, B. W.★, Private. Died September 21, 1862, at Iuka, Miss.

Whetstone, E. A., Private. Killed August 10, 1861, at Oak Hills, Missouri.

Williams, Alexander★, Private. Died July 7, 1863, at Vicksburg, Miss.

Webb, J. D., Private. Discharged June 30, 1861, Fort Smith, Ark.

Webb, T., Private. Discharged June 30, 1861, Fort Smith, Ark.

Wright, T. J., Private. Discharged April 18, 1862, Little Rock, Arkansas.

Wilkinson, Joe, Private. Discharged July 10, 1862, Tupelo, Miss.

Williams, G. B., Private. Discharged July 16, 1862, Tupelo, Miss.

Wadkins, James, Private. Discharged July 16, 1862, Tupelo, Miss.

Washburn , W. M., Private.

Yon, Joseph, Private. Died August, 1861, Maysville, Ark.

★Died of wounds.

Zimmerle, R., Private. Discharged July 10, 1862, Tupelo, Miss.

Caldwell, W. R., Private. Remained east† of Mississippi River, after fall of Vicksburg.

Edmonson, J. N., Private. Remained east of Mississippi River after fall of Vicksburg.

Edmonson, M., Private. Remained east of Mississippi River after fall of Vicksburg.

Finn, Terrence, Private. Remained east of Mississippi River after fall of Vicksburg.

Harrison, A. C., Private. Remained east of Mississippi River after fall of Vicksburg.

Kelley, Henry, Private. Remained east of Mississippi River after fall of Vicksburg.

Meyer, A., Private. Remained east of Mississippi River after fall of Vicksburg.

Sheffield, W. B., Private. Remained east of Mississippi River after fall of Vicksburg.

Sullivan, M. B., Private. Remained east of Mississippi River after fall of Vicksburg.

Stirces, S. H., Private. Remained east of Mississippi River after fall of Vicksburg.

Shumaker, W. V., Private. Remained east of Mississippi River after fall of Vicksburg.

Smith, James M., Private. Remained east of Mississippi River after fall of Vicksburg.

Thompson, J. A., Private. Remained east of Mississippi River after fall of Vicksburg.

Wilcox, J. J., Private. Remained east of Mississippi River after fall of Vicksburg.

Worley, S. N., Private. Remained east of Mississippi River after fall of Vicksburg.

Walker, N. E., Private. Remained east of Mississippi River after fall of Vicksburg.

All of the above were enlisted into the State Service at New Orleans, La., May 5th, 1861, and transferred to the Confederate States Service at New Orleans, May 17th, 1861.

RECRUITS

Alford, G. W. Enlisted February 10, 1863. Died at Ft. Delaware, December, 1863.

Brice, W. H.   "   July 30, 1861. Killed, Vicksburg, June 19, 1863.

Bosworth, G. P. "   December 5, 1864.

Biddle, H.   "   October 15, 1864.

Bearden, B. C.,   "   "   "   "

Elton, E. W.   "   August 15, 1863.

Emswiler, G. E. "   March 17, 1862.

Evans, G. R.   "   May 5, 1862. Discharged, Corinth, Oct. 17, 1862.

Fryor, H. C.   "   February, 1863. Lost a leg at Vicksburg.

Fluelen, J. G.   "   September 21, 1864.

Gray, T. T.   "   March 17th, 1862.

---

†These men, having homes or relatives east of the Mississippi River, after the capitulation of Vicksburg remained in that department, and were attached to the 21st or 22d La. Infantry.

Graves, P. S.   Enlisted November 26, 1864.

Grant, P.   "   April 10, 1863.

Howell, F. M.   "   July 30, 1861. Killed at Vicksburg, June 24, 1863.

Higginbotham, D. F. "   March 17, 1862.

Hammonde, E. H.   "   October, 1864.

Johnson, T. H.   "   February 10, 1863.

Mason, J. M.,   "   March 25, 1863. Accidentally killed September 24, 1863,
    at Home.

McFee, S. O.   Enlisted July 30, 1861. Killed at Vicksburg, June 16, 1863.

Maxwell, J. D.,   "   June 6, 1861.

Maxwell, J. N.   "   October 6, 1861.

McGuire, J. F.   "   January 5, 1865.

Kaff, J. B.   "   February 10, 1863. Killed at Vicksburg, June 25, 1863.

Risor, John.   "   May 5, 1862. Died at Grenada, December 24, 1862.

Sharp, A. F.   "   ———— 5, 1864.

Saunders, S. N.   "   February 10, 1863.

Sutton, Jos.   "   October 7, 1864.

Smith, J. W.   "   December 19, 1864.

Totle, Jacob.   "   February 10, 1863.

Wright, W. W.   "   "   "   "

White, G. B.   "   "   "   "   Died at Snyder's Bluff, June 26, 1863.

W. N. Washburn was elected Second Junior Lieutenant some time in October, 1861, while on the March for Carthage, Mo. This election was ordered to fill the vacancy occasioned by promotion, after the death of Captain Henson. At the time of the reorganization he was a prisoner, having been captured at the battle of Elk Horn, and consequently was not re-elected. After the death of Lieut. Beauchamp, Lieut. Renwick filled the vacancy, and Washburn was elected Second Junior Lieutenant.

ROLL OF COMPANY C, WINN RIFLES

Pierson, D., Captain. Wounded at Iuka, Sept. 19, 1862; wounded at Vicksburg. Promoted to Lieutenant-Colonel.

Emanuel, Asa, 1st Lieutenant. Re-elected May 8th, 1862.

Lurry, W. C., 2d Lieutenant.

Strather, W., 2d Lieutenant. Wounded August 10, 1861, at Oak Hills.

Middlebrook, N. M., 1st Sergeant. Wounded at Oak Hills, August 10, 1861; wounded at Vicksburg. Elected Captain May 8th, 1862.

McCain, A. W., 2d Sergeant. Elected 2d Lieutenant May 8, 1862. Killed at Iuka, September 19, 1862.

Alford, W. H., 3d Sergeant. Killed at Elk Horn, March 7, 1862.

Copeland, J., 4th Sergeant.

McCain, J. M., 1st Corporal. Wounded at Oak Hills, August 10, 1861.

W. T. Fagan, 2d Corporal. Elected 2d Lieutenant, May 8, 1862. Wounded at Vicksburg.

C. F. M. Befer, 3d Corporal.

J. Sholurs. Died August 3, 1861.

Benson, H., Private.

Brock, J., Private.

Bird, L. G., Private.

Bulger, W., Private. Died July, 1861, at Camp McCulloch, Ark.

Barnes, J. G., Private.

Bonnet, J. R., Private.

Bonnet, H., Private. Died August, 1861.

Brantley, E. C., Private.

Brantley, G. D., Private.

Belden, H. C., Private.

Black, B. F., Private.

Black, H., Private.

Benson, F., Private.

Collens, H., Private.

Collum, W., Private. Died June, 1861, at Fort Smith.

Carson, W. J., Private. Wounded at Vicksburg.

Curry, G., Private.

Cole, R. E., Private. Wounded at Vicksburg.

Cole, H., Private.

Carter, G. B., Private. Wounded at Vicksburg.

Canady, O. F., Private.

Carter, J., Private.

Crew, H. M., Private. Killed at Iuka, Sept. 19, 1862.

Crew, J., Private. Died August 1861.

Cockerham, H., Private. Killed at Oak Hills, August 10, 1861.

Campbell, R., Private.

Cockerham, W., Private.

Cockerham, B., Private. Died June 1861, at Fort Smith, Ark.

Calhoun, I. G., Private.

Cunningham, H. H., Private.

Davison, W. F., Private. Died May, 1862, at Corinth, Miss.

Dun, Geo. F., Private. Died June, 1861, at Fort Smith, Ark.

Evans, J. M., Private.

Evans, W., Private. Wounded at Vicksburg.

Furgerson, W. J., Private.

Huthnance, H., Private. Wounded at Corinth, October 3, 1862.

Houston, R. K., Private. Wounded at Vicksburg.

Hardee, B., Private.

Hoduett, G. W., Private.

Hallamon, W. A., Private. Killed at Vicksburg.

Hicks, I. N., Private. Appointed 4th Corporal, September 30th, 1861.

Howell, W. F., Private.

Harlen, ———, Private.

Holland, J. T., Private.

Halston, M. R., Private.

Inabinett, A. J., Private.

Jones, Jas. W., Private. Wounded at Vicksburg.

Kelly, D., Private.

Lockheart, A., Private.

Livingston, R. L., Private.

Leopard, F. M., Private.

Lovett, W., Private.

Little, G. B. N., Private.

Muirhead, H. C., Private.

Muirhead, Wm., Private. Wounded at Iuka, September 19, 1862.

Martin, E. P., Private.

McBride, J. M., Private. Wounded at Oak Hills, August 10, 1861; wounded at Vicksburg.

McDonald, G. N., Private.

Mooney, E. W., Private.

McCormick, J. N., Private.

Moody, N., Private. Wounded at Vicksburg.

Means, B. H., Private.

Mathis, John, Private. Wounded at Vicksburg.

Middlebrook, Wm., Private. Elected 2d Junior Lieutenant at Snyder's Mills, Miss., 1863.

Nickolson, J., Private.

Newman, A. H., Private. Taken prisoner at Corinth, October 3, 1862.

Nox, Geo., Private.

Oglesby, J., Private.

Oglesby, M., Private.

Phillpot, B. F., Private. Killed at Iuka, September 19, 1862.

Phillpot, G. W., Private. Died at Mt. Vernon, Mo.

Pierson, John H., Private.

Pierson, Jas., Private.

Pearre, A. J., Private. Wounded at Iuka, September 19, 1862; wounded at Corinth, Miss., October 4, 1862.

Powers, H. C., Private.

Ritch, Wm., Private. Wounded at Vicksburg.

Rudd, J. D., Private. Wounded at Vicksburg.

Smith, W. R., Private. Killed at Vicksburg, Miss.

Smith, Jas., Private.

Spillman, G. C., Private. Wounded at Vicksburg.

Thompson, V. B., Private.

Teagle, John, Private. Died July, 1861, at Fort Smith, Ark.

Teddlie, T. J., Private. Killed at Vicksburg, Miss.

Teddlie, W. J., Private. Wounded at Vicksburg.

Tannyhill, D. M., Private.

Tannyhill, W., Private.

Williams, Thos., Private. Wounded at Vicksburg.

Webb, J. D., Private.

Webb, J. C., Private.

Winner, M., Private.

Wilson, J., Private.

Warner, J. D., Private. Wounded at Oak Hills, August 10, 1861.

ROLL OF CO. "D,"
PELICAN RANGERS, NO. 2

Blair, J. D., Captain. Resigned, 1861.

Russell, S. D., 1st Lieutenant. Elected Major, May 8, 1862. Promoted to Colonel. Wounded at Corinth and Vicksburg.

Russell, W. E., 2d Lieutenant. Elected Captain, May 8, 1862. Wounded at Vicksburg.

Hyams, S. M., Jr., 2d Lieutenant. Elected Lieutenant-Colonel of Cavalry Regiment.

Morse, B. P., First Sergeant. Elected 2d Lieutenant, May 8, 1862. Wounded at Corinth.

Walmsley, H. B., 2d Sergeant.

Airey, F. W., 3d Sergeant. Appointed Sergeant-Major. Elected Captain of Louisiana Regiment. Afterwards A. A. G., Hay's Staff.

Peters, J. H., 4th Sergeant.

Charleville, J., 1st Corporal. Wounded at Iuka, September 19, 1862.

Grove, D., 2d Corporal. Wounded at Elk Horn, March 7, 1862.

De Russey, W. A., 3d Corporal.

Peters, J. H., 4th Corporal.

Blackstone, M. P., Private.

Bowling, W. T.,   "

Barksdale, A. H.,   "

Badt, W.,   "   Wounded at Vicksburg.

Bastick, W. R.,   "

Bassett, M. C.,   "

Carrell, J. N.,   "

Chambers, J.,   "

Cohn, M.,   "

Collins, W. M.,   "

Cobb, T.,   "   Killed at Vicksburg.

Creighton, W. B.,   "

Caradine, I.,   "   Wounded at Elk Horn, March 7, 1862.

Duke, H. J.,   "

Dodson, W. W.,   "

Davenport, J. A.,   "

Davis, W. P.,   "

Davis, B.,   "   Wounded at Oak Hills, Aug. 10, 1861.

Daly, T.,   "   "   " Iuka, Sept. 19, 1862.

Evans, D. N.,   "

Ely, V.,   "

Edmonson, H. V. C., "   Killed at Vicksburg.

Fonteneau, G.,   "   Wounded at Vicksburg.

Fox, G. W.,   "

Grillett, S.,   "   Wounded at Vicksburg.

Goodwin, J.,   "

Gandy, W. W.,   "   Killed at Vicksburg.

Gallion, E.,   "

Hilburn, W. H.,   "

Hammet, R. C.,   "   Killed at Vicksburg.

Ivy, W. W.,   "   Wounded at Iuka.

Jackson, C. H.,   "

Kimball, A. J.,   "

Hutchinski, W.,   "

Levasseur, E. B., Private.

Leplant, O.,   "   Died of wounds at Iuka, Sept. 19, 1862.

Leplant, A.,   "

Masley, J. M.,   "

Masson, E.,   "

Mattingly, G.,   "

McCaskey, T. H.,   "   Wounded at Iuka, Sept. 19, 1862.

McDowell, L. B.,   "

Matthews, T. J.,   "

McCarty, J.,   "

McDaniel, J. A.,   "   Wounded at Vicksburg.

McDaniel, H.,   "

McKerley, J.,   "

McMahon, J.,   "

Moore, P. S.,   "

Merritt, J.,   "   Wounded at Corinth, Miss., Oct. 3, 1862, and at
                                 Vicksburg, Miss.

O'Brien, M.,   "

Oliver, W.,   "

Powell, C.,   "

Read, J. L.,   "

Rachal, A.,   "

Ragon, P. H.,   "

Spragg, W.,   "

Shiff, J.,   "

Springer, F. H.,   "   Wounded at Elk Horn, March 7, 1862.

Trichel, G. L.,   "   Elected 1st Lieutenant, May 8, 1862. Wounded at Iuka,
                                 Sept., 19, 1862.

Trichel, E.,   "

Thomasie, O.,   "

Williamson, J.,   "   Died from wounds, Oak Hills, Aug. 10, 1861.

Wheitfield, G. W.,   "

Wolf, J.,   "

Waddell, H. J.,   "

Yost, J. B.,   "

ROLL OF CO. "E," MOREHOUSE FENCIBLES

James F. Harris, Captain.

C. P. Brigham, 1st Lieutenant.

    2d Lieutenant.

    3d Lieutenant.

Dannals, G. W., 1st Sergeant.

    2d Sergeant.

Brashear, C. H., 3d Sergeant. Elected Captain May 8, 1862.

Tucker, J. M., 4th Sergeant.

McGuire, G. W., 5th Sergeant.

Myers, J. P., 1st Corporal. Wounded September 19, 1862, Iuka and Vicksburg.

    2d Corporal.

Tomlinson, M. A., 3d Corporal.

    4th Corporal.

Anderson, H. D. B.

Ballard, D. C. Prisoner, September 19, 1862, Iuka.

Barton, J. R. Killed, Iuka, September 19, 1862.

Bradley, John.

Brice, W. T. Killed at Oak Hills, Aug. 10, 1861.

Bastic, A. G.

Brigham, T. Prisoner, September 19, 1862, Iuka.

Carter, J. J.

Carter, C. J.

Causey, W. S.

Crane, S. Killed at Vicksburg.

Culpepper, L. B.

Dawson, H. D.

Downey, T. D. Wounded at Vicksburg.

Dudley, G. W.

Esom, ———. Wounded at Vicksburg.

Gwinn, D. A. Killed at Vicksburg.

Faulkenburg, W. W. U.

Grubbs, John.

Henderson, Wm. Prisoner, September 19, 1862, Iuka.

Haldeness, James.

Hughes, H. S.

Halt, R. C. Wounded, Iuka, Sept. 19, 1862, and Vicksburg. Elected 2d Lieutenant, May 8, 1862.

Hurd.

Faw, W. H. Wounded, Aug. 10, 1861, Oak Hills.

Floyd, S. J.

Floyd, A. J.

Halt, H. H. Wounded at Oak Hills.

Jones, John.

Katon, T.

Kirkwood, J. H.

Lanier, R. H.

McIntire, J. A.

McDonough, J.

McGowen, A.

Murphy, C. C.

Miller, G. O.

Miller, D. L. Killed, Aug. 10, 1861, Oak Hills.

Massey, M. H.

Masterson, ———. Wounded, Sept. 19, 1862. Killed at Vicksburg.

Norwood, B. Killed, September 19, 1862, Iuka.

Miller, G. Wounded at Vicksburg.

Pierson, P. Wounded, September 19, 1862, Iuka.

Powell, J. S.

Powell, A. J. Wounded at Vicksburg.

Powers, J. W.

Quinn, R. L. Wounded at Vicksburg.

Riley, J.

Reardon, D.

Smith, E. W.

Stembridge, J. E.

Sullivan, T.

Thomas, A. J. Elected 2d Lieutenant March, 1863, Snyder Mills.

Tomlinson, J. E.

Tucker, W. C.

Turpin, J. G. Elected 2d Lieutenant May 8, 1862.

Wallace, T. H.

Woodbury, J. W. Killed, August 10, 1861, Oak Hills.

Zeagler, W. B.

ROLL OF CO. "F," SHREVEPORT RANGERS

J. B. Gilmore, Captain. Elected Lieutenant-Colonel May 8, 1862. Promoted Colonel. Wounded September 19, 1862, Iuka. Resigned.

W. A. Lacy, 1st Lieutenant. Resigned October 8, 1861. Disability.

O. J. Wells, 2d Lieutenant. Promoted 1st Lieutenant, October 8, 1861.

A. W. Jewell, 2d Junior Lieutenant. Promoted 2d Lieutenant, October 8, 1861.

Kinney, Wm., 1st Sergeant. Elected Captain May 8, 1861.

Davis, B., 2d Sergeant. Wounded August 10, 1861, Oak Hills, and Discharged October 6, 1861. Disability.

Hughes, W. W., 3d Sergeant. Transferred to McCulloch's Body Guard.

Dundon, L. M., 1st Corporal. Elected 2d Junior Lieutenant October 12, 1861. 1st Lieutenant May 8, 1861.

Jus, J. F., 2d Corporal. Wounded September 19, 1862, Iuka, and twice at Vicksburg.

Horne, J., 3d Corporal. Elected 2d Junior Lieutenant May 8, 1862. Died of wounds, Vicksburg.

Hicox, H., 4th Corporal. Died August 18, 1861, of wounds, Oak Hills, August 10, 1861.

Anderson, J. H., Private. Discharged October 9, 1861. Disability.

Attaway, E. M., Private. Mortally wounded Oak Hills, August 10, 1861.

Attaway, J. B., Private. Died June 10, 1861. Fort Smith, Ark.

Allen, J., Private. Killed August 10, 1861. Oak Hills, Mo.

Allen, S., Private. Discharged January 15, 1862. Camp Benjamin, Ark.

Brosi, J., Private. Wounded, Vicksburg.

Basser, J. H., Private. Wounded Oak Hills, August 10, 1861.

Brownwell, J. S., Private. Killed August 10, 1861, Oak Hills.

Breening, R., Private. Wounded at Vicksburg.

Bird, E., Private. Discharged.

Brown, J. S., Private. Killed August 10, 1861, at Oak Hills.

Bickham, T. C., Private. Wounded August 10, 1861, Oak Hills. Discharged.

Bell, W. C., Private. Discharged July 25, 1861, at Camp Jackson. Disability.

Charlton, J., Private.

Clark, M. O., Killed September 19, 1862, at Iuka.

Clark, J. O., Private. Elected 2d Senior Lieutenant May 8, 1861. Wounded at Vicksburg.

Cole, R. F., Private. Wounded at Vicksburg.

Collins, J., Private.

Cartwright, D., Private. Discharged July 19, 1862, Conscript Act.

Coon, J., Private. Died August 15, 1861, from wounds at Oak HIlls.

Craig, J., Private. Taken prisoner, never heard from.

Carroll, E. R., Private.

Chastein, W. J., Private. Died September 3, 1861. Mount Vernon, Mo.

Chastein, J., Private. Discharged.

Duvall, D. S., Private. Discharged July 19, 1862, Conscript Act.

Dill, T. N., Private. Wounded at Vicksburg.

Dodez, D. G., Private.

Davis, F. A., Private. Wounded August 10, 1861, at Oak Hills and Vicksburg.

Donahoe, J., Private. Died August 16, 1861, wounds at Oak Hills.

Dick, R., Private. Captured at Chickamauga and kept in prison.

Dwire, P., Private. Discharged July 19, 1862, Conscript Act.

Dougherty, J. P., Private. Died August 18, 1861, at Springfield, Mo.

Efner, G. M., Private. Wounded at Vicksburg.

Gray, A. Mc., Private. Discharged July 19, 1862, Conscript Act.

Gallagher, T., Private. Discharged July 19, 1862, Conscript Act.

Hudson, W. T., Private. Wounded at Vicksburg.

Howard, J., Private. Killed August 5, 1861, at Camp Stephens, Arkansas.

Hicox, J. W., Private. Wounded August 10, 1861, at Oak Hills.

Hudson, T. S., Private. Wounded September 19, 1862, at Iuka.

Jinks, J. D., Private.

Jones, J. W., Private. Died of wounds, Corinth, October 3, 1862.

Jefferson, J. F., Private.

Kidd, J., Private. Discharged July 19, 1862, Conscript Act.

Kelly, D., Private. Discharged July 19, 1862, Conscript Act.

Kimball, J., Private.

Larmier, J., Private. Discharged, disabiliity.

Lynch, M., Private. Discharged July 19, 1862, Conscript Act.

Lawson, M., Private. Discharged July 19, 1862, Conscript Act.

Lawson, Wm., Private. Discharged October 6, 1861, Conscript Act.

Liles, H. T., Private.

McGintry, J., Private.

Miller, J. J., Private.

Miller, M. F., Private.

McGray, A., Private.

Marr, T., Private

Mayes, J. W., Private.

Manning, S. J., Private. Wounded August 10, 1861, at Oak Hills.

Manning, G. W., Private.

Newland, C. W., Private. Wounded September 19, 1862, at Iuka.

Nicholas, A., Private.

Percell, W. H., Private.

Pennery, P. L., Private. Wounded at Vicksburg.

Patterson, J. P., Private.

Peisker, F., Private.

Pierce, F., Private. Discharged July 19, 1862, Conscript Act.

Poland, T., Private. Discharged January 8, 1862. Disability.

Parker, R., Private. Discharged July 19, 1862, Conscript Act.

Rosser, J. H., Private. Transferred.

Roberts, T. M., Private. Killed at Vicksburg.

Ruff, G. V., Private. Discharged October 6, 1861. Disability.

Reasoner, W. B., Private.

Singer, L. J., Private. Kiled at Vicksburg.

Simpson, B. L., Private. Died August 15, 1861, from wounds at Oak Hills.

Shelton, W. A., Private. Captured at Oak Hills.

Smith, T. D., Private. Died on steamer May 25, 1861. Buried at Napoleon, Ark.

Smith, J., Private.

Scanlan, J. S., Corporal. Wounded at Vicksburg.

Sheridan, W., Private. Discharged July 19, 1862, Conscript Act.

Sheridan, P., Private. Wounded at Vicksburg.

Sheffield, G. F., Private. Died.

Shows, J. M., Private. Discharged September 25, 1861.

Sewell, J. H., Private.

Scruggs, R., Private. Discharged July 25, 1861. Disability.

Thompson, J. Q., Private. Discharged July 19, 1862. Conscript Act.

Thomas, W. H. C., Private. Discharged.

Ward, R. A., Private.

Weaver, W., Private. Discharged July 19, 1862, Conscript Act.

Wilson, J., Private. Discharged July 19, 1862, Conscript Act, rejoined.

Walls, C., Private. Discharged July 19, 1862, Conscript Act.

White, T. J., Private. Discharged July 19, 1862, Conscript Act.

White, J. A., Private. Discharged July 19, 1862, Conscript Act.

Young, J., Private. Discharged.

ROLL OF COMPANY "G,"
PELICAN RANGERS, NO. 1

W. W. Breazeale, Captain. Resigned September 24, 1861.

W. O. Breazele, 1st Lieutenant. Resigned September 24, 1861.

G. W. Halloway, 2d Lieutenant. Resigned October 13, 1861.

L. Caspari, 2d Junior Lieutenant. Promoted 1st Lieutenant October 12, 1861; Captain February 18, 1862.

W. B. Butler, 1st Sergeant. Elected Captain May 8, 1862.

P. L. Prudhomme, 2d Sergeant. Elected 2d Lieutenant May 8, 1862.

J. C. Trichel, 3d Sergeant. Promoted 2d Sergeant May 15, 1862.

J. A. Derbonne, 4th Sergeant. Promoted 1st Sergeant May 15, 1862.

F. F. Chaler, 5th Sergeant. Died at Maysville, Ark., September 14, 1861.

R. W. McConel, 1st Corporal. Discharged July 16, 1862.

H. L. Tauzin, 2d Corporal. Discharged September 6, 1861.

T. W. Abbington, 3d Corporal. Appointed Color Guard September 20, 1861.

F. W. Sanchez, 4th Corporal. Promoted 3d Corporal November 1, 1861; 2d Corporal May 15, 1862.

Aleman, R., Private.

Bassier, P. Private. Elected 3d Lieutenant May 8, 1862.

Bassier, Placide, Private. Killed at Oak Hills, August 10, 1861.

Bassier, P. E., Private. Discharged July 25, 1862.

Breazeale, B. B., Private. Appointed 5th Sergeant May 15, 1862.

Barmes, M., Private. Discharged July 15, 1862.

Bordinave, V., Private. Died at Castillian Springs, October 3, 1862.

Behrman, Private. Joined March 3, 1862; captured at Iuka.

Bernes, F., Private. Taken prisoner at Elk Horn.

Charleville, J., Private. Appointed 3d Sergeant May 15, 1862.

Charleville, W. A., Private.

Castey, C. D., Private.

Craft, S. E., Private. Discharged July 16, 1862.

Cannon, D., Private. Prisoner at Elk Horn, March 7, 1862.

Cloutier, F., Private.

Charles, L., Private. Discharged December 9, 1861.

Despallier, B. P., Private.

Dell, L., Private. Discharged December 3, 1864.

Dew, L., Private. Taken prisoner at Elk Horn, July 16, 1862.

Dickens, A., Private. Joined March 3, 1862; captured at Iuka.

DeBaillion, B., Private. Discharged October 10, 1861.

Dozier, C., H.,   "   "   "   10,   "

Eshworth, J. L.,   "   "   "   10,   "

Escabeda, M., Private.

Espy, K., Private. Appointed Assistant Surgeon May 11, 1861.

Flores, L., Private.

Garcia, A., Private.

Gainnie, F., Private. Elected 3d Lieutenant October 12, 1861; 1st Lieutenant May 8, 1862.

Guimchamp, J., Private. Joined March 3, 1862.

Guimchamp, E.,   "   "   "   3,   "   Captured at Iuka.

Guiton, J.,   "   "   "   3,   "

Hyams, J. P.,   "

Haller, P.,   "

Haller, T.,   "

Hynes, S., Private. Discharged October 6, 1861.

Hughes, H., Private.   "   "   10,   "

Hernandez, S., Private.

Hitzman, J., Private. Taken prisoner at Elk Horn, March 7, 1862.

Hoffman, J. C., Private. Discharged October 6, 1861.

Hertzel, Samuel, Private. Joined March 3, 1861.

Hartman, M. S., Private.   "   "   3,   "

Jones, A., Private. Discharged July 16, 1862.

Johnson, J., Private. Discharged June 13, 1861.

Keyser, J. C. O., Private. Appointed 1st Corporal August 10, 1861.

Kyle, Jas., Private. Elected 3d Lieutenant December 28, 1861. Discharged May 24, 1862.

Lemoine, T., Private. Appointed 4th Corporal May 15, 1862.

Lowe, A., Private.

Lyons, H. L., Private.

Moss, Jas. W., Private. Elected 2d Lieutenant October 12, 1861. Promoted 1st Lieutenant December 28, 1861.

McKenna, H., Private.

McDaniel, F., Private.

Miller, H., Private.

Murphy, C. V., Private. Appointed 3d Corporal May 15, 1862.

Matthews, J. H., Private. Discharged July 16, 1862.

Nagle, J., Private. Captured at Iuka.

Norris, J. C., Private. Appointed 1st Corporal May 15, 1862.

Nores, J., Private. Appointed 4th Sergeant October 1, 1862.

Ourdin, F., Private. Joined March 3, 1862.

Prudhomme, J. A., Private. Wounded at Elk Horn, March 7, 1862. Discharged April 17, 1862.

Phillips, Ed., Private. Taken prisoner at Elk Horn, March 7, 1862.

Prue, F., Private.

Pine, F., Private.

Rachal, P., Private. Discharged July 16, 1862.

Rachal, J. B. D., Private.

Rachal, T., Private. Discharged November 8, 1861.

Rowe, A. H., Private. Wounded at Elk Horn, March 7, 1862. Wounded April 17, 1862.

Rivera, M., Private.

Richeson, R. A., Private. Discharged July 16, 1862.

Sasser, J. L., Private.

Shea, J., Private. Discharged July 16, 1862.

Schroeder, C. F. H., Private. Killed at Elk Horn, March 7, 1862.

Shaw, M. J., Private. Wounded at Elk Horn, March 7, 1862.

Sing. A. J., Private. Discharged January 13, 1862.

Smith, Thos., Private. Wounded at Elk Horn, March 7, 1862.

Tool, M., Private. Discharged November 28, 1861.

Tauzin, John M., Private. Killed September 19, 1862, at Iuka.

Wilson, P. Private. Discharged July 16, 1862.

Wrinkle, A. D., Private.

Warner, B. F., Private. Killed at Elk Horn, March 7, 1862.

Wright, John, Private.

ROLL OF CO. "H," MONTICELLO RIFLES

J. S. Richards, Captain. Re-elected May 8, 1862. Promoted Major.

W. D. Hardeman, 1st Lieutenant. Promoted Captain and A. Q. M., A. A. G., General Hebert's Staff.

A. A. Hedrick, 2d Lieutenant. Promoted 1st Lieutenant, May 8, 1862.

W. H. Corbin, 2d Lieutenant. Discharged.

H. Maynadier, 1st Sergeant. Discharged.

A. W. Currie, 2d Sergeant. Promoted Captain. Elected 2d Lieutenant, May 8, 1862.

J. W. Alexander, 3d Sergeant. Killed at Floyd, La., by Federals.

Dr. J. Chambless, 4th Sergeant. Appointed Surgeon, 1861.

T. G. Walcott, 1st Corporal. Discharged.

Dr. J. S. Herring, 2d Corporal. Discharged.

W. A. Page, 3d Corporal. Discharged. Rejoined.

C. E. Guy, 4th Corporal.

Anthony, S. L.

Atkins, J. M. Discharged, 1861.

Beard, W. A. 1st Sergeant. Killed, March 7, 1862, Elk Horn.

Beverly, J. J. Discharged, 1862, Fayetteville, Ark.

Bickman, J. D. Killed, September 19, 1862, Iuka.

Bonner, W. F. Discharged.

Bowles, J. E. Died, 1861, Fort Smith, Ark.

Bradley, W. C.

Briggs, H. D. Appointed 1st Sergeant, 1862.

Bruton, B. Discharged. Killed at Floyd, La.

Bullard, T. Discharged.

Byrd, H.

Byrd, J. Killed, Vicksburg.

Burns, W., Corporal. Killed, Vicksburg.

Cathron, J.

Crawford, F. A.

Canady, W. J.

Collins, G. Discharged. Killed by Federals.

Collinsky, P. Discharged.

Corbin, W. P. Killed, March 7, 1862, Elk Horn, Ark.

Corbin, J. J. Discharged. Afterward Lieutenant.

Davis, J.

Dawson, M. H.

De France, A.

Dempsey, ———. Died.

Dorsey, W. Died at Hospital, Quitman, Ala.

Drake, J. B. Discharged.

Eddins, L. S.

Ewing, A. G. Captain and A. C. S., 3d Louisiana Cavalry.

Fitch, W. P. Discharged.

Fitch, N. F. Discharged.

Green, W.

Gardner, T. B.

Guy, C. E.

Hedrick, J. E. C. Discharged.

Hedrick, P. P.

Hedrick, W. A.

Hargrove, W. J.

Hargrove, J. F. Wounded, Vicksburg.

Hash, B. F. Died.

Holbrook, ———. Discharged.

Holden, J. J. Discharged.

Horton, W. C. Killed.

Horton, H. T.

Holland, J. B.

Howard, J. Discharged, July 19, 1862, Conscript Act.

Humphreys, J. H.

Insley, T.

Irwin, E.

Irwin, J. J.

James, S. Died, June, 1861, Fort Smith, Ark.

Jeeter, C. S. Killed accidentally, 1863, Snyder's Bluff.

Jones, M. A. J. Discharged.

Keegan, Geo.

Kelly, J. Discharged, wounded.

Keeff, M. Discharged, 1862.

Knight, B. Died, 1862, Tupelo, Miss.

Landfair, J. L.

Leggett, E. H.

Mangum, W. S. Discharged.

Martin, J. A. Killed, Vicksburg.

Martin, T. D.

Murphy, M.

McCarty, F. B.

McCowen, J. Wounded, Vicksburg.

McDonald, J. Killed, September 19, 1862, Iuka.

McDonald, R.

McGrew, S. J. Killed at Floyd, La., by Federals.

NcNiel, J. Elected 1st Lieutenant.

McFadden, E.

Morrison, J.

Morehead, N.

Nash, J. R. Appointed 2d Sergeant.

Nolan, W. P. Discharged.

Only, J. T. Killed, March 7, 1862, Elk Horn.

Perry, J. E.   "   "   "

Perry, J. R.

Pope, W. P. Discharged.

Richardson, W. W. Discharged.

Richardson, L., Dr. Discharged.

Ravan, J. Discharged.

Ray, J. E. Discharged.

Reese, J. C. Killed, Vicksburg.

Reese, S. L.

Rollins, J. Discharged.

Rollins, R. Discharged.

Roland, J. F.

Scott, R. C. Transferred to McCulloch's escort, 1861.

Scott, H. L.

Sharplin, W. P. Killed, March 7, 1862, Elk Horn.

Smith, J. M.

Sherdan, B. F. Discharged.

Sherdan, J. M. Discharged.

Singleton, S. S. Killed, March 7, 1862, Elk Horn.

Sims, L. P.

Smithe, J. M. Killed, March 7, 1862, Elk Horn.

Smithe, N. B. Discharged.

Spurlock, J. L. Discharged.

Stuart, J. M. Elected 2d Lieutenant, May 8, 1862. Wounded at Vicksburg.

Tomlin, M. H. Killed on "Big Black," Miss.

Tompkins, J. B.

Wade, S.

Weatherly, W. W. Died.

Whatley, J. W.

Wilson, D. Discharged.

Veale, J. Killed, Vicksburg.

Young, S. Discharged.

Young, James. Died, 1861, Fort Smith, Ark.

Young, John.

ROLL OF CO. "I," CALDWELL GUARDS

W. L. Gunnels, Captain.

Evans, T. J., 1st Lieutenant.

Fluitt, S. B., 2d Lieutenant.

Humble, T. C., 2d Jr. Lieutenant. Wounded at Oak Hills. Elected Major 31st Louisiana, and killed at first siege of Vicksburg.

Stringer, J. J., 1st Sergeant.

Brinton, J. A., 2d Sergeant.

Guffy, H. M., 3d Sergeant.

Stutson, W. S., 4th Sergeant.

Broadway, T. J., 5th Sergeant. Taken prisoner at Elk Horn, March 7, 1862.

Blythe, T. J., 1st Corporal.

Bridger, J. C., 2d Corporal.

McClary, W. D., 3d Corporal.

Weatherford, 4th Corporal.

Brian, B. F., Private.

Breard, C. A.

Brooks, J.

Beale, W. H. Taken prisoner at Elk Horn. Died of wounds at Iuka, September 19, 1862.

Bliss, D. W. Taken prisoner at Elk Horn.

Banks, A. J. Wounded at Elk Horn, March 7, 1862.

Barnett, W. T.

Chandler, W. S. Discharged.

Crane, P. H. Discharged.

Cottingham, W. E.

Cottingham, J. R. Elected 2d Lieutenant, May 8, 1862. Wounded and taken prisoner at Snyder's Bluff, April, 1863.

Cartwright, M. P. Wounded at Vicksburg.

Cantelere, F. E. Taken prisoner at Elk Horn. Wounded at Iuka, September 19, 1862.

Cain, W. L.

Cain, L. L. Wounded at Iuka, September 19, 1862.

Cain, F. F. Taken prisoner at Elk Horn, March 7, 1862. Wounded at Iuka, September 19, 1862.

Craddock, J. D.

Dunn, D. F.

Dunn, T. J. Taken prisoner at Elk Horn. Killed at Vicksburg.

Downes, J. E.

Dowd, W. Taken prisoner at Iuka, September 19, 1862.

Douglas, E. M. Wounded at Corinth. Killed at Vicksburg.

Fluett, J. P.

Fluett, J. S. Discharged.

Faulks, W. C.

Fogle, W.

Fegart, E. W.

Freeman, D. Wounded at Elk Horn, March 7, 1862.

Ferrand, C. A. Taken prisoner at Elk Horn.

Flowers, J. M. Taken prisoner at Iuka, September 19, 1862.

Guffey, W. J.

Gregory, W. J. Taken prisoner at Elk Horn.

Girod, E. Taken prisoner at Elk Horn, and wounded at Corinth, October 3, 1862.
    Wounded at Vicksburg.

Gray, J. R. Wounded at Iuka, September 19, 1862, and Vicksburg.

Gray, ————.

Girod, F. Wounded at Vicksburg.

Greene, R. J.

Hines, J. Wounded at Vicksburg, and at Iuka.

Hough, H. C. Wounded at Vicksburg.

Howell, S. J. Killed at Iuka, September 19, 1862.

Hamilton, F. M.

Hargrove, W. P.

Heigdon, D.

Hough, T. J.

Haley, J. E.

Hanna, J. E.

Humble, G. W. Wounded at Vicksburg.

Hass, H.

Johnson, J. E. Elected Captain, May 8, 1862. Wounded at Iuka, September 19, 1862,
    and Vicksburg, July 1, 1863. Died from wounds.

Johnson, J. B. Wounded at Iuka, September 19, 1862.

Johnson, H. L.

Jenkins, W. Killed at Elk Horn, March 7, 1862.

Jones, J.

Killcrease, H.

Kelly, A. Killed at Vicksburg.

Kelly, J. F. Prisoner at Elk Horn.

Levy, L. Wounded at Oak Hills, August 10, 1861.

Landerneau, J.

Lilly, W. E.

Lawson, W. P. Wounded at Elk Horn, March 7, 1862. Killed at Vicksburg.

Landerneau, A.

Mason, S. W.

Mason, W. H. Died, July 30, 1861.

Mason, D. F. Taken prisoner at Elk Horn.

McCormack, J. O. Wounded at Iuka, September 19, 1862. Wounded at Vicksburg.

McFarland, W. L.

McFarland, G. T. Wounded at Vicksburg.

McFadden, J. M.

Moss, W. A.

March, D. Taken prisoner at Corinth, October 3, 1862.

Mayfield, J. W.

Michell, J. R.

Miller, H. J. Died July 17, 1861.

Moffit, S. J., Private. Wounded at Corinth, October 3, 1862.

Moffitt, J. W., Private.

Mourain, G. P., Private.

Madden, V. V.

May, W. B.

McQuarters, W. A. Wounded at Vicksburg.

Meredith, T. McB. Wounded at Oak Hills. Elected 1st Lieutenant, May 8, 1862. Promoted Captain.

Meredith, R. B. Wounded at Vicksburg. Prisoner at Elk Horn.

Meredith, B.

Noble, T. J. Discharged.

Noble, W. C. Wounded at Iuka, September 19, 1862.

Perry, A. J.

Rice, J. C. Wounded at Vicksburg.

Rundle, G. K. Taken prisoner at Iuka, September 19, 1862.

Rice, M. T.

Ray, M. V. Wounded at Vicksburg.

Ray, B. Wounded at Vicksburg. Prisoner at Elk Horn.

Ray, F. Wounded at Vicksburg.

Sapp, W.

Swain, G. B.

Sandridge, J. M. Wounded at Vicksburg.

Sweeny, W.

Stuart, L. P. Killed at Vicksburg.

Stephens, F. M.

Smith, P. R. Taken prisoner at Elk Horn. Wounded at Vicksburg.

Tegart, E. W.

Vaughn, J. L. Wounded at Elk Horn, March 7, 1862. Killed at Vicksburg.

Whittington, A.

Watson, J. G.

Walker, O.

White, M. Taken prisoner at Iuka, September 19, 1862.

Whittington, W. W.

Wooten, W. L.

Williams, J. R.

Weatherford, R.

Whitehurst, A.

Watsson, G. W. Died July 21, 1861.

ROLL OF COMPANY "K," PELICAN RIFLES

Tunnard, W. F., Captain. Elected Major May, 1861; taken prisoner at Elk Horn.

J. P. Viglini, 1st Lieutenant. Elected Captain May, 1861.

J. B. Irwin, 2d Lieutenant. Elected 1st Lieutenant May, 1862. Killed at Iuka, Sept. 19, 1862.

Watson, W., 1st Sergeant. Discharged, Conscript Act, July 19, 1862.

Waddell, G. D., 2d Sergeant. Appointed Hospital Steward.

Tunnard, W. H., 3d Sergeant. Appointed A. C. S. Sergeant, May, 1862.

Hurley, C., 4th Sergeant. Elected 1st Sergeant, May, 1862.

Bogel, J. C., 1st Corporal.

Gentles, H. H., 2d Corporal. Elected Junior 2d Lieutenant, October 12th, 1861; Captain, May 8th, 1862; wounded and taken prisoner at Iuka, Sept. 19th, 1862.

Brunat, F. R., 3d Corporal. Elected Junior 2d Lieutenant, May, 1861. Died, March, 1862.

Lewis, D., 4th Corporal. 3d Sergeant, May, 1862.

Patterson, R., Musician. Drum-major, by appointment, May 15, 1862.

Hersch, H. Musician. Transferred from Co. A, July 1st, 1862. Killed at Iuka.

Cambell, D., Musician. Discharged October, 1861, Camp Jackson, Ark., disability.

Aldrich, M. C., Private. A. C. S. Department, detached.

Allen, J. B., Private. Died July 15, 1861, Fort Smith, Ark.

Alexander, S., Private.

Alexander, A., Private. Discharged October, 1861, disability.

Addison, J. A., Private.   "   "   25th, 1862, disability.

Bovard, J. A., Private.

Bovard, W. T., Private.

Booth, A. B., Private.

Benton, L. J., Private. Killed June 9, 1863, Vicksburg.

Benton, E. J., Private. Wounded and died June 30, 1863, Vicksburg.

Burrows, P. Private.

Brandenstein, M., Private. 2d Corporal; killed May 22, 1863.

Boullion, J. R., Private. Died February 9, 1862, Fayetteville, Ark.

Boullion, J. J., Private. Discharged August 26, 1862, disability.

Barratt, J. E., Private.

Bell, A. J., Private. Discharged July 19, 1862, Conscript Act.

Burrows, A. P., Private.

Bills, J. T., Private. Discharged October, 1861, disability.

Bills, H., Private. Elected 4th Sergeant May, 1861.

Bellow, E. J., Private. Discharged January 1862, disability. Rejoined.

Caffreay, J., Private. Wounded and taken prisoner at Iuka, Sept. 19, 1862.

Crasson, J. P., Private. Discharged, disability.

Contini, F., Private.

Chambers, J. F., Private. Wounded at Vicksburg.

Cain, W. P., Private. Killed, Elk Horn, March 7, 1862.

Chambers, H. H., Private. Discharged July 19, 1862, Conscript Act.

Cameron, A. F., Private. Discharged September, 1861, Camp Jackson, Ark., disability.

Cameron, A. W., Private.

Curran, M., Private. Wounded at Oak Hills, August 10, 1861, and discharged September, 1861, Camp Jackson, Ark.

Crane, Jas., Private. Discharged September, 1861, Camp Jackson, Ark., disability.

Duffy, A. V., Private. Killed May 22, 1863, Vicksburg.

Dalsheimer, A., Private. Taken prisoner, Corinth, May 4, 1862.

Duggan, T., Private.

Denham, R. T., Private. Killed September 19, 1862, Iuka, Miss.

Elter, A., Private. Taken prisoner May 17, 1863, Snyder's Bluff.

Edmonston, W. L., Private. Taken prisoner and wounded October 4, 1862, Corinth. Wounded at Vicksburg, 1863.

Echols, D., Private. 4th Corporal. Taken prisoner March 7, 1862, Elk Horn, and May 19, 1862, Iuka. Wounded and died July 7th, 1863, Vicksburg.

Erwin, W., Private. Wounded March 7, 1862, Elk Horn, and discharged April 27, 1862.

Funke, F., Private. Discharged July 19, 1862, Conscript Act.

Fraenkel, F., Private. Discharged May, 1861, disability.

Finlay, H., Private. Went to England after siege of Vicksburg.

Gay, D. B., Private. Transferred to Point Coupee, October, 1862.

Hueston, J., Private. Discharged July 19, 1862, Conscript Act.

Hickman, B. F., Private. Wounded October 4, 1862, Corinth and Vicksburg. Died July 3, 1863.

Hughes, J. C., Private. Discharged April 27, 1862.

Heroman, F. M., Private. Discharged July 19, 1862, Conscript Act.

Hock, J., Private. Taken prisoner September 19, 1862, Iuka. Went to Germany.

Hall, C., Private. Wounded August 10, 1861, Oak Hills. Discharged September, 1861, Camp Jackson.

Hernandez, H., Private. Died September 5, 1861, Mount Vernon, Mo.

Hernandez, L., Private. Discharged May, 1861, N. Orleans.

Hardy, J. H., Private. Discharged August 20, 1861, Camp Jackson, Ark., disability.

Hackett, A., Private.

Henderson, R. L., Private. Discharged April 7, 1862, Fayetteville, Ark. Captain 8th La., Batn. H. Artillery.

Hyatt, J., Private. Left Company December, 1862.

Jolly, E., Private. 2d Sergeant.

Jones, Chas., Private. Discharged, May, 1861, N. Orleans.

Knox, N. L., Private. Wounded August 10, 1861, Oak Hills , and died September 15, 1861, Mt. Vernon, Mo.

Loyd, E. A., Private.

McGuinness, W., Private.

McFarland, W., Private.

McCabe, R. J., Private.

Monget, W., Private. Wounded, Oak Hills, August 10, 1861. Discharged, September, 1861.

Nelson, J. M., Private. Detached September 16, 1862, A. Q. M. Department.

Perry, J. G., Private.

Pino, A., Private.

Payne, A. B., Private. Elected 2d Junior Lieutenant, May 8, 1862.

Powers, J., Private. Discharged January 1, 1863, disability.

Roysdon, A. W. Private. Transferred to 25th La. Inf., 1865.

Robinson, G. L., Private.

Russ, S. P., Private. 1st Corporal. Wounded at Oak Hills and Vicksburg.

Robertson, J. H., Private. Wounded at Corinth October 4, 1863, and taken prisoner.

Roddy, J., Private. 3d Corporal. Wounded and taken prisoner September 19, 1862, Iuka.

Reams, D. B., Private.

Russ, V. C., Private. Discharged, July 19, 1862, Conscript Act.

Smith, Jed., Private. Discharged, January, 1862, Fayetteville, Ark.

Sparks, J. H., Private. Discharged, October, 1862, disability.

Stephens, J. G., Private.

Sanchez, J., Private. Discharged, September, 1861, Camp Jackson, Ark., disability.

Tunnard, F. D., Private. 1st Sergeant. Elected 2d Junior Lieutenant, May, 1861, N. Orleans. Resigned and returned to Regiment 1862. Wounded at Iuka.

Thomas, H., Private.

Taqueno, F., Private. Wounded and taken prisoner, October 4th, 1862, Corinth.

Walters, T. R., Private. Wounded August 10, 1861, Oak Hills. Discharged, September, 1861.

Williams, J. D., Private. Elected 2d Lieutenant, May 8th, 1862. Wounded October 4th, 1862, Corinth.

Watson, W. W., Private. Discharged, January, 1862, Fayetteville, Ark., disability.

Williams, J., Private. Wounded August 10, 1861, Oak Hills, and discharged, September, 1861, Camp Jackson.

ROLL OF CO. "H,"
22D LOUISIANA INFANTRY

Comprising members of the 3d Louisiana Infantry remaining
East of the Mississippi River.

Captain, C. H. Brashear.
1st Lieutenant, J. P. Parsons.
2d Lieutenant, W. T. Fagan.
2d Lieutenant, Jr., A. J. Thomas.

1st Sergeant, C. Hurley.	1st Corporal, W. E. Walker.
2d " A. B. Booth.	2d " J. F. Chambers.
3d " J. Roddy.	3d " W. B. Sheffield.
4th " T. Williams.	4th " R. J. Galloway.

PRIVATES

1. Aldrich, M. C.	26. Laundry, F. T.
2. Bellow, E. J.	27. Little, G. B. N.
3. Bills, J. H.	28. McCaskey, T. H.
4. Blankenship, W.	29. Minter, N.
5. Barrott, J. E.	30. Meyer, A.
6. Boyard, L. C.	31. Manning, S. J.
7. Caldwell, W. R.	32. Miller, H.
8. Cooper, T. E.	33. Moore, J. F.
9. Crawford, J. F.	34. Norton, C.
10. Downey, P. V.	35. Orman, C. J.
11. Farrell, M.	36. Orman, M. A.
12. Finn, T.	37. Phillips, E. B.
13. Foster, T. E.	38. Pugh, ———.
14. Grubbs, J. T.	39. Paff, C. W.
15. Gould, J. T.	40. Patterson, J. P.
16. Hackett, A.	41. Pierson, P.
17. Hubbard, J.	42. Robbins, M. C.
18. Holland, A.	43. Rogers, ———.
19. Hurd, W.	44. Swain, L. B.
20. Hall, J. B.	45. Saunders, W.
21. Hudson, W. T.	46. Shumaker, M. V.
22. Johnston, J.	47. Thompson, J. A.
23. Johnston, W.	48. Taquino, F.
24. Jones, M. D.	49. Walker, R.
25. Reilly, H.	50. White, R. R.

LIST OF CASUALTIES OF THE 3D REGIMENT LOUISIANA INFANTRY, AT THE BATTLE OF OAK HILLS (WILSON'S CREEK), MO., AUG. 10, 1861

T. R. Verbois, 2d Lieutenant, Co. A. Slightly wounded.

John McManus, Private, Co. A. Wounded slightly.

M. Coughlan, " " " "

N. Beard, " " " seriously.

E. Le Blanc, " " " "

R. H. Hinson, Captain, Co. B. Killed.

J. P. Renwick, Sergeant-major, Co. B. Killed

E. A. Whetstone, Private, Co. B. Killed.

C. E. Adamson, Sergeant, Co. B. Wounded.

J. W. Pettit, Sergeant, Co. B. Wounded.

J. W. Hewitt, Private, Co. B. Wounded seriously.

T. J. Potts, Private, Co. B. Wounded seriously.

B. Norton, Private, Co. B. Wounded slightly.

J. Sullivan, Private, Co. B. Missing.

H. Cockerham, Private, Co. C. Killed.

N. M. Middlebrooks, 1st Sergeant, Co. C. Wounded seriously.

M. McBride, Private, Co. C. Wounded slightly.

J. D. Warner, Private, Co. C. Wounded slightly.

Williamson, J., Private, Co. D. Died from wounds.

B. Davis, Private, Co. D. Wounded slightly.

D. L. Miller, Private, Co. E. Killed.

W. F. Brice, Private, Co. E. Killed.

J. W. Woodburn, Private, Co. E. Killed.

H. H. Halt, Private, Co. E. Wounded slightly.

W. H. Faw, Private, Co. E. Missing.

James Allen, Private, Co. F. Killed.

John S. Brown, Private, Co. F. Killed.

Thomas W. Hecox, Corporal, Co. F. Wounded seriously.

Ben. Davis, Sergeant, Co. F. Wounded slightly.

B. L. Simpson, Private. Co. F. Wounded seriously.

J. Donohue, Private, Co. F. Wounded seriously.

E. M. Altaway, Private, Co. F. Wounded seriously.

S. J. Manning, Private, Co. F. Wounded slightly.

J. Coon, Private, Co. F. Wounded slightly.

T. C. Bickman, Private, Co. F. Wounded slightly.

F. Davis, Private, Co. F. Wounded slightly.

J. H. Basser, Private, Co. F. Wounded slightly.

M. A. Sheldon, Private, Co. F. Missing.

Placide Bossier, Private, Co. G. Killed.

S. Eishworth, Private, Co. G. Wounded seriously.

L. Charles, Private, Co. G. Wounded slightly.

H. Hughes, Jr., Private, Co. G. Wounded slightly.

J. Hoffman, Private, Co. G. Wounded slightly.

Samuel Hynes, Private, Co. G. Wounded slightly.

A. J. Sing, Private, Co. G. Wounded slightly.

M. Toal, Private, Co. G. Wounded slightly.

T. C. Humble, 2d Lieutenant, Co. I. Wounded seriously.

L. Levy, Private, Co. I. Wounded slightly.

James Hines, Private, Co. I. Wounded slightly.

T. McB. Meredith, Private, Co. I. Wounded slightly.

J. B. Irvin, 2d Lieutenant, Co. K. Wounded slightly.

Charles Hall, Corporal, Co. K. Wounded seriously.

W. Monget, Private, Co. K. Wounded seriously.

J. C. Williams, Private, Co. K. Wounded seriously.

W. T. Board, Private, Co. K. Wounded slightly.

A. J. Bell, Private, Co. K. Wounded slightly.

M. Curran, Private, Co. K. Wounded slightly.

N. L. Knox, Private, Co. K. Wounded slightly.

E. A. Floyd, Private, Co. K. Wounded slightly.

J. M. Nelson, Private, Co. K. Wounded slightly.

T. R. Wallers, Private, Co. K. Wounded slightly.

Silas Russ, Private, Co. K. Wounded slightly.

RECAPITULATION

Killed 9

Wounded 48

Missing 3

Total 60

LIST OF CASUALTIES, 3D REGIMENT LOUISIANA INFANTRY, McCULLOCH'S BRIGADE, AT THE BATTLE OF ELK HORN (PEA RIDGE), ARK., MARCH 7, 1862

L. Hebert, Colonel. Prisoner.

W. F. Tunnard, Major. Prisoner.

Henderson, R., Private, Co. B. Prisoner.

Alford, W. H., Sergeant, Co. C. Killed.

Grove, D. E., Sergeant, Co. D. Wounded.

Caradine, J., Private, Co. D. Wounded.

Springer, H., Private, Co. D. Wounded.

Craig, J., Co. F. Killed.

Cain, F., Co. F. Wounded.

Miller, M. T., Co. F. Prisoner.

Singer, L. J., Co. F. Prisoner.

Jus, J. F., Co. F. Prisoner.

Duval, D. S., Co. F. Prisoner.

Wols, C., Co. F. Prisoner.

Kimball, J., Co. F. Prisoner.

Bernes, F., Private, Co. G. Prisoner.

Cannon, D., Private, Co. G. Prisoner.

Dew, L., Private, Co. G. Prisoner.

Hitzman, J., Private, Co. G. Prisoner.

Prudhomme, J. A., Private, Co. G. Wounded.

Phillips, E., Private, Co. G., Prisoner.

Rowe, A. H., Private, Co. G. Wounded.

Schroder, C. F., Private, Co. G. Killed.

Warner, B. F., Private, Co. G. Killed.

Beard, W. A., Sergeant, Co. H. Killed.

Corbin, W. P., Private, Co. H. Killed.

Only, J. T., Private, Co. H. Killed.

Perry, J. E., Private, Co. H. Killed.

Sharplin, W. P., Private, Co. H. Killed.

Singleton, S. S., Private, Co. H. Killed.

Smythe, N. B., Private, Co. H. Killed.

Broadway, J. T., Sergeant, Co. I. Prisoner.

Beale, W. H., Private, Co. I. Prisoner.

Banks, A. J., Private, Co. I. Wounded.

Cantelope, F. E., Private, Co. I. Prisoner.

Cain, F. T., Private, Co. I. Prisoner.

Dunn, T. J., Private, Co. I. Prisoner.

Freeman, D., Private, Co. I. Wounded.

Ferrand, C. A., Private, Co. I. Prisoner.

Gregory, W. A., Private, Co. I. Prisoner.

Jenkins, W., Private, Co. I. Killed.

Kelly, J. F., Private., Co. I. Prisoner.

Lawson, W. P., Private, Co. I. Wounded.

Mason, D. F., Private, Co. I. Prisoner.

Meredith, R. B., Private, Co. I. Prisoner.

Ray, B., Private, Co. I. Prisoner.
Smith, P. R., Private, Co. I. Prisoner.
Vaughn, J. L., Private, Co. I. Wounded.
Viglini, J. P., Captain, Co. K. Prisoner.
Cain, W. P., Private, Co. K. Killed.
Echols, D., Private, Co. K. Prisoner.

LIST OF CASUALTIES, 3D REGIMENT LA. INFANTRY, HEBERT'S BRIGADE, PRICE'S ARMY, AT THE BATTLE OF IUKA, MISS., SEPT. 19, 1862

J. B. Gilmore, Lieutenant-Colonel. Wounded.
J. H. Brigham, Adjutant.   "
J. Kinney, Captain, Co. A.   "
U. Babin, Lieutenant, Co. A. Missing.
J. Ramouin, Lieutenant, Co. A. Killed.
———— Joly, Sergeant, Co. A. Wounded.
D. Bridges, Corporal, Co. A. Killed.
J. Richard, Corporal, Co. A. Missing.
A. Gourrier, Private, Co. A. Killed.
J. H. Breaux, Private, Co. A. Wounded.
E. L. Breaux, Private, Co. A.   "
N. Gayarre, Private, Co. A.   "
T. Gourrier, Private, Co. A.   "
W. Sanders, Private, Co. A.   "
M. Landry, Private, Co. A.   "
M. Brassard, Private, Co. A. Missing.
    Renwick, Lieutenant, Co. B. Wounded.
    Brown, Sergeant, Co. B.   "
    Whittaker, Corporal, Co. B.   "
    Buckmaster, Private, Co. B.   "
    Bass, Private, Co. B.   "
J. Blankenship, Private, Co. B.   "
W. Cooper, Private, Co. B.   "
T. Cravens, Private, Co. B.   "
D. M. Evans, Private, Co. B.   "
W. S. Finley, Private, Co. B.   "
T. Finn, Private, Co. B.   "

A. C. Harrison, Private, Co. B. Wounded.

W. M. Washburn, Lieutenant, Co. B. Missing.

   Stewart, Sergeant, Co. B. Missing.

S. W. Whorley, Private, Co. B. Missing.

A. W. McKain, Lieutenant, Co. C. Killed.

B. F. Thelpal, Private, Co. C. Killed.

D. Pierson, Captain, Co. C. Wounded.

H. M. Crew, Private, Co. C.   "

W. Morehead, Private, Co. C.   "

A. J. Perry, Private, Co. C.   "

G. L. Trichel, Lieutenant, Co. D. Wounded.

B. Davis, Sergeant, Co. D.   "

T. H. McCaskey, Private, Co. D. "

A. Leplant, Private, Co. D.   "

W. W. Joy, Private, Co. D.   "

J. Charleville, Private, Co. D.   "

B. Norwood, Sergeant, Co. E. Killed.

R. Barton, Private, Co. E. Killed.

R. C. Holt, Lieutenant, Co. E. Wounded.

P. Pierson, Private, Co. E.   "

J. Myers, Private, Co. E.   "

—— Masterson, Private, Co. E. "

T. Brigham, Private, Co. E. Missing.

W. Henderson, Private, Co. E. Missing.

D. C. Ballard, Private, Co. E. Missing.

M. O. Clark, Sergeant, Co. F. Killed.

J. Horn, Lieutenant, Co. F. Wounded.

W. T. Hudson, Sergeant, Co. F. "

D. W. Manning, Private, Co. F. "

Jules Jus, Private, Co. F.   "

J. A. White, Sergeant, Co. F. Prisoner.

R. Dick, Corporal, Co. F. Prisoner.

L. J. Singer, Private, Co. F. Prisoner.

R. L. Perry, Private, Co. F. Prisoner.

J. M. Tauzin, Sergeant, Co. G. Killed.

M. S. Hailman, Private, Co. G. Killed.

F. N. Sanchez, Corporal, Co. G. Wounded.

C. V. Murphy, Corporal, Co. G. "

R. Alleman, Private, Co. G.   "

W. A. Charleville, Private, Co. G. Wounded

A. Dickens, Private, Co. G.   "

M. Escobeda, Private, Co. G.   "

J. Ginchan, Private, Co. G.   "

J. Guiton, Private, Co. G.   "

J. P. Hyams, Private, Co. G.   "

J. G. Norris, Private, Co. G. Missing.

M. S. Hartman, Private, Co. G. Missing.

W. S. Behrman, Private, Co. G. Missing.

E. Genehan, Private, Co. G. Missing.

J. D. Beckman, Private, Co. H. Killed.

J. McDonald, Private, Co. H. Killed.

S. Singleton, Private, Co. H. Killed.

H. T. Horten, Sergeant, Co. H. Wounded.

W. F. Bonner, Private, Co. H.   "

S. B. McCarty, Private, Co. H.   "

G. Higgins, Private, Co. H.   "

C. Hedrick, Lieutenant, Co. H.   "

N. Murfie, Private, Co. H. Prisoner.

J. Reese, Private, Co. H. Prisoner.

S. J. Howell, Sergeant, Co. I. Killed.

W. H. Beale, Private, Co. I. Killed.

J. E. Johnson, Captain, Co. I. Wounded.

J. O. McCormick, Private, Co. I. "

J. B. Johnson, Private, Co. I.   "

F. E. Cantelope, Private, Co. I.   "

L. L. Cain, Private, Co. I.   "

F. F. Cain, Private, Co. I.   "

W. C. Noble, Private, Co. I.   "

J. Hayne, Private, Co. I.   "

J. M. Flowers, Private, Co. I. Missing.

Geo. K. Runnels, Private, Co. I. Missing.

W. Dowd, Sergeant, Co. I. Prisoner.

M. White, Corporal, Co. I. Prisoner.

J. B. Irvin, 1st Lieutenant, Co. K. Killed.

H. Heasch, Musician, Co. K. Killed.

R. Denham, Private, Co. K. Killed.

H. H. Gentles, Captain, Co. K. Wounded.

E. Jolly, Sergeant, Co. K.   "

J. H. Bells, Sergeant, Co. K., Wounded.

J. Roddy, Corporal, Co. K.   "

M. Brandenstein, Corporal, Co. K. "

J. Caffrey, Private, Co. K.   "

F. D. Tunnard, Private, Co. K.   "

A. Roysden, Private, Co. K.   "

B. F. Hickman, Private, Co. K.   "

A. F. Cameron, Private, Co. K.   "

J. Hock, Private, Co. K. Prisoner.

D. Echols, Private, Co. K. Prisoner.

Field and Staff Wounded 2

RECAPITULATION

Killed 18
Wounded 71
Missing .14
Prisoners 10
—
Total .113

LIST OF CASUALTIES, 3D REGIMENT LA. INFANTRY, HEBERT'S BRIGADE, AT THE BATTLE OF CORINTH, OCTOBER 3 AND 4, 1862

S. D. Davis, Sergeant, Co. A. Missing.

W. Sanders, Private, Co. A. Wounded.

J. D. Maxwell, Private, Co. B. Missing.

D. Norton, Private, Co. B. Missing.

T. C. Higginbothem, Private, Co. B. Missing.

G. B. Quinn, Private, Co. B. Missing.

A. Neuman, Private, Co. C. Missing.

B. P. Morse, Lieutenant, Co. D. Wounded.

J. Merritt, Private, Co. D. Wounded.

D. Dodez, Private, Co. F. Wounded.

Jones, Private, Co. F. Wounded.

Marr, Private, Co. F. Missing.

Lowe, Corporal, Co. G. Wounded.

Keiser, Corporal, Co. G. Wounded

C. S. Jeter, Private, Co. H. Wounded.

S. L. Reese, Private, Co. H. Missing.

E. M. Douglass, Private, Co. I. Wounded.

E. Girod, Private, Co. I. Wounded.

S. J. Moffit, Private, Co. I. Wounded.

D. March, Private, Co. I. Missing.

J. D. Williams, Lieutenant, Co. K. Wounded seriously.

D. Lewis, Sergeant, Co. K. Wounded seriously.

J. H. Robertson, Private, Co. K. Wounded seriously

B. F. Hickman, Private, Co. K. Wounded slightly.

F. Taquino, Private, Co. K. Wounded slightly.

W. L. Edmondson, Private, Co. K. Wounded slightly.

A. Dalsheimer, Private, Co. K. Prisoner.

A. F. Cameron, Private, Co. K. Prisoner.

FIELD AND STAFF

Major S. D. Russell, wounded.

Sergeant-Major McFee, killed.

RECAPITULATION

Killed, Field and Staff 1

Wounded 1

Wounded 17

Missing and Prisoners 11

———

Total .30

LIST OF CASUALTIES, 3D REGIMENT LOUISIANA INFANTRY, HEBERT'S BRIGADE, FORNEY'S DIVISION, DURING THE SIEGE OF VICKSBURG, MAY 18 TO JULY 4, 1863

Field and Staff.—Lieutenant-Colonel S. D. Russel, seriously; Major D. Pierson, Slightly; General Hebert's Staff, Captain C. A. Bruslé, seriously.

COMPANY "A," IBERVILLE GREYS.—*Killed*—Captain J. Kenney, Lieutenant J. Randolph. *Privates*—N. Schade, F. Leonard, J. P. Chastant, Amidé Hebert, B. Berry,

C. Dupuy, J. Breaux. *Wounded Seriously*—Sergeant M. Bassac, L. D. Blanchard, C. Pruett, S. Allain, J. Connor, W. McGuinness, S. Kohn, M. O'Brien, *Wounded Slightly*—Sergeant H. Guidicé, Lieutenant U. Babin, P. T. St. Amant, P. C. Wellis.

COMPANY "B," MOREHOUSE GUARDS.—*Killed*—Sergeant J. T. Sharp, Sergeant W. H. Howell, Sergeant B. Brice, Corporal S. Smith, Corporal T. McFee. *Privates*— W. Finley, J. N. Hewett, J. Lee, F. M. Howell, J. W. Naff, J. C. May. *Wounded Seriously*—Lieutenant W. P. Renwick. *Privates*—H. C. Fryer, H. Kelly, J. M. Burke, A. Williams, T. H. Johnson. *Wounded Slightly*—Lieutenant W. M. Washburn, Lieutenant Joe Davenport, Sergeant J. M. Sharp. *Privates*—D. Buckmaster, W. McCallaghan, D. Shoemaker, J. W. Blankenship, S. W. Sanders, J. M. Smith, B. Q. Vaughn, —— Tatle, F. M. Worley, T. N. Higenbothem.

COMPANY "C," WINN RIFLES.—*Killed*—Corporal W. A. Hallowman, T. J. Teddlie. *Wounded Seriously*—*Privates*—G. C. Spillman, N. Moody, J. N. McBride, W. J. Carson, W. Evans, W. J. Tedley. *Wounded Slightly*—Captain N. M. Middlebrooks, Lieutenant W. T. Fagan, T. Williams, W. Smith, R. Cole.

COMPANY "D," PELICAN RANGERS, No. 2.—*Killed*—Sergeant W. W. Gandy. *Privates*—H. V. Edmonson, T. Cobb, B. Duke, R. C. Hammett. *Wounded Seriously*— P. Gillett, W. Badt, J. McDaniel, J. Fonteneau, J. Merritt. *Wounded Slightly*—Captain W. E. Russell.

COMPANY "E," MOREHOUSE FENCIBLES.—*Killed*—D. A. Gwinn, Silas Crane, —— Masterson. *Wounded Seriously*—Sergeant G. Miller, R. Quinn. *Wounded Slightly*— Lieutenant R. C. Halt. *Privates*—T. D. Downey, A. J. Powell, J. Myers, —— Esom.

COMPANY "F," SHREVEPORT RANGERS.—*Killed*—Sergeant T. M. Roberts, Lieutenant J. Horn. *Wounded Seriously*—Lieutenant J. O. Clark, P. L. Permery, L. J. Singer, J. Charlton, George Efner, Corporal Scanlan, J. Brosi, J. Jus. *Wounded Slightly*— F. A. Davis, P. Sheridan, T. N. Dill, R. T. Cole, W. Hudson, R. Brenning.

COMPANY "G," PELICAN RANGERS, No. 1.—*Killed*—D. Cannon, F. Escobeda, E. Carro, L. Floris, M. Escobeda, J. R. Howell. *Wounded Seriously*—N. Mora, J. Quinelty, J. Guiton, A. Garza, —— Escobeda, Sergeant J. A. Derbonne, J. Morin, C. D. Castex. *Wounded Slightly*—Lieutenant P. Bassier, —— Murray, A. Wrinkle, L. Hubbard, L. Floris, C. Castex, R. Alemand.

COMPANY "H," MONTICELLO RIFLES.—*Killed*—Corporal J. A. Martin, J. Veal, W. Burns, J. C. Reese. *Wounded Seriously*—J. McCowan, L. P. Simps, J. F. Hargrove, J. Byrd. *Wounded Slightly*—Lieutenant J. Stuart.

COMPANY "I," CALDWELL GUARDS.—*Killed*—Captain J. E. Johnson, Corporal P. Lawson, Corporal A. Kelly, T. J. Dunn, L. Stewart, J. L. Vaughan, E. Douglas, F. Ray. *Wounded Seriously*—Sergeant J. R. Gray, Sergeant J. Sandridge, E. Girod, G. W. Humble, W. A. McQuatters, J. A. McCormick. *Wounded Slightly*—Corporal

J. C. Rice, Corporal G. P. Mourain, M. V. Ray, A. Girod, H. C. Hough, J. Hines, G. T. McFarland, P. Smith, M. P. Cartwright, M. Sandridge.

COMPANY "K," PELICAN RIFLES.—*Killed*—Corporal M. Brandenstein, A. V. Duffy, E. J. Benton, L. J. Benton, B. F. Hickman, Corporal D. Echols. *Wounded Seriously*— Sergeant E. Jolly, J. F. Chambers, W. L. Edmonson. *Wounded Slightly*—Corporal S. P. Russ, H. Finlay.

This list is very imperfect, being compiled from private notes, without the aid of any official documents. The total loss in the regiment reached nearly, if not more than, 200 out of a total of not quite 400 men.

APPENDIX

I cannot close this volume without a special acknowledgment of my indebtedness to my friends for their interest in my labors, and for furnishing valuable documents and papers. I am under special obligations to Hon. Charles A. Bruslé, Iberville; Major J. M. Taylor, H. V. Babin, and F. D. Tunnard, Baton Rouge; J. Harvey Brigham, J. Davenport Bustrop, J. Leonard, Plaquemine; W. Kenney, Dr. G. W. Kendall, Colonel J. B. Gilmore, Shreveport; L. Dupleix, Esq., J. C. Trichel, Miss Jennie Barlow, Natchitoches; Colonel D. Pierson, Colonel S. M. Hyams, Colonel J. D. Blair, New Orleans; Major J. S. Richards Floyd, Captain W. B. Butler, Natchitoches Parish; G. W. Humble, T. McB. Meredith, Columbia, La.; A. B. Payne, and A. Booth, Baton Rouge.

To these friends, who have encouraged me in the prosecution of my labor in compiling this History do I feel deeply grateful, and thus make acknowledgment of my gratitude by the mention of their names. Many of the interesting records of this volume are due to their prompt assistance and kind remembrance. I sincerely trust that they may feel repaid by a perusal of its pages.

W. H. TUNNARD

INDEX